AGAINST COLONIZATION AND RURAL DISPOSSESSION

About the editor

Dip Kapoor is professor in international education and development at the University of Alberta and volunteer research associate and co-founding member of the Center for Research and Development Solidarity (CRDS), a rural Adivasi (original dweller) and Dalit small/landless peasant organization in Orissa, India. He is the co-editor of several book collections, including: *Learning from the Ground Up: Global Perspectives on Social Movements and Knowledge Production* (2010), *Beyond Colonialism, Development and Globalization: Social Movements and Critical Perspectives* (2015) and *NGOization: Complicity, Contradictions and Prospects* (2013). He has been engaged in popular participatory action research pertaining to adult education, organizing and trans/local social action addressing rural development-displacement and dispossession (land-, forest- and food-related politics) since the mid-1990s, involving several organized collaborations with Adivasi, Dalit and/or small and landless peasant social groups in eastern India.

AGAINST COLONIZATION AND RURAL DISPOSSESSION

LOCAL RESISTANCE IN SOUTH AND EAST ASIA, THE PACIFIC AND AFRICA

Edited by Dip Kapoor

ZED

Against Colonization and Rural Dispossession: Local Resistance in South and East Asia, the Pacific and Africa was first published in 2017 by Zed Books Ltd, The Foundry, 17 Oval Way, London SE11 5RR, UK.

www.zedbooks.net

Typeset in Plantin and Kievit by Swales & Willis Ltd, Exeter, Devon
Index by ed.emery@thefreeuniversity.net
Cover design by Kika Sroka-Miller
Cover photo © Andrew McConnell/Panos

A catalogue record for this book is available from the British Library.

ISBN 978-1-78360-944-4 hb
ISBN 978-1-78360-943-7 pb
ISBN 978-1-78360-946-8 pdf
ISBN 978-1-78360-945-1 epub
ISBN 978-1-78360-947-5 mobi

CONTENTS

About the contributors | vii

1 Local resistance to colonization and rural dispossession in South and East Asia, the Pacific, and Africa 1
Dip Kapoor

2 Waponahki anti-colonial resistance in North American colonial contexts: some preliminary notes on the coloniality of meta-dispossession 28
Rebecca Sockbeson

PART I: SOUTH AND EAST ASIA AND THE PACIFIC REGION

3 Sovereignty politics in Samoa: *fa'asamoa, fa'amatai,* and resistance to colonial capital and dispossession of customary land and place 43
Naomi Gordon

4 Adivasi, Dalit, and non-tribal forest dweller (ADNTFD) resistance to bauxite mining in Niyamgiri: displacing capital and state-corporate mining activism in India 67
Dip Kapoor

5 Our crops speak: small and landless peasant resistance to agro-extractive dispossession in Central Sulawesi, Indonesia . . 98
Hasriadi Masalam

6 Dispossession and neoliberal disaster reconstruction: activist NGO and fisher resistance in Nagapattinam, Tamil Nadu 122
Raja Swamy and Prema Revathi

7 Lumad anti-mining activism in the Philippines. 145
Robyn Magalit Rodriguez

8 Coal power and the Sundarbans in Bangladesh: subaltern resistance and convergent crises. 164
Sourayan Mookerjea and Manoj Misra

PART II: AFRICAN REGION

9 Resisting accumulation by dispossession: organization and mobilization by the rural poor in contemporary South Africa 187
Lalitha Naidoo, Gilton Klerck, and Kirk Helliker

10 Food sovereignty through ecofeminism: re-commoning as resistance to agribusiness dispossession in Kenya 209
Leigh Brownhill, Wahu Kaara, and Terisa Turner

11 Guided by the Yomo spirit: resistance to accumulation by dispossession of the Songor salt lagoon in Ada, Ghana 231
Jonathan Langdon and Kofi Larweh

12 Contesting dispossession: land rights activism in Gambella, Ethiopia, and Pujehun, Sierra Leone 251
Rachel Ibreck

13 Local resistance to large-scale agricultural land acquisitions in the Benishangul-Gumuz region, Ethiopia 275
Tsegaye Moreda

14 All that glitters: neoliberal violence, small-scale mining, and gold extraction in northern Tanzania 296
Zahra Moloo

15 'Oloibirinization', collective identity, and the future of multilocal resistance in the Niger Delta. 315
Temitope B. Oriola

Index | 335

ABOUT THE CONTRIBUTORS

Leigh Brownhill is an independent scholar whose research and teaching focus on ecofeminism, social movements and food and water sovereignty, especially in East Africa and North America. She teaches sociology and communication studies at Athabasca University and is the author of *Land, Food, Freedom: Struggles for the Gendered Commons in Kenya, 1870–2007* (Africa World Press, 2009). Her interest in post-oil organic/indigenous agriculture and her multi-ethnic kith and kinship ties (from the Kenyan coast, mountain and lakeside) have shaped her long-term research engagement in Kenya, as well as involvement in community-based education and political activism, over the course of three decades. With her co-authors in this volume, she is co-founder of First Woman: The East and Southern African Women's Oral History and Indigenous Knowledge Network, which has recorded life histories of elderly Kenyan women since 1994. She is also a senior editor of the journal *Capitalism Nature Socialism* and chair of the ecofeminist editorial group.

Naomi Gordon is currently completing her MEd thesis, which is a critical ethnographic exploration of anti-colonial resistance to dispossession in Samoa, in the Department of Educational Policy Studies at the University of Alberta, Canada. She was a journalist with the *Cook Islands Herald* and Cook Island's news and communications consultant to the Ministry of Gender Affairs, Cook Island, and for the Metis Nation of Alberta, Canada. Her family ties are to the village of Lepea in Samoa.

Kirk Helliker is an associate professor in the Department of Sociology at Rhodes University, South Africa. He also heads the Unit of Zimbabwean Studies based in the department. He has co-edited three books in recent years, on land reform in Zimbabwe, land struggles in southern Africa, and the land question in South Africa. His main research interests relate to agrarian studies, civil society, nongovernmental organizations, and social emancipation, with a particular focus on Zimbabwe. He is actively involved with NGOs and agrarian movements in seeking to bring about meaningful agrarian change in South Africa.

Rachel Ibreck is a lecturer in politics and international relations at Goldsmiths, University of London. Her research interests include civil society and social movements in conflict-affected countries in Africa; transnational human rights activism; and justice and memory politics after mass atrocities. She is interested in research collaborations between academics and activists and in action research methodologies. She has previously worked for human rights organizations, including Justice Africa. She was co-convener of a seminar with Christian Aid Ireland on 'The Politics of Land-Grabbing: Strategies of Resistance', bringing academics together with activists from Sierra Leone, Columbia, and the Occupied Palestinian Territory at the University of Limerick, June 2013. She is currently working with lawyers and community activists on researching everyday experiences of customary and statutory justice during the conflict in South Sudan for the Justice and Security Research Programme at LSE.

Wahu Kaara is a social justice activist, a university council member at Maseno University and Dedan Kimathi University of Technology, and a 2005 Nobel Peace Prize nominee from Kenya, along with 1,000 women activists from around the world. She is the founder of the Kenyan Debt Relief Network (KENDREN) and was a participant in the 'Freedom Corner' pro-democracy demonstrations for the release of 52 political prisoners along with several mothers, wives, and daughters.

Gilton Klerck is an associate professor in the Department of Sociology at Rhodes University, South Africa. His main research interests include industrial relations, workplace restructuring, labour law, and value chains.

Jonathan Langdon is an associate professor in the Development Studies Program and Adult Education Department at St Francis Xavier University, Canada. He holds a Social Science and Humanities Research Council Insight Grant supporting research concerning learning in social action in the Songor, Ghana. He has published a book on *Indigenous Knowledges, Education and Activism* and has authored articles in several journals, including the *Canadian Journal of Development Studies*, *McGill Journal of Education*, *Interface: A Journal for and About Social Movements*, *Action Research* and *Studies in the Education of Adults* (UK). Most recently, he and Songor movement members produced a collectively written book, *The Struggle of the Songor Salt People* (Comboni, Ghana) that uses oral testimony to share the people's story of the Songor. Langdon is the Canada research chair in sustainability and social change leadership.

Kofi Larweh is the former station manager for Radio Ada, Ghana, and lead trainer for the Ghana Community Radio Network. He has been an active member of the Songor artisanal salt movement for three decades. He has co-published articles in *Interface: A Journal for and About Social Movements* and *Action Research*. Most recently, he played a leading role in the production of the collectively written book *The Struggle of the Songor Salt People* (Comboni, Ghana).

Hasriadi Masalam is doing research concerning learning in social action in rural resistance to palm oil development dispossession in Sulawesi, Indonesia. He is a co-founder of ININNAWA Community, a federation of popular social action NGOs in South Sulawesi, Indonesia.

Manoj Misra is assistant professor of sustainable development at Hankuk University of Foreign Studies, Seoul, Republic of Korea. He was a visiting research fellow at the Agrarian Alternatives cluster at Heidelberg University, Germany. His writings have won best graduate paper awards at the American Anthropological Association and the Canadian Association for the Study of International Development. His research interests include agrarian change and food sovereignty, development dispossession, and coal power and climate justice movements in South Asia.

Zahra Moloo is an investigative journalist and documentary filmmaker from Kenya. She has worked with IRIN News as a reporter and producer, and with the Right Livelihood Award Foundation. Much of her work has focused on investigating the extractive industries in Africa. She also covers environmental stories, the war on terror and the impact of neoliberalism in Africa. She has reported from across East and Central Africa, Libya, and the West Bank. Her work has appeared in the BBC's *Focus on Africa* magazine, Al Jazeera English, IPS News, Agence France Presse, IRIN News, CCTV's Faces of Africa, CODESRIA, and Africa is a Country. Her film, *In the Shadow of a Gold Mine*, is an investigation into a multinational gold mine in Tanzania. She holds a bachelor of arts in history and development studies from McGill University and a master's in journalism from City University in London.

Sourayan Mookerjea is associate professor in sociology at the University of Alberta. He is a social and cultural theorist whose research explores contradictions of globalization, migration, urbanization, subaltern social movements, popular culture, new media, and class politics. Dr Mookerjea is co-editor of *Canadian Cultural Studies: A Reader* (Duke University Press, 2009) and director of the Intermedia Research Studio, Department of Sociology, University of Alberta.

Tsegaye Moreda is a postdoctoral fellow at the International Institute of Social Studies (ISS) in The Hague. His research interests are in the politics of natural resources: land, water, forests, sub-soil minerals – examined in the era of the global resource rush and climate change. His work has been published in the *Journal of Peasant Studies* and the *Canadian Journal of Development Studies*.

Lalitha Naidoo is director of the East Cape Agricultural Research Project in Grahamstown, South Africa. Her main research interests relate to agrarian political economy, social mobilization, labour markets, and minimum wages.

Temitope B. Oriola is assistant professor in criminology and socio-legal studies at the University of Alberta. A recipient of the Governor General of Canada Academic Gold Medal, Oriola is author of *Criminal Resistance? The Politics of Kidnapping Oil Workers* (Ashgate, 2013).

Prema Revathi has produced and directed documentary films detailing the exclusion of Dalits and other marginalized communities from the tsunami relief and rehabilitation process, the struggles of women against sexual violence, Dalits for housing rights, and the resistance of Adivasis against forced displacement in the Narmada valley. In addition, she has worked in television and film production, and published articles, poetry, and short stories for English and Tamil publications on peoples' struggles, the environment, and women's rights. Revathi presently writes a column for *The Hindu*'s Tamil edition. Following the tsunami of 2004, she co-organized public hearings on food security in eight coastal districts of Tamil Nadu. She also established Vanavil, a school for children from destitute communities affected by the tsunami in Nagapattinam. She has worked with the National Federation of Women in the slums of Chennai, convened an anti-child labour cell with the All India Trades Union Congress (AITUC), and served as an advisor to the Arunthathiyar Human Rights Forum.

Robyn Magalit Rodriguez is associate professor of Asian American Studies at the University of California Davis. Her research is broadly concerned with understanding how processes of globalization, particularly international migration, impact the societies that migrants leave and the societies to which they move. Her book, *Migrants for Export: How the Philippines Brokers Labor to the World* (University of Minnesota Press, 2010), won an Honorable Mention for Best Book in Social Science by the Association for Asian American Studies. She is the co-author of *Asian America: Sociological and Interdisciplinary Approaches* (Polity Press, 2014). Currently, she is finishing a book entitled *In Lady Liberty's Shadow: Race and Immigration in Post-9/11 New Jersey* to be published by Rutgers University Press. She uses the skills she has developed as a researcher to contribute to communities, and is currently working closely on different projects with the National Alliance for Filipino Concerns.

Rebecca Sockbeson is assistant professor of indigenous education at the University of Alberta and is of the Penobscot Indian Nation, Indian Island Maine, the Waponahki Confederacy of tribes located in Maine, United States, and the Maritime provinces of Canada. She is the eighth child of the Elizabeth Sockbeson clan, the auntie of over 50 Waponahki and Stoney Sioux youth, and the mother of three children who are also of the Alexis Nakota Sioux First Nation of Alberta. A political activist and scholar who has published works in the *American Indian Culture and Research Journal* and the *Canadian Journal of Native of Education*, she graduated from Harvard University, where she received an MEd degree. She worked for the University of Southern Maine for seven years with racially and ethnically underrepresented populations prior to commencing doctoral studies and accepting an academic appointment in Canada.

Raja Swamy is assistant professor of anthropology at the University of Tennessee. He is currently working on a book based on his research concerning the impact of the 2004 tsunami on economic development priorities in India's Tamil Nadu state. Exploring the contradictory outcomes of humanitarian agendas subordinated to the demands of a World Bank-financed and state-led reconstruction project, this work attempts to bridge the gap between political ecology and disaster studies by drawing upon an ethnographic study of displaced and resistant artisanal fisher communities on the margins of India's globalizing economy.

Terisa Turner is from the tar sands and natural gas fields of Northern Alberta, where growing up she experienced on all sides resistance to Big Oil from alliances of indigenous and settler peoples. Her Oberlin MA assessed the 1970 Black Power rebellion in Trinidad and an LSE PhD addressed the global oil market and Nigeria's oil industry. She was research assistant to C.L.R. James and co-founded the International Oil Working Group to help enforce the UN oil embargo against the racist regime in apartheid South Africa, with a focus on facilitating direct action by oil and transport workers in a context of workers' and communities' control over fossil fuels and feed stocks, especially at choke points such as export terminals and ports. This focus on popular control and re-commoning, especially over oil and food, has developed an appreciation of the world historic system transforming front-line direct action by specific indigenous and African women and their allies to keep fossil fuels in the ground and promote solar commoning instead. She has been a professor at universities in the USA, Nigeria, and Canada, and currently is Senior Policy Advisor, Energy Futures, Friends of the Earth Canada, and ecofeminist editorial collective member with the journal *Capitalism Nature Socialism*. *Oil and Class Struggle*, *Arise Ye Mighty People: Gender, Race and Class in Popular Struggles*, 'Why Women Are at War with Chevron', and the prize-winning graphic narrative *Nakedness and Power* are among her publications.

1 | LOCAL RESISTANCE TO COLONIZATION AND RURAL DISPOSSESSION IN SOUTH AND EAST ASIA, THE PACIFIC, AND AFRICA

Dip Kapoor

Contemporary contestation and resistance by indigenous peoples, forest dwellers, small or landless peasants, pastoralists, fishers, marginal castes and ethnicities, and precariously positioned farm labor addressing colonial capitalist development displacement and dispossession in parts of the Asia-Pacific and Africa, however politically (un)spectacular, is common but seldom acknowledged. This perpetuates the untenable notion, both politically and theoretically, of an uncontested compliance or resignation, or a willing acceptance of loss of territory and customary land, if not a sense of place, history, and sociocultural presence.

Euro-American experiences of development and progress realized through liberal conceptions of land as private property characteristic of capitalist social relations and modes of production are, in the alleged absence of contestation equated with this relative silence, positively affirmed and subsequently prescribed as the universally applicable political-economic destination. The role of the repeated violence (including genocidal) of multiple dispossessions and forced (or bribed and manipulated) occupations and political-economic restructuring continually enforcing five centuries of Western colonial capitalism is obscured in such a politics, which normalizes colonization as a necessary social force of constant and (un)civil compulsion in matters pertaining to the lives of the colonial-dispossessed, while denying any explicit recognition of resistance and contestation to such violence by those being dispossessed.

These Euro-colonial political and theoretical projects have always been resisted and challenged on material grounds by the 'wretched of the earth' (Fanon 1963), or those being compelled, manipulated, or invited to commit social and political-economic suicide in the face of a supposed inevitability regarding their necessary demise. Anti-colonial resistance has taken on various forms in different regions and scales over the course of five centuries of Western colonialism, including: (1) the defense of, and by, pre-existing states of their polities against Western expansion; (2) popular and often violent nativist uprisings and reactions to Western interference and imposition of institutions and customs via militant or missionary Christianity; (3) slave revolts (e.g. African and Creole) against plantation owners and masters; (4) issue-specific ameliorative uprisings exposing a colonial injustice in the interests of reform/concessions; and (5) organized movements and violence against colonial regimes for national independence (Benjamin and Hidalgo 2007: 59).

Engaged academics, activists, and journalists in *Against Colonization and Dispossession: Local Resistance in South and East Asia, the Pacific and Africa* attempt to register contemporary and predominantly organized and open democratic rural resistances, struggles, or movements addressing: primitive accumulation (Marx 1867/1990); ongoing accumulation by dispossession (ABD) (Harvey 2003);[1] and the exploitation of 'unfree' labor (landless and marginal peasants/exploited farm wage labor and fishers) (Brass 2011) as continued colonial theft integral to a coloniality of power exercised through the development project and a globalizing capitalism (Fanon 1963; Nkrumah 1965/1971; Quijano 2000; Rodney 1982) in the Euro-colonial political geographies of South and East Asia, the Pacific, and Africa.

Colonialism is understood as material and ideological racialized dispossession, domination, and exploitation that persists beyond the national achievement of official independence of the so-called Third World or the *Darker Nations* (Prashad 2008) in the twentieth century, to include continuing and new forms of neocolonialism (Nkrumah 1965/1971) on an international or global scale, contrary to the suggestion of postcolonial ruptures in the post-national independence period. Speaking to the situations of the indigenous, Huanani-Kay Trask (1993/1999: 102–103, emphasis added) expresses this as follows:

I have defined neocolonialism as the experience of oppression at a stage that is *nominally* identified as independent or autonomous. I use *nominally* to underscore the reality that independence from colonial power is legal but not economic [e.g. continued Anglo-American legal and land tenure systems in places as diverse as the Philippines, Fiji and parts of Africa]. . . . it is the ideological position that all is well; in other words, that decolonization has occurred. Therefore, problems and conflicts are post-colonial and the fault of the allegedly independent peoples. Nothing could be more inaccurate.

. . . we are surrounded by other, more powerful nations that desperately want our lands and resources and for whom we pose an irritating problem. This is just as true for the Indians of the Americas as it is for the tribal people of India and the aborigines of the Pacific. This economic reality is also a political reality for most if not all indigenous peoples. The relationship between ourselves and those who want to control us and our resources is not a *formerly* colonial relationship but an *ongoing* colonial relationship.

This process includes ongoing internal colonial relations (Casanova 1965) of domination (the source of such structural control is primarily from within national containers) between state-corporate actors, the comprador bourgeois classes and racialized social groups, and classes within states and regions, reproducing historical inequalities and projects of subjugation through development or market violence, land theft, exploitation, and cultural invasion (Benjamin and Hidalgo 2007; Fanon 1963; Guha 1983/1999, 1990). It is therefore generally understood, if not explicitly acknowledged across the contributions in this collection, that the current expression of this process as land grabbing and ABD is neither novel nor a break from the historical colonial capitalist project in these regions. ABD is continually reproduced as racialized colonial dispossession through an unrelenting project of developmentalism. That is:

much like our understandings of European conquest in the Americas, contemporary land grabbing is not simply an economic project. We would do well to remember that the myth of empty lands is a racial metaphor marking the racialized dispossession and genocide of the region's first inhabitants by European powers. . . . understanding land grabbing as a critique of development demands recognition of the spatial and temporal continuities of grabbing as a historical geography of race. (Mollett 2015: 427)

This observation is in keeping with and is variously utilized by several contributors to this collection in relation to specific histories and political-geographical contexts, and in terms of what the Black Radical Tradition (Hudson 2016) in the Caribbean and the United States (African diasporic contributions) has found noteworthy, which is that '[c]apitalism and racism, did not break from the old order (slavery, feudalism) but rather evolved from it to produce a modern world system of "racial capitalism" dependent on slavery, violence, imperialism, and genocide' (Kelley 2000: xxiii; Robinson 2000). Racial inferiority is concretized through the interlocking processes of racially targeted land theft and exploitation of colored labor,[2] as evidenced by the mercantile capitalist forced Atlantic slave labor migration of some 30 million Africans (only 11 million survived the journey) to the New World, including Jamaica and the British West Indies, described by the then British Secretary of State as 'a traffic so beneficial to the nation' (Delgado Wise and Veltmeyer 2016: 56).

Local rural resistance to colonization and dispossession

The revolt against colonial capitalism and imperialism has much to learn from the struggles and movements of communal peasant societies in rural geographies (Patel 2006) as it does from indigenous/land-based sovereignties that continue to be at the front line of dispossession, along with ongoing forms of ABD in peri/urban (rural extensions) locations and destinations in the 'planet of slums' (Davis 2006) and the struggles of variously racialized urban poor migrant workers (Choudry and Hlatshwayo 2016).

GRAIN (www.grain.org) and Food First (www.foodfirst.org) continue to support and document land, water, and green grabs, and the resistance by indigenous peoples, fisherfolk, pastoralists, farm workers, and migrant labor, and the implications for food and hunger (see *The Great Food Robbery*) and the politics of Food Sovereignty. War on Want, meanwhile, has documented and politicized (see *The Hunger Games*) the questionable role of DFID (Department for International Development, UK) aid and its alleged complicity with agribusiness (Monsanto, Unilever, Syngenta, Diageo, SABMiller) interests through public–private partnerships, dispossessing small and marginal farming groups in Sub-Saharan Africa. A study by Oxfam in 2011 suggests that an area the size of Western Europe (227 million hectares) has been sold or leased since 2001, involving mostly international state-corporate investors (e.g. 125 million hectares have been grabbed by rich countries for outsourcing agricultural production alone in Africa), while GRAIN's most recent study (July 2016), building on research from 2008, documents 500 current land-grab deals across 78 countries (around US$94 billion in farmland investments) and over 30 million hectares (the size of Finland).

> This period has witnessed a vast expansion of bourgeois land rights . . . through a global land grab unprecedented since colonial times . . . as speculative investors now regard 'food as gold' and are acquiring millions of hectares of land in the global South. (Araghi and Karides 2012: 3)

And this does not include, for instance, contemporary colonial capitalist dispossession via the global mining industry (Moody 2013).

Local resistance to colonial capitalist dispossession in South and East Asia, the Pacific, and Africa by indigenous peoples (nations), forest/tribes and ethnicities, pastoralists and hunter gatherers, small/landless (women) peasants, and fishers and farm workers facing precarious labor conditions in/out of small-scale peasant agriculture and wage labor includes cases addressing: colonial occupations of indigenous territories (lands and peoples) of genocidal implications and struggles for indigenous sovereignty/nations (Waponahki in North America; Samoa); mining (salt/Ghana; gold/Tanzania; oil/Nigeria; bauxite/India; gold-copper-nickel/Philippines; coal-conservation grabs/Bangladesh); agricultural/plantation land grabs and precarious farm/plantation labor (coconut plantations/Indonesia; citrus fruits and vegetables/South Africa; coffee plantations/Kenya; palm oil and rubber/Sierra Leone; rice/Ethiopia; maize/Ethiopia); and tsunami disaster relief and the dispossession of coastal fishers (India).

Local resistance is not used to suggest any kind of explicit spatial nor political binding or exclusivity. Activists and contributors work with a broad appreciation, vertical and horizontal, of resistance formations in relation to the spatial and political workings of colonial capital recognizing the challenges of organizing both horizontally across tribes/ethnicities, castes, gender, non/class, small landless cultivator-emergent wage labor, if not vertically with regional and inter/national actors. Similar attention is required vertically in relation to guerilla activisms, local or international political groups, civil society actors (I/NGOs and academic/research-activists), media, national organizations, and international actors (human rights coalitions/agents), if not pertinent state structures. Local resistance, if anything, is a political attempt to flag and make conspicuous the struggles of those who are being directly affected by colonial capitalist dispossessions in the rural belt as being the primary agents of (dis)organized and sporadic or planned long- and short-term push-back and resistance, given that this is where the brunt of primitive accumulation and colonial violence is continually felt. It would not be an exaggeration to reference the contexts being discussed in this collection as low- to high-intensity war zones; the daily reality for those who have to try to live, sleep, and eat in an atmosphere of continuous insecurity and prospects of being killed.

The importance of recognizing the primacy of the activism of those directly affected (and in the line of fire in the locale) has been brought up by activists in these locations for political reasons. A point made in this regard has to do with how co-optation or disarticulation of the aims of the struggle or the seizure of the political profile and achievements of the struggle by sympathetic actors at different scales can deflate activism at the heart of the movement formation. This also provides state-corporate actors with a chance to dismiss these struggles as being the work of foreign meddlers or as being instigated by more established left movements (see Chapter 7 by Rodriguez on the Philippines and Chapter 4 by Kapoor on India, on this tactic). With reference to the major mobilizations against capitalist globalization in North America more recently, Vijay Prashad (2003) illustrates the general point regarding recognition of primary political agency when he raises the question, 'Who is at the frontlines of the struggles?' in order to underscore the politics of activism as it relates to the importance of the front-line activism of people of color and the working poor versus other actors in major 'global justice' mobilizations:

> The question is not just about gaps that have opened up between those who demonstrate and those who don't, but between those who think they are at the frontlines when they toss the tear gas

canisters back at the police and those who face routine political disenfranchisement, economic displacement, social disdain, and yet spend their days in their own forms of fight-back. (p. 194)

Furthermore, the current political and theoretical insistence regarding the global or transnational scale and the unproblematic appreciations of scaling up imperatives (un)wittingly colonizes the material and ideological terms of protest and resistance by those waging the war at the points of dispossession on many an occasion, despite expressed political empathies and solidarities across multiple points of political and spatial differences. Aziz Choudry (2015), in a similar vein, refers to the tendency toward a colonial amnesia, for instance, when it comes to indigenous exclusions in social movement organizing in metropolitan centers.

In fact, in ideological and material terms, as global and transnational colonial capitalists reproduce the propagandist conception of placelessness or absorb place into the more ambiguous idea of space as a product of coloniality in the interests of a politics of capitalist accumulation, for those facing the prospects of potential eradication in these maneuvers, (re)establishing and (re)affirming a sense of place as specificity and the immediate local affiliation and meaning of land, ecology, history, ancestry, and spiritual grounding is understandably, and politically speaking, paramount. In fact, most front-line activists in these locations are wary of attempts by transnational activists to establish terms of resistance in more national or global terms, again out of political necessity for the latter perhaps, given that capital does not recognize such spatial limits. The political dismissal of such place-based struggles as ethnocentric or essentialist and conservative, however, demands (speaking in dialectical terms) that global-centric critics also scrutinize the essentialist and ethnocentric political-economic and socio-cultural impositions of a colonial capitalist modernity project over several centuries in multiple locations in relation to, as opposed to in isolation from, an anti-colonial politics of place-based pushback.

The struggles being considered in this collection are lesser known internationally, with the exception perhaps of the Niger Delta and the long-standing claims of the Lumad in Mindanao (see Chapter 15 by Oriola on Nigeria and Chapter 7 by Rodriguez on the Philippines, respectively). Contributors are all either engaged academics who have worked with the same struggles in one capacity or another or with similar struggles in these regions (Kapoor 2009), if not elsewhere, while contributing to political and research conversations for movements and academia. Some participants are activists or are engaged with popular media working for these struggles in whatever their stage of germination. Contributors have relied on first-hand experiences, research-based primary documentation, and secondary sources to illuminate, politically speaking, relatively inconspicuous struggles and to provide political insights concerning resistance to dispossession in remote locations where the strong arm of state-corporate agents of dispossession operates with impunity in the interests of accumulation. Direct action and open democratic resistance, with all their risks, expose these transgressions where and when possible. Developing the case studies for this collection has been a challenging exercise on many counts, a primary one being the political necessity to measure what is said or shared, and what should not or cannot be shared in the name of political vigilance, as these are ongoing long-term and contemporary struggles.

With the exception of two cases (see Chapter 13 by Moreda on Ethiopia and Chapter 14 by Moloo on Tanzania) and one that suggests a 'new land activism' led by chiefs and landowners (local elites) (see Chapter 12 by Ibreck on Ethiopia and Sierra Leone – one of two chapters that discusses rural 'elite-led' responses along with Chapter 8 by Mookerjea and Mishra on Bangladesh, where shrimp farm/landowners were instrumental), all the cases in the collection discuss resistance to dispossession by directly affected marginalized small and landless peasants, indigenous, tribes, castes, pastoralists and hunter-gatherers, fishers, and precarious farm laborers. Gendered struggles (horizontal and vertical) and the active involvement of women figure prominently in several chapters, including Chapter 10 by Brownhill *et al.* on Kenya, Chapter 11 by Langdon and Larweh on Ghana, Chapter 6 by Swamy and Revathi on Tamil Nadu, Chapter 4 by Kapoor on India, and Chapter 5 by Masalam on Indonesia. Similarly, caste/ethnicity/race and related questions addressing unity in organizing work are taken up in Chapter 4 by Kapoor on India, Chapter 5 by Masalam on Indonesia, Chapter 6 by Swamy and Revathi on Tamil Nadu, Chapter 9 by Naidoo *et al.* on South Africa, Chapter 11 by Langdon and Larweh on Ghana, and Chapter 15 by Oriola on Nigeria, on collective identity across ethnicities in the Delta. Wage/labor-small/landless peasant cross-class organizing is addressed in Chapter 5 by Masalam on Indonesia, Chapter 6 by Swamy and Revathi on Tamil Nadu, Chapter 9 by Naidoo *et al.* on South Africa, Chapter 10 by Brownhill *et al.* on Kenya, and Chapter 4 by Kapoor on India. Ecological politics and resistance-related deployments are evident in some chapters as well, especially Chapter 10 by Brownhill *et al.* on Kenya, as in Chapter 8 by Mookerjea and Mishra on Bangladesh.

Strategies and tactics used in organized activism are mostly forms of non-violent militant activism across cases (or hidden forms of violence as sabotage, if not implied use of violence – see Chapter 13 by Moreda on Ethiopia and Chapter 14 by Moloo on Tanzania for examples, or Chapter 5 by Masalam on Indonesia and Chapter 4 by Kapoor on India), while the mostly non-violent Anuak (see Chapter 12 by Ibreck on Ethiopia and Sierra Leone) have occasionally resorted to the use of counter-violence against the developmental violence of the state, if not in the established activism of the Lumad (see Chapter 7 by Rodriguez on the Philippines) or in the Niger Delta (see Chapter 15 by Oriola on Nigeria). Resistance also takes on the form of re-commoning (parallel politics interventions) in the face of *land-grab* threats to peasant agriculture and fisheries (see Chapter 10 by Brownhill *et al.* on Kenya and Chapter 6 by Swamy and Revathi on Tamil Nadu explicitly on this point, if not Chapter 3 by Gordon on Samoa, in relation to national efforts by Samoans regarding sovereignty assertions). All cases (with the exception of Chapter 12 by Ibreck on Ethiopia and Sierra Leone, Chapter 13 by Moreda on Ethiopia, and Chapter 14 by Moloo on Tanzania) address open democratic, semi-organized forms of resistance deploying various expressions of organized direct action and/or extrajudicial activism. While overt forms of organized resistance or pushback against colonial capitalist dispossession constitute what is referenced as resistance for the most part in this collection, authors were not asked to adhere to a fixed definition of what does or not constitute resistance. That is, covert forms of daily hidden resistances (Scott 1985), if not survival-related actions (see the case of small-scale miners in Chapter 14 by Moloo on Tanzania, for instance), are also addressed and included as constitutive of a political range of, for instance, peasant resistance in colonial contexts (Guha 1983/1999).

While a majority of the cases address the political importance of the primacy of the agency and organized responses of those who are directly affected by dispossession, some chapters conclude that these are a scattered and fractious (weak) politics, which would amount to little in the way of mounting an effective challenge without the frontal assistance of inter/transnational actors and agents such as human rights activists (see Chapter 12 by Ibreck on Ethiopia and Sierra Leone, a human rights activist and researcher's insights, or Chapter 8 by Mookerjea and Mishra on Bangladesh, regarding the significance of the role of inter/national environmental organizations in the Sundarbans). As pointed out already, these are also cases where the said struggles are primarily being led by local tribal/caste-class elites and cross-class hierarchical organizing efforts, unlike in the other cases where the focus is primarily on horizontal organizing. The mining activism of the Lumad (see Chapter 7 by Rodriguez on the Philippines), on the other hand, links all spatial and political possibilities, starting with the direct action of the Lumad and linked to/ with left political formations, including church-based human/political rights organizations and coalitions at inter/national levels. Chapter 6 by Swamy and Revathi on Tamil Nadu also addresses the instrumental if not frontal role of locally based social action NGOs in articulating fisher resistance around tsunami relief/relocations and shrimp farming. The role of NGOs is variously addressed in other chapters as well (see Chapter 8 by Mookerjea and Mishra on Bangladesh, Chapter 5 by Masalam on Indonesia, or Chapter 4 by Kapoor on India).

Also, in relation to agency and organized political (im)possibilities concerning colonial capitalist dispossession, several chapters address the role and contradictory place of indigenous or tribal chiefs and rural leaders, if not elites in non-capitalist class structures. In relatively egalitarian structures, such as the *Matais* in Samoa (see Chapter 3 by Gordon on Samoa), who exercised customary law in precolonial polities with the understanding that their legitimacy was established through their allegiance and service to the community, and have mostly remained so despite colonial occupation, the current efforts are toward rejuvenating and magnifying this politics. In Ghana (see Chapter 11 by Langdon and Larweh on Ghana), this is also the case but is an ongoing internal struggle for resistance to the appropriation of salt lagoons, whereas in the case of Sierra Leone (see Chapter 12 by Ibreck on Ethiopia and Sierra Leone) the chiefs appear to have capitulated to the distortions produced by a colonial system wherein they are now a part of what Mahmood Mamdani (1996) refers to as decentralized despotism, or a system of indirect neocolonial rule backed by the coercive power of the state, and no longer see the need to build or adhere to precolonial legitimacies established through shared norms and local consensus.

While the established struggles continue to adjust to changes in macro-political conditions and continue their political engagements (see Chapter 3 by Gordon on Samoa, Chapter 7 by Rodriguez on the Philippines, and Chapter 15 by Oriola on Nigeria), others are seeking to renew themselves some two decades later (see Chapter 5 by Masalam on Indonesia) and looking for ways to regain and build new momentum. Those struggles and movements that have continued to resist and disrupt colonial capitalist dispossession capitalize on this momentum to continue to strengthen the opposition as the agents of dispossession remain relentless (e.g. see Chapter 4 by Kapoor on India, Chapter 9 by Naidoo *et al.* on South Africa, and Chapter 11 by Langdon and Larweh on Ghana) and/or develop expanded forms of organization (e.g. see Chapter 6 by Swamy and Revathi on Tamil Nadu, and producer cooperatives and unionization of fishworkers) or create parallel re-commoning initiatives (e.g. see Chapter 10 by Brownhill *et al.* on Kenya, and ecofeminist food sovereignty initiatives). Newer (non)formations attempt to take on an organized approach or struggle to remain engaged even sporadically, but persist nonetheless (see Chapter 12 by Ibreck on Ethiopia and Sierra Leone, Chapter 13 by Moreda on Ethiopia, and Chapter 14 by Moloo on Tanzania), while others led by rural or national caste-class elites point to the political challenges of such cross-class organizing and representation, if not the futility of trying to organize locally for those being dispossessed, suggesting a need for a more transnational politics instead (see Chapter 8 by Mookerjea and Mishra on Bangladesh and Chapter 12 by Ibreck on Ethiopia and Sierra Leone).

Organization of the book

The collection aims to amplify the existence and knowledge for and about land-based (anti-colonial) struggles in the South and East Asian, Pacific, and African regions while recognizing the coloniality of ABD in these locations. The latter reality is addressed with a brief set of preliminary notes on what Rebecca Sockbeson in Chapter 2 refers to as *meta-dispossession* of her people, the Waponahki (or Wabanaki tribes of northeast United States and eastern Canada), given the genocidal objectives of European invasion and the colonial deployment of bounties and germ warfare to eradicate Wabanaki. Five out of 20 tribes remain, surviving population depletions of some 97 percent in some cases. Sockbeson briefly traces the historical connections between the theft of land and the attempts to erase the presence of her people, their culture, and language as part of a racist process of *meta-dispossession*, up to the present where contemporary native struggles in Standing Rock against the Dakota Access Pipeline (DAPL) and similar protests to clean the river and shut down paper mills on Waponahki land in Maine are meeting with some success. That said, the fact that the Waponahki are here today is a testimony to the failure of the colonial genocide project and the tenacity of the Wabonaki peoples.

The political geographies of Euro-American colonial dispossession potentially connect different locations, expressions, and experiences with coloniality and the violent theft of land and subjugation of peoples, if not contextually specific anti-colonial resistances across time and space. Given these preliminary notes on the prior and continued experience with the coloniality of dispossession in present-day North American colonial contexts, several contributors to the collection extend the colonial experience with dispossession in the South and East Asian, Pacific, and African regions with their respective contextual specificities. As several subsequent chapters demonstrate, (neo)colonization continues to be accomplished via the (neo)colonial and internal colonial vectors of state-corporate and upper class-caste-ethnicity and racialized violence, including via the means of partially revised and often harsher colonial land, forest, and mineral and mining laws. Attempts to divide marginal social groups and non-capitalist classes through state (non)recognition for the purposes (allegedly) of ameliorative measures or deliberate migration policies encouraging horizontal conflict between the *wretched of the earth* are part and parcel of ongoing racialized dispossession, as colonial theft persists with impunity in the postcolonial era in the name of development and progress. These analytics and experiences are sustained through subsequent chapters in one way or another and to different levels of amplification, including in: Chapter 3 by Gordon on Samoa, Chapter 4 by Kapoor on India, Chapter 5 by Masalam on Indonesia, Chapter 7 by Rodriguez on the Philippines, Chapter 9 by Naidoo *et al.* on South Africa, Chapter 10 by Brownhill *et al.* on Kenya, Chapter 11 by Langdon and Larweh on Ghana, Chapter 14 by Moloo on Tanzania, and Chapter 15 by Oriola on Nigeria.

South and East Asia, and the Pacific regions Naomi Gordon (Chapter 3) picks up the thread regarding the coloniality of ABD from Rebecca Sockbeson (Chapter 2) in relation to the ongoing struggles around the territories of indigenous peoples, and in this case Samoa and nineteenth-century colonization of the island. The chapter draws connections between colonial and neocolonial dispossession of land and Samoa's traditional systems of *fa'aSamoa* (Samoan way) and *fa'amatai* (way of chiefs) through colonial laws and financialization as 80 percent of customary land is currently being targeted as collateral for business loans being encouraged by the Asian Development Bank. A group of *matai* have taken up joint action to challenge this development and reassert indigenization through the *Fono* council and the centrality of the Samoan way and the way of chiefs.

Dip Kapoor (Chapter 4) addresses Adivasi (original dweller) or scheduled tribe (state recognition), Dalit (scheduled castes), and non-tribal forest dweller (ADNTFD) resistance to bauxite mining in eastern India (Orissa) in Lanjigarh being led by the Niyamgiri Surakhya Samiti (NSS), an ADNTFD social movement organization since 2003. After elaborating on the role of colonial, neocolonial, and internal colonial deployments of state-corporate violence, forest and land laws, and the criminalization of tribes along with the disproportionate impacts of colonial capitalist development on these social groups and mainly non-capitalist classes, the purpose, strategy, organization, and critical developments of the NSS-led struggle are considered in some detail, along with movement-relevant knowledge for similar anti-colonial struggles in forest belts. To date, the movement has successfully obstructed the Odisha Mining Corporation (OMC)-Vedanta/Sterlite (UK) bid to mine the top of Niyamgiri (Mountain of Law). However, the refinery remains operational and is the target of current activism.

Hasriadi Masalam (Chapter 5) considers small/landless peasant-organized resistance to coconut-plantation-related dispossession in Bohotokong village, Sulawesi province in eastern Indonesia. Another example of open direct organized activism under the leadership of ORTABUN, with a peasant farmer membership of 44 organizations linked to provincial networks such as the Sulawesi Agrarian Reform Struggle Front and the Peasants' Alliance Against Discrimination, this chapter considers the tensions of plantation labor and small/ landless peasant organizing, including Saluan ethnic groups, over a period of three decades and the current challenges associated with rejuvenating momentum. The chapter contextualizes these local developments by first examining the role of the neo/colonial Dutch initiated agro-extractive regime (especially in relation to lucrative palm oil) in Indonesia to the current-day situation under Chinese (and Arab) planters in relation to coconut.

The tsunami of 2004 was deployed as a strategy by a neoliberalizing developmentalist Indian state to wrest coastal lands from artisanal fishing communities of the mainly Pattinavar sub-castes in Nagapattinam district in the state of Tamilnadu, intensifying struggles between local fisher communities and the state. Raja Swamy and Prema Revathi (Chapter 6) examine what the push for commercial exploitation of the coast, which began in the 1980s, and now increasingly driven by the prerogatives of neoliberal (capitalist) globalization has engendered in the manner of coastal commoning as a foundational political strategy of coastal fishers in framing their interactions with the state or private capitalists. The chapter also considers the instrumental if not frontal role of SNEHA (Social Needs Empowerment Humane Awareness), a community-based social action NGO, in relation to coastal fisher resistance and its gender–economy dual strategy (and associated challenges) concerning both tsunami reconstruction and dispossession and anti-shrimp farming resistance in the region. The chapter addresses the challenges of establishing a broad fishworkers' union and of organizing a federation of self-help groups (SHGs initiated by SNEHA) into a producer cooperative.

Robyn Magalit Rodriguez (Chapter 7) historicizes the mature resistance struggles/formations of the Lumads of Mindanao and the broader transnational Philippine left movement in relation to US neo/colonialism and continued para/military harassment and violence against Lumad communities in the southern Philippines in the mining belt. The chapter demonstrates how, regardless of regime changes over the decades, the labor and land of the Philippines and the Lumad have always been up for grabs for multinational capital, a process that has always been actively facilitated by the Philippine state. Traversing local, regional, national, and international scales, Lumad activism demonstrates the centrality of colonial violence in this process of dispossession as indigenous activists resort to multiple strategies of intervention, including reinventing/providing state services in these communities (e.g. education and the Alternative Learning Center for Agricultural and Livelihood Development); services withdrawn as part of punitive action by the colonial capitalist state. Mining companies and state-corporate violence have pushed the Lumads into armed resistance, and some 70 percent of the New People's Army are from Lumad tribes.

Sourayan Mookerjea and Manoj Mishra (Chapter 8), in the final chapter in this section addressing the South/East Asian and Pacific region, consider subaltern resistance to coal power in the Sundarbans in Bangladesh. Cheap fossil fuels, such as coal, the authors point out, lie at the heart of industrial capitalism's spatial expansion from the nineteenth century onward, generating convergent crises that are both ecological and sociopolitical (dispossession, livelihood loss, and poverty inequality), which subsequently finds Bangladesh among the top five climate-vulnerable countries on the Global Climate Risk Index. Coal power is central to this colonial capitalist development paradox, as are related struggles by grassroots and civil society groups in relation to the Rampal plant. Considering the Rampal power plant (resistance) in the neoliberal vortex, the authors demonstrate the implications of this development for the Sundarbans, the largest contiguous mangrove forest in the world and the natural habitat of the Royal Bengal tiger. The Rampal land grab has been facing what the authors refer to as a 'network resistance of the multitude', initially led by landowners and shrimp farmers under the Association for the Protection of Agricultural Land who were members of a prior association of shrimp farm owners. The chapter considers the subsequent entry of middle-class environmental groups (green capitalists) and ENGOs, and the development of a network-of-networks-type resistance formation, with its peculiar challenges as a moment of tactical solidarity between small farmers and landless laborers, was soon broken up (now made invisible through colonial capitalist development dispossession) by the state's repressive apparatus and other class (feudal and capitalist) interests, which have taken over the politics of this agitation around Rampal.

African region Apartheid-era land laws restricted 80 percent of South Africa's population (blacks) to 13 percent of the land base. Reframing dispossession and reparation in terms of both a social wage and a secure livelihood, Lalitha Naidoo, Gilton Klerck, and Kirk Helliker (Chapter 9) address the precarious labor/wage (exploitation) of farm workers resembling what they reference as a pre-industrial proletariat, including widespread employment of children 14 years and younger, and wages as low as US$39/month, with almost a third of children on farms at risk of hunger. This chapter considers opposition to (mainly white) employers and the state (on citrus and vegetable farms) by (mainly black) farm workers and small/landless peasants (90 percent of whom used to be farm workers) through organized direct action by Phakamani Siyephambili (a Xhosa phrase meaning 'rise up and move forward') in the Eastern Cape province. Consideration is given to describing the emergence of organized action, the structure of this social movement organization, key developments/tactics and forms/modalities of resistance, and contestation in relation to the state-corporates while addressing questions concerning the possibility of unifying farm workers, dwellers, and small/landless peasants with a common history/experience with apartheid, prompting one farm worker (a belief shared by small-scale farmers and dwellers alike) to critique the 2011 program of white commercial farmer mentorship as a program that 'will continue to make us slaves to white farmers as we will never be able to own land of our own for housing, to graze our livestock and for ploughing'.

Leigh Brownhill, Wahu Kaara, and Terisa Turner (Chapter 10) take up re-commoning as resistance to agribusiness dispossession accomplished through finance capital and new enclosures (postcolonial colonizations of land) in Kenya through ecofeminist food sovereignty initiatives in Maragua (Shiriki farm), mobilizing cross-gender and intergenerational alliances, including young farmers stewarded by elderly rural women helping to reproduce, popularize, and preserve ancient seeds. The authors argue that Kenyan re-commoning initiatives prefigure a global transition to post-fossil fuel farming systems by relinking commoners' value chains (seeds, finance, and markets), as opposed to corporate value chains, and pursuing ends that are both socially and ecologically just, and using means that create peaceful possibilities. The process draws on Kenya's thousands of small-scale producer and peasant farmer self-organized farmer's groups engaged in food sovereignty activities, networks, and campaigns. Their work goes beyond critiquing and lobbying against the corporate (Big Ag) agenda for agriculture, toward replacing it in practice by re-commoning and re-establishment of local food sovereignty. The chapter contextualizes these developments, including the Shiriki case, by discussing the post/colonial race-gendered (male deals) anatomies of agricultural dispossession in Kenya, from British colonization to the current controls exercised by Monsanto, Syngenta, USAID, the Gates Foundation, and the IFIs in the agricultural sector.

The Songor salt lagoon is West Africa's largest alluvial salt-producing lagoon and a major source of livelihood for the 90,000 Adas or 35 communities and four clans living around the lagoon. Tracing the attempts of the British and the post-independent state-corporate actors to wrest control and dispossess the Adas of this communal resource from colonial times, Jonathan Langdon and Kofi Larweh (Chapter 11) discuss two contemporary periods of social movement mobilization by the Adas concerning the defense of the salt lagoon, despite or in spite of the contradictory role of the local chiefs and their vertical involvements with state-corporate attempts to dispossess the clans. From the adverse ecological impacts of the Volta Dam and national development that affected the natural flooding cycles and salt yields to the current corporatization intrusions by Vacuum Salt Ltd, this chapter demonstrates how the Adas and artisanal salt-winning cooperatives have engaged in semi/organized activism from colonial times. Currently, an educated activist fringe and a people's community radio initiative (Radio Ada) have contributed toward the building of the campaign and the Ada Songor Advocacy Forum (ASAF) to defend the lagoon as a communal resource and source of livelihood for the clans. Women's cooperatives and activism have been central to the development of these resistance formations.

Rachel Ibreck (Chapter 12) explores resistance to land grabs in Sierra Leone (Pujehun district) and Ethiopia (Gambella region), largely dependent on a new breed of land rights activists (new social formations and strategies of resistance) engaged in mainly non-violent place-based struggles, but with networks stretching into transnational movements and the human rights diaspora. Critics and land rights activists face the constant risk of becoming implicated in violent local ethnic or patronage politics of chiefs. While land leases (many not transparent) today amount to 248,294 hectares and 225,012 in Pujehun and Gambella, respectively, the chapter examines these new forms of resistance (involving or led by local educated elites) in relation to the Socfin palm oil and rubber project acquisition of 30,000 hectares in Pujehun and Saudi Star and Karituri rice-farming-related acquisitions in the Anuak zone in Gambella. The new land rights activism in the former case coalesces around the Malen chiefdom of the Mende ethnic group and the Malen Land Owners and Land Users Association (MALOA) and legal and civic methods of contestation. Anuak activism, led by educated Anuak in Gambella or in exile in Kenya, is via a covert informal network based in Gambella with strong diasporic connections to the Anywaa Survival organizations (UK) and Anuak Justice Council (US), and is an example of a fragmented political struggle.

Also in relation to Ethiopia, Tsegaye Moreda (Chapter 13) discusses local forms of covert and overt resistance by the indigenous lowland communities or Gumuz to large-scale agricultural land acquisitions in the Benishangul-Gumuz region through a state large-scale investors' pact. Land grabs for commercial crops and biofuels in the lowland regions affecting pastoralists, indigenous and ethnic minorities, and peasants are to the tune of some 3.6 million hectares as of 2011. Gradual encroachments by highland plough cultivators and the Derg regime's forced resettlement program from the highlands to the lowland areas have created a diverse range of social groupings in the Gumuz region. Resistance against investors is covert (e.g. arson) and overt, wherein Gumuz re/occupied land and cultivated it, regardless of its investment status in Dangur, Yaso, and Belojiganfoy *woredas*. The chapter also considers horizontal (violent) conflicts with seasonal migrant agricultural labor from the region/ highlands and resistance to the state motivated by land loss but also the failure to provide Gumuz with an opportunity to avail of wage employment and development possibilities. The state's attempt to relocate (dispossess) project-affected Gumuz is being contested with flight as a response as Gumuz flee to more remote areas. Resistance in this context is mainly unorganized and unstructured, though persistent and ever-present.

Zahra Moloo (Chapter 14) underscores the growing significance of small-scale miner everyday resistance, judicial activism, and the trans/national if not local role for investigative journalism/ media activism synergies in building the prospects of an emergent organized resistance possibility against the gold-mining enclave of mineral extraction (AngloGold Ashanti Geita Gold Mine and Acacia Mining's North Mara Gold Mine) in northern Tanzania. Contextualizing these developments in relation to the coloniality of capitalism and mining incursions into Tanzania up to the present day, including the complicit role of NGOs receiving funding from mining corporates and restricting interventions to corporate social responsibility and best practices to better penetrate local communities and aid in the process of colonial capitalist mining dispossession, the chapter makes current practices of corporate/intermediary (and state) violence against small-scale miners conspicuous in mining concession areas. It does so while underscoring an instrumental role for investigative journalism and media activism to bring this violence to light and cement opportunities for organized responses that front-end local resistance while connecting these efforts and raising the prospects for Global North–South solidarity activism such as the 'Yes to Life, No to Mining' movement and allied campaigns such as 'Protest Barrick' in addressing mining corporate colonial penetrations.

In the final chapter rounding off the collection, Temitope Oriola (Chapter 15) takes up the internationally recognized predicament and resistance related to the Niger Delta and ongoing, since 1958, ecological and social crises produced by petro-capitalism (Shell, Chevron, Texaco, Agip, Mobil, etc.), and colonization and dispossession of the peoples of the Delta. The chapter traces the role of British colonial expansion, TNCs, and national/local elites in a process of *Oloibirinization* or decline and oblivion in developmental, political-economic and sociocultural terms named after *Oloibiri*, the town with the dubious distinction of being the first place where oil was struck in Nigeria. Using this model to assess and expose how colonial capitalist dispossession has traveled through time and space in this region, the chapter focuses on the multilocal resistance politics of the Delta, questions of pan-Niger identity, and the tensions around unity in a seasoned politics involving multiple ethnolinguistic social groupings and clans or ethnicities. Current political developments and changes in state-party politics are assessed in relation to the various tensions and prospects affecting the dominant resistance formations, such as MOSOP, MEND, and the NDPVF, and the relative public (de)merits of movement counter-violence.

Colonialism, dispossession, and land-based anti-colonial struggles: reflective considerations

Karl Marx acknowledged European colonialization as an indispensable necessity and advantage in advancing world historical and revolutionary progress; an important modernizing force (Benjamin and Hidalgo 2007) necessary for the 'transformation of the feudal mode of production into the capitalist mode', that is, '[i]n actual history it is a notorious fact that conquest, enslavement, robbery, murder, in short, force, play the greatest part' in ensuring 'primitive' or 'original' accumulation of wealth and capital (Marx 1867/1990: 874, 915–916):

> The discovery of gold and silver in America, the extirpation, enslavement and entombment in mines of the aboriginal population, the beginning of the conquest and the looting of the East Indies, the turning of Africa into a warren for the commercial hunting of black-skins, signalized the era of the rosy dawn of the era of capitalist production. (p. 823)

Marx simultaneously (and predictably, given his position on colonialism and progress) dismissed rurality and the peasantry as politically inert and counter-revolutionary in sociopolitical terms, and the idea of revolution (if not a supposedly futile rural resistance to colonial capital dismissed as 'militant particularities' by David Harvey 1996) became preoccupied with the political agency of an industrial proletarian class project. The continued political presence and importance of land-centered (autonomy or indigenous sovereignty) anti-colonial projects of the indigenous and small/landless peasants based on a territorial solidarity (including a cultural and religious significance pertaining to peoples, ancestors, place, and history) and an attendant material interest to ensure that the economic activities (including the use value of labor) on a given *land* are indeed supporting its inhabitants, were ejected to an anachronistic space of the pre-political. Although he found slavery abhorrent, according to Cedric Robinson, author of *Black Marxism*, 'their role in capitalist production, Marx believed, was an embarrassing residue of a precapitalist, ancient mode of production, which disqualified them from historical and political agency in the modern world' (Robinson 2000: xxix).

Hernando de Soto, a market-Friedmanite, on the other hand, laments the failure of Third World governments to legally register individuated land titles (via post/colonial property laws) and subsequently use land as a marketable commodity now capable of being divided and thereby mobilized for market transactions (including as collateral for loans to 'the poor'), as 'dead capital' (de Soto 2000: 157). Similar to the colonial *terra nullius* (empty lands Doctrine of Discovery) basis for Western imperial colonization (racialized theft as dispossession), the insinuation here is that pre-existing ethnic land arrangements (communal and territorial collective tenure arrangements and understanding of land), in addition to being deemed relatively unproductive, are also an impediment to development that assumes land to be, above all, an economic or marketable asset, 'virtually conflated with formal titling which empowers them to dispose of their land in a market context as a private commodity' (Assies 2009: 574). Such 'extra-legal' land arrangements (outside state institutions) are then subject to forced/ bribed commodification and are under attack and risk of seizure as current neoliberal initiatives to modernize property registries and facilitate land markets (e.g. market-assisted land reforms being promoted by the World Bank over the past decade) continue to inform dispossession in the long history of coloniality, that is, '[o]nce again, such a project exalts white bodies, capitalist investment and private property and while simultaneously condemning brown and black bodies, subsistence production and collective and customary property arrangements' (Mollett 2015: 425).

The contemporary examples of rural resistance and contestation (Kapoor 2013) addressed in this collection mostly seek to register a (anti-colonial) land-based and/or precarious labor politics, if not provide a corrective by disturbing political silences in this regard. For one, anti-colonialism is first and foremost about the political contradictions (conflicts) generated over land, that is, derived from the Latin word *colere*, colonialism after all means to cultivate, inhabit, and guard land. Second, anti-colonial domination and resistance are internally constituted and part of the dialectic (internally interpenetrated and mutually constitutive of each other) of colonial (non)relations, as are state-capital or the social relations of capitalist production and class conflict. Contemporary colonizing materialist-theoretical accounts and political projects ignore the former contradiction and associated conflicts and resistance, that is, selectively abandon dialectics, while continuing to emphasize the later political dialectic in the interest of propelling (theoretically, if not politically) the inevitability thesis pertaining to the case for proletarian possibilities and (agrarian) class formations in relation to capital alone.

Raul Delgado Wise and Henry Veltmeyer (2016: 43), in their consideration of migration dynamics and 'pathways out of rural poverty', mention wage labor and migration as the only two ways out, and subsequently expand on these dynamics, while 'resistance' is curtailed in brackets. In this Marxist political and theoretical analysis, a politics of (labor) exploitation is thereby advanced as the only route toward the eventual revolutionary demise of capitalism, and deemed as the sole project of any real political significance. The attendant political terra-nullification of (pre)existing land and territorially based peoples and communal modes of production, and their continuities and struggles against ongoing projects of colonial capitalist theft and destruction, or the land-based politics of dispossession and resistance against primitive accumulation and ABD, are neither affirmed in terms of their anti-colonial political merit nor as having any real potential for posing a significant challenge to colonial capitalism.

That said, others have recently suggested that struggles around 'coercive commodification' of land (or continuing colonization, as suggested by several authors in this collection) in India and the struggles of 'those that reject commodification altogether', that is, are not negotiating better terms of incorporation 'within the terrain of commodification', 'are less easily institutionalized than labor struggles and may therefore constitute a significantly disruptive force for capitalist development in many countries for the foreseeable future' (Levien 2013: 355–356).

Western Marxist critics of 'left eurocentrism' (Biel 2015: 16–18) have until recently begun to acknowledge, what has already been understood in Third World resistances (Patel and McMichael, 2004), some of these tendencies, pointing out, for instance: the underplaying of colonialism and the slave trade as a basis for the historical origins of ongoing accumulation under the capitalist mode of production, if not the failure to recognize the main contradictions of the capitalist mode as being those between oppressor (imperialist) and oppressed nations (colonized 'Third World'); a concomitant condescension toward national movements for liberation given the sole focus on the proletarian movement in industrial countries; and a 'corrupted vision' where the Euro-American world continues to lead a socialist world order that is supposed to replace capitalism. David Harvey, meanwhile, in a similar vein, attempts a revisitation of his earlier dismissal of 'militant particularities' (Harvey 1996), while apparently trying to rescue Marx/ism on this point as follows:

> Above all, the connectivity between struggles within expanded reproduction [proletarian] and against accumulation by dispossession [e.g. indigenous anticolonial or anti-proletarian communal land-based] must assiduously be cultivated. Otherwise there is the danger of re-creating the lacunae in Marx's account of primitive accumulation and failing to see the creative potential that resides in what some regard dismissively as 'traditional' and non-capitalistic social relations and systems of production. (Harvey 2003: 179)

Zoomers' (2010) comprehensive but euphemistic reference to this process of colonial development dispossession as the 'foreignization of space' today, for instance, includes, in addition to the traditional types of foreign/internal investments related to mining and export-oriented agribusiness (and land purchases for cattle farming): (1) offshore farming and foreign direct investments (FDIs) in food production; (2) FDI in non-food agricultural commodities and biofuels; (3) development of protected areas, nature reserves, ecotourism, and hideaways; (4) special economic zones (SEZs), large scale infrastructure works (e.g. dams), and urban extensions; (5) large-scale tourist complexes; (6) retirement and residential migration; and (7) remittance-based land purchases in countries of origin. Such characterizations (foreignization of space) are euphemistic not only because they avoid references to the contemporary colonization of land but because this discussion is intended for better land governance, capacitation of 'the poor' and inclusive/sustainable development concerned with rights and economic progress, or versions of neocolonial justice as fairer incorporation into ongoing unequal terms of incorporation into the colonial capitalist development of agriculture.

Failure to acknowledge the historical geographies of race and the coloniality of capitalist power in relation to these forms of ABD (land grabbing) and related ongoing anti-colonial indigenous and land-based communal resistances today, struggles marked by political and existential differences pertaining to the implications of colonization by racial-capital in relation to land, labor, and cultural continuities, reduces the scope of the political reproductions of critical agrarian studies. While making the important political case for food sovereignty given the penetration of the agribusiness complex and state-corporate land grabs and acknowledging Via Campesina, the largest indigenous and peasant network organization today in this regard or recognizing the importance of indigenous-left formations (Petras 2013) with yet emergent or conflicting political potential for realizing (state-popular) socialism (e.g. Bolivia), similar concern for wider claims pertaining to a politics of indigenous sovereignty and for other land-based communal economies are yet to be taken seriously.

While critical agrarian studies acknowledges the political significance of what has been referred to as 'land sovereignty' or 'the notion of a people's counter(enclosure) campaign' ('re-grounding (re)possession'), which considers 'actually existing land-based social relations' (Borras and Fanco 2010: 32–36), such recognition veers toward cross/class relations (class projects – *peasantizing* the indigenous) alone, thereby ignoring related indigenous sovereignty (also *actually* pre/existing land-based social relations) projects. Given the insistence on a class politics signaling the importance of class/wage labor struggle, while resorting to appeals to a 'rights-based approach' to 'allow a social justice framework', and subsequently leaning toward a politics of governmentality within capital/imperialism, the political limitations of which have been considered by Marxists (Brass 2011) and others in a similar vein (Williams 2010), if not various indigenous colonial critiques (Alfred 2001; Trask 1993/1999; Veene 2013), is ironic at best if not a contradictory political proposition on most counts. The United Nations Declaration on the Rights of Indigenous Peoples (UNDRIP) affirms the right to self-determination (Article 3), including the right to determine political status, if not secession. The purportedly anti-colonial vision of Via Campesina, for instance, expressed in the Final Declaration in March 2006, seems to go well beyond (extends) the claims of 'food sovereignty' and such limiting politics and definitions of 'land sovereignty':

> No land reform is acceptable that is based only on land redistribution. We believe that the new agrarian reform *must*

include a cosmic vision of the territories of communities of peasants, the landless, indigenous peoples, rural workers, fisherfolk, nomadic pastoralists, tribes, afrodescendants, ethnic minorities and displaced peoples, who base their work on the production of food and who maintain a relationship of respect with Mother Earth and the oceans. (Via Campesina 2006, emphasis added)

Perhaps these political formations well recognize that 'to identify with white liberty and white justice; that is, values secreted by their masters', is to become 'emancipated slaves' because 'the terms of recognition remain in the possession of the powerful to bestow on their inferiors as they see fit' (Fanon 1967: 220–222). Furthermore, these appeals to a human rights, inclusive citizenship, and social justice politics defined and administered by various Ministries of Empowerment, embedded in ruling relations reproducing colonial capitalist disempowerment, now help sanitize an ongoing process of land usurpation and exploitation with more impunity, buttressed by such neo/colonial conceptions and administrations of justice (Ngugi 1967). To identify with colonial justice (an oxymoron in a colonized context), the colonized would have failed to re-establish themselves as truly self-determining, that is, as the creators of the terms by which they are to be recognized, or else they limit the realm of possibility of their freedom (Fanon 1963: 9).

Notes

1 Primitive accumulation refers to the process of (violent) separating the direct producer from the land and other means of production, and is the starting point for capitalist development as it is presumed that this will be followed by a process of proletarianization or the conversion of the resulting surplus population in to a working class (free wage labour). Accumulation by dispossession suggests that this process is recurring, and not over, and redefines Marx's temporal assumption. Furthermore, 'when the thieves use the stolen land and bodies (usually as labor) to make money for themselves, you have accumulation by dispossession' (West 2016: 24).

2 'This dispossession is, of course, connected to race and the deeply ingrained European, American, and Australian racist ideologies about Pacific Islanders in general and Melanesians in particular. In finely grained rhetorics and practices these racist ideologies are embodied on a daily basis for people from Papua New Guinea. These racist legacies are lived and, in various ways, feed into the structural inequality that both creates and limits indigenous modes of being and social reproduction' (West 2016: 24).

References

Alfred, T. (2001). 'From sovereignty to freedom: towards an indigenous political discourse'. *Indigenous Affairs*, 3. Copenhagen: IWGIA.

Araghi, F. and Karides, M. (2012). 'Land dispossession and global crisis: introduction to the special edition on land rights in the world system'. *Journal of World Systems Research*, 18(1): 1–5.

Assies, W. (2009). 'Land tenure, land law and development: some thoughts on recent debates'. *Journal of Peasant Studies*, 36(3): 573–589.

Benjamin, T. and Hidalgo, D. (2007). 'Anticolonialism'. In T. Benjamin (ed.), *Encyclopedia of Western Colonialism Since 1450*. Farmington Hills, MI: Thomson Gale, pp. 57–65.

Biel, R. (2015). *Eurocentrism and the Communist Movement*. Montreal: Kersplebedeb.

Borras, S. Jr. and Franco, J. (2010). 'Towards a broader view of the politics of global land grab: rethinking land issues, reframing resistance'. *Initiatives in Critical Agrarian Studies (ICAS) Working Paper Series No. 001*. Published by the ICAS, Land Deal Politics Initiative and Transnational Institute and the financial support of the Inter-Church Organization for Development Cooperation (ICCO), Netherlands. (39 pages).

Brass, T. (2011). *Labour Regime Change in the Twenty-first Century: Unfreedom, Capitalism and Primitive Accumulation*. New York: Brill.

Casanova, P. (1965). 'Internal colonialism and national development'. *Studies in Comparative International Development*, 1(4): 27–37.

Choudry, A. (2015). *Learning Activism: The Intellectual Life of Contemporary Social Movements*. Toronto: University of Toronto Press.

Choudry, A. and Hlatshwayo, M. (2016). *Just Work? Migrant Workers' Struggles Today*. London: Pluto.

Davis, M. (2006). *The Planet of Slums*. New York: Verso.

Delgado Wise, R. and Veltmeyer, H. (2016). *Agrarian Change, Migration and Development*. Winnipeg: Fernwood.

de Soto, H. (2000). *The Mystery of Capital: Why Capitalism Succeeds in the West and Fails Everywhere Else*. New York: Basic Books.

Fanon, F. (1963). *Wretched of the Earth*. New York: Grove Press.

Fanon, F. (1967). *Black Skin, White Masks*. New York: Grove Press.

Guha, R. (1983/1999). *The Elementary Aspects of Peasant Insurgency*. Durham, NC: Duke University Press.

Guha, R. (1990). *The Unquiet Woods: Ecological Change and Peasant Resistance in the Himalaya*. Berkeley, CA: University of California Press.

Harvey, D. (1996). *Justice, Nature and the Geography of Difference*. Malden, MA: Blackwell.

Harvey, D. (2003). *The New Imperialism*. Oxford: Oxford University Press.

Hudson, J. (2016). *The Racist Dawn of Capitalism: Unearthing the Economy of Bondage*. Available at: https://bostonreview.net/books-ideas/peter-james-hudson-slavery-capitalism [accessed 1 October 2016].

Kapoor, D. (2009). 'Participatory action research (par) and People's Participatory Action Research (PAR): research, politicization and subaltern social movements in India'. In D. Kapoor and S. Jordan (eds), *Education, Participatory Action Research and Social Change: International Perspectives*. New York and London: Palgrave Macmillan, pp. 29–44.

Kapoor, D. (2013). 'Trans-local rural solidarity and an anti-colonial politics of place: contesting colonial capital and the neoliberal state in India'. *Interface: A Journal for and About Social Movements*, 5(1): 14–39.

Kelley, R. (2000). 'Foreward.' In C. Robinson (ed.), *Black Marxism: Making of the Black Radical Tradition*. Chapel Hill, NC: University of North Carolina Press.

Levien, M. (2013). 'The politics of dispossession: theorizing India's land wars'. *Politics and Society*, 41(3): 351–394.

Mamdani, M. (1996). *Citizen and Subject: Contemporary Africa and the Legacy of Late Colonialism*. London: James Currey.

Marx, K. (1867/1990). *Capital: A Critique of Political-Economy*, Vol. 1, trans. B. Fowkes. London: Penguin.

Mollett, S. (2015). 'The power to plunder: rethinking land grabbing in Latin America'. *Antipode*, 48(2): 412–432.

Moody, R. (2013). *Rocks and Hard Places: The Globalization of Mining*. London: Zed Books.

Ngugi, J. [wa Thiong'o]. (1967). *Weep Not, Child*. London: Heinnemann.

Nkrumah, K. (1965/1971). *Neo-Colonialism: The Last Stage of Imperialism*. Rhodesia: Panaf Books.

Patel, R. (2006). 'International agrarian restructuring and the practical ethics of peasant movement solidarity'. *Journal of Asian and African Studies*, 42(1/2) 71–93.

Patel, R. and McMichael, P. (2004). 'Third Worldism and the lineages of global fascism: the regrouping of the Global South in the neoliberal era'. *Third World Quarterly*, 25(1): 231–254.

Petras, J. (2013). *Social Movements in Latin America: Neoliberalism and Popular Resistance*. New York: Palgrave Macmillan.

Prashad, V. (2003). *Keeping Up with the Dow Joneses: Debt, Prison, Workfare*. Cambridge, MA: South End.

Prashad, V. (2008). *The Darker Nations: A People's History of the Third World*. New York: New Press.

Quijano, A. (2000). 'Coloniality of power, eurocentrism, and Latin America.' *Nepantla*, 1(3): 533–580.

Robinson, C. (2000). *Black Marxism: The Making of the Black Radical Tradition*. Chapel Hill, NC: University of North Carolina Press.

Rodney, W. (1982). *How Europe Underdeveloped Africa*. Washington, DC: Howard University Press.

Scott, J. (1985). *Weapons of the Weak: Everyday Forms of Resistance*. New Haven, CT: Yale University Press.

Trask, H-K. (1993/1999) *From a Native Daughter: Colonialism and Sovereignty in Hawai'I*, revised edition. Honolulu, HI: University of Hawai'i Press.

Veene, S. (2013). 'NGOs, Indigenous Peoples and the United Nations'. In A. Choudry and D. Kapoor (eds), *NGOization: Complicity, Contradictions and Prospects*. London: Zed Books, pp. 76–101.

Via Campesina (2006). *Final Declaration for a New Agrarian Reform Based on Food Sovereignty*. Available at: https://viacampesina.org/en/index.php/main-issues-mainmenu-27/agrarian-reform-mainmenu-36/165-final-declaration [accessed 6 January 2017].

West, P. (2016). *Dispossession and the Environment: Rhetoric and Inequality in Papua New Guinea*. New York: Columbia University Press.

Williams, R. (2010). *The Divided World: Human Rights and Its Violence*. Minneapolis, MN: University of Minnesota Press.

Zoomers, A. (2010). 'Globalisation and the foreignization of space: seven processes driving the current global land grab'. *Journal of Peasant Studies*, 37(2): 429–447.

2 | WAPONAHKI ANTI-COLONIAL RESISTANCE IN NORTH AMERICAN COLONIAL CONTEXTS: SOME PRELIMINARY NOTES ON THE COLONIALITY OF META-DISPOSSESSION

Rebecca Sockbeson

> Waponahki resistance is deeply manifested in the reminder from our Elders that we were not intended to be here via colonial efforts to eradicate us, but most importantly we are still here, and that has required distinct resistance and fight back strategies. There were and continue to be systematic efforts to annihilate my people and dispossess us of all that we have ever known and understood . . . . We are still here.

Before European invasion, the Waponahki[1] people numbered over 20 tribes throughout Maine and the Maritimes. Entire tribes were wiped out via genocidal bounties and germ warfare. On top of this overt violence, tribes also faced systematic efforts to have colonialists rob them of their land and ancestral ways of knowing and being as a people. The effects of this historical legacy have severely dispossessed our people of ancestral ways of knowing and being, and the destruction this has caused is evident in the trauma and loss of Waponahki people today. The people survived population depletion of 97 percent (Paul 2000; Thornton 1987). Today, five tribes remain: the Penobscot, Passamaquoddy, Mi'kmaq, Maliseet, and Abenaki. Our survival depends on our ability to fight back against the historical legacies of colonialism.

These struggles are misrepresented by accounts of colonial historiographers and writers who depict our story as one of 'loss'. In their story, we have 'lost' our land and cultural knowledge. These are colonially blurred, minimizing, if not euphemizing, versions of the history of my people. In our experience, these things have not been lost, but 'taken'. These extensive and intensive experiences of a collective people so heavily and systematically dispossessed require a deeper understanding than the nouns 'loss' or 'dispossession' can only begin to offer.

The following chapter outlines the historical context of the dispossession of the Waponahki, which generally reflects similarly timed colonial experiences of other Indigenous peoples in the northeastern United States. In doing so, I introduce the term *meta-dispossession* as a way to more accurately name the underpinnings of the state of the current socioeconomic crisis my people face today. The addition of 'meta' speaks to the transcendence beyond dispossession. This history offers some perspective on the contemporary realities of the legacies of *meta-dispossession*, and the ways in which my people continue to take up the fightback and resist the coloniality of dispossession. The relevant historical context presented here makes sense of this meta-dispossession on Indigenous terms as it relates to the current socioeconomic and epistemicidal crisis my people face.

Relevant historical context

Much of the documented history has been recorded by non-Waponahki anthropologists and historians, and is considered by many Waponahki to be inaccurate and biased (Paul 2000; Wagner *et al.* 1993). The history of the Waponahki, who are Indigenous to the land, existed far before European invasion: the people have lived on what is now known as the State of Maine in the United States and Atlantic Canada in New Brunswick and Nova Scotia since time immemorial. As peoples of oral tradition, Waponahki ways of knowing and being have been passed down from generation to generation.

The following dates and accounts provide relevant context for the discussion of dispossession and the ongoing fight back. The Waponahki initially served as guides and hosts, teaching the Europeans how to survive and thrive on the land. The Waponahki values of generosity and hospitality were quickly taken advantage of by the Europeans, who began their abusive treatment of the Waponahki as early as the mid-1500s. As the Europeans began taking over Waponahki lands, kidnapping and murdering the people, the Waponahki began to defend themselves and fight back. The Waponahki became highly skilled at using European guns they had acquired through trade, with the result that, in 1632, English authorities prohibited gun sales to the Waponahki. Yet another way of taking power away from the Waponahki, this act also furthered their intended decimation. From the seventeenth to the early eighteenth centuries, the history of the people includes massive massacres and wars with the Europeans (Prins 1995). During this time, Indigenous leaders developed a political alliance to challenge European warfare, the Waponahki Confederacy, which lasted into the 1860s (Francis *et al.* 2008). In the early 1700s, Queen Anne of England commenced compensating her people for Native American scalps, and bounties began to be paid for the scalps of Waponahki. Issuing such bounties after prohibiting gun sales to Native people grossly disadvantaged them in defending themselves and made it easier to kill off the Waponahki (Paul 2000). A specific bounty for Penobscot scalps was issued in 1755, about 100 years after the Waponahki gun prohibition. Similar bounties existed all along the eastern seaboard of both the United States and Canada, and account for some of the most densely populated massacres and removals of Indigenous people (Paul 2000; Thornton 1987).

In an attempt to halt the decimation of Penobscots from the 1775 scalping bounties, Penobscot Chief Joseph Orono, accompanied by a delegation of Penobscots, pledged an alliance with the English in Watertown, Massachusetts. In 1818, the Waponahki and the State of Massachusetts signed a treaty establishing and allocating reservation lands (AFSC 1989).

During the mid-1700s, the Wabanaki were resisting the seizures of land, particularly those lands that afforded access to the life ways of ocean and river fishing. The genocidal bounty was enacted in 1755 during this same era. Today, Indigenous people in both Canada and the United States are the least likely to be homeowners or off-reservation property owners than any other group. Ocean- and riverfront property is even more unlikely to be owned by a Waponahki tribal member today, and this is deeply rooted in initial colonial land dispossession (Bear-Nicholas 2015; Brooks and Brooks 2010; Sockbeson 2011). The coast of Maine is identified as one of the most beautiful places in the world (Beckett n.d.). There are over 4,000 islands off the coast of Maine, which accounts for more islands than the rest of the eastern coast combined. The majority of these islands are privately owned and considered prime real estate today (Maine Bureau of Parks and Lands n.d.). Early colonial records indicate that land seizure was based upon the successful capture and

By His HONOUR

SPENCER PHIPS, Efq;

Lieutenant-Governour and Commander in Chief, in and over His Majefty's Province of the *Maffachufetts-Bay* in *New-England.*

A PROCLAMATION.

WHEREAS the Tribe of *Penobfcot* Indians have repeatedly in a perfidious Manner acted contrary to their folemn Submiffion unto His Majefty long fince made and frequently renewed ;

I **Have therefore, at the Defire of the Houfe of Reprefentatives, with the Advice of His Majefty's Council, thought fit to iffue this Proclamation, and to declare the Penobfcot Tribe of Indians to be Enemies, Rebels and Traitors to His Majefty King** *GEORGE* **the Second : And I do hereby require His Majefty's Subjects of this Province to embrace all Opportunities of purfuing, captivating, killing and deftroying all and every of the aforefaid Indians.**

AND WHEREAS the General Court of this Province have voted that a Bounty or Incouragement be granted and allowed to be paid out of the Publick Treafury, to the marching Forces that fhall have been employed for the Defence of the *Eaftern* and *Weftern* Frontiers, from the *Firft* to the *Twenty-fifth* of this Inftant *November* ;

I **Have thought fit to publifh the fame ; and I do hereby Promife, That there fhalt be paid out of the Province-Treafury to all and any of the faid Forces, over and above their Bounty upon Inliftment, their Wages and Subfiftence, the Premiums or Bounty following, viz.**

For every Male *Penobfcot* Indian above the Age of Twelve Years, that fhall be taken within the Time aforefaid and brought to *Bofton, Fifty Pounds.*

For every Scalp of a Male *Penobfcot* Indian above the Age aforefaid, brought in as Evidence of their being killed as aforefaid, *Forty Pounds.*

For every Female *Penobfcot* Indian taken and brought in as aforefaid, and for every Male Indian Prifoner under the Age of Twelve Years, taken and brought in as aforefaid, *Twenty-five Pounds.*

For every Scalp of fuch Female Indian or Male Indian under the Age of Twelve Years, that fhall be killed and brought in as Evidence of their being killed as aforefaid, *Twenty Pounds.*

Given at the Council-Chamber in *Bofton,* this Third Day of *November* 1 7 5 5, and in the Twenty-ninth Year of the Reign of our Sovereign Lord *GEORGE* the Second, by the Grace of GOD of *Great-Britain, France* and *Ireland,* KING, Defender of the Faith, *&c.*

By His Honour's Command,
J. Willard, Secr.

S. Phips.

GOD Save the KING.

BOSTON: Printed by *John Draper,* Printer to His Honour the Lieutenant-Governour and Council. 1755.

2.1 British 1755 proclamation offering £40 for an adult Penobscot male, £20 for the scalp of Penobscot woman or child

Note: £40 in 1755 is approximately $8,869 in 2016 US dollars: 'Pounds to Sterling Dollars, Historical Conversion of Currency', Dr. Eric Nye, U. of Wyoming, https://www.uwyo.edu/numimage/currency.htm

or decimation of Wabanaki people. The scalp bounty was enacted in 1755, and shortly after the American Revolution (1765–1783) lands seized by the British were either allocated to soldiers or, in the case of coastal property, sold to the highest bidders (Brooks and Brooks 2010; Maine Bureau of Parks and Lands n.d.; Prins 1995). The following colonial account of one of the most coveted fishing areas, where the rivers meet the ocean, reveals how specific towns were named after the individuals responsible for the genocide, and this colonial oppression celebrated through the naming. Here, we see how the prosperous town of Westbrook, Maine, came to be named:

> Thomas Westbrook . . . was charged with scouting Wabanaki territory in the east, including patrols between the Presumpscot and Saco Rivers. His commission, as given to him by Lieutenant Governor Dummer, was: 'You are to take, intercept, kill & destroy the Indian Enemy in all Places where they may be found'. (Brooks and Brooks 2010:18)

Brooks and Brooks further show how the seizure of waterfront lands heavily compromised Indigenous traditional ecological knowledge (ITEK). They identify ITEK as that critical body of knowledge that is transferred intergenerationally and is inextricably linked to the ecology of the territory, rooted in the belief system associated with the land and waters. The dispossession of primary fishing areas has had devastating impacts on the ITEK and feeds the beast of epistemicide, which is the intention to eradicate a people's epistemology, their ways of knowing and being. These waterfront land seizers marked the beginning of the end of critical access to the ocean that the Wabanaki once had and furthered the colonial epistemicidal agenda of meta-dispossession.

Native people are the most heavily legislated against group than any other group in both the US and Canada. More laws have been created to control or dispossess us than any other group. From the early 1880s until the early twentieth century, Waponahki children were sent to federally operated residential schools, primarily the Carlisle Indian Industrial School, where students were not permitted to speak any Native language (Francis *et al.* 2008). During this time, reservation life was imposed. With the people no longer able to move throughout the region and live off the land, the Waponahki way of life and the traditional economic system was disrupted. A dramatic shift in work and economic subsistence occurred as the people moved from traditional hunting and fishing to a heavier reliance on making and selling baskets, guiding, logging, and construction (AFSC 1989). In 1924, Native Americans won citizenship status, but were not given the right to vote in federal elections until 1954.

The Second World War and the 1950s marked many transitions and further dislocation for the Waponahki. The Waponahki endured severe poverty and unemployment during this time. Many Waponahki men enlisted in the military and joined the war effort overseas, while wartime disruptions forced numerous remaining Waponahki families to leave their reservation communities for factory jobs located in the Boston, Bridgeport, and Hartford areas. These migrations off-reservation had the result of imposing a significant shift from Native languages to English, as off-reservation schools enforced English-language-only policies, and teachers went so far as to approach parents in their homes to encourage them to speak only English with their children (Francis *et al.* 2008). In 1952, the first bridge was built between the home of the Penobscot Indian Nation, Indian Island, to Old Town on the mainland (also known as Marsh Island) (Ranco 2000). The right to vote in state and local elections was granted to the Waponahki in 1967, 12 years after the right to vote in national elections. Maine marks the last US state to grant Native people such as the Waponahki the right to vote (AFSC 1989).

The 1970s and 1980s saw a series of legal challenges for land and changes in legislation. In 1972, the Passamaquoddy tribe and Penobscot Nation filed a lawsuit claiming two-thirds of the State of Maine (AFSC 1989). The claim included 12.5 million acres of land granted in treaties that had not been ratified by Congress. The Penobscot and the Passamaquoddy were relying upon the Indian Nonintercourse Act of 1790, which dictates that Indian (Indigenous) lands can only be acquired with the approval of the United States Congress (Francis *et al.* 2008). The land in question thereby would remain under the continuing ownership of the Passamaquoddy and Penobscot. In 1975, the Penobscot and Passamaquoddy were granted federal recognition, which gave reservation communities access to much-needed federal funding for housing, education, and infrastructure. In 1980, the Maine Indian Claims Settlement Act was signed into law. The act recognized the treaties had not been ratified by Congress, but it did not award the tribes ownership of their previous landholdings. Instead, monetary compensation was granted so they could buy back certain lands within their traditional territories (Ranco 2000). This has been deemed one of the largest legal land claim suits in the history of the United States. Although this may appear as an act of repossession of the land, it came at a continued cost of our rights (Ganter 2004). The lands purchased back by the Penobscots have both state and federal regulation and are categorized as either 'trust' or 'fee' land. The US government controls the tribal land purchased back in 'trust', as they hold the title to the land for the 'benefit' of the tribe. Ultimately, it is also the US government who deems what is beneficial for the tribal nation. The 'fee' land is under authority of the tribal nation, as the tribe secures actual title to the land, however the tribal nation is required to pay annual taxes to the state in order to keep this land (TEEIC n.d.). This has created an ongoing tension within the tribal community as many want to convert our trust land into fee land, particularly as the newly elected federal government under Donald Trump's administration embarks upon us and will have authority over trust lands. Tensions are high and outcomes uncertain. The land dispossession is extensive and deeply felt within our communities. My reservation, the Penobscot Indian Nation, sits on a six-mile-diameter island with over 500 residents; it is one of four reservation communities in Maine. Maine Indian people face the highest rates of poverty, unemployment, and incarceration rates than any other group in the state, and this is reflective of the national statistics for American Indians in general. What does the land dispossession have to do with the socioeconomic crisis? It has everything to do with it. The fact that one of the largest claims to land in the history of the US occurred in the whitest, least diverse state in the nation is no coincidence; such coloniality is meta-dispossession. I see so many white people in my state as a haunting indicator of the vast and massive genocide my people have survived.

Waponahki generosity in the face of meta-dispossession

The meta-dispossession of coloniality imposed a destructive legacy. The process of acknowledging and naming this legacy and its destruction offers new perspective on today's reality, and begins to help us make sense of the nonsensical. The current high rates of death and addiction are legacies of this dispossession giving it the 'meta' understanding. It is within the context of this history that the Waponahki people are returning to their ways of thinking and working diligently to dismantle the frame of colonization that has held them tightly within institutions and systems that were crushing and overpowering the Waponahki people. My own story as a Waponahki woman and researcher is only one of many as we move along that path toward our own renewal and repossession.

The absence or dramatic decline of the ancestral rituals and ceremonies associated with how we come into this world and how we leave this world are being wrongfully identified as cultural 'loss'; the act of renaming such experiences as a dispossession is at the heart of resistance. Legislation against Indigenous peoples has dispossessed us of land, ways of knowing, and ways of being. The American Indian Religious Freedom Act of 1978 attempted to make it legal once again for Indigenous knowledge to be transferred by allowing ancestral ceremonies and rituals to be practiced (NARF 1979). Up until this point, Indigenous knowledge transfer was either practiced underground or not at all. Federal and state prohibitions of our human rights to speak our languages and practice our ways of being have been central to meta-dispossession, and our peoples' misunderstanding of it all as a loss feeds the coloniality. The rethinking of 'lost' or 'forgotten' as colonial rhetorics of dispossession are fundamental to the fighting back. This rethinking process and more accurate engagement with dispossession is required in order for the political will and mobility to enact effective resistance. Making more accurate sense of the painful legacy of colonialism opens the pathway to continued repossession and revitalization of our ancient knowledge systems and imbedded languages.

The people's creation stories are rooted in the land and cosmos. The knowledge about this has been heavily subjugated, hence dispossessed. It has been identified by our elders and traditional knowledge holders that the most significant dispossession felt and experienced today is the way in which we come into the world and leave this place, birth and death, and the associated rituals and ceremony have been 'lost'. Currently, the here and now is endemic of lack of past and future ritual. Lack of accountability associated with the colonial rhetoric of 'loss' prevents knowledge mobilization about systemic dispossession. So long as we misperceive the lack of practice of these significant ceremonies as a 'loss', we will continue to remove colonial dispossession as a cause and increase the likelihood of internalization of these concepts. In the course of my studies at Harvard University, I attended a lecture of an anthropology postdoctoral fellow. The presentation was about language loss, and I hoped for insight into the Waponahki experience. However, the word loss kept poking me in the eye, straight through to my nerves. I finally raised my hand and explained that our languages had not necessarily been lost, and that perhaps 'taken' was a more suitable term. I had reached clarity on the issue of our people not speaking their own language. If it were as simple as a loss, we could take full blame, we could gather search parties to find it, and once it was retrieved we could identify a process so as to not be so forgetful next time, something as simple as purchasing a key hanger to place by my door so I won't lose my keys. However, language and cultural loss is not that simple, nor is land loss.

Revitalization of language and Indigenous knowledge recovery works against undercurrents of oppression; this needs to be addressed by both our Waponahki communities and mainstream society. If I view something as taken from me, there is an implication that it is still there, that it can be retrieved. However, if I lost it, I am to blame for its disappearance. As Native people, blame can be so paralyzing that we become immobilized. That is yet another easy justification to remain speaking the English language and privileging Euro-Western epistemology. Loss is not a strong enough word to describe the history of Indigenous languages and the lack of ceremony and ancient ritual practice, and it does not accurately represent what happened. Language and cultural loss supports the mentality of disempowerment and immobility on the parts of Indigenous peoples themselves. The truth is, as Mary Bassett (1997) says so profoundly about the low fluency in our communities, 'it is not our fault'. Similarly, the meta-dispossession and its associated socioeconomic crisis is not our fault either. Reality is, it is our meta-responsibility, our burden to be the victors in the fight back and that we continue to be; we do not have time to be victims. Revolutionary thinking compels us to know that we are so much more than the meta-dispossession that attempts to define and oppress us. Winona LaDuke, an Indigenous warrior, writes about responsibility: 'And there it is a fundamental question for all of us: If a people disappear in seven generations, does that mean responsibility disappears too?' (LaDuke 2016: 178).

I recently joined other tribal members in a ceremony to pray for the thousands of water protectors out at Standing Rock who are challenging the Dakota Access Pipeline (DAPL). The Penobscot Nation is all too familiar with water protection. The key idea here is protection from capitalism and its associated greed and human rights deprivation, identified in this movement as the *Black Snake*. Texas-based Energy Transfer Partners Oil Company has been building a crude oil pipeline through Standing Rock Sioux Nation, in North Dakota. The residents of Bismarck and their city council denied Texas-based Energy Transfer Partners access to build the pipeline through their town, and their wishes were honored. However, the Standing Rock Sioux Tribal Nation also voted to deny access, but because colonial regimes such as the US government are still heavily intact, Texas-based Energy Transfer Partners began their pipeline construction on tribal land without the permission of the tribal nation, and the US government has been letting this happen since April 2016.

Trust lands were put in place by the federal government so that the non-Natives could not take land away from us, and now the federal government doesn't have to get our permission to put a pipeline down. Putting a pipeline through the Standing Rock Sioux's only source of drinking water and sacred sites is the same as genocide.

Generosity is a coveted ancestral value of the Wabanaki, so the concept of greed is traditionally looked down upon. Within the past 5–10 years, like many other Indian reservations or First Nations communities, our rates of violent death and addiction has felt an all-time high. Our communities are devastated by the rates of death and the associated contexts of drug addiction. One of the horrific implications of greed is addiction, and addiction is birthed from the colonial processes of dispossession, making it a meta-dispossession. Passamaquoddy Elder Wayne Newell reminded a group of tribal members of the importance of generosity to our people, and in the same discussion Passamaquoddy Elder Mary Bassett cautioned us that the same generosity gave leverage to the colonizer to take advantage of our people (personal communication, 1 November 2009). The colonial implications of this greed includes the potential to compromise a fundamental value of the Wabanaki people: generosity. In fact, generosity is so deeply valued that greed, on the other hand, is considered to be an evil force (Sunlight Media Collective *et al.* 2015):

In the beginning, these newcomers were welcomed as guests to their homeland. But soon, they would be committing the most

egregious crime of Penobscot society: greed. And so began a
centuries old clash of cultures. Penobscots survived enormous
losses from colonization. Death and displacement of ancestors,
destruction of fisheries, degradation of water, deforestation of
traditional hunting grounds, and destruction in their traditional
forms of governance. (Sunlight Media Collective *et al.* 2015)

Late Penobscot Elder ssipsis writes extensively about dispossession
and resistance in her poems and story collections; she too cautions
our people about what greed does to our land and river. She is writing
specifically about the pulp and paper mills that emitted dioxin, which
is a highly carcinogenic toxin that whitens paper, into the river. For
several decades, the seven pulp and paper mills upstream from my
reservation, Indian Island, were allowed to dump dioxin into the
river that my people survived on the fish from, and came to have
higher rates of cancer and other associated health problems from.
ssipsis writes about this:

The taste of greed: Metallic vomit, hissing and streaming by day
and belching at two a.m. the deadly dioxin overloads. The river
streams continuously as floating curds and residue, endless puffs
of pulp washed down with chlorine, flushed down the Penobscot
River Sewer Basin. (ssipsis 2007: 59)

Today, the Penobscot Nation has experienced some significant
victories in the river restoration project and getting the state to shut
down the paper mills. My reservation community, the Penobscot
Nation that sits on our ancestral territory of Indian Island, recently
won a court battle that confirmed our ancestral fishing rights in the
water surrounding our little island of six miles in diameter. However,
in 2012, the State of Maine Attorney General attempted to assert
that the water was not part of our reservation property, a violation of
the Land Claims Settlement Act. In 2015, the State of Maine court
ruled against the Penobscot Nation in my people's attempt to protect
our treaty rights to the water that surrounds our reservation lands.
The tribe has appealed this decision to federal courts, and this legal
battle is ongoing. The political mobility surrounding this particular
issue is much like the history of the Wapohnaki, and this time many
non-Native allies have come forward in support of the Penobscot

Nation in the upholding of the treaty rights to the water (Sunlight Media Collective *et al.* 2015).

Generosity is at the root of the resistance, and gives the fight back the teeth necessary to take down the *Black Snake* that so many of us are up against in our respective Indigenous communities. The fight back necessitates generosity; the dispossession relies on greed. This generosity is ancestral to my people, the Waponahki, and our resistance is deeply informed by this value, serving as a critical reminder that the epistemicide is not complete . . . we are still here.

Notes

1 Also known as Wabanaki Tribes of Northeast United States and Eastern Canada.

References

American Friends Service Committee (AFSC) (1989). *The Wabanakis of Maine and the Maritimes: A Resource Book About the Penobscot, Passamaquoddy, Maliseet, Micmac and Abenaki Indians*. Philadelphia, PA: American Friends Service Committee.

Bassett, M. (1997). *Re-Evaluation Counseling Workshop*. Presentation at Waponahki Language Gathering Conference. Indian Island, ME.

Bear-Nicholas, A. (2015). 'The role of colonial artists in the dispossession and displacement of the Maliseet, 1790s–1850s'. *Journal of Canadian Studies/Revue d'études canadiennes*, 49(2), Spring: 25–86.

Beckett, K. (n.d.). 'Ten beaches to visit now: Gooch's Beach, Maine'. *National Geographic*. Available at: http://travel. nationalgeographic.com/travel/ beaches-to-visit-now/#/kennebunk-beach-maine_94257_600x450.jpg [accessed 14 November 2016].

Brooks, L. and Brooks, C. (2010). 'The reciprocity principle and traditional ecological knowledge: understanding the significance of indigenous protest on the Presumpscot River'. *International Journal of Critical Indigenous Studies*, 3(2): 11–28.

Francis, D., Leavitt, R. and Apt, M. (2008). *Peskotomuhkati Wolastoqewi Latuwewakon: A Passamaquoddy-Maliseet Dictionary*. Orono, ME: University of Maine Press.

Ganter, G. (2004). 'Sovereign municipalities? Twenty years after the Maine Indian Claims Settlement Act of 1980'. In B. Johansen (ed.), *Enduring Legacies: Native American Treaties and Contemporary Controversies*. Westport, CT: Praeger, pp. 25–43.

LaDuke, W. (2016). *Chronicles: Stories from the Front Lines in the Battle for Environmental Justice*. Ponsford, MN: Spotted Horse Press.

Maine Bureau of Parks and Lands (n.d.). *Coastal Island Registry*. Available at: www.maine.gov/dacf/parks/ about/coastal_island_registry.shtml [accessed 21 December 2016].

Native American Rights Fund (NARF) (1979). *We Also Have a Religion: The American Indian Religious Freedom*

Act and the Religious Freedom Project of the Native American Rights Fund. Announcements, Winter. Available at: www.narf.org/nill/documents/nlr/nlr5-1.pdf [accessed 14 November 2016].

Nye, E. (n.d.). *Pounds to Sterling Dollars, Historical Conversion of Currency.* Available at: www.uwyo.edu/numimage/currency.htm [accessed 14 November 2016].

Paul, D. (2000). *We Were Not The Savages: A Mi'kmaq Perspective on the Collision Between European and Native American Civilizations.* Halifax: Fernwood.

Prins, H. (1995). 'Turmoil on the Wabanaki Frontier, 1524–1678'. In R. Judd, E. Churchill and J. Eastman (eds), *Maine: The Pine Tree State from Prehistory to the Present.* Orono, ME: University of Maine Press, pp. 97–119.

Ranco, D. (2000). *Environmental Risk and Politics in Eastern Maine: The Penobscot Indian Nation and the USEPA.* PhD Dissertation, Harvard University.

ssipsis (2007). *Prayers, Poems, and Pathways.* Knox, ME: Robin Hood Books.

Sockbeson, R. (2011). *Cipenuk Red Hope: Weaving Policy Toward Decolonization and Beyond.* PhD Dissertation, University of Alberta. Available at: https://era.library.ualberta.ca/files/c2v23vt49r [accessed 16 November 2016].

Sunlight Media Collective (Producer), DeFrances, M. and Girouard, M. (Directors) (2015). *Penobscot: A Fight for Ancestral Waters.* Indian Island, ME: Sunlight Media Collective.

Thornton, R. (1987). *American Indian Holocaust and Survival: A Population History Since 1492.* Norman, OK: University of Oklahoma Press.

Tribal Energy and Environmental Information Clearinghouse (TEEIC) (n.d.). *Tribal and Indian Land.* Available at: https://teeic.indianaffairs.gov/triballand/ [accessed 16 November 2016].

Wagner, D., McInnis Misenor, K., Attean, E., and Sockbeson, R. (1993). 'Penobscot Nation Oral History Project'. Unpublished manuscript, Penobscot Nation and University of Southern Maine, Portland, ME, USA.

PART I

**SOUTH AND EAST ASIA AND
THE PACIFIC REGION**

3 | SOVEREIGNTY POLITICS IN SAMOA: FA'ASAMOA, FA'AMATAI, AND RESISTANCE TO COLONIAL CAPITAL AND DISPOSSESSION OF CUSTOMARY LAND AND PLACE

Naomi Gordon

Introduction

For Samoa,[1] exploitation and dispossession works across socio-cultural and political-economic axes dating back to nineteenth-century colonial conquest and the effort to erode the traditional systems of *fa'asamoa* (Samoan way) and *fa'amatai* (way of chiefs) in an attempt to disarticulate the Samoan way of life and understanding, and in order to weaken customary laws that govern and protect Samoan land and peoples. Historically, and today, the systems and practices of *fa'asamoa* and *fa'amatai* have attenuated coloniality and capital's infiltration into Samoa's political economy, as is the case in Samoa's current struggle to protect customary land.

As signatory to neoliberalizing policies, the Samoan state promotes land and labour, as instruments for economic growth and social prosperity. Over the last two decades, customary land, accounting for 80 per cent of all land in Samoa, has become the target of capital with the state's introduction of legislation to mobilize and securitize customary land. At issue is the alienation of customary land vis-à-vis the undermining of customary land ownership rights, which for Samoa has deep implications that threaten the nation's traditional political framework, and ostensibly Samoa's sovereignty. While the state has largely been successful at stemming consultations and dialogue on the issue, decreeing any mention of land alienation as asinine, dissension continues to grow on the ground. A group of *matai*[2] have taken up joint action to challenge the Asian Development Bank's (ADB) project of commodifying customary land through a finacialization process that expands the scale of collateralized lending to business by using customary land as collateral. Most fervidly, the group opposes the imposition of economic and legal frameworks that jettison customary laws and systems that have safeguarded the interests of Samoans for millennia. This is documented in a complaint letter to the accountability mechanism of the ADB as follows:

> Customary land is not merely untapped collateral. Rather, it sits at the heart of the *fa'asamoa* – of the Samoan political and electoral mainstream, as well as its cultural core and family life. Accordingly, customary land rights are entrenched and securely enshrined in the Constitution. (Elisara *et al.* 2014)

Typifying what Harvey (2005a) coins accumulation by dispossession, the state has worked in concert with the ADB to privatize and commodify collectively owned land, suppress subsistence economies and traditional practices, and entrench credit systems vis-à-vis collateral mortgaging. The usurping of customary landowner rights, however, is not new terrain for Samoa, and is linked to colonial agendas that worked to displace collective ownership and subsistence economies for individualized ownership/property rights, agricultural cash economies, and wage labour. Samoa's current struggle for protecting customary land and sovereignty needs to be understood as emerging from the interrelated and historical contexts of colonialism and global capitalism. This analytic and the experiences and memories of Samoa's cultural and political subjugation and emancipation together suggest a historically situated and place-based response that critiques the continuities and discontinuities of the colonial project while enabling a potentially more complete understanding of colonized life in Samoa (Rabaka 2003).

This chapter, drawing on critical ethnographic research that the author conducted in Samoa in 2014, works to advance the idea of dispossession as a recurrent process occurring differentially across space and time while underscoring capital's assault against the material and the social. For indigenous peoples and struggles, social and material interactions and transgressions by global institutions and local functionaries are indivisible. What is taken up here are the terrains of Samoan resistance and modes of organization and action, grounded in a politics that disrupts imperialist structures and systems of power through indigeneity – *fa'asamoa* and *fa'amatai* – tangible avenues of resistance against the machinations of colonial capital seeking to assimilate and extinguish indigenous economies, knowledges, and ways of life.

Terrains of dispossession: repudiating *fa'asamoa* and *fa'amatai*

To understand the mechanisms and experiences of accumulation by dispossession in Samoa is to talk about the continuities of colonial structures and systems of domination and imposition. It is to talk about situating struggles in specific historical contexts that take into account places and relations of power that work to shape the internal dynamics, and structural and social conditions necessary to entrench systems of economic individualism and property rights, and to disarticulate customary systems and meanings. It is to understand that the enclosure of the commons is inseparable from the enclosure of customary social and political systems – *fa'asamoa* and *fa'amatai* – as both are mutually inclusive in a reciprocal relationship. For Samoans dispossession signifies a collision of two forces – one *palagi* (European), the other Samoan – where the former is inherently incompatible with the social and political organization of *fa'asamoa* and *fa'amatai*. The continuities of dispossession are considered here briefly, and key points of contention and colonial imposition are highlighted to explicate the recurrent processes of colonial dispossession.

Colonial dispossession in Samoa Compared to other areas of the globe, Samoa's encounter with colonization came late, abated by the nation's remote geographic location, the island's lack of natural resources, and, moreover, Samoa's indolence to foreign agendas, rejection of wage labour, and largely impenetrable institutions of *fa'amatai* and *fa'asamoa* (Linnekin 1991; Meleisea 1987a). However, by the middle of the nineteenth century, waves of colonial dispossession were advanced through the modus operandi of legal and financial mechanisms that aimed to reorganize the system of *fa'amatai* and diffuse the values and principles of *fa'asamoa* to transform customary land tenure, and displace and commodify Samoa's agrarian political economy.

Samoa's early colonial period was marked by missionaries who endeavoured to embed the spiritual and physical institution of the Church into Samoa's districts and villages, entrenching its practices into Samoans' way of life and capitalizing on traditions, such as the customary practice of gift giving – *fa'alavelave*.[3] This period also saw Samoa's insertion in to the market economy, instigated by commercial entrepreneurs who introduced new forms of economic organization and activity that sought to commodify land and labour and accumulate surplus economic profits (Macpherson and Macpherson 2009). Through coercive methods of taxation and land mortgaging, the development of large-scale plantations and monopolies flourished, such as the German trading company Godeffroy & Sohn, who in over a decade acquired roughly 100,000 acres of land (Moses 1973). By the late 1870s, Europeans had claimed all land around Samoa's capital, Apia.

During the period of colonial rule, both German and New Zealand regimes concentrated on expanding agricultural cash economies, instituting wage labour, increasing commodification of land, simplifying kinship rules, and attempting to weaken the power of *fa'asamoa* and *fa'amatai*, whose systems and practices were seen as impediments to economic development. Under the Treaty of Berlin, the western islands of Samoa were ceded to Germany, with formal annexation the following year in 1900. Prevailing German policy aimed to convert Samoans into submissive objects to become a passive and productive labour force for German enterprises (Moses 1972). Moses (1972) writes that the attitude of the German administration was not to advance civilization; rather: 'It was expected that they (natives) would supply a cheap steady source of labour in return. Indeed the natives had to learn the obligation of work' (Moses 1972: 43).

However, as Firth (1977) asserts, Samoans were not willing labourers and regularly demanded high pay, which resulted in the rise of indentured labour of Melanesians and later Chinese, and the institution of racialized labour (Castille 2012). Where capital struggled with labour, it excelled in land dispossession, with European settlers and planters amassing large sections of land. To secure this land, a central constituent of the Treaty of Berlin included the formation of an international Land Commission and Supreme Court, which adjudicated settler claims to Samoan land, granting over 135,000 acres (14 per cent of Samoa's land area) to European settlers (Meleisea 1987a). Fortifying German interests involved the reorganization of Samoa's customary political framework into an interventionist style of government and establishing the Land and Titles Commission to adjudicate all land matters, which was a task formerly controlled through the *matai* system (Meleisea 1987b). With a legal land entity in place, colonial powers focused on monopolizing agricultural commodification, export production, and initiating full-scale development of the plantation economy, which was sustained by indentured Chinese labour.[4]

Under New Zealand's administration, three events are of particular significance. The first is the 1918 Spanish influenza epidemic that resulted in the death of 8,500 Samoans, decimating most of the high-ranking *matais* and orators (Hempenstall and Rutherford 1984). The second is the stripping of *matai* titles to secure the administration's political control and indigenous containment. Together, the first and second events crystallized Samoan rebellion by a younger generation of *matais* and would come to represent the third major event, the *Mau* independence movement, which symbolized a united front against New Zealand's colonial rule (Maxwell and Liu 2010). Throughout New Zealand's rule, the question of labour remained tenuous, as Samoans remained resistant to wage labour and indentured labour was deemed improvident, and moreover was unwelcome given the racialized policies of New Zealand (Meleisea 1987a). In conjunction with labour, land matters remained priority, with the administration's emphasis on implementing legal apparatuses and polices of dispossession. The most prolific was the Samoa Act, which introduced civilian public service and a Westminster parliamentary system, both crucial factors in the shift away from subsistence economies and the uptake of wage labour[5] (Davidson 1967). This Act also reclassified all land in Samoa: crown land (85,000 acres), freehold land (45,000 acres) belonging to the church and Europeans, and customary land (599, 000 acres). Under the Act, all customary land was inalienable. However, with the enactment of the Samoan Individual Property Ordinance a year later, customary land was bestowed as if it was freehold land (Nayacakalou 1960). Instituting the Samoan Offenders Ordinance aimed to weaken *fa'asamoa* and *fa'amatai*, giving power to the administration to banish *matais* and prohibit the use of *matai* titles, which led to the formation of Samoa's *Mau* movement. Following the Second World War, global policies shifted and agendas of 'decolonization' emerged alongside the establishment of the United Nations, which would impact the course of Samoa's sovereignty. On 1 January 1962, Samoa became the first sovereign Polynesian state of the twentieth century.

Post-independence neoliberal dispossession in Samoa Harvey (2005a, 2005b) describes accumulation by dispossession as an extension of primitive accumulation, emphasizing accumulation as an ongoing process executed by sets of 'predatory practices' that exploit and commodify natural resources, labour power, and cultural forms, all of which have gained increasing significance under contemporary capitalism as neoliberalism. In Samoa, accumulation by dispossession targets land, labour, food production, culture and meaning, customary laws and practices, and ways of relating to the land. As illustrated, dispossession has a colonial history that has continued to flourish in political and social spaces following Samoa's independence. As the first independent nation in the Pacific, Samoa faced new challenges from international and regional economic actors. The nation would experience new forms of legal and financial mechanisms of dispossession; of particular importance in this regard were two land acts.

The Taking of Land Act 1964 provided the ability for government to take land for public purposes and for the payment of compensation, including customary land. The Customary Land Alienation Act 1965 prohibited the alienation of customary land; however, amendments were soon made for the Minister of Lands, Surveys and Environment to grant lease over customary land without permission from customary owners. These Acts set the tone for the national challenges Samoa faced as it worked to define the relationship between traditional authority and law with that of state authority. Constitutionally, Samoa adopted a hybrid political system that combined Westminster-style democracy with traditional political institutions and systems, whereby all members of parliament were required to hold the title of *matai*. Until the late 1970s, the political system was based on consensual decision-making without political parties and with deference shown to the *Tama-a-Aiga* (highest-ranking chiefs). This changed with the emergence of political factions and the formation of the Human Rights Protection Party (HRPP) and the Samoa National Party (Toleafoa 2013). Since winning office in 1988, the HRPP has maintained power, ostensibly making Samoa a one-party political system with near absolute power.

Until the late 1980s and early 1990s, Samoa was heavily supported by international and regional aid, propped up by a growing remittance economy. Guided by neoliberal policies, Samoa's economy underwent intensive reformations vis-à-vis structural adjustment programmes that worked to streamline the public sector, increase private sector development, support existing commercial agriculture through incentivization schemes, and expand communications, manufacturing, and tourism (ADB 2002). These schemes significantly affected the Samoan way of life and propelled migration to the urban centre of Apia:

> Our people still have the opportunity to live off the land. But the policies of government today is such that it's not providing the right incentives to the farmers to continue, working the land. Because they [government] now provide policies that continue to prioritize tourism as a revenue earning sector for Samoa, but when you look it is exploiting our customary owners. Many of them are now being pushed out of working the land. Many would rather go and work in these tourism sectors becoming yes sir, yes sir, what do you want for your lunch, sir, people. They become servants and I don't need to tell you, you can see the infiltration of this country with all these foreign business interests. (interview notes, Fiu Mata'ese Elisara, 2014)

By the end of the 1990s, the government, in concert with the ADB, developed the nation's first planning document, *Strategy for the Development of Samoa*, which intensified its focus on the private sector and attraction of foreign capital. Ostensibly, this plan and subsequent plans[6] have laid the foundation for a succession of government-led and ADB-sponsored projects that explicitly target customary land, and which have been supported and implemented through legal mechanisms.

In 1997, an amendment to the Lands, Surveys and Environment Amendment Act 1989 outlined the modes by which government lands could be alienated by way of lease or sale. This was followed one year later by the ADB report *Improving Growth Prospects in the Pacific 1998*, which examined ways to create individual freehold and leasehold tenure. In the early 2000s, the ADB provided US$3.5 million to support the expansion of micro and small business enterprises (MSEs) under the project Small Business Development. This project focused on improving access to credit for MSEs and facilitating private-sector-led growth with a commitment from Samoa's government to open up the market to land for investment, and to use customary land as collateral (ADB 2011). Associated with this project was the technical assistance for Capacity Building of Financial and Business Advisory Services, which aimed to improve the private sector's legal environment and debt recovery process for reforms to customary land (ADB 2005a). From 2005 onwards, the government of Samoa increasingly focused on land for development schemes with support from the ADB's technical assistance on Economic Use of Customary Land Phases I, II, III to support greater investment through leasing of customary land as collateral for financing (ADB 2015).

Building on the work of previous projects/technical assistance *Small Business Development* and *Capacity Building of Financial and Business Advisory Services*, Phase I was approved in 2005 with a focus on establishing a working group on the economic use of customary land (ADB 2005b). In 2008, the state passed the Land Titles Registration Act that introduced the Torrens Land system to customary land, enabling for registration of customary land under individual ownership. This was followed in 2009 by Phase II of *Promoting Economic Use of Customary Land*, which further explored leasing of customary land and options for development. A main output of Phase II involved the formation of the *Customary Land Advisory Committee*, which aimed to help with the coordination and implementation of national customary landowner coordination, build capacity to support customary land reformation, and act as a vehicle to provide public information (ADB 2009). In 2012, a second amendment was made to the Customary Land Alienation Act 1965 to legalize mortgages over leases of customary land granted by the Minister (Customary Land Advisory Commission Act 2012), thereby setting the stage for Phase III of the project. Phase III of the project aims to improve access to credit for business investment with the expected outcome of using customary land leases as collateral. Central to Phase III is a leasing framework that allows for:

(i) creating a security interest in leases, (ii) establishing priority for the lender, (iii) publicizing security interests in leases so that interested parties can establish if a lease has already been pledged as security, and (iv) creating a process for repossessing and selling the lease in the event of default. (ADB 2013: 2)

In 2014, the ADB approved a US$5 million grant to the government of Samoa for an agribusiness project to promote the commercialization and export of agricultural produce and processed products with provision of $1 million in funds for financial intermediaries to lend to agribusiness (ADB 2014). This project expected to provide financing for 10–15 agribusinesses. The following year, the government of Samoa introduced the Citizenship Investment Bill 2014, which enables citizens of any country to apply for Samoan citizenship by investment of 4 million tala (US$1.6 million). It also gives legal access to land for any individuals who have a net worth of 2.5 million tala (US$1 million).

Terrains of indigenous resistance: reassertions of *fa'asamoa* and *fa'amatai*

While Samoa has been lauded as a successful example of agricultural and economic reform in the Pacific (IMF 2003), the attempt to penetrate Samoa's traditional governance system and laws, and the dispossession of Samoans from their land through the interjection of capital, has not gone unnoticed nor uncontested. Historically and today, spaces of (re)indigenization are taken up, extolling the values and practices of *fa'asamoa* and *fa'amatai*, in repudiation to dominance and victimry, and in struggle for sovereignty. These spaces are mapped along trajectories of colonial machinations and capitalist accumulation marked by points of compliance, negotiation, and struggle. To understand the spaces of re-indigenization, or more aptly Samoanization, it is imperative to define the systems that confront colonial practices by generating a Samoan sociopolitical geography of space, reasserting the *va* (social space) and *fa'asamoa* and *fa'amatai*, and which are negotiated within the terrain of indigenous resistance.

For Lilomaiava-Doktor (2009), the Samoan concept of *va* 'engages the power within and between spaces and places arrayed in opposition to each other' and is only understood within the context of *fa'asamoa* and *fa'amatai* (p. 1). *Fa'asamoa* is a political and social system that is all-encompassing of meaning, culture, tradition, rituals, values, and principles (Huffer and So'o 2005; Iati 2009). It prescribes and governs Samoan life and customs, determining social interactions between kinship, and outlining behaviours and obligations. Lilomaiava-Doktor (2009) suggests that to understand one's place in Samoan cosmology is to learn and connect with the protocols and dimensions of the *aiga* (kin group), and the principles of *tautua* (service), *alofa* (love, care), *fa'aaloalo* (respect), *fa'alavelave* (obligation), and *pule* (authority). For Samoans, social identity and *I'inei* (home) is rooted in the indivisible bond between kin group and *fanua* (communal land).

Embedded within *fa'asamoa* is *fa'amatai*, the political system of *matais*, which refers to the political and governance sphere that centers on the *aiga* (extended family) and the position of the *matai* (chief), the elected leader of the *aiga* (Iati 2009). The authoritative power structures are built around the political framework of *nu'u's* (local polities), which are divided into districts and villages, each attached to a *Fono* (village council) and *matai sufa* (high chief titles) who were elected by and who governed all social and material relations of their *aiga* (extended families). Within *matai* titles, there are distinct hierarchal rankings, the highest titles belonging to *Tumua* and *Pule* (orator titles) (Iati 2009; Meleisea 1987a, 1987b). Ostensibly, *fa'amatai* comprises the processes and institutions within and between kin groups, as administrator to family interests, such as land, *matai* titles, and honour of the family and village. Today, *fa'amatai* remains the system of government at village and district levels, retaining power and authority, as noted by Dr Telei'ai Sapa Saifaleupolu (2014),[7] one of the four *matai* defending customary land: 'Village autonomy has the authority to stop any community members from cutting down mangroves or if somebody applies to the government for a permit to a claim, they (village) have that right to intervene, even against government'.

For many Samoans, *fa'amatai* is largely incompatible with Western systems, and for many *matais fa'amatai* is the only system for Samoa. Le Tangaloa Dr Pitapola Alailima (2014) laments:

Democracy is nothing but a tyranny of the majority. There is no difference between the power of one and a million . . . . Is there any wonder why in democracy of majority you need weapons, outside forces, outside strength to enforce the will of the majority . . . now, how about the will of equal voice of the Samoan, matai system where no decision is made unless there is absolute one hundred percent consensus of the decision makers. Complete unanimity – in Samoa it's holistic decision-making.

As articulated by Le Tangaloa Pitapola, *fa'asamoa* and *fa'amatai* are living systems that are continuously shaped by external and internal dynamics. As such, they have not been immune to change and are not unproblematic, being both complicit and resistant to coloniality and capitalist encroachments. For many Samoans, *fa'asamoa* is a financial burden, driven by pressure to fulfil obligations to the *aiga*. There are also obligations to the Church, which is woven into the social and political fabric of *fa'asamoa*, and in the case of *fa'alavelave* has become competitive, and for many has spiralled out of control, with families spending upwards of 1.4 million tala per week on donations/contributions to churches and customary obligations:[8]

> I guess some people say they survive by faith. I was just thinking of that phrase 'man does not live on bread alone' . . . . It's very difficult for people to . . . change their mindset . . . of how to spend, so that they can spend some money on their children's education and medical rather than spending all that you know on custom, but the killer stone is the church and all that. I go to church but it's very difficult . . . .. The same people who gives and prays are the same people who mourn and suffer. (small-scale farmer, 2014)

For many *matai* today, changes to *fa'asamoa* have been substantive, as described by Maulolo Tavita Amosa (2014), Managing Director of Samoa Cultural Centre:

> The way I see it, it's kind of slipping away from the traditional culture and the thing is as you all know culture is not static its dynamic and the external factors that make culture dynamic is mainly due to our values from time to time. Today we look at our values, which are very much influenced and impacted upon by the dollar . . . . So, Samoans today they are looking at the way of maximizing the accumulation of their monetary capacity in order to meet modern value demands . . . but I still think *fa'amatai* is strong.

Similarly, Fiu Mata'ese Elisara (2014)[9] laments that the co-optation of Samoa's traditional systems and laws strike at the heart of Samoan identity:

We don't seem to have the capacity to stand up and defend what has worked for us for generations and more or less the political economic powers [Samoan government] are coopted by the views of the Western model and have succumbed to that pressure. And we ended up serving the very structure that we belong. Sure there are some issues we need to address I mean no society is perfect but don't touch the structure of the society that has made our identity for generations and links us to who we are.

This issue of co-optation is central to the *matai* struggle against the legal and financial apparatuses of accumulation by dispossession, in which the physical is indivisible from the social. *Fa'asamoa and fa'amatai* are the embodiment of the physical and spiritual collective, grounded in *I'inei*, in the land, in the sea. These laws and institutions connect people with each other and with the natural world, based upon principles of reciprocity and collectiveness. Chairman of the Samoa Farmers Association, Afamusunga Toleofa (2014), articulates that:

Land is the very core of who we are and what our identity is . . . this government has been carried away by its own cleverness, egged on by donors who do not understand Samoa's traditions. They [international institutions] do not understand the stability comes from the traditional, the land, the cultural *fa'asamoa*.

To frame *fa'asamoa* and *fa'amatai* within indigenous resistance connects Samoa's struggle over protecting land and cultural/political sovereignty to a long lineage of indigenous resistance against the systemic violence of globalizing capitalism and the coloniality of power (Quijano 2000). Indigenous knowledge as a cornerstone of indigenous resistance is a site of embodied experience situated in local histories that work to rearticulate power for social change, and in Samoa resistance as a point of struggle for sovereignty is embedded within Samoan ways of knowing and doing, and has evolved to envelop anti-imperialist politics. Resistance is also manifest in the guarding of customary knowledges to protect Samoan ways of knowing and doing, occurring at the intersections of power between coloniality and Samoan indigeneity. As Meleisea (1987a, 1987b) writes, challenges to *fa'asamoa* have historically provided Samoans with the impetus to resist colonial imposition, in which *fa'asamoa* came to symbolize 'resistance' against colonization. It is under such impetus that the current struggle for protecting customary land is being waged.

Historical modes of organizing: matai system While the apparatuses of accumulation by dispossession aim to sever and silence the experiences and memories of resistance, Samoans have stood their ground. Early forms of opposition to *palagi* (European) imbrications were largely uncoordinated and waged along everyday acts of resistance. This was seen in acts against plantation economies and trade, which were carried out by filling copra baskets with rocks to skew the scales, harvesting crops based upon convenience of Samoan planters versus settler patterns, and disengaging from the market system entirely influencing supply and demand. Under the German regime, labour was a contentious issue for the administration, who were faced with continual shortages of plantation labour. Firth (1977) asserts that this was because Samoans preferred trade to labour, and under *fa'asamoa* and *fa'amatai* were obligated to work in the village; moreover, it was beneath contempt for Samoans to participate in paid work for the individual over collective service to the village. Furthermore, there was also the threat of strikes, as seen in 1902 when the Samoan *malo* (indigenous government) ordered road workers to strike for better pay and food. Samoa's history of armed resistance and the administration's belief that the commercial economy would suffer without Samoan trade further pacified German policy to enact forced labour (Firth 1977).

As the waves of capital encroachments intensified, Samoan organization became more formalized, as evidenced in the first coordinated agrarian resistance to German colonial rule in 1904 under the banner '*Oloa* movement' to contest the corrupt practices of colonial traders. This movement signalled a new dimension in Samoan political consciousness springing from Samoan discontent over inequitable market systems and exploitation, and resulting in the establishment of a cooperative copra trading company based on Samoan ownership and collective profit-making (Moses 1972). Quintessentially, the *Oloa* movement symbolized 'Samoan protest at the domination of capital by Europeans and an attempt to assimilate part of that factor of production to themselves through self-reliance'

(Hempenstall and Rutherford 1984: 29). In 1909, Luaki Namulau'ulu Mamoe, an orator from Safaotulafai in Savai'I, led an insurgency against the German administration, in response to the dismantling of the *Malo* (indigenous government) and the prohibition of using 'the names and privileges of *Tumua* and *Pule* by legislating against any reference to them in the *fa'alupenga*, the traditional formal salutation of Samoa which expressed their political precedence' (Hempenstall and Rutherford 1984: 26–27). The movement referred to as '*Mau a Pule*' called for the reinstatement of *Tumua* and *Pule* and the return of *Faipule*, and as a movement was inscribed with sovereignty politics under a charter that demanded the restoration of Samoan political institutions and the nation's independence from colonial rule. Soon after, the Toeaina Club emerged in response to the manipulation and profiteering of the colonial copra market, advocating for Samoan food sovereignty, regulation of copra production and sale, and protest against impacts on traditional agricultural practices (Meleisea 1987a).

In late 1926, Samoa's independence movement, *O le Mau*, emerged, symbolizing Samoan demand for sovereignty and protection of traditional institutions and systems (So'o 2008). Formalizing in 1927, the *Mau* declared its political intent, demanding 'a government of the people in accordance with the will of the people' under the mantra of 'Samoa mo Samoa' (Davidson 1967: 119). *Mau* responses of passive resistance included discontinuing meetings by district councils, women's committees and village committees, the withdrawal of Samoan children from government-run schools, neglect of plantations, and the ceasing of payments for taxes, diverting money instead to the *Mau* (Davidson 1967). The *Mau* were bitterly opposed to the manipulation and restructuring of traditional governance systems, particularly the *Faipule*, the administration's attempt at individualizing land tenure and appropriating customary practices (Davidson 1967; Meleisea 1987a). As a political body, the *Mau* outwardly challenged through protest, making a case for Samoan self-governance contesting colonialism's paternalistic rendering of a people that were racially and culturally inferior to Europeans (Davidson 1967; Hempenstall and Rutherford 1984; So'o 2008).

While the *Mau* movement marked the last large-scale movement in the colonial period, the *Tumua* and *Pule* and *Aiga* (TPA) protest movement in the 1990s marked the first and largest movement of the postcolonial period. The TPA arose in contestation to the value-added goods and services tax (VAGST), and operated under the objectives of abolishing VAGST and changing the HRPP government. On 2 March 1994, approximately 20,000 people participated in the protest, half of whom held the title of *matai* (So'o 2008). In 2012, protests would erupt at the villages of Satapuala and Magiagi. In the case of Satapuala, untitled men of the village took to the street, blockading the Faleolo Road over land disputes between the government and the village, which was met with a force of more than 100 armed police. The land in question involves 10 acres that was set aside by the government to build a hospital (Netzler 2012b). However, the alienation of the land in question dates back to the Second World War, when American military occupied this land. A *matai* from the village of Satapuala recounts the historical dispossession of land in question:

> In 1942, the marine army came to Samoa for the Second World War and they stay here at the Satapuala village . . . . The deal was marine will use the land of Satapuala and when they finish they give it back . . . . But the land went to the government, so now my village asked the government – well there are a lot of stories a lot of things happening in there makes things different and that's what happen in 2012. They [people of Satpuala] get tired of keep going. We travel to NZ to get some help we been all over. There no point in travel go look for help, stay here this is our land. The government should give us something and then the government said oh no the navy left so the government step in and take the land. That's not the deal. When the navy left give it back . . . and that's why the road block happen. (*matai* from the village Satapuala, November 2014)

In the same year, the village of Magiagi erected a roadblock in response to a government decision for the village to switch from free to prepaid electricity or cash power. According to the Ilalio (2012), the village claimed that an agreement had been made in 1983 between the Electric Power Corporation and the village, in which village lands would be used to develop government-sponsored hydropower projects, in exchange for the village receiving free power. Fighting for their rights, the village set up barriers to block access to the hydropower station, which was met with a threat from government of cutting off power supply to the entire village if they refused to agree to cash power (Ilalio 2012).

In 2014, a group of *matai*, including Fiu Mata'ese Elisara, Lilomaiava Dr Ken Lameta, Dr Telei'ai Sapa Saifaleupolu, and Leuluaialii Tasi Malifa, working outside the dominant forms of civil society or social movement resistance, mobilized knowledge and collective action to disrupt and engage directly with neoliberalizing policies of the state and international economic institutions through meeting with village *Fonos*, hosting conversations locally to discuss the agendas of private property rights, finacialization, and alienation of customary land, and lodging a formal complaint through ADB channels. In the official complaint letter to the ADB, the group of *matai* declare 'the cumulative long-term impact of these ADB interventions will be severely detrimental to our people, including land alienation and dispossession. These reforms are incompatible with the indigenous culture and political institutions of Samoa, and they are inconsistent with the needs and aspirations of the Samoan people' (Elisara *et al.* 2014).

> And yet they [government] say they can't stop it now because they are already co-opted to trade policies . . . . In terms of food security the capacity is there to provide food, but the way it's being done now, unfortunately, we are seeing a lot of our own traditional knowledge being lost. The fact that we are now so much more comfortable after how many years of being introduced to foreign policies that we think this is the right thing to do. And who dare, the four of us dare to question the government about these things, you know we get trodden on and pointed at . . . we don't care about the perception of people as far as we are concerned as long as we know in our own minds that we are doing this work to raise awareness about the reality of the people and our people needs. (Fiu Mata'ese Elisara, 2014)

Resistance: spaces of learning and social action to re-indigenize *fa'asamoa* and *fa'amatai*

The right for Samoans to speak to their own experiences of colonialism and capitalist dispossessions based on their own memories lies at the core of Samoan resistance. Indigenous knowledge production as a site of resistance and resurgence of collective identities and self-realized ways of doing and being recovers narratives of the past and charts a future of indigenous design (Tuhiwai-Smith 2012). *Fa'asamoa* and *fa'amatai* are spaces for re-indigenization, spaces where knowledge and culture are ever-evolving, and spaces to re-engage with Samoan indigeneity to confront the narratives and violence of colonialism. As illustrated here, the assaults against *fa'asamoa* and *fa'amatai* were intentional and calculated to displace collectivity and sacredness of indigenous knowledges for the idolization of trade and market. Across the Pacific, indigenous ways of knowing and living sustain people, connecting them to places, land, and identity. Hawaiian scholar and poet Haunani-Kay Trask (1993/1999) articulates this sense of bond and story:

> But because the West has lost any cultural understanding of the bond between people and land, it is not possible to know this connection through Western culture. This means that the history of indigenous people cannot be written from within Western culture. Such a story is merely the West's story of itself. Our story remains unwritten. It rests within the culture, which is inseparable from the land. To know this is to know our history. To write this is to write of the land and the people who are born from her. (p. 126)

Learning through the Fono council The *Fono* (village council) represents the process of maintaining or re-establishing village harmony, and is called when a breach of social norms has occurred or will occur. It is also the place where decisions are made for the village. For the group of *matai*, these two points are crucial – land alienation is a breach of social norms, and decision-making and consensus building occurs through the sharing of knowledge. The *Fono* itself is a physical and social space that is a space of Samoan indigeneity.

Its physical construction is without walls, it is open, transparent, connected with the land, the sea, the air, with four distinct sides: the front for orators, the back for untitled men, and two sides for *matai*. Its social space is guided by strict protocols that bind Samoan indigeneity in history, and lineage, always circling back to the connections to the land. The *Fono* begin with the *fa'alupega*, a ceremonial greeting that recognizes the *Fono* and the naming of *matai* titles, which connects individuals and families to land and to their origin history. Only *matai* – orators and chiefs – can attend a *Fono* and only a small number of those in attendance actively participate. The proceedings begin with a *kava* ceremony, which is ritually prepared and served based on rank with an honorific oratory given as the *ipu* cup is shared. As explained by Fiu Mata'ese Elisara (2014), the sharing of the *ipu* cup represents trust and unity by all those who share and drink from the same cup. This ritual opening then begins the long oration and discussion of the matter at hand. Fiu Mata'ese Elisara (2014) discusses the importance of engaging in such a way:

> This ritual and political process is very important to Samoans, Samoan way of life. It enshrines our history, how we do things and represents accountability. We engage with the *Fono* because it is our traditional system, because there is power in the decisions. For example, when we went to a village and shared the long term impact of ADB and government's so called visibility study on hydroelectric power, overnight they changed their whole affirmative response to government saying no forever, nobody is going to touch that. So, the power of information and power of awareness and good information can really be the power of the people. If those guys clearly understand from trusted sources because you can have people go and brainwash them and then make decisions from some false information and that's the danger of it and therefore the responsibility is on us to make sure that we do take that challenge because at the end of the day if we don't advocate the issues that we know with the peoples that we love and with the land we love then we are also guilty.
>
> So that's the attitude of here if all this about customary lands and ADB and government we have advocated our issues with the people of this country, meaningful consultation they understand the long term impacts of mortgaging customary lands and they still go ahead and say yes then we are in the clear and time will tell for the generation of the future.
>
> I hate the word education when you start to deal with our customary land owners because who are we to go and educate our leaders (customary/village) I mean they are the professors

of their own resources and they know best. Its basically sharing with them what we know from a perspective that they might not appreciate and then once when we lay down clearly for them the issues, they are the best people to decide because they are the resource owners. They know exactly the solutions to any problems they have with the lands and whatever we share with them they might be able to actually generate solutions for.

Collective agency and learning through conversations Collective agency is foundational to the historical fabrics of indigeneity, the root of Pacific thought and way of life, and catalyst for resistance to colonial dispossession and exploitation. Collective agency in the context of collective learning is an interconnected process of shared, experiential learnings, and knowledge production that is simultaneously individual and collective. The exchange and reclamation of power initiates a transformational process that flows across material and social relations, empowering Samoan thought and action. Collective learning through resurgence of Samoan indigeneity invokes a reclamation and rearticulation of autonomous power mobilizing people and setting the foundation for resistance against the intrusions of capital. In Samoa, collective agency lay at the heart of *fa'asamoa*. In the current struggle for customary land and sovereignty, the four *matai* have used the spaces of *fa'amatai* to engage in collective learning, using the mechanisms and language of ABD – co-opting the concept of consultations. As explained by Lilomaiava Dr Ken Lameta (2014), the ADB said their consultations were critical to this process, so we are doing consultations our way to get the message to the people:

> Government they are really smart when they introduced the legislation they used the chairman of the national council of churches as chairman of the commission, this land commission. And of course as you know, Samoans will never say anything against a *Faisiapo* [church leader] I have heard that the process was just more or less telling the people, this will be done, this is what we are going to do. It was never fully explained to the people, the impact on ownership of the land. So we are getting to those groups here not just the villages but we are getting out, our concern is the young ones, the youth they should understand

what is happening. We are getting to the women's group, and we will leave the Matai for the village meetings and go to meet the matais there. Everybody else we are working on that. We want to cover as much, if not all the people as we can. Particularly, our focus is on the youth so they understand what's happening here this will really effect them.

Learning in action The mobilization of knowledge and indigenous resurgence to disrupt and engage directly with neoliberalizing policies of the state and international economic institutions has been successful, as seen in the village of Sili and described by Fiu Mata'ese Elisara (2014):

> The issue was that Sili had probably a 15 million dollar US project that they have already invested ADB and that's why ADB is continually pushing government to actually do something about Sili. We kept on telling government that hydroelectric power is not a renewable energy option for a small country like Samoa. They didn't even tell the people that they were going to damn off about four intakes in the river and run dry the whole thing. You see whole biodiversity, the river biodiversity is gonna be lost and they never told them that. And they were only going to have one trickle little system to flow through and then they were going to drive stuff down to the hydro power. And there was only about 5 miles inland from the village itself. So any man made infrastructure is going to fail and then what happens to the villages? So we our leaders (village) have already said yes to government and we went there and made a presentation and when the people understand the real plans they open their eyes and stopped it forever. We need to make sure people will understand the magnitude of the problem and the thing they don't realize right now and the things that government is not telling them.

As noted earlier, learning and action is reflected in the work of the group of *matai* challenging the ADB, employing the tactics of collective agency and practices of *fa'amatai*. This group has also employed the modern colonial political process, lodging a formal complaint to the ADB Complaints Review Panel. Their message is consistent: while leasing of lands is not forbidden, the length of land leases currently required to secure a mortgage amounts to land alienation, which is forbidden by both customary laws and the constitution. To date, the *matai* have been successful in stalling full implementation of Phase III, through social action aimed at the channels of *fa'amatai* and the ADB process, which has found that the government did not sufficiently meet the consultation requirements as set out in the agreement:

> Vesting unfettered power to enter into long-term lease agreements to be used as collateral in a single aiga member with authority, the *matai* or *sa'o*, in a manner that bypasses traditional consultative and consensus-seeking processes is tantamount to alienation of customary lands. This is the hidden danger. (Elisara *et al.* 2014)

Fiu Mata'ese Elisara (2014) says through conversation, through dialogue, through learning, people are beginning to understand the issues at heart, to understand the devil in the detail:

> There might be few of us but there is a lot of support there, who might be latent support quiet support but I know when a lot of this comes up, they will join forces with us. We are not interested in making any names for ourselves but we fundamentally believe in the value of this and we hope that this being a god given country will find a way to move forward.

Conclusion

Colonialism and capitalism are inextricably intertwined, and enacted through racialized forms of dispossession in Samoa. In our current epoch, accumulation by dispossession brutalizes and strips indigenous peoples of their land and their way of life. Accumulation by dispossession is not new; rather, it is recurring in spaces across the globe and in Samoa. Through the complicit actions of the state and the neoliberalizing agendas of the ADB, accumulation by dispossession is occurring through legal and financial means. As Harvey (2005a, 2005b) laments, financialization and debt is perhaps the most tragic and destructive of accumulation by dispossession mechanisms.

This chapter aimed to show the continuities of dispossession, the assaults against Samoa's customary systems and practices, and the modes of organization and mechanisms of resistance to dispossession. Through basing resistance upon customary systems and practices, the group of *matai* has opened new spaces of mobilization and learning. The principal lessons to be learned from the experiences in the struggle to protect customary land and Samoan sovereignty, both historically and presently, is the vital importance for collective action and learning. The practices of *fa'asamoa* and *fa'amatai* have worked to safeguard Samoan interests and ensure a continued Samoan sense of place despite ongoing attempts to colonize customary institutions, land, labour, and spirituality. It is this learning that is the catalyst for action and anti-colonial empowerment in the face of continuous co-optation and the weakening of customary systems. With Samoa and other small Pacific nations, the questions that keep bubbling to the surface are around absolute loss – for when the land is taken, where will Samoans go and where will the culture go?

Notes

1 The Independent State of Samoa is commonly known as Samoa, and up until 1997 was known as Western Samoa.

2 *Matai* is the Samoan word for chief and is part of the *matai* system of Samoan social organization.

3 *Fa'alavelave* refers to ceremonial and family obligations, which entails gift giving in the form of labour or resources.

4 Between the years 1903 and 1913, approximately 3,800 Chinese labourers were brought to Samoa.

5 Employment in public administration is Samoa's leading employment sector (Samoa Bureau of Statistics 2016).

6 Strategy for the Development of Samoa (Ministry of Finance 2002, 2005, 2008, 2012).

7 Dr Telei'ai Sapa Saifaleupolu is a *matai* from the village of Samatau and is one of the four complainants against the ADB.

8 Samoa Bureau of Statistics (2013) and reflects the national expenditure.

9 Fiu Mata'ese Elisara is a *matai* from the village of Sili who has headed the complaint process against the ADB.

References

Asian Development Bank (ADB) (2002). *Country Strategy and Program Update (2003–2005)*. Manila: Asian Development Bank.

Asian Development Bank (ADB) (2005a). *Technical Assistance to Samoa for Capacity Building of Financial and Business Advisory Intermediaries.* Manila: Asian Development Bank.

Asian Development Bank (ADB) (2005b). *Technical Assistance to Samoa for Promoting Economic Use of Customary Land.* Manila: Asian Development Bank.

Asian Development Bank (ADB) (2009). *Samoa: Promoting Economic Use of Customary Land, Phase II*. Manila: Asian Development Bank.

Asian Development Bank (ADB) (2011). *Samoa: Small Business Development Project*. Manila: Asian Development Bank.

Asian Development Bank (ADB) (2013). *Independent State of Samoa: Promoting Economic Use of Customary Land, Phase III*. Manila: Asian Development Bank. Available at: www.adb.org/sites/default/files/project-document/79101/46512-001-sam-tar.pdf [accessed 28 March 2015].

Asian Development Bank (ADB) (2014). *Samoa: Samoa AgriBusiness Support Project*. Manila: Asian Development Bank. Available at: www.adb.org/printpdf/projects/46436-002/main [accessed 28 March 2015].

Asian Development Bank (ADB) (2015). *Reform Renewed: A Private Sector Assessment for Samoa*. Mandaluyong City, Philippines: Asian Development Bank.

Castille, J. (2012). 'The last phase of the South Sea slave trade: Jack London's adventure'. *Pacific Studies*, 35(1): 325–341.

Davidson, J. (1967). *Samoa mo Samoa: The Emergence of the Independent State of Western Samoa*. Melbourne: Oxford University Press.

Elisara, F.M., Malifa, L.T., Lameta, L.K., and Saifaleupolu, T.S. (2014). *Samoan Matais Complaint to the Asian Development Bank*. Available at: www.adb.org/sites/default/files/page/42458/complaints-sam-matais-sep14.pdf [accessed 28 March 2015].

Firth, S. (1977). 'Governors versus settlers: the dispute over Chinese labour in German Samoa'. *New Zealand Journal of History*, 11(2): 155–179.

Harvey, D. (2005a). *The New Imperialism*. Oxford: Oxford University Press.

Harvey, D. (2005b). *A Brief History of Neoliberalism*. New York: Oxford University Press.

Hempenstall, P. and Rutherford, N. (1984). *Protest and Dissent in the Colonial Pacific*. Suva, Fiji: University of the South Pacific.

Huffer, E. and So'o, A. (2005). 'Beyond governance in Samoa: understanding Samoan political thought'. *The Contemporary Pacific*, 17(2): 311–333.

Ilalio, M. (2012). '2 chiefs sacked over Magiagi power meter dispute in Samoa'. *Samoan Observer*. 27 August. Available at: http://pidp.org/pireport/2012/August/08-28-12.htm [accessed 14 April 2017].

Iati, I. (2009). *Controversial Land Legislation in Samoa: It's Not Just About the Land*. Available at: www.devnet.org.nz/sites/default/files/IatiIatiLandLawSamoa.pdf [accessed 28 March 2015].

International Monetary Fund (IMF) (2003). *Public Information Notice: IMF Concludes 2003 Article IV Consultation with Samoa*. Available at: www.imf.org/external/np/sec/pn/2003/pn0380.htm [accessed 28 March 2015].

Lilomaiava-Doktor, S. (2009). 'Beyond "migration": Samoan population movement and the geography of social space (VA)'. *The Contemporary Pacific*, 21(1): 1–32.

Linnekin, J. (1991). 'Ignoble savages and other European visions: the La Perouse affair in Samoan history'. *The Journal of Pacific History*, 26(1): 3–26.

Macpherson, C. and Macpherson, L. (2009). *The Warm Winds of Change: Globalisation in Contemporary Samoa*. Auckland: Auckland University Press.

Maxwell, G. and Liu, J. (2010). *Restorative Justice and Practices in New Zealand: Towards a Restorative Society.* Eugene, OR: Wipf & Stock.

Meleisea, M. (1987a). *The Making of Modern Samoa: Traditional Authority and Colonial Administration in the History of Western Samoa.* Suva, Fiji: Institute of Pacific Studies of the University of the South Pacific.

Meleisea, M. (1987b). *Lagaga: A Short History of Western Samoa.* Suva, Fiji: University of the South Pacific.

Ministry of Finance (2002). *Strategy for the Development of Samoa 2002–2004: Opportunities for All.* Apia: Government of Samoa.

Ministry of Finance (2005). *Strategy for the Development of Samoa 2005–2007: For Every Samoan to Achieve a Better Quality of Life.* Apia: Government of Samoa.

Ministry of Finance (2008). *Strategy for the Development of Samoa 2008–2012: Ensuring Sustainable Economic and Social Progress.* Apia: Government of Samoa.

Ministry of Finance (2012). *Strategy for the Development of Samoa 2012–2016: Boosting Productivity for Sustainable Development.* Apia: Government of Samoa.

Moses, J. (1972). 'The Solf regime in Western Samoa: ideal and reality'. *New Zealand Journal of History*, 6(1): 42–56.

Moses, J. (1973). 'The coolie labour question and German colonial policy in Samoa, 1900–1914'. *The Journal of Pacific History*, 8: 101–124.

Nayacakalou, R. (1960). 'Land tenure and social organization in Western Samoa'. *Journal of the Polynesian Society*, 69: 104–122.

Netzler, J. (2012). 'Samoa government sacks Satapuala mayor after road blockade'. *Samoan Observer*. Available at: http://pidp.org/pireport/2012/August/08-21-05.htm [accessed 14 April 2017].

Quijano, A. (2000). 'Coloniality of power, Eurocentrism and Latin America'. *Nepantla: Views from South*, 1(3): 533–580.

Rabaka, R. (2003). *Deliberately Using the Word 'Colonial' in a Much Broader Sense: W.E.B. Du Bois's Concept of 'Semi-Colonialism' as Critique of and Contribution to Postcolonialism.* Available at: http://social.chass. nesu.edu?Jovert/v7i2/rabaka.htm [accessed 28 March 2015].

Samoa Bureau of Statistics (2013). *Household and Income and Expenditure Survey (HIES) 2013/2014.* Apia: Government of Samoa.

Samoa Bureau of Statistics (2016). *Employment Statistics, September 2016 Quarter.* Apia: Government of Samoa.

So'o, A. (2008). *Democracy and Custom in Samoa: An Uneasy Alliance.* Suva, Fiji: Institute of Pacific Studies.

Toleafoa, A. (2013). 'One party state: the Samoan experience'. In D. Hegarty and D. Tryon (eds), *Politics, Development and Security in Oceania.* Canberra: Australian National University Press, pp. 69–76.

Trask, H. (1993/1999). *From a Native Daughter: Colonialism and Sovereignty in Hawaii.* Monroe, ME: Common Courage Press.

Tuhiwai-Smith, L. (2012). *Decolonizing Methodologies: Research and Indigenous Peoples.* London: Zed Books.

4 | ADIVASI, DALIT, AND NON-TRIBAL FOREST DWELLER (ADNTFD) RESISTANCE TO BAUXITE MINING IN NIYAMGIRI: DISPLACING CAPITAL AND STATE-CORPORATE MINING ACTIVISM IN INDIA

Dip Kapoor

Introduction

Invoking the sanctity of the Niyamgiri hills (Mountain of Law), the abode of Niyam Raja (Lord of Law), the Dongria Kondhs residing on the upper reaches and slopes (Dongrias are recognized as Particularly Vulnerable Tribal Groups or PVTGs among some 635 Scheduled Tribes or STs by the state) and the Niyamgiri Surakhya Samiti (NSS or Niyamgiri Protection Society) movement organization continue to be engaged in a 15-year struggle against the Odisha Mining Corporation (OMC) and London-based Vedanta/Sterlite bid to exploit bauxite deposits of some 73 million tons of mineable ore (23–25-year life span) from Niyamgiri in Kalahandi and Rayagada districts in the state of Odisha.[1] The NSS includes mining-affected STs (Dongrias, Kutias, Majhi and Jharanias), Dalits (Scheduled Castes or SCs, in Constitutional terms), non-tribal forest dwellers (NTFD) and small/landless peasants. Described by global mining expert Roger Moody of Mines and Communities as 'the world's most damaging mining company',[2] or 'dacoits' in colloquial NSS activist lingo, state-corporate mining activism (Vedanta's corporate slogan is 'Mining Happiness in Odisha', along with promises of 'zero pollution') in a constitutionally protected area[3] has been a duplicitous exercise in state-sponsored corporate dispossession of ADNTFDs in a country with the world's largest number of forest-dependent peoples.

In a series of contradictory developments since 1997 (when a MOU was signed for mining and the refinery) for or against opencast mining involving a 700-hectare claim by Vedanta/Sterlite including the pinnacle or Niyam Dongar, the tallest mountain in Niyamgiri, the latest bid by the OMC to go it alone, was rejected by the apex court (Supreme Court of India) in May 2016 by a three-judge bench headed by Justice Ranjan Gogoi. The gradually widening and deepening support by directly affected ADNFTD's for the Dongria and the NSS at the epicenter of resistance has continued to contribute to such developments. The court rejected OMC's claim (among others) that the leaders of the movement and the composition of Gram Sabhas (village councils) had changed since the unanimous decision by 12 Gram Sabhas (as opposed to the 112 villages potentially affected by the project, according to the NSS) against mining Niyamgiri in 2013, thus warranting a Gram Sabha process for a second time, and hence the petition from the Government of Odisha (GoO).

This chapter considers resistance by bauxite-mining-affected ADNTFDs (those at the 'rock face') to related development dispossession in Lanjigarh, resistance that is currently directed at closing down the company's refinery, which was built in 2006, with environmental clearance from the Ministry of Environment and Forest (MoEF) in 2004 on the assurance from the company that no forest land would be diverted. In retrospect, some 58 hectares of forest land were diverted as part of the 723 hectares of land needed for the refinery at the foot of the mountain, not to mention that application and clearances for opencast mining on Niyamgiri were yet to be secured (delinked from the refinery development, given that this would require 672 hectares of forest land), suggesting the impunity of state-corporate actors in affecting ADNTFD dispossession (primitive accumulation) for mining.

The insights developed here are based on the author's long-term research and applied interests concerning ADNTFD's and small/landless peasant development marginalization, dispossession, and resistance in South/East Orissa since the mid-1990s. They are intended for similar social movement actors and contexts (and variously engaged academic activists), that is, struggles involving indigenous/other forest dwellers and small/landless (under 2 acres) subsistence peasants/labor in hilly regions where the state exercises *eminent domain*. This includes primary and secondary research developed from: interviews with the leadership of the NSS (Kondh, Jharania, and Dalit) and some of their closest allies (e.g. locally based Dalit lawyers/advocates and experienced anti-displacement political activists from these districts in the state) and their ongoing assessments through solicited/self-reporting over time. NSS participation in a nascent Adivasi-Dalit landless/small peasant and development-displaced trans/local social network effort of some 14 movement organizations or the Lok Adhikar Manch (LAM) (see Kapoor 2015) has also informed this analysis, as have documentaries on the 'Referendum' and 'Niyamgiri-The Mountain of Law' produced and publically distributed by Samadrusti TV (www.samadrusti.org) and secondary documentation (academic and activist sources, e.g. see www.foilvedanta.org and www.sanhati.com) regarding mining and resistance in Niyamgiri and Odisha.

After considering colonial capitalist state-corporate dispossession of ADNTFD, and small/landless peasants in Odisha and Niyamgiri in particular, including a brief history of resistance to dispossession in the state, the chapter focuses on the political resistance of the NSS. This includes considerations pertaining to: movement evolution, purpose(s), and aims; organization and material/financial support; strategy, mobilization, and tactics (and the Gram Sabha politicization); and elaborations around the consistent reliance on a core localized non-violent political mobilization or persistent direct action by ADNTFDs (OMC-VAL mining-affected social groups) in Niyamgiri and Lanjigarh.

Colonial capitalist dispossession in the forest belt: state-corporate mining activism and resistance

In the Indian context, the coloniality of capitalist power was first realized under British colonization in the 1880s and the restriction of ADNTFD rights over land and forests through the various Forest Rights Acts, reducing them to encroachers on their own territories. Rich forests were plundered for timber for shipyards and railways as forests were cleared to make room for plantations of sugar cane, coffee, tea, indigo, and cotton. The eighteenth- and nineteenth-century exploits of the British East India Company in Bengal, the richest state at the time, included the introduction of English landlordism, the tripling of land taxes, the dispossession of some 20 million smallholders, including forced conversions to growing opium for export to China, the eventual destruction of the local textile industry, and the subsequent famine-related deaths of a third of the population (10 million people), prompting then Governor-General William Bentinck to suggest that the bones of cotton weavers were bleaching the plains of India, and that such misery could hardly be found in the history of commerce (Davis 2002).

Initially, the British allied with the feudal structural arrangements whereby ADNTFDs were exploited through feudal systems of revenue assessment under *zamindari, ryotwari,* and *princely state* arrangements, but it was the subsequent introduction of the Permanent Settlement Act of 1894 that dealt a devastating blow to ADNTFDs by introducing the alien concept of land as private property, demarcated and sanctified by a piece of paper (Sahu and Dash 2011). Not receptive to the concept of land as private property and ill-equipped to deal with the official process for recognition, this Act strengthened land theft by upper-caste classes in the state of Odisha, and neither were ADNTFDs prepared to deal with the colonial state's land classification/legislation schemes. Colonial land laws and the use of state-sanctioned violence and harassment under the Criminal Tribes Act (criminalizing some 500 nomadic tribes, or 80 million people today with no state recognition beyond the status of criminals) together effectively dispossessed these subordinate (racialized/caste-stigmatized) groups from land and forests, while reducing them to 'coolie' labor for plantations (Davis 2002; Gadgil and Guha 1992; Guha 1997).

The colonial extractive model moved from imperial to commercial and conservation-related post-independence state control, whereby forests were now conceived as a strategic national resource under the National Forest Policy of 1952 and eminent domain of the state, that is, villages located closest to a forest could not preclude the right of the country to receive the benefits of a national asset. The post-independence state took over an additional 21 million hectares of land as Reserve Forests controlled by the Forest Department bureaucracy, while in Odisha the Forest and Revenue departments together 'own' 50–80 percent of the land in the Scheduled V Areas (mainly populated by Scheduled Tribes and Castes), continuing to disenfranchise ADNTFDs on their own lands. Relatively progressive state land legislation, such as the Orissa Government Land Settlement Act of 1962, wherein 70 percent of state land is supposed to be distributed among the landless, remains mainly unimplemented, if not at a standstill, post-liberalization of the Indian economy since 1991, as average Adivasi landholding across the state is just over 1 acre, which is considered landless (Sahu and Dash 2011).

While Adivasis constitute 22 percent of the population in Odisha, they account for 42 percent of development-displaced persons (DDPs), and at the national level, of the 21.3 million people estimated to be DDPs between 1951 and 1990 due to mines, dams, industry, and parks, they account for 40 percent, while 20 percent are Dalits (Fernandes 2006; Nag 2001). This trend has been accelerated post-1991 neoliberalization of the Indian economy (New Economic Policy) and the establishment of over 500 special economic zones. According to the Dilip Singh Bhuria Commision's report (2000–2001), the state, which is supposed to protect tribal interests as per constitutional guarantees in Scheduled Areas (Schedule V), has contributed to their exploitation through the location of industries and other development projects in tribal areas that are rich in mineral resources, while the De-Notified and Nomadic Tribes Act (replaced the British Criminal Tribes Act) is still used to criminalize, harass, and humiliate an estimated 150 million semi-nomadic or nomadic tribes belonging to some 400 groups (Munshi 2012). That said, in Odisha, Forest Department landlordism (*zamindari*) is being challenged as over a third (some 2 million hectares) of the state's forest area is under 'Community Forest Management' (CFM), as the Forest Department seeks to weaken community control (potentially enhanced under the revised FRA of 2006) through 'Joint Forest Management' (JFM) (Sahu and Dash 2011).

> In post-colonial societies, decolonization merely changed
> the direction but not the goal of this violent hunt for natural
> resources. As countries that were once formal or informal
> colonies gain political independence, the more successful among
> them join the march of civilization in the name of 'development'
> only to become colonizers themselves. . . . If a lack of strength
> does not allow them to conquer other lands and people, regions
> inside the country are identified for the hunt of natural resources.
> Imperialism turns inwards; and the latecomers in the race wage
> war against their own citizens, but this time in the name of
> developing them. (Bhaduri 2010: 12)

In the words of an NSS activist: 'We all know that our problems today are because of colonialism [*samrajyobad*] and capitalism [*punjibad*] and these MNCs [Vedanta], NGOs, DfID [Department for International Development, UK] and the government are its forces' (Lingaraj Azad, NSS activist, interview notes, February 2011).

Post/colonial dispossession has always been met with stiff resistance in the state of Odisha, which has a rich history and contemporary experience[4] with ADNTFD pushback (including the NSS in Niyamgiri), along with a persistent organizing presence, guerilla movements, and party political institutional arrangements inclusive of the Marxist-Leninist and Maoist left. In the 1960s, the Food Liberation movement supported by the Communist Party of India (CPI), which sought to return land to the Dalit/tiller through forced reappropriations from *zamindars* (landlords) was succeeded by the CPI (Marxist-Leninist) responsible for the Chitrakonda Labour Movement (armed reappropriations of land for the poor). The later sowed the seeds for Adivasi non-armed resistance in the state, including the current non-violent Narayanpatna land rights struggle active in South Odisha since 1994 under the banner of the Chasi Mulia Adivasi Sangh (CMAS), which has returned some 3,000 hectares of land to the Adivasi. Similarly, the CPI (ML) steered non-violent, militant land-rights movements, has also distributed thousands of hectares of usurped land to Adivasi-Dalits in south Odisha (Sahu and Dash 2011: 263–264) The Niyamgiri struggle of the ADNTFD in Lanjigarh is also in the heartland of this region of protest, and the *individual* participation of experienced activists from left party political persuasions in concert with the NSS is apparent.

The Niyamgiri Surakhya Samiti (NSS) and ADNTFD resistance to the bauxite refinery and mine

Vedanta, a name derived from the ancient wisdom of the Vedas going back some 3,000 years, promulgating a non-materialist philosophy, made its first bid for mining wealth in Odisha (the land of farmers) in 1997 as Sterlite, when the company signed an MoU for the Niyamgiri refinery (just prior to Niyamgiri being declared a National Park) with the GoO, including some 77 percent of reserved forests in the potential mining lease area. In June 2002, the company applied to acquire the land of 12 villages (on the plains beside the Niyamgiri mountains) in the Lanjigarh block of Kalahandi district for its refinery, a decision that was immediately challenged by hundreds of villagers (including Majhi Kondhs), who filed petitions at the Revenue Office in Bhawanipatna, an event that marked the commencement of the first signs of the possibility of collective response to dispossession and increasing state-corporate repression and manipulation to affect dispossession for the mine.[5]

Origins of the NSS: the refinery, dispossession, and initial resistance at the foot of the mountain Despite the repeated attempts of the District Collector (DC) to get people to accept compensation, jobs, and new houses (some 300 people were told their land would be acquired through these measures, while 60 families were *displaced*), 4 of 12 villages agreed to the terms, while the remaining villages were walled out by the company.

The latter got together to form the NSS in 2003 at around the same time that Vedanta/Sterlite signed an MoU with the GoO to mine Niyamgiri on 7 June 2003.[6] The NSS was galvanized by the likes of Adivasi leader and first President Dai Singh Majhi, made famous for his popular retort to the DC at Belamba village where he said, 'we cannot eat your money'. Similarly, village elder and founding member Bhim Majhi from Turiguda is known for bringing up climate warming impacts of the refinery and the project's effects on rainfall and the resulting ridicule in the form of racialized replies from the DC, 'What are you Kondhs up to? What do *you* know about these things?' Or by the 12–13 villages who wrote a letter expressing their refusal to leave Niyamgiri, which prompted a similar dehumanizing colonial derogation from the District Magistrate, quote, 'Who has written this? A pig or a goat? Does he have a name or an address?' (Padel and Das 2010: 148–149).

According to Siddhartha Nayak, a lawyer from Lanjigarh who is also from a village in this locale, and an instrumental NSS supporter, activist, and founding member of a local lawyer's collective called the Kalahandi Sachetan Nagarik Manch (KSNM or *Conscious Citizen's Forum*) set up to provide legal aid for NSS leaders (e.g. moving for bail petitions, advocating on their behalf or filing cases and FIRs by those being subjected to state/corporate violence related to the project) and supporting small local land claims, when survey work concerning the refinery first began in 2003, there was considerable enthusiasm among some people in the town as they looked forward to securing project-related jobs as company agents went around saying that 'Lanjigarh will become a big city comparable to Mumbai, Delhi and Kolkata' (interview notes, January 2016). According to

Nayak, when Adivasi and Dalit traditional holders (*sukho basi*) began to realize that they could not gain land ownership recognition from the government, and that only a few people who had *pattas* (deeds) had such recognition and were prepared to sell their land, initial questioning of the project began. Prompted by Adivasi NSS activists such as Kumuti Majhi and others, who began to educate *sukho basi* around who would likely get the 10,000 jobs being touted around the locale by company supporters – namely the more educated if not landed Other Backward Castes (OBCs) and General Castes (GCs), who were also mainly migrants/outsiders, opposition began to grow more vocal from the SC-ST majority.

When the talk in town shifted from just three villages (starting with Kinarigan) to the possibility of more (Nayak said the company's strategy was to start with two or three and move four or five at a time) facing displacement and land loss without compensation, followed by the news that bauxite for the refinery was to come from mining Niyamgiri (as opposed to external sources), the stage was set for open confrontation and vocal opposition by Adivasi-Dalits at the foothills in the path of the refinery – an opposition channeled by the NSS. '*Ame amo jameen chariboo nahi* (we will not leave our land) became a common refrain in the language of protestors' (interview notes, January 2016).

As opposition to village displacement mounted, the company decided to take the land of six villages. The remaining villages near the boundary wall (in the case of Kopaguda, just 50 yards away) were inundated with refinery construction, including having to tolerate around-the-clock floodlighting. Public hearings (as per the MoEF requirements) were held regarding the mine, refinery, and power plant in February 2003 at the Kutia Kondh Development Agency in Lanjigarh, minus any Dongria participation, even though this group was living in and around the proposed mine site, given that the project was going beyond refining to mining Niyamgiri and Niyam Dongar. Becoming increasingly aware of the implications of the project for those on the mountaintops through NSS-led public education efforts and the social rumor mill, Dongria protested outside the March hearings of the Odisha State Pollution Control Board in Muniguda, since they were barred from participating.

Despite growing resistance to the refinery in Lanjigarh, a 'groundbreaking ceremony' went forward on 30 March 2003 with the assistance of the local member of the legislative assembly (MLA) and member of parliament (MP) amidst widespread anger and protest, resulting in the beating (by the 'company's musclemen', according to the victim) and eventual arrest of a local Dalit activist from Kalahandi district, Lingaraj Azad,[7] who is an instrumental leader in the emergence and development of the NSS, if not wider process of growing opposition to the mining project. His arrest and detention in Lanjigarh police station prompted people (predominantly women concerned about their families in the wake of the project) from Turiguda, Boringpadar, Kapaguda, Belamba, and Basantpadar to march to the police station to express their solidarity with him and to file a First Information Report (FIR), only to be beaten with cricket bats and stumps by members of a Vedanta/Sterlite-funded youth cricket club (reported in *Samaj*, 9 April 2003), while a People's Union for Civil Liberties (PUCL, 16 May 2003) report found that the Lanjigarh police colluded in this attack and had threatened Adivasi protestors attempting to file an FIR with dire consequences. The attack on the protestors lasted all the way from Lanjigarh to Basantpadar, resulting in severe injuries to 17 (mainly women) and the death of an old Dalit man, Maya Nayak, two days later.

On 8 June 2003, Odisha's Chief Minister, Naveen Patnaik, laid the foundation stone for the Lanjigarh refinery. According to Azad and other NSS leaders, a leaflet campaign was used to make people aware of this event, but as people from neighboring regions and the affected villages attempted to move toward the spot, they were intercepted by police at 12 different points (e.g. Bartlima, Kansari, Chatarpur), and a massive police deployment encircled affected villages to prevent protestors from venturing out. According to NSS activists, MLA Balabhadra Majhi's (an Adivasi voted into office with the substantial support of Adivasis) musclemen (*goondas*) and representatives stationed themselves at police points/camps to identify those opposed to the project, people who were then detained and prohibited from even quenching their thirst or attending to other needs, for as long as the Chief Minister was there. Two days later, angry protestors demolished the foundation stone in a symbolic effort to say no to the refinery and the mine. Adivasi activists Abhi Majhi and Bhima Majhi were arrested and released a few days later.

In early January 2004, police gave the villages a couple of days' notice to leave their homes. The Kondh villages of Kinari,

Borabhata, Sindhabahali, and Kotduar were razed to the ground by bulldozers. The villagers were taken away in trucks to Vedantanagar, the rehabilitation and resettlement colony, along with the previous year's supply of grain from their fields and some cash in a bank account, and now spatially removed from wider community links and social relations, their land, and their Gods, who were embedded in the stones and posts at the center of those villages that were now part of the rubble. Located between the mountain and the refinery, they provided a readily available captive labor supply for menial work and stone quarrying, and the new colony was constantly surveilled by guards, allegedly for the protection of these displaced villages from those who did not accept compensation for land or who were forcibly displaced (Padel and Das 2010). Between 2002 and 2004, the refinery development had acquired the land earlier used by Adivasis for farming, displacing 118 families and forcing approximately 1,200 families to sell farmland for the refinery (Amnesty International 2010).

An Oath March of about 2,000 protestors took place on 7 April 2004 from Belamba village to Lanjigarh town, an occasion where the political party leader of the popular socialist SJP, the late Kishen Pattanaik, gave his first and last speech (he passed away thereafter):

> A month ago, four villages were destroyed under the direction of the company and the support of the government – they think they can invade anything with the government's help – we have to learn not to be afraid. They think the state can be run with company money so they are handing it over to the company – our fight is not just for a few villages but to save the nation from slavery. (Break the Silence: Niyamgiri – The Mountain of Law, Samadrusti TV Production)

The following day, police arrested 15 protestors for setting fire to Vedanta/Sterlite machines. While people for and against the project had started quarreling among themselves, and even though there was a realization among some that educated youngsters from the area would likely secure jobs, according to Nayak (interview notes, January 2016), a majority viewpoint against the project soon grew in strength as people felt only a few such educated youngsters would benefit through employment with the company. Nayak shared the following quote (paraphrased) by the NSS's first President, Dai Singh Majhi, in his response to District Collector (DC) of Kalahandi Saswat Mishra's promise of jobs, and his suggestion that all would benefit if they accepted the company and the project:

> I am not literate, what job could you give me? Not a single government officer has ever come to our villages and now the DC has come here today, why? Have you come to plead [*okilati*] before us on behalf of the company? What job can you give me? What job can you guarantee my son who is illiterate and so might his son be too? The place on which you are standing here today, these forests, streams, the land you see around us and the air you breathe – in this place my grandfather was employed [*chakri*] and on this soil I too have found *chakri* and I can guarantee my son and his sons can also find *chakri* in like manner because this land does not leave anyone unemployed [*ehi mati thahakoo chakriya nor kori chare nahi*]. Vedanta nor any company can promise the same to us.

The threat of mining Niyam Dongar: growing the NSS up and down the mountain slopes[8] The combination of increasing land dispossession and lack of transparency, if not the active use of deception and stealth associated with this process of organized usurpation (from the point of view of those losing land and place) by the company and the OMC (and the DC), combined with the non-recognition of traditional dweller claims, enhanced the prospects for an oppositional politics and accelerated organizing among *sukho basi* and initial NSS mobilization efforts linked to the refinery at the foot of the mountain. The continued spread of more concrete information regarding the perceived attack on the sanctity of Niyam Raja's abode, Niyam Dongar and Niyamgiri, for mining by NSS activists and others spurred NSS mobilization efforts up the slopes of the mountain to the villages of the more remote hamlets of the Dongria and Kutia Kondh 'primitive tribal groups'.

Purpose and aims
The continuous political education (*jono shikhya*) and organizing work of NSS Majhi Kondh Adivasis and Dalit activists from the Lanjigarh refinery development area at the foot of the mountain

initiated and drove the organizing effort up the mountain, along with an evolving if not multifaceted emergent sense of political purpose. From an initial focus in relation to the refinery development around prospects related to jobs and social services (e.g. company-provided health and education promises) and compensation (or not) in relation to land claims prospects for *sukho basi*, or essentially material concerns 'within the terrain of commodification' (Levien 2013: 381), a gradual and eventually more enduring, if not all-encompassing, sacral and political solidarity around the specificity of the Dongria Kondh Adivasi belief in the mountain (in conjunction with other Adivasi/local beliefs in the area with regard to *Darni Penu*, or Earth Goddess) as the sanctified abode of Niyam Raja, and the non-commodify able source of all life itself, began to emerge. According to Nayak, 'this is no more a fight/struggle [*lodhai*] for livelihood alone. It is a struggle for Niyamraja whom some have tried to hurt and Niyamraja is the symbol of our life and dignity [*amo jibono abong atmo somanoro protiko atonthi*]' (interview notes, January 2016).

Indeed, as explained by NSS activists, the fight for livelihoods and the fight to protect the sanctity of the mountain were one and the same, as the destruction of the mountain also meant the loss of livelihoods, as it did the destruction of *Niyam Raja* and *Darni Penu*, that is, 'More than livelihoods, Niyamgiri is the source of life. Some of us are forest/firewood pickers, some collect leaves, fruits, nuts and roots and live on that; some of us do agriculture (millet, rice, pulses, seeds) – we have everything in Niyamgiri that we need in our life'.

> Our aim is to keep our mother alive. We will not enter into the so-called development process or development talks [*vikaso katha abong vikaso dharare posibu nahi*]. The way the government is talking about development from 2003 till today (2011), we will ask, what is development [*vikas*]? If we accepted their version and did not go for the movement, our mother would have died. The hills and the forests wouldn't have been there. This would become a desert. Is this *vikas*? (NSS activist, interview notes, February 2011)

> Our development is in our hands. We need not depend on any company or government as our ancestors never depended on any company or government for their existence. We want Niyamgiri

to stay as it was and as it is [*n jemthi thila shemathi rohibata ame chahoo*]. Niyamgiri has given a wakeup call for all of us [*amoku othaiba pai daki chi*]. If we listen, many Niyamgiris will be saved. (NSS activist, interview notes, January 2016)

Straddling two districts, Dongrias (meaning those who belong to the mountains) inhabit the upper reaches of Niyamgiri in Kalahandi (mainly hunter-gatherers), Jharanias (meaning those by the streams/waterfalls) or agriculturalists live along the slopes by waterfalls, and Kutias (or those who reside lower down the mountain) are on the Rayagada side, along with Dalits and other non-tribal forest dwellers. While Dongrias were initially suspicious of the intentions of NSS activists from the plains, disbelieving their claims to being as effected as Dongrias might be in the eventuality of mining development, the Kutias on the Rayagada side criticized the NSS for permitting outsiders (including political party leaders from the Congress and the communist parties/left) from supporting the movement. NSS leaders had to explain that these parties were not part of the core movement, but supporters who were welcomed as and when they came to express solidarity and help out:

I was going from village to village like a thief or a beggar with few clothes in Kalahandi and Rayagada to speak to as many people as possible about the movement because in those early days Vedanta and its goons and police were ruling the place . . . you can't imagine how much of a beating we have all taken [*kee bholia mado khaichu, apno bhabhi paribe nahi*].

I used to tell them [Kutias], Niyamgiri has given birth to 136 streams and rivers – nobody can hold them back – as Jharanias or people who live close to the streams as agriculturalists we know this. Unless Nagabali and Vansadhara rivers come together, Vansadhara would not be a big river. Likewise, to become a big movement, we, the Jharanias, Kutias, Dongrias, and Dalits, must come together from Rayagada and Kalahandi. Since 2003, we have toiled hard to build this unity and struggle. That's when people were shouting development [*vikas*], but some of us understood *vikas* means forsaking our land and forest and allowing it to become a desert. . . . there was a time when NSS was a small entity, but today it has a presence in all the villages in this area and people are coming forward on their own to protect and preserve Niyamgiri . . . today Adivasi and Dalits are the main pillars [*mukhyo khonta*] of the NSS. (NSS Adivasi leaders, interview notes, January 2016)

Organization and material/financial support
Dongrias, Kutias, Jharanias, and Dalits in 112 villages and 10,000-plus households from either side of Niyamgiri (Rayagada and Kalahandi) form the core base of the NSS-led struggle (85 percent of those in the proposed mining region are Adivasi) and are represented through village-level organizations, or *gaon sangathans* (led by village elders), where all are members (since the mine is seen to be everyone's issue), followed by 25–30 village zonal clusters (regular meetings with dates planned in advance, with an NSS leadership team covering each zone once every three months), which are in turn linked to representative leadership teams from Rayagada (led by Lada Sikoka) and Kalahandi (led by Kumuti Majhi after Dai Singh) sides, respectively, who are in turn part of a central (apex) body of a smaller group of key leaders. Besides this more formal structuring, there are other leaders who number close to 100 or more individuals (female and male) spread across the region, and who have taken an oath for Niyamgiri and have 'come out and openly declared with courage [*sahas ke saath*] that they are ready to give up their life and blood but will not give up the land/hills' (NSS leader, interview notes, January 2016).

Meetings are hosted in turn by villages. '*Muththi*' (handful) collections from all in the form of rice and dal (lentils) are collected to feed everyone, including visitors. People come of their own accord from villages and pool these handfuls, despite 'Vedanta-wallas' (local or external goons paid by the company) efforts to strike fear around such participation by going around with loudspeakers telling them that they will be beaten (by the police, according to the NSS) for joining in and supporting these gatherings. If people are not in a position to contribute in kind, 30 rupees or 45 US cents (maximum) is a suggested cash contribution, including additional funds raised from the small-scale selling of agricultural and minor forest products – all funds raised go into a collective (village-level) fund to support meetings and more (e.g. when leaders need financial support in times of medical/legal need). 'People were never given money for supporting the movement – even transportation costs were born by each or they came by cycle.

A movement can only run if people participate spontaneously [*swotho propruto*]' (NSS activist, interview notes, January 2016).

Additionally, personal donations and contributions in kind from Lanjigarh town, including (and eventually) from OBC and GC petty traders facing the ecological impacts of the refinery (e.g. water and air/noise pollution) and the inflow of migrants who started to set up competing businesses, also facilitated the movement as the expansion of ADNTFD participation increased the caste-class ambit of the NSS (for material and cultural reasons) back into the town (plains/foothills) from where initial mobilization began around refinery dispossession.

Strategy, mobilization, and tactics
The ADNTFDs at the core of the NSS provided the glue for the struggle, wherein the sacred, the ecological, and the productive became one and were propagated as the primary purpose for the movement (for Niyamraja) by the Dongria, the group facing the grimmest prospects in the event of the mine being established on Niyam Dongar. This message was constantly affirmed at closed ceremonial gatherings on the mountain in February (every three months, a white rooster was sacrificed for Niyam Raja), where *Darni Penu* was worshipped and ties strengthened, along with expressions of solidarity and decisions regarding the composition of the NSS leadership, while also being an occasion where long-term directions for the struggle were established. Select supporters were invited to attend (mainly the key activists working with the NSS) as observers.

Plans and counterplans are adjusted and developed by the NSS leadership in conjunction with veteran anti-mining/dispossession activists who are part of a committee that consistently discusses and reviews directions and necessary action based on emergent information from NSS sources regarding police-company tactics. NSS strategy and tactics are also informed by: (a) the experience of these activists from similar anti-dispossession struggles in the state (Baliapal, Gandhamardan, Kashipur, POSCO); (b) cross-pollination (knowledge) from these movements as the leaders of current struggles (e.g. anti-POSCO) attend rallies, give speeches, and express inter-movement solidarity while NSS leadership visits these sites to both raise awareness about the struggle in Lanjigarh and to learn from these movements; and (c) national level participation in New Delhi with anti-displacement movements from across the country (some 50,000 people on one occasion with mining-related movements from Chennai and Goa, for instance, where judicial insights were shared among these movements, including public assessments of key justices/decisions).

A conscious strategy to grow the movement and widen the scope of the NSS constituency (mobilization tactics) was to continually embrace the ADNTFD social groups and those Adivasi-Dalit-OBC-GC caste/class groupings living in the vicinity of the refinery zone at the foot of the mountain, even when these people were reluctant, anti or two-timed the efforts of the NSS. Mobilization was consistent and unflagging (if not 'forgiving') in this regard, as was the spreading of the analysis and message/purpose of the movement. Several successful attempts around such expansions occurred around movement building at key moments when Vedanta's efforts (real and propagandist) proved to be counterproductive. Four such examples concerning Adivasi-Dalit relations, the role of women, youth, and petty trade/small business OBC-GCs (and land sellers) in town are considered in this regard to demonstrate how the NSS continually increased its scope as a sociopolitical formation contesting mining dispossession.

Whether or not Adivasi-Dalit relations are always rendered problematic due to a caste politics of interlocutors and opinion brokers (usually of the upper echelons) or a result of *real* horizontal conflicts among the marginalized and exploited, which in turn is never too far from a vertical politics of caste and class, is debatable. Speaking to the NSS/Lanjigarh context, however, Adivasi and Dalit leaders attest to the historical and continued close cultural and economic relations between these social groups, despite what are dismissed as petty differences incurred around the struggle to make a livelihood (Adivasi as gatherers and agriculturalists and Dalits as petty traders and middlemen in market transactions for Adivasi produce). 'In our area, Kondhs and Dombs (Dalits) have lived together as good neighbors [*bhallo parosi*]. I cannot speak for other areas, but here we have always had good relations despite some cheating by those engaged in small business relations, which we don't worry about as people are doing this for their livelihood – I say this as an Adivasi elder – we are immediate friends' (Adivasi NSS leader, interview notes, January 2016). Adivasi and Dalit NSS leaders and activists attest to the ancestral bond between both groups, between Kondh kings and

Domb ministers and as 'spiritual people' (*dharmaro loko*). The NSS leadership acknowledges that despite initial difficulties in some areas to convince Dalits to permit rallies/protest marches, there has never been a significant separation around this struggle, and if 'any one of us was not in the process, then the company would have been able to dig up the entire area by now'. They point to the fact that at meetings and rallies, all ADNTFD groups are present and active, and that 'wherever there is a Kondh, there is a Domb', and that all ADNTFD move freely in and out of each other's villages.

Women leaders have played a crucial role in relation to the prospects for the NSS mobilization.

> We have always realized the importance of women in our movement and their participation and numbers are always more. In our movement, women are as active as the men. It is the women who come in big numbers during rallies and processions. The company targets men's weakness for liquor and supplies free liquor but this does not work with the women. (NSS male activist, interview notes, January 2016)

Most women (mainly Dalits and Jharanias on the lower reaches of the mountain – closer to/in Lanjigarh) were initially cautiously supportive of the project because they felt it would provide jobs and money and educational opportunities for their children, and this created tensions in the NSS along the lines of gender. However, as they realized that neither jobs, money, nor education were forthcoming, and that the free supply of liquor was socially debilitating and destructive of family relations, women turned against the company and the project, that is, the company's plans to disrupt male participation through the free supply of liquor in the hope that women would then not be able to participate (no men to accompany them) was counterproductive:

> Rather, more women started going and attending these demonstrations because they were upset with the company for promoting alcoholism among their men. Gato Majhi, who is a women's leader, a Dongria who lives in the mountains, was given an umbrella and slippers [*chappals*] by the company – she received it and then burnt it in front of them [*tako tharonela, tanko moohore podi dela*]. There are many more women leaders in the Dongria villages as well as Jharania, and they have all come forward today. They

also compel the men to leave liquor, which helps with movement participation. (NSS male activist, interview notes, January 2016)

Youth, especially Dalit-Adivasi living closer to Lanjigarh at the foot of the mountains, were keen on the prospects for education, jobs, and careers with the company, and were easily persuaded by the state-corporate effort to spread their message in the region to undermine anti-mining sentiments and organizing efforts, if not motivate youngsters (as a dispossession tactic, as was the case with women and liquor) to champion state-corporate mining development in the region. Youth sporting clubs and cricket have been instrumental in this regard on multiple fronts, including with perpetuating violence against NSS activists/opponents of the project by acting as a company-funded 'sports club' cum alleged goon-squad.

The educated youth initially thought that Vedanta would open a factory and give them jobs. There was no proper understanding on how it would be destructive or harmful. But when we saw the company had actually started destroying the forests, it was an eye-opener [*akhi kholidela*] for us youth. Our elders had understood this much earlier, and it's said the truth always wins [*satyoro joyo sobu bele ochi*]. We had to accept that. We also understood that if some of us could get employment, probably we would have earned 100 rupees/day or more, but hundreds of thousands of families would have perished for good. That is why we had to follow the movement. (NSS youth activist, interview notes, January 2016)

The company took around 200 youth (mainly Dalits and Jharanias who have some formal education) to industrial training institutes (ITIs) to train them as fitters, plumbers, electricians, welders, and trades in general – when they came back, there was no job for them in the company or anywhere. Today, they have all turned against the company. (NSS activist, interview notes, January 2016)

Speaking of earlier days, the middle-aged and elderly leaders make mention of how youngsters (who are now a part of the movement) used to stay away or actively obstruct NSS leaders and team members from visiting the Dongria villages in the interior, blocking them at every opportunity. However, NSS leaders knew it was a matter of time and did not chastise the youth, but dealt with them patiently and encouraged them to think about wider issues for the ADNTFD in the interior, for instance:

Later, when the company actually set up the refinery and its vehicles were all around us, lots of outsiders came to settle in Lanjigarh with the help of jobs from Vedanta. They were contractors, truck drivers, coolies/laborers – they did not give these jobs to the local youth because they were always afraid the local youth could turn against them being from the area – the youth got disillusioned in time. Even then, some still had some hope and kept running behind government officers like Rakesh Mishra and S.K. Patnaik, the human resources head at Vedanta till their slippers [*chappals*] wore out [*daori daori chappal cheri gala*]. They would say, 'sir, are the bosses here?' [*hai kya, sahib hai kya*] – months and years passed but the sirs and *sahibs* were not accessible. . . . I was one of those land losers who thought that because they took my land they would give me a job and could feed my family better and send my children for studies, but all my dreams were shattered. Even a graduate like me who is a land loser has not got a peon [*chaprasi*] job in the company. And what about the thousands of people who are illiterate or semi-literate – what job can Vedanta give them except making them into coolies for some time on their own land? Like me, many felt cheated [*mo pori anek loko tokho re parile*]. We all joined the movement, and today NSS leaders are seen as people who were sent by *Dharni* to protect all of us. (NSS youth activist/leader, interview notes, January 2016)

Speaking of earlier days, NSS Adivasi leader (elder) Kumuti Majhi remembers how hard the movement had to try to convince youngsters to join and lead rallies when the Dongrias came down from the hills. He is visibly emotional when speaking of a promising Dongria youth leader, Jithu Jakeska, who turned the tables on the NSS and became a pro-Vedanta mining activist and agitator:

I was trying my best to develop him – we told him we are growing old, we may die any time, so you should lead us eventually. I gave him my *dhoti* and *lachi* [clothing]. But Vedanta played a crooked game and bought him over.

Kumuti and other NSS leaders blame the company and still do not reject youth like Jithu (who was promised a job, a vehicle, money for studies, and was sent to Bhubaneswar, the state capital), who are now unable to 'come to us nor go to his Dongria people' (having realized otherwise today), but is feeling personally cheated and now attends NSS meetings. But 'youth feel welcome by the NSS and many more have come from Jaganathpur village, for example, who were behind the success of the Gram Sabha process/mobilization'.

According to Siddhartha Nayak (interview notes, January 2016), OBC-GCs (petty traders/small business castes in Lanjigarh town) and those who had signed on for selling their land, were implicated in 'false cases' by the company and other middle men and 'spread anger against the company', as those implicated in these cases often had to stay in jail for months and make 60-kilometer-plus trips to Bhawanipatna repeatedly for court dates. Despite free legal aid from KSNM, all this cost money, time, and emotional energy, and strained families who were not cash rich as these were all cash demands. Migration to the region and the establishment of competing businesses also added to these strains on local small business owners. Even those who had been displaced with assurances of post-displacement compensation were forced to run after government officers and *dalaals* (company middlemen) and give bribes for same. When money was transferred to banks and post office deposits were made, most of those displaced did not know how much and were faced with situations of false withdrawals by bank and postal staff (fraud/theft), and didn't get anything in the end. It was not hard for the NSS, in time, to mobilize these disillusioned OBC-GCs and other townspeople against Vedanta, who, in time, as stated already, even provided financial support to the NSS. The situation of some of those being resettled and rehabilitated in places such as Vedantanagar has not helped the company or the state in this regard either:

Those who did get money could not handle their money properly and in no time finished it off. Today they are on the streets of Lanjigarh. Those who once had land and lived happily, today have to work in street side hotels to clean plates and cups or collect fuel wood and depend on public distribution rice to feed themselves and their families. . . . The settlement area does not even have minimum facilities. It's not a livable place [*banchiba eori jaga nahi*]. Water problems, drainage problems, no proper roads, and people are kept there as if in prison [*bandhi sala pori*] and under constant surveillance. (Nayak, interview notes, January 2016)

These difficulties and the destruction of the local environment, including the accelerated (post-refinery) drying up of the River Tel, the inorganic mining waste pollution of the Vamsadhara and subsequent deaths, skin/eye diseases, the rising incidences of TB, and the death of cattle have also helped the eventual backlash and the NSS mobilization against the company and the government, instigating the villagers of neighboring Chatrapur to even break pipelines laid by the company.

When it comes to such direct action, the NSS has relied on generating a display of strength in numbers, if not the non-violent (but always violent in appearance, as Dongria descend from the hills in thousands bearing traditional weapons/arms) storming of the town, the factory (refinery) gates, and local government offices (District Collector), including similar participation in demonstrations at the capital city Bhubaneswar, and even in Delhi, the nation's capital.

When the Dongrias and the Jharanias decide to take up movement action through collective walks, they come down from the forests in numbers of up to 5,000 at a time beating drums, blowing horns, and holding traditional weapons [bows and arrows, axes, spears, sticks/*dandas*] singing angry songs. The sound of drums and the walk is enough to strike fear [*bhaiyo shrushti kore*] in the hearts of people below. In fact, the people in the town would shut their doors and windows and remain inside. People in the streets would run here and there and leave their cycles and scooters on the roadside. Dongrias would not hurt the locals, but would not hesitate to march aggressively to the factory gates and to the police station. That was a display of the strength of the movement. We do this and meanwhile, our intellectual friends Bhawanipatna and Lanjigarh area file cases in the Supreme Court and the KSNM helps activists and locals with legal aid and education to deal with police and government officials and to get us out of jail. (NSS activist, interview notes, January 2016)

Examples of direct action and non/confrontational tactics used over time included: bicycle rallies with billboards and loudspeakers ('Vedanta go back, go back!' 'Niyamgiri Charibo Nahi – we won't leave Niyamgiri!'); leafletting villages or horn/conch-calls to mobilize Adivasi from across the mountains to join impromptu demonstrations/*andolans*; *padyatras* (village-to-village foot marches); *rasta rokos* (drop trees/boulders blocking roads); *dharnas* (sit-downs) at police stations/DC's office, prompting mass arrests (and jail crowding); and human chains (10,000 strong around Niyam Dongar in 2009 to protest mining post Supreme Court clearance. *Gheraos* or encirclements of officials and police by women and children were not uncommon as when the women of Chatrapur encircled/held the police and local MLA's wife accusing her of supporting Vedanta or when the women of Bandhaguda village demanded the release of all their men who had 'been disappeared overnight' demanding to be arrested with their children, squatting in the police station till they were beaten and forcibly transported out in trucks. Public shaming of Kondh MLA (voted in to office by Adivasi) as a 'company stooge who follows the money trail as a Cuttackia' (city person/traitor from Cuttack), sabotaging company equipment/vehicles (as is suggested by police but denied by the NSS activists); and continued 'squatting' (refusal by anti-displacement families) to disrupt forced resettlement plans are other examples of direct action. On the subject of violence, according to one leader:

In the initial days when the Dongria understood the danger, they said we will kill the police and other officers who come. We told them, no, we shall not kill them because if we did, we would fall in to their trap and we cannot face them because they have a bigger force [*bara shakti*] – we will be killed. Slowly they understood that our strength was in our numbers – when people of Bargarh village readily went to jail, many more villages came into the movement to support us, as did people from struggles against POSCO, from Kashipur, Gandhmardhan, and Kalahandi – experienced activists from these struggles joined us as well.

Gram Sabha mobilization as a critical incident

When the Supreme Court of India eventually issued a verdict in 2013 requiring mining development ratification by Gram Sabhas in the potentially affected region as per the PESA Act, this provided the NSS with a further opportunity for widening and deepening the movement and support for its 'no to mining' message, despite the state-corporate attempt to manipulate the process of village selection down to 12 (by the NSS's calculation, 112 villages), including a Gouda (Dalit) village (Tadijhola) of one family. A display of official and state power (if not intimidation) through the deployment of armed elite CoBRA forces and a heavy police presence,[9] with constant surveillance of all proceedings, including cameras trained on villagers present at these respective gatherings in the 12 villages, was constantly accompanied by ADNTFDs from all 112 villages who provided moral support in numbers to their fellow participants in the 12 villages. The Gram Sabha process widened and deepened the resistance to the mine in unexpected ways, producing an unprecedented political multiplier effect for the NSS-led struggle in the region and unified constituencies in a way that no amount of village-to-village door knocking alone could ever have hoped to have accomplished. All 12 villages unanimously rejected mining on Niyamgiri; youth and women leaders played an active role in providing testimonies and questioning Sarat Chandra Mishra (Rayagada district judge in charge) on matters of process, omissions, and distortions (including the de-registering of leaders like Lado Sikoka from the eligible voters list); and every attempt by the officials to delimit and quantify land (commodify/privatize/state-categorize) was challenged with claims for Niyamgiri as one indivisible territorial entity for all ADNTFDs.

External agents/supporters (individual and organizational)

NSS leaders and activists such as Lingaraj Azad acknowledge the selective importance of outside individuals and organizations (national and international) in augmenting and amplifying the resistance, but are quick to point out that this is a resistance 'whose success is only a result of the struggle of local people – it is not a victory of either the Congress or any political party or NGO. It is a victory of the people'.

The NSS remained open to but critically vigilant when it came to relations with various supporters, whether individual or organizational or from political parties, other national anti-displacement movements, local advocacy groups and inter/national NGOs, all of whom provided support and variously enabled or used the local movement for their own aims at inter/national levels at different points in time. These individuals and groups provided: media/publicity and public education; political/moral support (human rights claiming and shaming); scientific/knowledge and legal capacity to develop reports and make formal submissions to the courts (including the Supreme Court of India); accompaniment at key political moments around ground-level developments; shareholder, human/cultural rights, and environmental concerns related pressure on the company (leading to key divestments from Vedanta and a general discrediting of the company through public campaigns in the UK – see FoilVedanta – if not affecting business risk ratings for Odisha); and providing official contacts in government and related background networking to enforce environmental, forest, *panchayat*, religious, and cultural legislations, and to push forward a process of continued judicial activism via the court system. Direct action and continuous organizing in Niyamgiri by ADNTFD and the NSS regardless of the above types of unsolicited support, has been unflagging and dogged to date, despite interjecting moments of despair and silencing (e.g. the 2008 Supreme Court decision to permit mining while ignoring the recommendations of the Central Empowered Committee or CEC was particularly debilitating).

Directions for the near future: refinery activism and building forward
As stated in the introduction to this chapter, the Odisha Mining Corporation (OMC) once again filed a petition challenging the 2013 resolutions of the Gram Sabhas. The Supreme Court scrapped the petition on 6 May 2016. This is likely to sound the death knell for state-corporate capital mining activism in Niyamgiri as the company has no other viable source of bauxite to feed its 5 million ton per annum (mtpa) capacity refinery, not to mention a 1.6 mtpa aluminium smelter and 1,200 Mw captive power complex at Jharsuguda, in the hopes of sourcing bauxite from Niyamgiri.

With the recent ploy by the OMC, the NSS has escalated its involvement since 2015 and is demanding closure of the refinery, while leaders plan to gather some 10,000 ADNTFDs at the site and cram the jails with thousands of arrests should the company decide to continue with what the NSS allege as being an illegal development. In June 2016, a week-long *padyatra* (including the 12 villages involved with the Gram Sabha process) led by the NSS celebrated the recent Supreme Court decision and demanded the decommissioning of Vedanta's Lanjigarh refinery. September 2016 demonstrations at Muniguda by the NSS are also demanding an end to harassment and false arrests and murder of youth leaders and Dongria activists (and their relatives, as is alleged in the February shooting of 21-year-old Manda Kadraka by police as a Maoist sympathizer) by police and paramilitary forces and the closure of CRPF camps around Niyamgiri. In October, some 100 Dongria Kondhs torched a temporary camp of the CRPF at Parsali while protesting the building of roads to Niyamgiri that the Dongria feel are being constructed to facilitate the mining of Niyamgiri. Police, meanwhile, have blamed this on Maoists, who they claim are using Dongria as a cover to this effect. The NSS are also rejecting NGOs, demanding that foreign and local NGOs duping us should 'Go Back!'

> Earlier we had to run around day and night to make people understand, but today we don't have to tell anybody – every person in the village will tell you about Mother Earth, water, forests and air – everyone knows the company is a thief come from outside [*baharo ashithiba chor*]. And we are now alert enough not to allow Vedanta or any other bigger corporate force – it makes no difference to us [*amopain ologa kichu nahi*]. (Kumuti Majhi, interview notes, January 2016)

Local activism and resistance to mining in 'protected areas': some concluding reflections and insights for and about ADNTFD struggles in the forest belt

The NSS struggle to protect nature as God is inadvertently a form of resistance to land theft (colonial dispossession) and the proletarianization of racialized ADNTFD labor by mining. It represents an anti-colonial capitalist development politics to the extent that such claims by ADNTFD attempt to remove (block or extricate) land and labor from the colonizing economy of exchange and the alienation of labor, subsequently short-circuiting the process of accumulation and exchange value through such resistance. Needless to say, this poses a problem for those who subscribe to

Marx's colonial prognostications that 'England has to fulfill a double mission in India: one destructive, the other regenerating – the annihilation of old Asiatic society, and the laying of the material foundations of Western society in Asia' (Marx 1968: 125).

The NSS struggle against state-corporate activism to advance mining at all costs (state-corporate mining activism) demonstrates the indispensability of organized direct action and resistance by those (ADNTFD) at the mining *rock face* confronting the immediate prospects of land theft (colonial dispossession), the exploitation of labor, and the destruction of the ecological basis for life and regeneration in the region, in warding off such incursions. It demonstrates the feasibility and reality of organizing work across Adivasi-Dalit caste/class (forest dweller Adivasi communal-small/landless peasant agriculturalist) lines (including wider *temporary* mobilizations with OBC-GC/petty bourgeoisie caste-classes in Lanjigarh) for immediate and long-term political gains. There has been no mining on Niyam Dongar some two decades later in the forest belt, demonstrating the ability of an Adivasi-Dalit-peasant primitive communal (in pejorative Marxist terms) politics to disrupt and even halt (and especially if the current effort to shut down the refinery also succeeds) the process of primitive accumulation and the subsequent process of capitalist accumulation by dispossession (Harvey 2003; Marx 1975). Organizing ADNTFD or land-/cash-poor and subsistence-production-oriented social groups with meager dependence on (labor) markets/capital (productive-culture of the commons is relatively intact) in contexts where landlordism is not pervasive does not reinforce the regressive social relations of feudalism (and related synergies with capitalism) aptly critiqued by Marxists. This critique should not, however, be confused with the real egalitarian social prospects of an anti-colonial (capitalist) ADNTFD politics of the commons (not equated with communes), which also does little to significantly disrupt (if not coalesce with) a working-class revolutionary socialist politics in the terrain of capital, assuming the latter does not regress toward similar political-economic and social compulsions of the capitalist colonization of ADNTFDs.

Key to this process of direct action and organizing work, and noteworthy for movement praxis, are some of the following possible insights, as shared by NSS activists: (1) the presence and (constant) development of an NSS leadership team of experienced elders (and women and youth) and left political activists with a history of anti-mining/dispossession resistance in the locale; (2) persistent education and movement constituency building over time, including remaining open to detractors from ADNTFD groups; (3) establishing and reiterating a sense of movement purpose across constituencies, which makes political sense across ADNTFD and caste-class groups in the town; (4) self-financing/material supports (minimize need for same); (5) direct action with litigation/judicial activism and movement-media counter-hegemonic messaging; (6) selective and circumspect acceptance of assistance from outsider individuals/organizations, including disengagement when called for (e.g. with I/NGOs); (7) controlling the representation and the political aims of the core formation at all times to ensure an ADNTFD-driven politics; and (8) constant exposition and overt opposition and negation of state-corporate development violence through militant non-violent activism, despite the severity of retaliations.

While national and transnational actors/agents were instrumental in and around judicial and wider political action, the NSS decided on how to work/not with these actors at all times, discrediting those whose political aims were discordant/counter-productive, thereby maintaining a distinct center of movement gravity consistently embedded in the immediate concerns of ADNTFD and their action and representation of their own demands at all times. Trans/national vectors were, for the most part, contradictory elements in the resistance formation serving as un/invited sporadic augmentations or even as disruptions of continuous open direct action by mining affected marginal social groups who were always the primary protagonists (they put their lives on the line) given that they had everything to lose. Inter/national support on many fronts has had a reverse boomerang effect, un/intentionally enhancing the institutional political prospects of these various agents (e.g. Action Aid and its successful Niyamgiri-related St. Paul's Cathedral fundraising/campaign or the Congress/Green Kalahandi electoral spin-offs from their decision to latch on to the NSS struggle of ADNTFDs).

Niyamgiri gives much cause for pause to the current fetish pertaining to the alleged indispensability if not presumed instrumental necessity for a purported transnational/global social movement activism replete with the tendency towards achieving various political aims at all times and places; an unquestioned insistence that often leads to the silencing and attempted erasure of the primary political place of resistance by those actually being dispossessed and exploited, whatever the sympathetic politics and actions (and purported risks) being taken by those protesting in metropolitan settings at a distance. This mostly welcomed solidarity (circumspect or otherwise, as in the case of the NSS) as augmentation cannot replace nor become (nor should be politically confused with) the movement of the colonially dispossessed who struggle on regardless of whether or not such solidarity is forthcoming and are compelled to take on (or are forced aside) the continuous response to incessant state-corporate colonial capitalist development and the relentless pursuit of the mining of happiness.

While Marx somewhat nostalgically dismissed rurality and peasants as counter-revolutionary subjects in sociopolitical terms, and the idea of revolution was appropriated by the Marxist industrial (proletarian) working-class-based project, Frantz Fanon recognized that in 'colonial countries only the peasantry is revolutionary' given that (and speaking from the Algerian context) all the colonized 'has ever seen on his land is that he can be arrested, beaten, and starved with impunity' (Fanon 1963/2005: 9). Anti-colonial politics affirms the political and anti-colonial revolutionary possibility (historical-continued necessity) of the indigenous and the small/landless communal peasantry based on the politics of land and territories always in the way of the colonial capitalist accumulation project. This is because 'the land is the most meaningful . . . and it is land which must provide bread and natural dignity' (Fanon 1963/2005: 9). The basis for political-economic unity is a unity around territory and whether or not the economic activities (production) on a given land are supporting its inhabitants. These struggles and movements will continue to reference an anti-colonial (or parallel) political difference, contrary to the globalist white-stream colonial theoretical and political project that continually obscures/denies their material implications by insisting that these political formations are nothing more than an ethereal cultural difference, a superficial/malleable identity politics. Prying material and cultural logics apart in this manner is yet another example of a gesture toward facilitating territorial usurpation by making the material immaterial, and thereby enabling colonial capitalist accumulation designs of violent occupation, un/intended absorption, and rejection/disposal.

In the end, as the NSS experience seems to demonstrate, perhaps the only thing better than being exploited by capital is not being exploited by capital, that is, the relative freedom (from colonization) of unfree labor and from the usurpation of land through force and commodification – a colonial/anti-colonial dialectic produced in the political-economic (material) struggle (sacral politics/culturalisms included or not) of ADNTFDs against capitalist colonization of land, water, forests, and labor in Niyamgiris here and elsewhere. Liberation through the revolutionary overthrow of capitalism and the promise of an emergent socialist alternative, all at the necessary (or Marxist inevitability) cost of the colonization of indigenous and land-based egalitarian-communal societies of the landless (relatively so because land is not understood as a commodity to be owned, bought and sold) and their potential proletarianization (exploitation), is understandably uninspiring and of little comfort to those who are being forced or persuaded to destroy (negate) themselves as an alleged anachronism. Hence, in dialectical and material terms, it is only non/compliant struggle and resistance engendered by this colonial theft that becomes the inevitable.

Notes

1 Adivasi, or original dweller/persons, is a contested term in the Indian context (for a useful discussion, see Karlsson 2003), as are claims to indigeneity elsewhere for that matter, given the racialized politics of neo/colonization and the attendant projects of erasure by post/colonial states imposing the dominant myth of post/industrial capitalist development as progress through unfettered, neither by ecology nor by sociocultural and political-economic heterogeneity, materialism predicated on the profit-incentive and accumulation project. Claims to being 'Adivasi' are allegedly also harder to establish with any degree of certainty when compared to contexts of continued white settler-colonial exploitation (in the American and Oceanic contexts – see preceding chapters by Sockbeson and Gordon in this collection), given multiple waves of colonization in the Indian subcontinent, if not the colonial epistemic politics of anthropological and historical record purportedly de/legitimating fact from fiction.

2 See www.grain. org/article/entries/725-roger-moody.

3 Schedule-V prohibits transfer of tribal land to non-tribals; Article 25 also guarantees rights to religion and religious practices; forested regions are subject to further stipulations under the Forest Rights Act or FRA of 2006 and the Environmental Protection Act or EPA of 1986; and the Panchayat (Extension to Scheduled Areas) Act (PESA, 1996) empowers Gram Sabhas (village councils) to make primary decisions regarding (mining) development in the Scheduled Areas.

4 In the post-independence period, these include movements against:

Hirakud dam (Sambalpur, 1960s); Baliapal missile testing range (1980s–1990s); Gandhmardan bauxite mines (Baragarh, 1980s); Gopalpur port development for Tata Steel (1990s); Chilika Bachao Andolan and Integrated Shrimp Farming (Chilika Lake, 1990s); Lower Suktel dam (Bolangir, 2005); Kashipur bauxite mining (Kashipur, 1990s); POSCO mining/iron and steel (Jagatsinghpur, 2005) (see also Kapoor 2013, 2015, for more on similar movements in Odisha).

5 For example, NSS activists allege that the company was responsible for the death of Sukru Majhi, a prominent and respected veteran leader of the NSS, who was run over by a truck in March 2005, which reversed over him again to ensure he was dead.

6 Including a 1 MTPA alumina refinery, a 75 MW coal thermal power plant, and 2 MTPA red mud waste ponds.

7 A veteran popular political activist with considerable experience around similar anti-bauxite mining displacement struggles and movements such as Kashipur and Gandhamardan and a member of the Samajvadi Jan Parishad or SJP, which is yet to secure a seat in the national parliament. According to

Azad (interview notes, March 2009 and February 2011), the Niyamgiri struggle is being led by the NSS and not the SJP, and his participation is as a local activist affected by these developments in his home district. Other SJP activists have also helped the NSS initiatives on occasion.

8 This section has been developed with the help of several NSS leaders and their supporters for the most part, through discussion, formal interviews, and focus group sessions conducted episodically in 2009, 2011, and 2016.

9 Justified in terms of the (Naxalite) Maoist guerilla movement in Odisha (and the Red Corridor), often used (as shared by activists) as a pretext for arresting NSS leaders/activists as sympathizers (if not leaders and villagers in similar anti-dispossession movements in the state), and in keeping with what is being called Operation Green Hunt, commissioned by the Manmohan Singh-led government in this Corridor (an unprecedented internal deployment of para/military, police, and air force) to address what the Prime Minster referenced as the single greatest threat to India's internal security.

References

Amnesty International (2010). *Don't Mine Us out of Existence: Bauxite Mine and Refinery Devastate Lives in India*. London: Amnesty International.

Bhaduri, A. (2010). 'Recognize this face?' *Economic and Political Weekly*, 45(47): 10–14.

Davis, M. (2002). *Late Victorian Holocausts: El Nino Famines and the Making of the Third World*. London: Verso.

Fanon, F. (1963/2005). *The Wretched of the Earth*, trans. C. Farrington. New York: Grove Press.

Fernandes, W. (2006). 'Development related displacement and tribal women'. In G. Rath (ed.), *Tribal Development in India: The Contemporary Debate*. New Delhi: Sage, pp. 112–132.

Gadgil, M. and Guha, R. (1992). *This Fissured Land: An Ecological History of India*. Cambridge, MA: Harvard University Press.

Guha, R. (1997). *Dominance Without Hegemony: History and Power in Colonial India*. New Delhi: Oxford University Press.

Karlsson, B. (2003). 'Anthropology and the "indigenous slot": claims to and debates about indigenous peoples' status in India'. *Critique of Anthropology*, 23(4): 403–423.

Kapoor, D. (2013). 'Trans-local rural solidarity and a politics of place: contesting colonial capital and the neoliberal state in India'. *Interface: A Journal for and About Social Movements*, 5(1): 14–39.

Kapoor, D. (2015). 'Subaltern social movements and development in India: rural dispossession, trans-local activism and subaltern re-visitations'. In D. Caouette and D. Kapoor (eds), *Beyond Colonialism, Development and Globalization: Social Movements and Critical Perspectives*. London and New York: Zed Books, pp. 40–77.

Levien, M. (2013). 'The politics of dispossession: theorizing India's "land wars"'. *Politics and Society*, 41(3): 351–394.

Marx, K. (1968). 'The future of British rule in India'. In S. Avineri (ed.), *Karl Marx on Colonialism and Modernization*. Garden City: Doubleday.

Munshi, I. (2012). *The Adivasi Question: Issues of Land, Forest and Livelihood*. New Delhi: Orient Blackswan.

Nag, S. (2001). 'Nationhood and displacement in the Indian subcontinent'. *Economic and Political Weekly*, 1 March 1.

Padel, F. and Das, S. (2010). *Out of This Earth: East India Adivasis and the Aluminium Cartel*. New Delhi: Orient Blackswan.

Sahu, S. and Dash, M. (2011). 'Expropriation of land and cultures: the Odisha story and beyond'. *Social Change*, 41(2): 251–270.

5 | OUR CROPS SPEAK: SMALL AND LANDLESS PEASANT RESISTANCE TO AGRO-EXTRACTIVE DISPOSSESSION IN CENTRAL SULAWESI, INDONESIA

Hasriadi Masalam

Introduction

The agro-extractive regime pursued by the corporatized state and the pervasive expansion of capital accumulation has turned the rural frontier of Indonesia into agrarian war zones. The fall of the Suharto authoritarian regime in 1998 encouraged the escalation of agrarian conflicts and resistance to land dispossession in Indonesia. In the world's fourth most populated country, where more than half the people live on small-scale family farming in the rural areas, with almost half of these landless, the victims of violent agrarian conflicts are mounting, as is revealed by the numbers referencing death tolls, heavy injuries, imprisoned peasants, and activists (Lucas and Warren 2013). This is indicative of serious challenges by subaltern struggles around modes of production and meaning making that are 'in the way' of the neoliberal state apparatus and market imperatives being imposed by a globalizing colonial capitalism. It would be a political oversight to continue to remain oblivious to this perseverance of small and landless peasants in suggesting localized and indigenous ways of resisting dispossession and the violence of the 'postcolonial' developmental state, on their own terms or in relation to their potential for engaging with wider challenges by labor against capital (Kapoor 2015; Prashad 2008; Rajagopal 2003).

This chapter outlines small and landless peasant resistance against coconut plantation-led dispossession by identifying the key actors, modes, and impacts of dispossession, followed by an examination of the germination, stagnation, and prospects for rejuvenation of organized contestation, including judicial activism in conjunction with direct action and village-to-village efforts. The chapter is based on current participatory action research with marginal peasants

and indigenous ethnicities involved in an anti-dispossession struggle (Kapoor and Jordan 2009) in Bohotokong Village, Bunta Sub-
District, Banggai District, Central Sulawesi Province, in the eastern
part of Indonesia.

Capital accumulation and the neo/colonial agro-extractive regime in Indonesia

The process of capital accumulation (Harvey 2003) by the
corporatized state and rent-seeking elites relies on institutions and
practices of natural resource extraction from the era of the colonial
capitalist East India Company to today's neoliberal 'Indonesia Inc.'[1]
This explains the emergence and the continuities of the neo/colonial
agro-extractive regime that Sukarno, the founding father and the
first president, had characterized decades ago as colonial curses, that
is, positioning Indonesia as the market for colonial products, as a
source of raw materials for colonial capitalists, and an investment site
for the capitals of colonial powers, turning this resource-abundant
archipelago into 'a nation of coolies and a coolie amongst nations'.[2]
Since the Dutch colonial administration stipulated the *Agrarische Wet*
(Agrarian Law) in 1870, which granted them the right to issue *erpatch*
compatible with *Hak Guna Usaha* (large-scale land concessions)
scheme under the postcolonial state, the colonial curse continues
to be among the key factors explaining land dispossession in rural
Indonesia, particularly in the plantation sector. Indeed, large-scale
plantations are the most tangible living legacy of colonial agrarian
capitalist policies in the archipelago today (Alatas 1977).

The data released by Transformasi untuk Keadilan (TuK)
Indonesia[3] on February 2015 demonstrate the enormous extent
of land control by the 29 biggest palm oil tycoons in Indonesia,
controlling 5.1 million hectares of land worth US$69.1 billion in total,
and equivalent to 45 percent of the total Indonesian state budget in
2014. Being the world largest producer of crude palm oil with 7.3
million hectares of plantations, Indonesia is now expecting to expand
by a further 20 million hectares, 'an area the size of England, the
Netherlands and Switzerland combined' (Marti 2008: 7). During
Suharto's authoritarian regime, the key actors of palm-oil-induced
development dispossession mostly involved the 'Suharto palm oil
oligarchy' (Aditjondro 2001), where political actors were business
players utilizing modes of crony capitalism, aligning economic and

political interests between the Indonesian palm oil business, the government, and Sino-Indonesian business people, which included companies such as Astra, Sinar Mas, Raja Garuda Mas, Musim Mas, and the Salim Group/Indofood.

Both domestic and international creditors play an important part in the rapid expansion of palm oil plantation by the private sector. In addition to multilateral financial institutions such as the World Bank and Asian Development Bank, oil palm corporations also obtain credit from Indonesian national banks, as well as private international banks such as Rabobank, Citicorp International Ltd, Citibank, Shanghai Banking Corporation, Union Bank of Switzerland, Sumitomo Bank Ltd, Bank of Taiwan, Indosuez Bank-France, ABN-Amro Bank N.V., Japan Asia Investment, the Hong Kong Shanghai Banking Corporation, and Bank of Tokyo-Mitsubishi Ltd (Prasetyantoko and Setiawan, cited in Julia and White 2012). With the continuous support of loans from these financial institutions, there seems to be no end in sight when it comes to the constant expansion of this agro-extractive regime, despite the associated dispossession, impoverishment, and exploitation of peasant labor and associated conflicts, including environmental calamities.

Moreover, since the mid-1970s, to equip large-scale plantations with cheap labors and with loans from the World Bank, the Suharto regime continued the colonial project of transmigration to Outer Islands under the pretext of populating the relatively sparsely populated islands of Kalimantan, Sumatra, Sulawesi, and Papua, with people from overpopulated Java. Highlighting the involvement of the World Bank and the ecological damage to the lives of indigenous peoples, Survival International (1985) called the transmigration program in Indonesia 'the World Bank's most irresponsible project'. The policy of supplying the plantation with organized migrant labor and integrating smallholders in capitalist plantation agriculture by means of contract farming was well suited to the Suharto regime's vision of modernity and social control (Bissonnette 2013). It resembles the colonial vision of populating the outer islands with people from overpopulated Java and reinvigorates the Coolie Ordinance Acts of 1880, providing lawful rights to the planters in accessing and controlling labor through a coercive system.

The continuous capital accumulation and neo/colonial agro-extractive regime generates massive dispossession and multifaceted exploitation in the rural frontiers. As far as some of the related social impacts are concerned, some documented issues include: widespread land conflicts (Semedi 2014); exploitative labor conditions (McCarthy 2010); landlessness and land concentration (Bissonnette 2013); smallholder indebtedness (Semedi and Bakker 2014); food insecurity (Marti 2008); social displacement (Semedi 2014); and denial of the rights of indigenous peoples (Sirait 2009). Gendered effects of palm oil expansion have also been documented, which include: the payment of compensation and royalties to men; diminishing capacity to provide food and clean water; increase in workload; more prevalent social and health problems; no maternity provided; and women returning from childbirth or caring for children may struggle to regain employment (Julia and White 2012).

With the immense expansion of large-scale plantations, the resistance of the affected rural social groups is also escalating, particularly after the fall of Suharto. As 'one of the most conflict-ridden industries in Southeast Asia', the number of plantation-related social conflict accounts, as reported by various NGOs, are staggering (Cote and Cliche 2011: 121). Down to Earth (2002) reported a study during the period of 1998–2001, which documented over 800 arrests, over 400 cases of torture, and 12 deaths in connection with land conflicts with plantations.

Coconut plantations and dispossession in Bohotokong

Coconut plantations in the Indonesian archipelago are emblematic of the agro-extractive regime and are the most tangible living legacy of the colonial capitalist mode of production, which led to the creation of an economic enclave system with large export-oriented plantation estates as the centers of exploitation. Throughout history, the cultivation of coconut in the archipelago was mostly planted spontaneously by peasants, yet from the 1880s the increasing demands for copra, the dried kernel of the coconut, as a raw material for the production of soap and margarine in the European market ignited the interest of the Dutch colonial administration to add an element of compulsion in some areas. Due to this intervention, the growing of coconut expanded rapidly, and by 1939 approximately one-third of world copra exports originated in the Netherlands Indies, and copra constituted 80 percent of the total volume and 60 percent of the total value of exports of East Indonesia (Rasyid 2015).

The direct involvement of European planters in coconut cultivation and the coconut trade remained limited, as the majority of coconut growing was done by the indigenous population, while Chinese merchants dominated the intermediate trade in copra, linking the overseas trading networks with local indigenous networks (Heersink 1994). Gradually, Chinese traders contributed indirectly to the massive expansion of this crop through the mechanisms of lending money and goods against the future yield of trees, which they obliged their borrowers to plant. In 1891, the Chinese in the coastal commercial town of Banggai, now the administrative district of Central Sulawesi, controlled the export and import trade completely, where copra was the most important bulk commodity. Gradually, Chinese and European *onderneming* (commercial plantations) established themselves on land leased from the colonial state in many parts of Sulawesi Island, including in Banggai, particularly in the coastal region. In order to meet the demand for labor, the planters had to rely on the organized migration of labor and the native population in neighboring regions. Some Chinese and, later on, Arabian planters recruited the early dwellers, the Saluan ethnic, as labor to clear the forest, and plant and harvest the coconuts. In addition, with the support of the colonial regime, the planters also organized labor migration in large numbers from the neighboring regions, primarily from Gorontalo and Sangir, northern Sulawesi, and Buton, southeastern Sulawesi (Velthoen 2002).

Land dispossession in the Sulawesi Island today is inexorably linked to this regional and global history of capital expansion into the rural frontiers. This was indeed an aggressive process of land transformation, whereby the state claimed the rights to grant *erpatch* or concession licenses to private companies; a prerequisite for facilitating expansive capital accumulation. The conversion of the land into plantation changed the structure of land control in the region by creating the new social stratification of the Chinese and Arabian descents as capital owners and the native population and migrants as labor. The unequal social and economic structure generated by asymmetrical land control and ownership were reproduced in the postcolonial era. The policies to nationalize the foreign companies under Sukarno's Old Order era did not change the unequal control over the means of production.

Coconut plantation dispossession and peasant resistance in Bohotokong In the case of Bohotokong, the nationalization policy only perpetuated the transfer of the ex-colonial plantation (around 400 Ha) to the hands of Chinese planters, that is, Ong Soen Hie who controlled Away Estate (KOA), Toi Gen Keng controlling Bohotokong Estate (KOB), and Sioe Tje controlling Lompongan Estate (KOL), through the HGU mechanism issued by the state for a 12-year period (1968–1980). Before the concession license expired, the three planters transferred the land to their descendants, respectively T.K. Mandagi (KOB), Rudi Rahardja (KOL), and Budi Tumew (KOA). Prior to this handover and during the possession of these three new landlords, the plantation was largely abandoned until the expiration date of the HGU on 24 September 1980. By this time, the status of the land was supposed to return to *tanah negara* (state land). Yet, in 1988, Rudi Raharja, and, respectively, in 1989, TK Mandagi granted the concession to a new Chinese planter, Theo Nayoan, a Chinese businessman residing in Bunta Sub-District with strong ties to the local ruling elite.[4]

TABLE 5.1 Chronicle of land dispossession in Bohotokong

1891	Chinese and European *onderneming* (commercial plantations) established on land leased from the colonial state in Banggai
1960	Agrarian Law No. 5/1960, article 55 point 1, declared all ex-colonial concession ended
1968–1980	Ong Soen Hie, Toi Gen Keng, and Sioe The secured new HGU for 12-year period, plantation abandoned during this period
1979	Presidential Decree No 32/1979, declared all ex-colonial concession occupied by the local population will be redistributed to them
1980	HGU for the three Chinese planters expired
1982	Villagers of Bohotokong occupied the abandoned plantation
1984–1994	Peasants submitted land certification request four times (1984, 1986, 1991, 1994), yet no results
1988–1989	Rudi Raharja and T.K. Mandagi granted the concession (8–9 years after the license actually expired) to Jhony Nayoan (son of Theo Nayoan)
1991	Provincial BPN distributed form of certification request to villagers
4 April 1991	Jhony Nayoan threatened the head of Bohotokong village with gun to forbid him supporting the peasants claim over the land
1996	PT Lompongan (now owned by Theo Nayoan) forced the peasants to share 40 percent of their coconut trees for planting on the land he claimed
1997	BPN issued HGU for PT Anugrah Saritama Abadi (new company owned by Theo Nayoan)
26 April 1999	Peasants group reoccupied the contested land until today
2001	Establishment of ORTABUN (*Organisasi Tani Buruh dan Nelayan/* Peasant Labor and Fishermen Organization)

In 1960, the government issued Agrarian Law No. 5/1960, where article 55 point 1 declared that all ex-Western concession had ended, and in 1979 a Presidential Decree was issued mentioning that all ex-Western-controlled land already occupied by the local population (*rakyat*) would be redistributed to them. In 1982, local peasant families occupied the abandoned *onderneming*, which had now turned into forests, as revealed by the big trees and rattan, and then submitted letters of request to the local BPN (*Badan Pertanahan Nasional*/National Land Agency) several times to get the land certified on their behalf. Instead of responding to the peasants' requests, in 1997 the BPN issued a new concession license (HGU) to PT Anugrah Saritama Abadi (ASA), a new coconut plantation company owned by Theo Nayoan.

PT ASA is a copra supplier for PT Salim Ivomas Pratama Tbk (SIMP), a leading company producing Bimoli, the best-selling cooking oil brand, which has been a household name in Indonesia since 1978, a subsidiary of PT Indofood Sukses Makmur Tbk,[5] owned by Salim Group, the notorious conglomerate with a long history of being a crony of the Suharto authoritarian regime. Two copra processing facilities operated by PT SIMP in the region are located in Luwuk, capital of Banggai District (about 140 km from Bohotokong) and in Ampana, capital of Tojo Unauna District (about 100 km from Bohotokong). Other major copra processing companies where the copra produced in the region supplied to are PT Multi Nabati Sulawesi, subsidiary of Wilmar, one of Asia's largest integrated agribusiness groups, and PT Cargill Indonesia, the subsidiary of Cargill, the global agricultural giant.[6]

The official data available on the size of PT ASA landholding only registered 110 hectares, yet the BPN also issued additional individual licenses on behalf of four of the company's laborers to a total of 83 hectares. In addition, from the spread of land controlled by this company under individual land entitlements by Theo Nayoan and his large landholder relatives in three sub-districts,[7] that is, Bunta, Nuhon, and Simpang Raya, it is not an exaggeration that the affected peasants estimate the actual landholding to be up to 100 hectares of coconut plantation alone.

Land dispossession in Bohotokong was entering a new phase with the release of the new concession license (HGU) to PT Anugrah Saritama Abadi in 1997. The peasants occupying the land were constantly being intimidated by the thugs hired by the company and were criminalized by police officers for harvesting the crops that they planted on that contested land, whereby 12 villagers were jailed and numerous other cases of harassment and intimidation have taken place. The company utilized various means to dispossess farmers from their gardens, including divide and conquer (*adu domba*) through compensation schemes and criminalization of peasants using the police apparatus to arrest them and send them to jail. Another mode of intimidation was labeling the peasant group as *komunis gaya baru* (new-style communist), which for many villagers reminded them of the 1965 mass massacre of rural peasants for being accused of being members of the Indonesian Communist Party, a label that could generate disastrous consequences under the Suharto regime. Some farmers were under threat to sell their coconut trees through compensation schemes that the company offered. The militaristic authoritarian regime of Suharto encouraged such threats, intimidation, kidnappings, and unlawful arrests that Bohotokong peasants were subjected to:

> Before the HGU was issued in 1997, Koh Toe's [owner of PT ASA] ordered his men to come to me to demand for share from my coconut trees for several times (in 1992, 1995, and 1996), claiming that the land is now in his possession. Therefore as I have planted on his land then I have to share the harvest of my coconut fruits. I finally signed the agreement in the police office, that's how they get my consent to take my coconut trees. But we never sell our land. Can you imagine what kind of disaster occurred in this village when everyone here suddenly sells their land? (Bohotokong villager, interview note, October 2016)

The criminalization and continuous threats from the company had a serious impact on the social fabric of the village. The company created a sense of hostility and suspicion among the villagers, who were being divided between those who were for and against the land struggle. The constant intimidation created a sense of insecurity among villagers who dared to challenge the company's claim over the land:

> We the peasants are supposed to unite and get rid of the company. This is a struggle against monopoly of the powerful

rich people. Look at them, they control hundreds even thousands hectares of land. Unfortunately, for some villagers, the mentality of being labors had been deeply ingrained. In fact many of the villagers here are working as labors for live, since the time of their parents, that they come to believe that they can't make a living without depending on the company [*tidak bisa hidup kalau tidak dengan perusahaan*]. (Saluan elder, interview notes, October 2016)

Struggle and organized resistance through ORTABUN

The key actors engaged in the land struggle are small and landless peasants coming from different ethnic backgrounds, including the indigenous Saluang ethnic, the early dwellers that originally lived in the mountainous region before they gradually moved to the present coastal area of Bohotokong since the colonial period. Yet, they are now a minority in Bohotokong as many of them live in separate administrative villages. In fact, the majority of the population today are the descendants of migrant laborers that came under the migration scheme organized by the colonial Dutch to supply labor for the coconut plantations in the late eighteenth century, including the Gorontalo, Buton, Bugis, and Mandar. The struggle also involved women, local labor, and fisher groups facing land dispossession engineered by the coconut plantation company.

Despite the different ethnic backgrounds of the social groups involved, the main impetus behind the struggle is the aspiration of the small and landless peasants to own the land they till. For the descendants of Saluan ethnic, they are inspired by the cultural/historical fact that 'this *onderneming* is indeed our land long before the colonial Dutch conquered our territory'. The long history of fighting against the appropriation of their land by the coconut plantation within their family represented by typical comments such as '[m]y late father was also a land fighter [*orang perjuangan*], for many years in his life he was resisting the plantation owned by an Arabian descent' (Saluan woman, interview notes, October 2017).

For the generation of migrant labor, their engagement with the struggle is precipitated by the 'long dreams to have land' (Bohotokong village head, interview notes, October 2017). The fact that approximately 80 percent of Bohotokong villagers do not have land, and have to count on their labor to make ends meet, is what inspired them to seize any opportunity to occupy land they deemed as a prerequisite for the peasant life. When they found out that the concession license had actually expired, about 170 peasant families took the initiative to distribute the land for farming, 'wishing the law will really provide some protection for us [*mumpung ada undang undang yang lindungi kita*]' (Bohotokong elder, interview notes, October 2016). Indeed, the land struggle in Bohotokong was legally regulated under two pieces of legislation, including the Basic Agrarian Law (*Undang-Undang Pokok Agraria*) 1960 and the Presidential Decree (*Keputusan Presiden*) 32/1979, both of which permitted the redistribution of ex-colonial plantations to small landless peasants tilling the land in the locale. Some considered the struggle as 'fighting against the oppressive rulers [*penguasa zalim*]' and resisting colonization with the ultimate aim of being 'the master of our own homeland [*tuan rumah di negeri sendiri*]'.

Indeed, since the colonial era, it was the popular resentment to the colonial capitalist agrarian policy and the peasant's 'deep emotional urge to own the land [they] till' (Jacoby 1961: 30), which ignited the revolutionary struggle for independence. After the proclamation of independence in 1945, the founding leaders recognized the fact that the only way to get out of rampant poverty, which colonialism had bequeathed to postcolonial Indonesia, was to ensure that the poorest of the poor had access to the main means of production for an agrarian society, that is, land. The Basic Agrarian Law (BAL) was legally stipulated in 1960 that limited maximum and minimum land ownership, and regulated the implementation of land redistribution for: excess land, absentee land, land under self-government, and other state land. Under the leadership of the nationalist President Sukarno and his *Berdikari* (standing on own feet) policy, and the support of the Indonesian Peasant Front (BTI), the largest peasant organization at that time, established by the Indonesian Communist Party, the agrarian reform made steady progress initially. The related social unrest led to the mass killings of more than a million peasants and intellectuals under the pretext of the anti-communism war, launched by the US and its allies, who relied on local and national military factions, in alliance with various paramilitary groups. The massacre totally halted the demand for agrarian reform and paved the way for General Suharto, supported by Western allies, who together opened the gate for foreign direct investment. In effect, the mass killings of

1965–1966 served the purposes of primitive accumulation by literally clearing the ground for capitalist development, while laying the foundations for what some have defined as post-1966 'hyperobedience' (Heryanto 2006) and 'rural depoliticization' (Mas'oed 1983).

The memories of the peasant occupations as part of the land reform of the early 1960s revived after the fall of the General Suharto-led New Order authoritarian regime on 21 May 1998, which triggered the escalation of agrarian conflicts in the rural frontiers. In many parts of the archipelago, a dramatic resurgence of direct action targeting the reoccupation of a thousand hectares of land allocated for development projects and conglomerate interests became a widespread phenomenon, whereby dispossessed peasants resolved their grievances over decades of land disputes through such occupations. In West Java alone, the land-reclaiming actions involved over 28,000 households, occupying a total of 17,229 hectares during the immediate post-Suharto period (Lucas and Warren 2013).

Confrontational strategies and the maturation of the struggle The rising euphoria of reformation and the opening up of political opportunities immediately after the fall of the Suharto regime inspired the Bohotokong peasants to turn individualized struggles into collective and organized resistance against the private company and the state apparatus deemed as key actors of land dispossession. On 26 April 1999, about 170 families reclaimed the disputed ex-*onderneming* land by destroying the coconut trees planted by PT ASA. The company immediately responded by reporting the land reoccupation to the local police, and as a result nine Bohotokong villagers who led the land occupation were arrested and imprisoned. This situation instigated the peasant group to occupy the Provincial Legislative Assembly (DPRD) Office in Palu, capital of Central Sulawesi, about 500 km away from Bohotokong. In September 1999, for almost one month, the open rally demanded the release of their fellow peasants and the cancellation of the concession. The DPRD occupation and open rallies were supported by student organizations, local NGOs, and involved villagers from all over Central Sulawesi who were also involved in other agrarian conflicts.

Prior to the land reclamation, the villagers developed a leadership system called *pemandu* (team of counsels) appointed among leading individuals from the mixture of social groups, based on ethnicity groups, and/or geographical divisions where the peasants dwell. Their main role was managing fair land redistribution, dealing with the state apparatus and other external actors, as well as facilitating the decision-making and settling internal affairs. During the rallies in Palu, the *pemandu*, for instance, assigned some members of the struggle to stay in the village and continue the land occupation while also providing logistics for other villagers who were assigned to join the occupation of the DPRD Office. The strategy for 'not leaving the fortress empty' (leader of ORTABUN, interview notes, October 2016) was deemed important in order to avoid leaving any chances for the company to return and take the land back. Due to this protest, the arrested villagers were released by the police, but their demand for the cancellation of the plantation permit was not fulfilled.

The partial success of occupying the DPRD Office boosted the confidence of the struggle (*perjuangan*), and peasants continued with village-level consolidation by constructing a gathering point on the reclaimed land. Most villagers recognized the center as camp (*kem*), as the structure was initially a temporary plastic tent, before being replaced with bamboo construction and later on with more permanent wooden materials, following the need for larger meeting space to accommodate a growing membership. As the popularity of the camp grew, it gradually developed into a process of village-to-village organizing along with neighboring peasant groups that were also engaged in various conflicts against the ex-*onderneming* plantations in Bunta Sub-District.

The emerging village-to-village organizing eventually led to the establishment of *Organisasi Tani Buruh dan Nelayan* (ORTABUN/ Peasant Labor and Fishermen Organization), wherein villagers involved in the land reclaiming organized their struggle in cooperation with local labor and fisher groups engaged in similar agrarian conflicts in the region, and to serve as an umbrella for some local farmer organizations in Bunta Sub-District. ORTABUN was declared through a peasant congress (*kongres petani*) on 4 October 2001. ORTABUN declared that its aim was to form a collective action organization for the struggle of the marginalized and oppressed peasants, laborers, and fishers being dispossessed and exploited by an unjust political and economic system.

Despite the legalistic nature of the process of land dispossession initiated by the plantation company, ORTABUN constituents relied on direct action from the point of germination and toward the maturation of the struggle. In facing constant intimidation and threats from the state apparatus, which was reinforcing the company's interests, the *perjuangan* members often resorted to extra-institutional processes in facing the fragile and corrupt judicial system. For instance, in confronting intimidation by the police and/or army together with the company's laborers and/or hired thugs mobilized by the company to harvest the contested coconut trees, they created a creative strategy of hitting the electric poles (*toki tiang listrik*) whenever the 'enemy' was entering their villages. On several occasions this tactic actually succeeded in getting the police and the company's laborers or hired thugs to retreat when they heard that sound, as they know it meant that all ORTABUN members had gathered with machetes in their hands ready to confront them.

As the constituents of ORTABUN have to confront the criminalization every time the company reported a case of theft, encroachment, and destruction of the contested coconut garden, the educational and organizing processes taught about strategies 'to get the police confused' (*strategi kasi bingung polisi*) and developed argumentational skills to counteract legal ploys used by the police/company. For instance, they learned that their perennial crops (coconut, cocoa, etc.) that they planted are indeed strong evidence that can be used to challenge the questionable administrative procedures (legalese) of the licenses issued by the state to the company. For ORTABUN, 'our crops speak! [*tanaman kami sudah bicara*]' (focus group notes, October 2016). The company and the state cannot continue to ignore the fact that they were the ones who planted those crops and have continued to cultivate the land for more than three decades.

The establishment of the camp was frequently mentioned by ORTABUN members as an important turning point for the emergence of organized resistance and in relation to developing strategies and tactics, as well as chalking out roles in implementing a plan of action. It is a commonly recognized place to nurture collective courage and tenacity, despite the continuous attempts of the company and the police's spies (*mata-mata*) to overhear their conversations. In dealing with the spies, who were often their own relatives, ORTABUN members 'tr[ied] not to be hostile to [their] fellow villagers who are in favor of to the company as laboring [*ba'upah*] is their only source of living [*cuma cari makan*]. In fact, some of the laborers [whose lands were appropriated by the company] are actually more than willing to try and get their land back but they are indebted and therefore do not dare to speak up. Some even covertly support the struggle [*diam-diam dukung gerakan*]' (ORTABUN member, interview notes, October 2016). Their non-confrontational approach to the local laborers and fishermen, especially those who were working for the company, helped elicit some useful information about the company's plans and efforts to weaken peasant claims over the land, thus helping to prepare counter-strategies.

In 2005, the women members of ORTABUN managed to prevent the mass arrest of peasants involved in a big harvest in the contested coconut garden. The garden owner who lived in the neighboring village had been arrested earlier by police who brought him to the house of the company's owner for interrogation. Afterward, 27 police personnel came to the village with a truck to confiscate the harvested coconuts and to arrest anyone present in that garden. The women then stood in a line as a fence of shins (*pagar betis*) to stop the truck. Some even climbed the truck to unload the confiscated coconuts, while others seized and hid the truck's keys. They took the police as hostages and demanded the release of their fellow villagers. Some women involved in holding the police hostage admitted that the spontaneous action was to avoid bloody fights if they let their husbands physically attack the police – so they asked their men to stay behind while they took the lead. They even provoked, if not cautioned, the police by accusing them of trying to sexually harass them. The experience of taking the police as hostages emboldened them to confront the constant threats and intimidation from police and company laborers/hired thugs, especially when their husbands were imprisoned and they were vulnerable. The land is 'my shelter, a place for me to live and die', is a common remark among women members of ORTABUN, who have always played an instrumental and active role in the struggle against dispossession in the locale:

My husband had been jailed for three different periods of times, more than three years in total of imprisonment. Actually I was on the wanted list too [*Daftar Pencarian Orang*]. But I have lost my fear, so for the whole period of being jailed, I visited my husband every time I could afford the costs of going to Luwuk [about 145 km from Bohotokong]. Afterward I went home and took care of my garden with the help of other wives whose husbands were also arrested. We felt ashamed for ignoring the garden while our husbands were jailed for noble cause. Once he wrote me a letter asking to sell our cows if there's nothing else left at home to feed our children. Luckily our cocoa crops were ready for harvest at that time. Yet still it was a tough time. Our daughter had to quit her school as we couldn't afford it. (woman member of ORTABUN, interview notes, October 2016)

The women members also shared songs of struggle (*lagu perjuangan*), which nurtured a common platform of this anti-dispossession struggle and helped create a sense of unity among the different social groups involved. Singing those songs during rallies and open demonstrations, or while waiting for their regular gatherings to get started, served as rituals to continue sharpening the focus of their resistance and strengthening group solidarity. In fact, the deeper meanings of these songs represent a peasant political consciousness (*hati nurani petani*), which maintained a historical memory in their decadal struggle of going through the ups and downs of resisting land dispossession. One such song composed by a female member of ORTABUN is called 'Mother Sorrow' and describes the difficulties of a mother in raising her children while her husband was imprisoned due to false criminalization by the company and state apparatus.

Sengsara ibu	Mother in sorrow
Sengsara ibu merawat anaknya	Mother nurture her children in sorrow
Pada masa onderneming	During the onderneming days
Beberapa orang ditangkap polisi	Some people arrested by the police
Disangka melanggar pidana	Accused as criminals
Siang malam anak bertanya ayahnya	Night and days children are waiting for their father
Oh ibu di mana ayah	Oh mother where is father
Dengan tangis ibu menjawab anaknya	With tears mother replies her children
Ayahmu di dalam penjara	Your father is in jail
Ayahmu di dalam penjara	Your father is in jail

Another popular song that raised spirits, actually adapted from a children's rhyme, calls for the peasants to refuse the compensation offered by the company, and is directed at those who may be willing to surrender their claim over the land to stand up together, as well as to challenge the constant intimidation, threats, and bribes.

Minggir dong, minggir dong	Get away, get away
Petani Bohotokong mau lewat	Bohotokong peasants are coming
Jangan dipecah-pecah, mari kita bersatu	Don't get divided, let us unite
Minggir dong, minggir dong	Get away, get away
Bangkitlah, bangkitlah petani Bohotokong	Raise up, raise up Bohotokong peasants
Jangan mau disogok, jangan takut digertak	Accept no bribe, beware of intimidation
Minggir dong, minggir dong	Get away, get away

Role of external allies and networked supports As the Bohotokong peasants' resistance against PT ASA was transformed from hidden transcripts (Scott 1990) to overt modes of response and resistance aimed at land dispossession, the elders of the struggle (*pemandu*) also began to establish some connections with external allies and supporters. Such relations commenced in the late 1990s when government-funded university-based poverty researchers suggested that they present their land dispute case to LBH Bantaya,[8] a legal aid organization based in Palu. Instead of advising for pursuing a judicial approach to the Bohotokong dispossession, Bantaya activists suggested reconsolidation at the village level by establishing a Legal and Human Rights Information Centre (*Pos Informasi Hukum dan HAM*) on the occupied land. The terms 'law and human rights' were utilized as a ploy to avoid any harsh reactions from the local police.

Besides being a meeting space, the camp, as the villagers called it, also served as an information center where villagers consulted on their issues related to agrarian conflicts with a paralegal and accessed pertinent resources, particularly in relation to agrarian reform plans. Thus, it functioned as a key educational and organizing point where Bantaya provided training to paralegals recruited from among the ORTABUN members themselves. In addition, the regular case study sessions based on emerging themes organized and facilitated by the trained paralegals helped them in building their argumentational skills against legal usurpation of land:

> The regular sessions in our camp were like attending a college for us. I even spent time reading the resources that Bantaya supplied for us when I was in jail. There was one small handbook that I particularly remember on responding to illegal arrest and interrogation. I found it useful because I realized that every time a new police head posted in Luwuk and Bunta, they will issue warrant letters in responding to company's report. The police will always told me 'I am new here' whenever I refused to sign the interrogation minutes as this is the same old case. So I responded, 'You must have some archives here in this respected office, right, sir?' In our camp, we even rehearsed non-linear responses [*jawaban melintang*] in the police interrogation room or in the court. Don't let them silenced you, instead get them exhausted with your questions! (Saluan elder, interview notes, October 2016)

For Bantaya activists, the suggestion to establish the camp was a two-prong and simultaneous educational and organizing strategy in order to help the villagers understand the wider context of the state and connect the same to matters they were involved in or their own day-to-day experiences. Furthermore, the deliberation to bypass the litigation tactic in dealing with an agrarian conflict emerged from joint reflections with the Bohotokong peasants after observing a tendency of some lawyers toward enjoying a stardom syndrome, while the peasants directly affected by the dispossession were advised 'to stay behind and let the lawyers solve their problem' (Bantaya activist, interview notes, July 2016). In fact, legal aid often ends up pacifying the peasants' spontaneous direct action. The educational and organizing work around extrajudicial political processes through collective discussion and case study also proved to be an invaluable role played by Bantaya in promoting creative information dissemination within the internal circles of the land struggle in Bohotokong village, and to the neighboring villages and towards continuously strengthening their reclaiming strategies over time.

ORTABUN members also mentioned the role of Bantaya in introducing the idea of people-based organization (*organisasi rakyat*) through planned visits with such organizations in Jenggawa, Tapos, and some other places in Java to learn about the successes and failures of land-reclaiming actions in those places; visits that were organized by Bantaya in cooperation with LBH Surabaya. A solid people's organization is expected to strengthen the claim of people's rights in light of the ignorance of the corporatized state, instead of a patchwork (*tambal sulam*) approach focusing on a case-by-case push back. ORTABUN has managed to widen its membership into 44 farmer organization members today, where each organization has about 20–25 individual constituents in three sub-districts (Simpang Raya, Nuhon, Bunta) in Banggai District, Central Sulawesi. The peasants' organization has also been involved in a provincial-level network through *Front Perjuangan Pembaruan Agraria Sulawesi* (Sulawesi Agrarian Reform Struggle Front) and *Aliansi Anti Diskriminasi Petani* (Peasants' Alliance against Discrimination) that connect Bohotokong peasants with similar struggles in Central Sulawesi.

To complement judicial activism, in cooperation with the Indonesian Farmers Alliance (*Aliansi Petani Indonesia*, API), ORTABUN has organized training in natural farming and diversification of coconut products other than copra, such as coconut shell briquette, and virgin coconut oil (VCO). However, the organizing and educational process in this regard is not making substantial progresses in terms of developing productive economic opportunities for local peasants. The technical assistance regarding natural farming that API delivered has not generated tangible interest among members to practice the new skills to date, and warrants further discussion.

ORTABUN members generally agreed to a role for external actors, including local and national NGOs, in legal activism and with respect to improving the visibility of the Bohotokong struggle through media campaigns and legal advocacy, especially in relation to police harassment. However, some members saw engagements with NGOs sympathetic to their cause as a distraction from their most pressing issues as each NGO usually presents their own specific programmatic focus as being of central importance. In fact, the financial support that ORTABUN received from NGO projects (*cari modal lewat LSM*) created distrust among members, who questioned the lack of transparency and vested interests of some leaders in ORTABUN.

Currently, ORTABUN plans to seize the opportunity for blocking the renewal of the concession license of the company that will expire in 2017. ORTABUN organized the village head of the neighboring villages to send a petition expressing their objection to the pertinent government offices, as one prerequisite for the renewal will be getting approval from the village government. In pursuing the agenda, ORTABUN also tried to make sure that in the upcoming village head elections in ex-*onderneming* areas, there will be someone supportive of their struggle for land. Another possibility is proposing the occupied land as part of the recent Objects of Agrarian Reform (*Tanah Obyek Reforma Agraria*, TORA), a program announced by President Jokowi. This scheme opens up the possibility of canceling the concession license and the redistribution of the land to small/landless peasants. For this specific purpose, ORTABUN established cooperation with a local NGO to support them in conducting counter-mapping as a prerequisite for the national land redistribution scheme. The organizing around these two evolving possibilities might rejuvenate the state of exhaustion and key challenges facing a long-term struggle against dispossession and an agrarian structure premised on inequality and the disappearance of the peasant.

Maintaining momentum and shifting identities and political-economic interests: challenges for ORTABUN The anti-dispossession struggle through land reclaiming in conjunction with the judicial activism of the small/landless peasants in Bohotokong has now lasted for more than three decades. Despite their persistence to defend their land and organized resistance challenging state-endorsed dispossession by the plantation company, the ORTABUN constituents admit that there is a sense of fatigue setting in around pursuing defensive strategies and in responding to the ongoing intimidation, as well as the long list of unlawful arrests and imprisonments.

The anxieties over the legal status of the land they cultivated has discouraged some members of *perjuangan* as they reflect on the real possibility of passing on their piece of land to their children, not to mention the rising costs of farming due to increased dependence on chemical pesticides, fertilizers, and seeds, as well as the fluctuating market price for their main commodities – copra, cocoa, and corn. For most of them, what matters today is getting back the land, and has little to do with improving the productivity of their land. The challenges posed by an increasing dependence on cash and wage labor, along with the precarity around holding land that is an ongoing and hard battle, as discussed, challenges the peasant way and other economic activities, where they can earn money faster by, for instance, selling their labor to harvest and process coconut into copra. The increasing reliance and experience of wage labor makes it difficult to reawaken their character as peasants, if not their reliance on a peasant economy. Without sufficient efforts to tackle this issue, as one ORTABUN member reflected, 'our struggle for land might go astray as even after we manage to secure the legal recognition, people might end up selling their land due to economic pressures' (interview notes, October 2016).

The alliance building with plantation laborers and fishers has yet to generate promising possibilities either. For the fishers, due to expansion of modern fishing trawlers in their fishing territory, the numbers of those depending on fishing as their main source of livelihood continues to decline. Most fishers decide to abandon their traditional fishing gear as they can't compete with the larger boats coming from other regions, and focus more on being sharecroppers, selling their labor at the coconut plantation or working as three-wheeler motorcycle (*bentor*) drivers. Some families are working on these occupations interchangeably by working as labor early in the morning, before moving to the sharecropping coconut gardens until noon, and then later in the evening they go out fishing, mostly for personal consumption. ORTABUN actually initiated advocacy action to prevent the larger fishing boats from entering the territory by mapping the fishing territory of the local fishers with small boats. With the diminishing number of fishers, however, these attempts have not been explored further.

The same is the case with the plantation labor members, many of whom are in a vicious circle of bonded relations with their employers. So far, the labor organizing on this front has involved sporadic attempts in responding to individual cases of violence against the plantation laborers. In one case where ORTABUN had been particularly active when a company laborer was murdered within the company premises in December 2002, they organized open rallies protesting the slow response of the police, but the police responded by arresting some workers, who were finally released after being violently interrogated. In fact, as the demonstrations escalated into physical clashes, two protestors were shot by the police. Even the media campaigns involving some national NGO networks had no tangible results. Until today, no one from the company has been interrogated by the police, under the pretext of no evidence found.

The unequal agrarian structure, together with market pressure toward coconut commodification, exacerbated the general patterns of rural identity, shifting from a land-based peasant mode of communal production to a labor mode being exploited by capital. The prevalent new attitude toward land as property has also turned the direction of the struggle into a single focus of demanding the cancellation of the commercial plantation permit and getting legal recognition from the state for individual property. Some members, especially the Saluan ethnic women, who are less receptive to entrepreneurial pursuits compared to migrant labor groups, argue that it is the traumatic experience of dealing with the criminalization that convinced them of the importance of securing land title, and not so much because of the pressures toward the commodification of land. For these women, the value of land as a place 'to live and die' encouraged them to pursue the dual mode of production for market and own consumption as a strategy.

Concluding reflections for small/landless peasant activism

The persistence of the small/landless peasant to defend their land has been largely solidified by a reliance on localized direct actions. The legalistic nature of an agrarian contestation, however, ironically traps peasants seeking 'legal recognition' inside the ruling relations of colonial capital and all while challenging the state's 'monopoly over violence and definitions of legality' (Harvey 2003: 145). In fact, the judicial activism could potentially end up in an elitist legal struggle by generating dependence on the generosity of the external actors, sympathy and solidarity aside, to deal with a complex and puzzling judicial activism defined in the urban centers of the ruling elite, far beyond the political-geographical span of small/landless peasants in the rural peripheries. The measures to integrate juridical actions into broader political mobilization targeting multiple scales and arenas, bringing together localized organizing efforts with urban-based campaigns, have indeed been proven to generate some successes in confronting the agro-extractive regime pursued by the corporatized state in this case and in others (Rajagopal 2003). The counter-hegemonic organizing and educational efforts engendered from the engagement with external supporters helped the germination of organized resistance against land dispossession in Bohotokong, particularly in dealing with the immediate needs for defying the state-corporate criminalization of peasants working to feed themselves and their communities.

Reflecting on the escalation of agrarian wars in the Global South, the ORTABUN struggle demonstrates the resilience of rural social groups in confronting the colonization of local land. It provides some hints on the challenges for the resurgence of their affinity to land not solely as means of production, but also as means of meaning making in achieving the collective aspiration of a good rural life they have historical and cultural reasons to value. For that to happen, the resurgence of peasant affinity to land needs to shift away from the tendency toward the distracting outward-looking strategies in contesting the hegemony of state-corporate civil society nexus toward the terrain of commodification, and instead seek direction for the struggle from inward perspectives to rejuvenate collective action and the strengthening of claims over land in a constant subversion of prevailing neo/colonial capitalist agrarian ruling relations.

Notes

1 In a speech before the Asia Pacific Economic Cooperation (APEC) Summit 2013 at the Bali International Convention Center, on 6 October 2013, President of Indonesia (2004–2014), Susilo Bambang Yudhoyono, referenced himself as 'the chief salesperson of Indonesia Inc.', while extending the invitation 'to seize the business and investment opportunities in Indonesia'. See www.kemlu.go.id/Lists/SpeechesAndTranscription/DispForm.aspx?ID=807&ContentTypeId=0x01003EA9EEAD2C809F49A8A9E2B6786925C3.

2 Sukarno's presidential speech before the National Policy Council meeting on 28 August 1959. See http://old.bappenas.go.id/get-file-server/node/8258/.

3 See www.tuk.or.id/wp-content/uploads/2015/02/Tycoons-in-the-Indonesian-palm-oil-sector-140828-Tuk-Summary.pdf.

4 Two of Nayoan's relatives were currently serving as local parliament members, and the wife of one of his sons was a strong candidate for *Bupati* (District Head) in the last 2015 election in Banggai District.

5 According to the company's 2012 annual report, the total sales value of the Edible Oils & Fats Division alone in 2011 is IDR 9.07 trillion, mainly attributable to higher sales of cooking oil and copra-based products.

6 The increasing popularity of coconut water as a healthy drink generates further demand on the supply of this commodity, as demonstrated by the involvement of two global giant soft drink players, Pepsi Cola and Coca-Cola, through the acquisition of Zico Beverages, who gets its coconuts from Indonesia, Thailand, and Brazil. In addition, the various incentives and subsidies for the development of coconut oil as biofuel

might also intensify the global demand and accelerate land dispossession in coconut-producing regions.

7 Another major coconut plantation company in the Bunta area is PT Tobelombang, subsidiary of PT Nyiur Mas Inti Group, who also own PT Banggai Sentra Shrimp, a joint shrimp-farming venture with a French company, PT Delta Subur Permai, a cacao plantation of about 8,000 hectares in Saseba, and PT Nyiur Mas, a logging company.

8 Established in 1996, with a central office in Palu, the capital of Central Sulawesi province, Bantaya (in Kaili language, meeting place) was initially a legal aid organization, before it was transformed into Bantaya Association, focusing on gender equality and environmental protection on a community level, as well as strengthening of autonomy and rights of local communities.

References

Aditjondro, G.A. (2001). 'Suharto's fires: Suharto cronies control an ASEAN-wide oil palm industry with an appalling environmental record'. *Inside Indonesia*, 65, January–March. Available at www.insideindonesia.org/suhartos-fires [accessed 24 June 2015].

Alatas, H. (1977). *The Myth of the Lazy Native: A Study of the Image of the Malays, Filipinos and Javanese from the 16th to the 20th Century and Its Function in the Ideology of Colonial Capitalism*. London: F. Cass.

Bissonnette, J F. (2013). 'Development through large-scale oil palm agribusiness schemes: representations of possibilities and the experience of limits in West Kalimantan'. *Sojourn*, 28(3): 485–511.

Cote, D. and Cliche, L. (2011). 'Indigenous peoples' resistance to oil palm plantations in Borneo'. *Kasarinlan: Philippine Journal of Third World Studies*, 26(1–2): 121–152.

Down to Earth (2002). 'Stop human rights violations against peasant farmers!' *Down to Earth*, 52, February. Available at: www.downtoearth-indonesia.org/story/stop-human-rights-violations-against-peasant-farmers [accessed 12 August 2015].

Harvey, D. (2003). *The New Imperialism*. Oxford: Oxford University Press.

Heersink, C.G. (1994). 'Selayar and the green gold: the development of the coconut trade on an Indonesian island (1820–1950)'. *Journal of Southeast Asian Studies*, 25(1): 47–69.

Heryanto, A. (2006). *State Terrorism and Political Identity in Indonesia: Fatally Belonging*. London: Routledge.

Jacoby, E.H. (1961). *Agrarian Unrest in Southeast Asia*. London: Asia Publishing House.

Julia and White, B. (2012). 'Gendered experiences of dispossession: oil palm expansion in a Dayak Hibun community in West Kalimantan.' *Journal of Peasant Studies*, 39: 995–1016.

Kapoor, D. (2015). 'Subaltern social movement and development in India: rural dispossession, trans-local activism and subaltern re-visitations'. In D. Caouette and D. Kapoor (eds), *Beyond Colonialism, Development and Globalization: Social Movement and Critical Perspectives*. London: Zed Books, pp. 27–48.

Kapoor, D. and Jordan, S. (2009). *Education, Participatory Action Research and Social Change:*

International Perspective. New York: Palgrave Macmillan.

Lucas, A.E. and Warren, C. (2013). *Land for the People: The State and Agrarian Conflict in Indonesia*. Athens, OH: Ohio University Press.

Marti, S. (2008). *Losing Ground: The Human Rights Impacts of Oil Palm Plantation Expansion in Indonesia*. London: Friends of the Earth, LifeMosaic, and Sawit Watch.

Mas'oed, M. (1983). *The Indonesian Economy and Political Structure During the Early New Order, 1966–1971*. Athens, OH: Ohio University Press.

McCarthy, J.F. (2010). 'Processes of inclusion and adverse incorporation: oil palm and agrarian change in Sumatra, Indonesia'. *Journal of Peasant Studies*, 37(4): 821–850.

Prashad, V. (2008). *The Darker Nations: A People's History of the Third World*. New York: New Press.

Rajagopal, B. (2003). *International Law from Below: Development, Social Movements and Third World Resistance*. Cambridge: Cambridge University Press.

Rasyid A.A. (2015). 'Makassar copra as a trigger of struggling for power between central and local government: a historical study of regional political economy in Indonesia'. *TAWARIKH: International Journal for Historical Studies*, 6(2): 197–212.

Scott, J.C. (1990). *Domination and the Arts of Resistance: Hidden Transcripts*. New Haven, CT: Yale University Press.

Semedi, P. (2014). 'Palm oil wealth and rumour panics in West Kalimantan'. *Forum for Development Studies*, 41(2): 233–252.

Semedi, P. and Bakker, L. (2014). 'Between land grabbing and farmers' benefits: land transfers in West Kalimantan, Indonesia'. *The Asia Pacific Journal of Anthropology*, 15(4): 376–390.

Sirait, M.T. (2009). *Indigenous Peoples and Oil Palm Plantation Expansion in West Kalimantan, Indonesia*. Amsterdam: Amsterdam University Law Faculty and Cordaid.

Survival International (1985). 'Indonesian transmigration: the World Bank's most irresponsible project'. *The Ecologist*, 15: 300–301.

Velthoen, E.J. (2002). *Contested Coastlines: Diasporas, Trade and Colonial Expansion in Eastern Sulawesi 1680–1905*. PhD Thesis, Murdoch University, Perth.

6 | DISPOSSESSION AND NEOLIBERAL DISASTER RECONSTRUCTION: ACTIVIST NGO AND FISHER RESISTANCE IN NAGAPATTINAM, TAMIL NADU

Raja Swamy and Prema Revathi

Introduction

Home to hundreds of artisanal fisher communities, India's vast coastline has in recent years become a tense battleground over the control and use of coastal lands and the nearshore marine fishery. Following decades of state-led efforts to encourage commercial fisheries, the 1980s witnessed a radical shift, with the Indian state aggressively pursuing neoliberal economic priorities, most notably coastal shrimp aquaculture. In addition to commercial fishing, various other activities, such as tourism, industries, and private construction, were either actively or tacitly encouraged by state policy, now markedly attuned to the demands of economic liberalization. If the 1990s witnessed an intensifying conflict between state-promoted shrimp farms and artisanal fisher communities, the first decade of the twenty-first century brought forth a new set of challenges presented by the devastating tsunami of 2004 and its aftermath. Deployed as a strategy to wrest coastal lands from fishing communities with the intention of relocating them inland, reconstruction intensified ongoing struggles between local fisher communities and the state.

The authors of this study conducted research in Nagapattinam in the aftermath of the tsunami, and documented the manner in which fisher communities were able to stave off mass relocation, continuing to thrive on the coast despite state efforts. A critical factor in enabling this form of resistance to state efforts was the role played by one community-based nongovernmental organization with an active long-term presence in the region.[1]

**Accumulation by dispossession in a South Indian
coastal economy**

Nagapattinam district spans a large section of the Cauvery River's
delta plains, the agriculturally rich heartland of northern Tamil
Nadu state. Alongside Tanjavur district, from which Nagapattinam
was separated only in the 1990s, Nagapattinam is part of the Tamil
country's historic rice-producing region, associated for centuries
with various empires, most famously the Cholas, who made
Nagapattinam their chief naval base in the tenth century. The
district's coastal stretches are also notable for their thriving artisanal
fisher communities, belonging mostly to the Pattinavar sub-caste,[2]
interspersed and often in close proximity to urban centers and their
markets. Artisanal fishing provides for the subsistence needs and
material well-being of fishers and is a major source of food for the
region's urban and rural populations. Yet, as an economic activity,
it is viewed by policymakers as an archaic and primitive way of life
destined to be transformed by modern capitalist uses of coastal land
and marine resources. Thus, efforts to 'modernize' India's artisanal
fishers with development projects beginning in the 1960s focused
on the mechanization and technological modernization of fisheries,
favoring a private-owner-led commercial push for increasing scale
and volume of catch. In Nagapattinam, however, the push for the
commercial exploitation of the coast began in earnest in the late 1980s,
as an economic development priority driven by the prerogatives of
neoliberal globalization.

Dispossession by commercial shrimp farms When the government of
India, at the behest of the World Bank, encouraged the proliferation
of coastal shrimp farms in the 1990s, it marked a radical shift in
development policy. Coastal shrimp farms were promoted by the
FAO as a solution to the problem of food insecurity, while they were
viewed as an economic growth strategy by the World Bank. The FAO
(1999) extolled the virtues of aquaculture as a means to achieve food
security by enabling the production of a protein-rich food source
by small operators already living in coastal areas. Brackishwater
aquaculture requires the infusion of seawater into ponds along the
coast where shrimp are raised with the help of a variety of inputs,
including those that facilitate growth (nutrients) and prevent diseases

(antibiotics). This food-centric argument, however, receded once the World Bank's focus on growth – and its necessity for debt servicing – took center stage in the 1990s.

As Martinez-Alier (2002) notes, the World Bank's strong support for shrimp aquaculture until at least the mid-1990s had to do with its 'drive for non-traditional exports to repay the external debts and to enter the path of export-led growth' (p. 80). This meant that aquaculture had to be directed toward generating higher values, a goal that could be achieved only by serving export markets. Thus, shrimp farms from their early beginnings were devoted toward the quick generation of high-value products that were less likely to be directed toward local consumption – especially by those populations deemed to require urgent nutritional assistance. Food security gave way to the logic of rapid commercial exploitation and degradation of the coast and the nearshore marine zone, both of critical importance to artisanal fishers. Nagapattinam led the rest of Tamil Nadu state with 996 farms and a total area of 2,384 hectares under shrimp acquaculture.[3]

Shrimp farms violated common-property conventions governing coastal land use, conventions that enable fishers to accommodate multiple claimants. Aquaculture pond clusters were exclusive spaces, fenced-off private property enclaves that in many cases hindered beach access for local fishers. When fishers attempted to cross these fenced-off enclaves, they were often violently stopped by guards posted by the shrimp farms. The most serious impact of shrimp farms, however, was in their environmental degradation both of the coastal land and the nearshore waters.

Brackishwater ponds required pumping into the land vast quantities of salty seawater that frequently made the soil saline, adversely affecting small farmers. Groundwater too was badly affected in this manner, with many villages having no option but to fight back when already meager water sources were becoming endangered due to shrimp farm inputs and effluents. With ponds needing to be periodically drained, effluents were simply pumped out to the sea. Moreover, since pumped out toxic water was substantially warmer, it affected nearshore fish stocks, making it harder for artisanal fishers to rely upon traditional fishing grounds and requiring them to search farther out for fishing grounds, resulting in increasing conflicts as marine common resource management conventions were threatened (Stonich and Bailey 2000).

The 2004 tsunami and reconstruction and fisher displacement and dispossession[4] Nagapattinam was the worst hit of all districts in the state of Tamil Nadu, and accounted for at least 6,000 of the estimated 10,000 deaths in India directly resulting from the tsunami's devastating waves on 26 December 2004. Many coastal villages were devastated, with few houses still standing. Despite the scale of devastation, it should be noted that there were also significant differences in the effects of the tsunami on coastal fisher villages. Sections of fisher villages located on elevated dunes or behind bioshields or built structures were relatively unaffected, and only partially damaged if at all. This is important to note because it helps put in sharp perspective the manner in which the state government's World Bank-financed reconstruction agenda deployed distance criteria to require mass inland relocation without regard for locational specificities of the sort noted above.

Reconstruction was premised on a strategic distinction drawn between economic development and humanitarian aid, with the former considered a prerogative tied to state and national development goals that necessitated the 'opening up' of coastal space via inland relocation, and the latter focused on building houses and managing the process of moving households inland. Under the post-tsunami reconstruction program, the state government of Tamil Nadu sought to ensure that recipients of housing would be faced with few options but to accept inland relocation. NGOs were tasked with the construction and delivery of houses for coastal recipients, while the government identified and procured land, often at significant distance inland from the coast, for this purpose. Most NGOs accepted and adhered to the limits imposed by the PPP, focusing their efforts on timely construction and delivery rather than on addressing the locational concerns of recipients. The political ramifications of humanitarian aid should therefore be considered in light of the mutual constitution of economic development and humanitarian aid, and not on its own terms as reflected in the voluminous documentation and critical evaluation of NGO practices, which tends to focus on questions of efficacy and accountability.[5]

Government Order 25 (GO 25) was the first clear indicator that the state government intended to use the devastation as an opportunity to respatialize the coast – primarily by making it difficult for fishers to continue living in their settlements spread across the sandy beaches of the state. The Order, issued on 13 January 2005, barely two weeks after the tsunami, presumed the 'permanent relocation' of coastal communities and laid out the terms for housing construction involving 'non-Government organisations, voluntary agencies, corporate houses, charities, public and private sector enterprises etc.' While NGOs were invited to participate in 'public private partnership' with the government for housing construction, they were expected to build on land that was to be identified and procured for that purpose by the government. In other words, NGOs were not to engage with questions of location, and had to abide with whatever locational choices the government made for the recipients of new housing.

While GO 25 laid out the basic framework for the entry of NGOs into the reconstruction program, a subsequent Order issued in March, GO 172, made explicit the criteria governing relocation. Invoking the Coastal Regulation Zone Notification of 1991, the Order focuses attention on two related criteria for relocation: proximity to the water's edge, marked by the high tide line (HTL), and quality of housing – ranging from low-quality structures built with locally available materials, *Kucca*, to brick and mortar structures, *Pucca*. As would be expected, poorer fisher households tend to live closer to the water's edge in structures that more closely fit the *Kucca* category than *Pucca*. Therefore, for these fisher households, the lure of new housing was as much a question of establishing safe distance from the water's edge as it was about acquiring a more robust and permanent structure for a home.

Yet, the government's Order did not merely offer relocation as a possibility, but stacked the odds against attempts by poorer fishers to retain coastal habitations. The distance criteria implied that only houses beyond the 200-meter mark could qualify for *in situ* reconstruction. For structures within the 200-meter zone, *in situ* reconstruction was prohibited, citing the CRZ's stipulation that only 'repair of structures authorized prior to 1991 is permissible and no new construction is possible'. In invoking the CRZ thus, the Order conveniently ignored the fact that the same Notification in fact recognized 'customary' uses of land by fisher communities as permissible exceptions to its prohibition of new constructions within 200 meters of the HTL. Moreover, since most fishers in this zone were already technically on government-owned *poromboke* land, there was little to no likelihood that any significant number of structures could claim to be authorized, and that too prior to 1991. In other words, GO 172 presented the vast majority of fishers few options but to accept relocation and abandon the coast.

The offer of legal recognition as a benefit of relocation was therefore weighed against the precarity of receiving no governmental assistance with rebuilding *in situ* and facing possible evictions now that the matter was being framed in terms of the CRZ, an ironic development given that the CRZ was itself invoked by fishers for decades as they sought to stave off various threats to the coast posed by shrimp farms, industries, and various commercial interests.

An important facet of GO 172 was the deployment of abstract criteria without reference to local specificities. Not all coastal villages suffered damages equally; many households escaped the ferocity of the tsunami waves because they lay on elevated land, atop dunes for instance, or were located behind natural vegetation, or, as in the case of a cluster of fisher households in Tarangambadi/Tranquebar, behind the seventeenth-century Dansborg Fort. This uniform application of the CRZ's zone-based stipulations regarding the construction of structures was useful for the purpose of enforcing the mass relocation of coastal communities more than it was intended to enforce the Notification. In fact, the post-tsunami reconstruction process unfolded even as the government of India instituted an expert panel to replace the CRZ with a 'management' model of the coast that would be more responsive to the plethora of demands of commercial interests, overcoming whatever remained of the ecological protections offered by the CRZ.

The critical condition that made relocation an act of formal dispossession was written into GO 172, tying the formal acceptance of a new house to the abandonment of all claims to coastal lands and properties. These the state would take control of, despite assurances that such lands would be documented in a 'prohibitory order book'. Such a condition was viewed as necessary by officials and many NGOs concerned that fisher recipients would view new houses as assets to acquire and maintain for purposes other than relocation. The contradiction between the moral expectations of the state and NGOs, on the one hand, and the goals and intentions of recipients, on the other, was referred to frequently in language reminiscent of colonial constructions of the 'primitive'. Fishers, it was argued, were prone to acquisitive behavior, and needed to be held accountable, in a moral calculus intended to inculcate the types of behaviors becoming of a responsible homeowner whose ownership now was less an entitlement and more a favor bestowed by the state.

The vast majority of new housing sites were significantly inland. While data compiled by the NCRC utilized straight-line distances from the coast, GPS data collected by Swamy (2011) showed that actually traveled distances were significantly greater for most relocated communities. Relocation imposed several constraints on fisher households that attempted to live in new sites. Added distance meant that fishers now had to factor in costs for auto-rickshaws or buses, and if they could not afford these, it meant rescheduling daily routines by adding significant amounts of time required for walking to beaches, markets, or the home village, especially when significant numbers of fishers remained there.

The tsunami house was a contested problem of location and meaning for artisanal fishers. While it included the promise of formal ownership, and the advantages of brick-and-mortar construction, its constraints proved too daunting for fishers already struggling to sustain livelihoods in a competitive and tough fishing economy. Moreover, despite NGO efforts to instill new disciplinary regimes pertaining to bodily and social care – the use of attached bathrooms and toilets, for instance – the problems of poor construction, structural limitations, and, most importantly, locational disadvantages made such a transition to instant urbanity problematic and undesirable. In some instances, entire groups of families returned to the coast instead of trying to struggle in new houses located kilometers away from their sites of work and markets.

Fishers and the state: power and communing as resistance

Over several decades, artisanal fishers utilized a variety of strategies in response to attempts by state and private interests to alienate them from the coast. These included both state-level legal action and mass mobilization. These strategies were grounded in a strong sense of attachment to place, staking claims on the basis of historical memory, for instance, but also a sophisticated and historically grounded ecological understanding of the coast. Coastal lands are not only sites where fishers reside in settlements – many believed to be of considerable antiquity – but also sites where economic and social life are woven into close relationships with specific resources. These coastal resources include beaches, dunes, groves, and freshwater sources. One outcome of relocation that was viewed with considerable regret by fishers was the loss of coastal resources such as Casuarina groves where twigs are collected by women. Often these groves are claimed by the state under the aegis of the Forest Department, making commoning at the same time a subversive act. Nevertheless, this was an abundant resource that coastal fisher communities could depend on even if in an uneasy relationship with the state. Numerous other examples abound, such as the use of dunes for fish drying and beaches for a range of fishing-related activities, as well as various cultural and social uses of the beaches, water bodies, flora, and fauna of the coast.

The defense of coastal *commoning* – practices referred to as *customary use* in official discourse – are important to consider as strategies of resistance. For example, when nearshore marine fishing was threatened by the entry of mechanized boats, fishers invoked traditional practices of resource regulation based on the principle of sustainable sharing of the common property. Similarly, when shrimp farms threatened to pollute and block access to coastal resources, fishers invoked commoning practices as the basis on which their claims to shared and pluralistic use of coastal resources was contrasted with the exclusive private property regime of shrimp aquaculture. Commoning therefore represents a foundational political strategy of coastal fishers in framing their interactions with more powerful players such as the state or private capitalists.

The state's view of fishers in the postcolonial era centered on the question of development. Various five-year plans in 1950s and 1960s promoted the modernization of fisheries, and active promotion commenced with the introduction of mechanized boats, which could ply deeper waters, expanding the range of fishing, as well as the volume and variety of catch. Yet, the history of modernization of the fisheries in the Coromandel coast suggests that the developmental state's efforts failed to transform the fisheries as intended, and instead was forced to enter into an uneasy relationship with artisanal fishers, a relationship that continues to shape the dynamics of state efforts and fisher responses in the present.

When, in the 1960s and 1970s, the government encouraged the growth of mechanized fishing boats as a means to 'modernize' the fisheries, it anticipated that mechanized boats would ply in fishing grounds farther out at sea. However, these new entrants found it easier to simply fish the nearshore, setting off violent conflicts with artisanal fishers. For mechanized boat operators, the challenge of fishing centered on maximizing yields and externalizing costs. For artisanal fishers, however, the management of the nearshore resource was a matter of long-term viability, and therefore bound to highly developed practices of regulated use between fishers within villages, and between adjacent villages that share the same fishing grounds. This common-property understanding could not coexist alongside a model of resource exploitation that focused on maximization and externalization of costs, especially those associated with destructive trawling. The resulting conflict inspired political mobilizations as artisanal fishers demanded curbs to the activities of trawlers, sometimes engaging in direct action. The state's response to the conflict was that of a peacemaker, and sought foremost to end violence between the contending fishers. But as peacemaker, the state had to concede to artisanal fishers the collective right to maintain their systems of regulation of the nearshore fishery. As Bavinck (2001) points out, in comparison with those of the state and the mechanized fishing sector, artisanal fishers' regulatory systems governing the nearshore fishery are the most advanced in terms of their knowledge base, grounding in historical practice, and democratic and localized control. Moreover, since artisanal fishers have a long-term interest in the sustainable management of the nearshore marine resource, their practices would have to serve as the basis for any viable long-term system of regulation.

But defending commoning practices against the assumptions and claims of modernizing states is not an easy task. Viewed strictly in terms of production, it can easily be argued that small-scale locally controlled production strategies are comparatively inferior in terms of output and scaleability. Such a view easily fits within elite discourses around development and shapes not only initiatives pursued by the state, but also responses on the ground. Thus, the push for comprehensive coastal regulations came primarily from ecologists, who clumped the protection of vulnerable ecosystems on the coast facing the combined onslaught of industries, urban development, destruction of beaches and mangroves, and pollution from shrimp farms with the protection of 'customary uses' of beaches, a reference to artisanal fisher communities and their settlements and economic activities on the beaches of India. While this did provide an opening for fishers, it echoed an elitist understanding of how fishers relate to their ecology, as 'traditional' users, not necessarily as economic agents with a specific set of productive and sustainable relationships with their environment. SNEHA's work with fishers from the 1980s enabled an understanding that linked the 'customary' with the economic. The organization took for granted that fishers are already integrated into a wider political economy, and sought, instead of a conservationist goal or 'protecting' fishers and their 'customary' interests, an activist goal of empowering fishers to better the terms of their economic and political engagement with the market and the state. Thus, the defense of commoning as a strategy of resistance required first and foremost the move from a static conception of rights – enshrined in 'customary' protections, to a dynamic one centering on fishers as custodians of the coast and nearshore fishery, defending claims using the language of rights, while demanding better conditions for production and exchange.

SNEHA and its gender–economy dual strategy: anti-shrimp farm and tsunami-displacement-related resistances

SNEHA (*Social Needs Empowerment Humane Awareness*) began supporting *Mathar Sangams* (women's self-help groups) in Karaika-lmedu, the main fishing village in Karaikal District,[6] from 1984.[7] These SHGs had been initially organized by Marie Chetty, a local schoolteacher who, with the permission of the village *panchayat*,[8] sought to help women improve their economic standing in the fish economy, of which they controlled the entire circulation side. As vendors, women were at a severe disadvantage on account of a lack of credit and various social barriers within fisher communities, as well as in their interactions in markets where they bought and sold fish. Efforts to improve their standing in the fishing sector required SNEHA's women SHGs to also take on long-standing social inequalities that women experienced within fisher society. Thus emerged a dual focus on *sectoral* and *social* interests. The effectiveness of tying sectoral interventions, such as reducing dependence on exploitative moneylenders and enabling the autonomous control of credit, depended upon and increased the organized cohesiveness of women addressing marginalization within and outside fisher society.

This dual focus in effect transformed fisher communities in profound ways. For one, it enabled women to challenge the centralized authority of the male *panchayat*, by providing a feasible alternative to moneylenders and the impacts of perpetual and worsening indebtedness. In addition, it enabled women for the first time to become direct participants in dialogue with the state, thereby increasing their political capital vis-à-vis fisher society's male-centric political order, but also by building a means to better articulate demands of the state, and engage with the state's developmentalist claims. This latter impact was most strikingly borne out by the mass movements that coalesced against the proliferation of shrimp farms in Nagapattinam and Karaikal through the 1980s and 1990s, as well as in SNEHA's efforts to assist fishers against displacement from the coast after the tsunami of 2004.

Anti-shrimp resistance Protests against shrimp farms began in fits and starts and soon grew into a regional and national campaign of fishers, farmers, agricultural workers, ecologists, and activists united in pushing back state promotion of destructive shrimp farming. In Karaikal and Nagapattinam districts, fishers led by women and organized by SNEHA joined agriculturalists mobilized by LAFTI (Land and Freedom for Tillers), a grassroots Gandhian organization working with local Dalit and other marginalized agriculturalists under a rights-based framework. A host of organizations coalesced under the *Campaign Against Shrimp Industries*, which played a critical role in moving the Supreme Court of India to issue an order effectively banning all industrial shrimp farms on 11 December 1996 (*S. Jagannath v. Union of India* 1996). While this was a powerful victory for coastal communities, resistance to the Supreme Court directive came from a powerful lobby of shrimp farm operators and a central government dedicated to pushing through its economic agenda of export-led commercial aquaculture. The government of India almost immediately thereafter introduced an *Aquaculture Authority Bill* to dilute the authority of the supreme court restricting coastal industrial shrimp farms. Thus, the result after more than a decade of struggle was mixed: while it became much more difficult for industrial shrimp farms to proliferate without challenge, the number of farms did in fact grow, mostly in violation of the order. Nevertheless, the campaign against shrimp industries serves as a powerful illustration of how a rights-based organization working with local natural-resource-dependent communities can in practice build a durable alliance linking such communities with a network of local, regional, and national allies, including ecologists and rights activists, and engage with institutions of the state as rights-bearing constituents.

While SNEHA did take on the leadership of CASI on the national stage, it was the local fisher communities, and particularly the women's groups mobilized under the rubric of SNEHA's 'self-help groups', that set the tone for the political confrontations on the ground. These engagements spanned a host of defensive struggles – against shrimp farms, but also against polluting or encroaching industries, as in the case of the women of Karaikal successfully taking to task Kothari Sugars in 1991. The struggles against shrimp farms found fishers routinely at the receiving end of physical violence by guards, but also police who sympathized with shrimp farm owners as they did with locally powerful industries. Undeterred, SNEHA's women used their collective strength to protest but also engage in physical actions, including the destruction of fencing built around shrimp farms. The effectiveness of SNEHA's mobilizations also illustrates the changing relationship between fishers and the state, and the assertion of what Subramanian (2009) calls *fisher citizenship*. As recounted by a veteran of the anti-shrimp farm struggles of the 1990s, the first step toward realizing that one could do something about them was to learn that one had rights.[9] This grounding of action within a discourse of rights had profound effects not only on the relationship between fisher communities and the state, but also within fisher communities between male *panchayats* and organized women. Thus, while the SNEHA SHG won the grudging approval of men because it helped alleviate the problem of indebtedness to ruthless moneylenders, its organizational potential extended into the sectoral domain further by positioning women-led mobilizations into direct engagements with the state.

Tsunami reconstruction and the struggle to defend coastal claims In the immediate aftermath of the tsunami's destruction the first responders in Nagapattinam were local community members and activists working with a handful of local organizations.[10] Prominent among these local organizations was SNEHA, with an active membership among fishers in dozens of villages spread across

Nagapattinam and Karaikal. When a plethora of NGOs descended on Nagapattinam within a week, their sheer numbers and the eagerness of their representatives to aggressively compete for 'territory' led to confrontations. In one instance, the RSS-affiliated Sewa Bharati attempted to set up checkpoints into Keechankuppam village and almost provoked a violent conflict with SNEHA workers as they tried to deliver supplies to the beleaguered village. In addition to the fight over territory waged by many NGOs that had no inkling about the region or the needs of its population was the emerging problem of aid delivery.

Many NGOs simply dumped enormous quantities of goods, such as clothes, food, utensils, and so on, without so much as conducting basic surveys to assess needs. This led to the problem of oversupply of often unwanted materials in some areas and utter neglect of other areas. SNEHA's role in the first weeks after the tsunami, therefore, was as a coordinator of relief, owing primarily to the fact that it alone maintained a large member-based presence in the affected villages, and through this network was able to quickly assess the needs of communities and match these to the burgeoning supply of materials. Thus was formed an NGO Coordination Center in Nagapattinam, with its temporary headquarters on the grounds of the District Collectorate under the leadership of SNEHA. What is significant here is the fact that SNEHA had at its disposal information about coastal fisher communities that the local arms of the government did not, including the numbers of households in villages, the range of material losses incurred, and so on. The coordination center also brought to heel many NGOs that, in their eagerness to act, ended up presenting more problems for those engaged in relief efforts. Thus, from a haphazard mode of delivery, SNEHA enabled the local administration to coordinate relief, bringing to bear its long-term experience with the affected communities.

However, in the weeks that followed, the entry of multilateral agencies involved in assessing damage and recommending reconstruction premised on the slogan 'build back better' raised the specter of relocation. At this juncture, SNEHA pushed for a strong NGO-led position on the question of location, but was quickly rebuffed by an emerging consensus that brought together the state government, the UNDP, and NGOs in partnership under a revamped and repurposed NGO Coordination and Resource Center. NCRC quickly shifted the focus away from thorny political issues such as relocation and placed the emphasis on coordinating the mammoth NGO-led housing construction projects that were to commence under the rubric of humanitarian aid. At this point, SNEHA reduced its involvement within NCRC and shifted its attentions to local interventions to stave off potential risks of mass relocation. What is interesting is that SNEHA did not directly challenge the reconstruction program's emerging consensus around relocation, but instead focused its energies on aiding local communities in efforts to defend their coastal habitations. Involvement in housing construction and repair centered, therefore, on ensuring that large-scale relocation was avoided, and local *in situ* construction and repairs preferred.

Working with a much smaller budget than several major players such as World Vision and other international NGOs, SNEHA's housing intervention was smaller in scale but also quite differently conceived. While the dominant model of housing construction employed by NGOs relied on a 'service delivery' model whereby the project is completed by hired contractors, SNEHA adopted an 'owner–driven' model that advanced installments to recipients, who then could identify their own contractors or utilize one recommended, and were free to use their own labor when feasible. Each of four stages of construction was inspected by engineers and SNEHA staff before a subsequent installment for the next stage could be advanced. This approach was flexible, attentive to local needs and aspirations, and cost-effective. It also afforded a flexible set of parameters for recipients, who could choose to invest in aesthetic considerations with their own funds if necessary. Assistance with *in situ* repairs and modifications in many villages across Nagapattinam and Karaikal helped communities re-establish their claims to the coast, avoiding inland relocation. Moreover, in addition to locational and structural issues, the slow and often uncertain pace of NGO-led construction made *in situ* repair an attractive option for many. The choice turned into whether families should continue struggling to live in squalid temporary shelters while waiting for new houses, or return to the coast and attempt to repair old damaged houses.[11]

Fisher resistance to accumulation by dispossession: political pointers for local activism

Several critical issues arise in considering fisher resistance to accumulation by dispossession on the coast. We consider three distinct and related areas – state/fisher relations, fisher/non-fisher relations, and the possibilities and limitations of NGO activism, in order to assess the challenges and possibilities of a politics of resistance. We begin with an illustrative case that embodies all three, drawn from the post-tsunami housing construction process. Between late 2007 and early 2008, the international NGO World Vision completed a massive housing complex for the residents of the fisher village of Nambiyarnagar, in an inland location in Nagapattinam. The village, while predominantly Pattinavar, was also home to a few Dalit families for whom the District Collector decided to allot a cluster of houses at the entrance to the new complex. Shortly after Dalit families had moved into their new houses, fishers of Nambiyarnagar protested and began agitations, threatening violent eviction of the Dalit families. The Collector initially attempted to stand his ground, but relented after a large demonstration and road blockade by fishers threatened to spin out of control. Eventually, with a small cordon of policemen guarding the entrance of the housing complex, and despite pleas for help to the administration, as well as NGOs including SNEHA, the families had to agree to relocate to a location further inland.

While fishers are considered a socially marginalized sub-caste, their local standing in Nagapattinam is also one of relative social and political power over Dalits. Despite efforts by left political parties and the state over the years, Dalits remain socially marginalized and subjected to everyday forms of humiliation and social degradation throughout Nagapattinam.[12] Thus, the effort of the local Collector to address the needs of Nambiyarnagar's Dalits was significant, and represented at the very least a proactive step toward addressing their marginalization. The ownership of new brick-and-mortar houses for Nambiyarnagar's Dalits was a direct means to social upliftment, and since all these houses were identical to those offered to fishers, it meant a claim to status that equaled that of fishers. Nambiyarnagar's fishers, on the other hand, were claiming both a stake in the housing complex – the houses at the entrance to the complex should, after all, be fisher houses, was the most common argument – as well as reasserting their claims to social superiority over Dalits. Fisher arguments centered on the idea that since they had to bear the brunt of locational distance to their sites of work, they should have first choice over houses near the entrance of the complex. Thus, their locational demands became interwoven into the fabric of the social contradictions of caste relations. However, Dalit families that were forced to vacate to houses farther inland ended up bearing the burden of distance, since these houses were adjacent to agricultural fields, whereas their work and social lives were tied to Nagapattinam's urban center. State–fisher relations in Nagapattinam are characterized by significant ambiguity. On the one hand, in the above incident, the collector and his administration were viewed as being unfriendly to fishers, and biased toward Dalits. Yet, in the annual Thiruvizha temple festival conducted in Nambiyarnagar, his deputy was invited to be the chief guest of the village. While poorer fishers in Suryanagar complained about the administration trying to drive fishers off the coast, *panchayat* leaders in Nambiyarnagar were more nuanced, arguing that they needed to work with the administration to get the best outcomes for their village's residents. Local officials had to contend with enforcing the requirements of the reconstruction program, answering to their superiors in Chennai, while also navigating the fraught terrain of multiple claimants to relief and reconstruction aid. In short, maintaining cordial ties with fisher communities remains a challenge of governance at the local level, and top-down efforts to redress problems locally can quickly be read as a challenge to the tacit, fragile cordiality existing between fisher leaders and the local officials of the state.

Dalits work in the commercial fisheries as wage workers alongside Pattinavar fishers. With the growth of the mechanized sector, the expansion of activities, including ice-making, diesel transportation, boat construction, and repairs, opened up opportunities for Dalits as well as other non-Pattinavars in urban Nagapattinam.[13] Thus, while the share-system operates as a 'traditional' means of apportioning catch equitably among exclusively Pattinavar fishers, the wage-labor economy tied to mechanized fishing offers a space for the mobilization of Pattinavar and Dalits as a *class* of fishworkers. Such an expansive definition of fishworker was utilized in 2004 by a fishworker union formed in Akkarapettai, the village with the largest number of mechanized boat owners in Nagapattinam. The *Akkaraipettai Visaipadagu Kattumara Meenpidi Thozilalar Sangam* (Akkaraipettai Motorized Boat and Kattumaram Fishworkers Union) brought together Pattinavar and Dalit fishworkers in the mechanized sector alongside artisanal fishers in a united struggle against owners, with demands for better wages and conditions of work alongside demands to end destructive trawler fishing in the nearshore. In the aftermath of the tsunami, the union won the support of SNEHA and succeeded in mounting a successful challenge in the village's *panchayat* elections, winning a position on the council. Partly the result of the general perception that the owner-dominated *panchayat* had favored powerful members in distributing tsunami relief materials and houses, this success was, however, short-lived for several reasons. Within the *panchayat*, the union's demands had to be translated into the language of governance, most importantly negotiating with the powerful alliance of owners with the state. Owners enjoyed political patronage as well, with the most powerful of them, K.A. Jayapal, contesting on the AIADMK ticket in local elections, and today Minister of Fisheries for Tamil Nadu. The inability of the local union to expand its base also had to do with union members themselves struggling with the effects of the tsunami, and the problems and promises of relocation and new housing. Moreover, the direct action model of engagement that the union could utilize in the context of its struggle within Akkarapettai was insufficient for the task of developing a politics that could engage with the threats posed by intensified efforts by the state to promote industrial and infrastructure development along the coast. It is for this reason that SNEHA launched the *Vanga Kadal Meen Thozilalar Sangam* (Bay of Bengal Fishworkers Union) in 2005, aiming to bring together fishworkers across the Nagapattinam-Karaikal coast in a broad alliance against state policies threatening the coastal and nearshore commons. While one might be tempted to read this shift as a softening of local politics in the classic Foucauldian formulation, we think it signifies the structural limitations of state-level politics for marginalized fishers and the activist NGO. For fishers, as evidenced in the case of the Akkarapettai union's short-lived success, winning a measure of control at the local level required a simultaneous diminution of political strategies honed in direct struggles with identifiable class opponents such as owners.

Yet, such a shift did not in itself preclude other forms of effective action, such as broadening the scope of fisher resistance beyond the conflict with owners, especially in relation to the state. SNEHA could bring to bear its own long-term efforts to broaden the struggle against state-led efforts to alienate fishers from the coast. In addition, while the Akkarapettai union succeeded in mobilizing the common outrage of fishworkers across caste boundaries, it could do little to translate unities achieved in mobilizations into socially meaningful changes. Dalit social relations with fishers continued to remain circumscribed by fisher assertions of social superiority.

The activist NGO in effect is most effective when mobilizing populations around demands on the state. In this context, mobilizations, legal campaigns, and broadening alliances can achieve successes, as they did most spectacularly against shrimp farms. However, addressing structural social inequalities is a harder, longer-term struggle, as borne out by SNEHA's efforts to push for gender equality within fisher society. In both cases – gender and caste relations – the central role of the village *panchayat* in constraining possibilities for social change should be considered an important indictment of the romanticized idea of 'traditional' governance. Thus, while the *panchayat* can be credited with being an effective institution when it comes to fisheries regulation or in responding to natural disasters, as Bavinck (2008) has argued, it remains a problematic institution at the center of gender, caste, and class inequalities.

The contradictory character of caste identity among fishers poses a major challenge to an activist NGO such as SNEHA. Fisher identity provides a basis for economic and political autonomy in relation to claims over coastal land and nearshore marine resources, but it also expresses itself as a caste identity in the social exclusion and marginalization of Dalits. Yet, such a notion of fisher identity does not easily overcome the structural contradictions of class within fisher society either. The agitation itself had begun as the result of complaints by a few dozen households that had been relocated to a shabby, poorly constructed complex called 'Suryanagar' about a year earlier. These fishers had endured a host of structural and locational problems, but had little luck convincing village leaders and local administrators to reallocate new houses for them. When news spread of Dalits being allocated the cluster of houses at the entrance of World Vision's new complex, these poorer fishers succeeded in convincing village leaders that this was a direct challenge to all fishers. Within weeks of the agitation and subsequent eviction of Dalit households from the new complex, however, the cluster was reoccupied, not by households who survived tottering Suryanagar, but by some of the more affluent households from Nambiyarnagar. In a final twist of irony, the poorer fishers who initiated the agitation ended up being allotted houses further inland, like the evicted Dalit families. In effect, fisher identity mobilized in this manner – as a caste in stark opposition to Dalits – ended up serving the needs of affluent fishers.

Conclusion: SNEHA, fishers, and the challenge of resistance under limits

While there were major differences between SNEHA's role in anti-shrimp mobilizations and its role in post-tsunami reconstruction, there are important continuities that are relevant to questions of resistance to accumulation by dispossession. As an NGO, its antecedents are different from those associated with the onset of neoliberalism. In the 1980s, organizations such as SNEHA emerged as a response to the social and economic marginalization of millions of producers in rural India, especially as the development state imposed its agendas, violently usurping land, resources, devaluing labor, and despoiling the environment in a push for GDP-based growth. Marginalized communities such as fishers could therefore only defend themselves from such an onslaught if they could engage with the state in its own language, principally the law. The elementary step necessary for this transformation was the adoption of the language of rights, rights that extended inward into the community in the sphere of gender relations, and outward into the domain of the non-fisher world of the market and state. Thus, in its early years, SNEHA organized campaigns against domestic violence even as it mobilized fishers against anti-fisher discriminatory practices prevalent in public transport. Winning the right to utilize public transport provided the sort of victory that cemented the contention that the rights of women within fisher society are indeed not distinct from, but constitutive of, fisher rights in the wider world.

A similar push toward combining the social and sectoral thrust of rights can be seen in SNEHA's expansion of the term *fishworker* to denote not only male fishers, but also women fish vendors and others involved in the petty fish trade. Since the economic interests of women fish vendors are ignored by the state, even as it affords diesel subsidies and off-season compensation to male fishers, the inclusion is aimed at enabling women to make visible their critical role in the fish economy, and thereby strengthen their ability to make demands on the state. The harvest side of the artisanal fishing political economy itself presents a challenge for conventional Marxist definitions of workers and owners, since many artisanal fishers own small boats. Yet, boat ownership should also be seen against the precarious conditions of perpetual indebtedness, which many such owners face. Despite ownership, however, the critical determining issue is that of labor, since artisanal crafts require teams that apportion catch on an equal basis, with the owner getting an extra share if he joins the team. While the traditional share system marks the artisanal sector from the mechanized sector, it also poses an inherent limitation to developing broader solidarities. Since commercial fisheries rest largely, though not entirely, on the basis of wage labor, fishers working in this sector are more easily definable as *fishworkers*. What is interesting with the definition is that it enables a perspective that transcends the sectoral distinction between artisanal and mechanized fishing, and enables two simultaneous forms of engagement with the market and the state. On the one hand, artisanal fishers as *fishworkers* defend their claims as custodians of the nearshore fishery and the coastal commons, while, on the other, fishers employed on mechanized boats fight for better conditions and returns as *fishworkers*. The inclusion of women fish vendors in the definition of *fishworker* further extends the term's radical meaning, by linking the political economy of catch/harvest with the realization of its value.

While efforts by SNEHA to organize fishworkers into a broad union have only achieved partial success, one arena where the organization has had more success is in its efforts to organize its federation of SHGs into a *producer cooperative*. The idea helps address one problem that is central to the artisanal fish economy, namely the low value of fish. When fish exporters scour the beaches of Nagapattinam for fresh catch, they pay artisanal fishers only a minuscule portion of the value they obtain by freezing, packaging, and shipping fish to lucrative markets overseas. SNEHA's producer cooperative is intended to help women increase the value of catch by pickling, packaging, and selling them locally and domestically through the cooperative model. While further studies need to be undertaken to assess the impacts of this initiative, it should be noted that it presents at least two important possibilities. First, it marks an effort to renegotiate the terms by which artisanal fishers engage with the market. If the struggle to get higher values for fresh catch is hampered by the steep inequalities between fishers and buyers – in addition to (and exacerbated by) the lack of storage, packaging technologies, and transportation options – such an approach offers a feasible and promising alternative. Second, the fact that the producer cooperative, like the SHG federation, is a women-led entity that is not profit-driven helps further strengthen the connection between the social and sectoral dimensions of the artisanal fishing political economy. Women are now key players in a struggle not only to defend the coast, but to also contest the terrain of the market against global commercial players who rely on the economic weakness of fishers to enhance profit margins. The longer-term strategic positioning of initiatives such as the producers cooperative by SNEHA presents an example of tying the domain of rights-based activism to staking and consolidating claims on the political economy of coastal fishing. As a renegotiation of power and a contestation of structural marginality, the producer cooperative embodies a model directly opposed to that promoted by the neoliberal state.

Notes

1 Revathi volunteered as a relief worker and organizer in the immediate aftermath of the tsunami. Her efforts include working with SNEHA as a relief coordinator, and conducting research and workshops focusing on the condition of women in post-tsunami Nagapattinam and Karaikal. Swamy conducted doctoral fieldwork in Nagapattinam in 2007–2008 on the effects of the 2004 tsunami on economic development priorities in coastal Nagapattinam. SNEHA (Social Need Education and Human Awareness) is an NGO active in Nagapattinam, Tamil Nadu, and Karaikal, Pondicherry, since the mid-1980s. SNEHA's work focuses primarily on coastal artisanal fisher communities, particularly women. In the aftermath of the tsunami of 2004, SNEHA was instrumental in organizing relief efforts, and shortly thereafter in defending fisher communities from state efforts to relocate them inland.

2 Pattinavars are considered a 'backward caste' by state and central governments, a designation arising from their economic and social marginalization as fishers within caste Hindu society.

3 See Central Institute of Brackishwater Aquaculture (2005).

4 The authors draw on doctoral dissertation fieldwork conducted in Nagapattinam between 2007 and 2008 (Swamy 2011), as well as several years of activist research conducted under the auspices of SNEHA and various civil society initiatives in Nagapattinam (Revathi) for several of the arguments advanced in this chapter.

5 A focus on humanitarian efficacy and financial accountability dominates the official documentation of NGO practices, as, for instance, in ACFID (2005) and UNICEF (2008).

6 Karaikal district, though an administrative unit of Pondicherry state, occupies a stretch of the Coromandel coast enclosed by Nagapattinam. Karaikal and Pondicherry were French colonial possessions, but their coastal

fisher populations share cultural and social ties. In short, there are cultural and social continuities between fisher communities spread across the Coromandel coast, regardless of whether these communities are to be found in Tamil Nadu or Pondicherry. We also include Karaikal in this study because SNEHA, the most important organization working among fishers of the region, built its base first in Karaikal's fisher villages in the 1980s, villages that also were important sites for struggles of the region's fishers against shrimp farms and industrial pollution in the years preceding the tsunami of 2004.

7 See Sharma (2007) for a detailed institutional account of SNEHA's post-tsunami work. See also annual reports from the 1990s (SNEHA 1997, 1998, 1999).

8 The local political body consisting of five elected customarily male leaders who manage the village's domestic affairs, but also its dealings with the political agencies and representatives of the state.

9 Interview with Indrani, SNEHA Coordinator, Karaikalmedu, 2007.

10 Revathi notes that in the days following the tsunami, the demanding task of retrieving bodies and consoling traumatized survivors fell upon SNEHA-affiliated and other local activists, working together with village residents. State and NGO agents arrived in significant numbers only in early January.

11 For a detailed account of structural and locational issues in NGO-built post-tsunami housing, as well as SNEHA's 'owner-driven' housing efforts, see Swamy (2011).

12 See Kandasamy (2014) for a riveting fictionalized account of the horrific massacre of Dalits in the village of Kelvenmani in 1968. Nagapattinam's agrarian political economy rests on the shoulders of Dalit agricultural workers, rural proletarians whose mildest efforts to achieve a measure of social dignity are often met with terrifying brutality at the hands of the propertied castes.

13 We are indebted here to insights into the internal dynamics of the commercial fishing sector from Dr V. Kumaravelu, who served as head of the *Vanga Kadal Meen Thozilalar Sangam* in 2008.

References

Australian Council for International Development (ACFID) (2005). *NGO Tsunami Accountability Report*. Deakin: ACFID. Available at: http://reliefweb.int/sites/reliefweb.int/files/resources/93D5012FAD469DAD49257014000F41C4-acfid-sasia-1jun.pdf [accessed 14 April 2017].

Bavinck, M. (2001). *Marine Resource Management: Conflict and Regulation in the Fisheries of the Coromandel Coast*. New Delhi: Sage.

Bavinck, M. (2008). 'Collective strategies and windfall catches: fisher responses to tsunami relief efforts in South India'. *Transforming Cultures eJournal* 3(2). Available at: http://epress.lib.uts.edu.au/journals/index.php/TfC/article/view/923/904 [accessed 14 April 2017].

Central Institute of Brackishwater Aquaculture (2005). *Assessment of Loss Due to Tsunami to Brackishwater Aquaculture and Fisheries Sectors in Coastal States of Andhra Pradesh, Tamil Nadu and Kerala*. Available at: www.ciba.tn.nic.in/divisions/tteis/ASSESSMENT_TSUNAMI.pdf [accessed 7 March 2010].

Food and Agriculture Organization (FAO) (1999). *The State of World Fisheries and Aquaculture –1998*. Rome: FAO.

Kandasamy, M. (2014) *The Gypsy Goddess*. New Delhi: Fourth Estate.

Martinez-Alier, J. (2002). *The Environmentalism of the Poor*. Northhampton, MA: Edward Elgar.

Sharma, A. (2007). *Enhancement of Women's Livelihoods and Group Solidarity in Karaikal District, Pondicherry* (No. Tsunami Reconstruction / Rehabilitation Initiatives Programme Publication No. 2).

S. Jagannath v. Union of India, WP 561/1994 (1996). Environmental Law Alliance Worldwide (ELAW). Available at: www.elaw.org/node/1974 [accessed 23 March 2016].

SNEHA (1997). *Annual Report*. Nagapattinam, Tamil Nadu, India: SNEHA.

SNEHA (1998). *Annual Report*. Nagapattinam, Tamil Nadu, India: SNEHA.

SNEHA (1999). *Annual Report*. Nagapattinam, Tamil Nadu, India: SNEHA.

Stonich, S.C. and Bailey, C. (2000). 'Resisting the blue revolution: contending coalitions surrounding industrial shrimp farming'. *Human Organization*, 59(1): 23–36.

Subramanian, A. (2009). *Shorelines: Space and Rights in South India*. Stanford, CA: Stanford University Press.

Swamy, R. (2011). *Disaster Capitalism: Tsunami Reconstruction and Neoliberalism in Nagapattinam, South India*. Doctoral Dissertation, University of Texas.

UNICEF (2008). *Humanitarian Action Report 2008 – Tsunami Response: Lessons Learned*. Available at: www.unicef.org/haro8/index_tsunami.html [accessed 23 March 2016].

7 | LUMAD ANTI-MINING ACTIVISM IN THE PHILIPPINES

Robyn Magalit Rodriguez

Introduction

In late 2015, international human rights groups and media outlets called attention to an issue that Filipino social justice activists, particularly indigenous activists, have long been engaged with: military and paramilitary harassment and violence against Lumad communities in the southern Philippine region of Mindanao, in response to their anti-mining activism. 'Lumad' is a broad umbrella term that used to describe indigenous communities in the area. It includes a wide range of indigenous groups. According to a Human Rights Watch report, Philippine military forces killed five members of a Lumad family, including children between the ages of 13 and 17, in Bukidnon province. Just a few weeks following this horrific incident, government-supported paramilitary forces in the province of Surigao Del Sur killed another three individuals, one being the director of a tribal school. Philippine military officials deny involvement in the Surigao killings, but admit that the killings in Bukidnon, even though they included the killing of two minors, were part of its campaign to eliminate communist insurgents of the New People's Army (NPA) in the region. The NPA, however, denies that the killed Bukidnon Lumads were members of their ranks. To be sure, the Lumads of southern Mindanao have actively resisted the (il)legal incursions by mining companies on their lands, and the Philippine military have 'red-baited' the Lumads, linking them to the NPA or the Communist Party of the Philippines to justify military and paramilitary harassment and violence.[1] This chapter historicizes the dispossession of the Lumads of Mindanao, placing it within the historical context of US colonialism and neocolonialism in the Philippines. It then reviews resistance struggles led by Lumads and the broader transnational Philippine left movement.

Neocolonialism, neoliberalism, and dispossession in the Philippines

Accumulation by dispossession, according to geographer David Harvey, is among 'the features of primitive accumulation that Marx mentions', which 'have remained powerfully present within capitalism's historical geography' (Harvey 2003: 145). In other words, the disruption of indigenous forms of exchange and the displacement of peasant populations through the extraction of natural resources on which the rise of capitalism depended are processes that continue apace in the contemporary moment. This is due to the global dominance of neoliberalism, that is, the doctrine of unregulated and unrestrained markets for the benefit of capital. For geographers studying the Philippines, mining operations in the Philippines' south is an especially stark example of accumulation by dispossession (Holden *et al.* 2011).

In the global popular imagination, the Philippines is perhaps most known for the US-backed Marcos dictatorship. Indeed, the present socioeconomic status of the Philippines, which is characterized by chronic crisis, is generally attributed to the ostentatious and opulent lifestyle of both the dictator and his wife due to ill-gotten wealth. For many around the world, this was often characterized (and caricatured) by First Lady Imelda Marcos' thousands of pairs of shoes. While they certainly lined their pockets and filled their closets with goods secured through the theft of the national coffer, much of the country's economic problems are attributable to its adherence to the dictates of the so-called 'Washington Consensus'. This consensus, propagated by the US-headquartered and -influenced institutions of the World Bank and the International Monetary Fund, is one that secures the requirements of global capital by encouraging Third World states (with both incentives and sanctions) to engage in export-oriented industrialization (EOI) (Hawes 1987). By shifting to EOI, Third World governments such as the Philippines orient their economies to foreign investors (rather than local capital) to build the industrial sector in their countries. At the same time, they rely on institutions such as the World Bank and the International Monetary Fund for loans to build the infrastructure global capitalists require. By the 1980s, the Philippines was among the world's largest debtor nations (this status was no doubt exacerbated by the first couple's graft and corruption). In 1983, the country's total foreign debt amounted to $42.8 billion. Consequently, the Philippines became one of the most structurally adjusted economies in the world as the Philippines' creditors imposed stringent repayment requirements.

The fall of the dictatorship, however, did not spell the end of the Philippines' economic woes. President Corazon 'People Power' Aquino assured the Philippines' foreign creditors that she would continue to adhere to the structural adjustments they demanded. Within only a year of her election to office, debt service under her leadership would consume nearly 40 percent of the national budget. At the same time, Aquino maintained the Philippines' export orientation. Successive regimes put the country firmly on a course consonant with the increasingly dominant, global, neoliberal agenda.

One of the most defining features of contemporary Philippine society is the out-migration of Filipino workers throughout the globe. In 2015, nearly 5,000 Filipino men and women left the Philippines to work as low-wage, low-status laborers in nearly 200 countries and territories around the world. The out-migration of Philippine workers is actively encouraged by the Philippine state as part of its neoliberal program. On the one hand, Philippine migrants bolster the government's foreign exchange reserves through the billions of dollars they generate in remittances. On the other hand, overseas employment serves to quell domestic political unrest, which always simmers under the surface of political life as a consequence of the multiple displacements Filipinos experience due to neoliberal reform. Trade liberalization, flexibilization, and privatization, among the key pillars of a neoliberal agenda, leave Filipinos landless, underemployed, and with basic social safety nets such as access to affordable healthcare completely bankrupt (Rodriguez 2010).

Even as the Philippine state exports labor, it continues to entice foreign corporations to enjoy profits by extracting surplus value from those who are left behind. Propagated as an alternative to overseas employment, the Philippine state has attempted to position itself as a site for business process outsourcing (BPO) for global firms (Padios 2012). The state has often drawn on the Philippines' status as a former US colony to make its claim that the Philippines is a more appropriate site than India, for example, for the conduct of particular kinds of business needs, including call center work. Of course, the

Philippines continues to entice foreign corporations to open up garments and electronics factories in its export processing zones (McKay 2006). Moreover, the Philippines attracts businesses in the tourism industry to profit from the Philippines' underdevelopment (Gonzalez 2013).

Just as significantly, the Philippines works to bring in corporations in the extractive industries to tap the mineral wealth of the archipelago, which is quite vast. Indeed, in the early 1990s, the Asian Development Bank had determined that the country was not sufficiently tapping its potential for foreign investment in the industry and called for greater liberalization of its mining laws. Moreover, multilateral institutions such as the World Bank also played a role in encouraging countries such as the Philippines to promote the mining industry as an extension of structural adjustment programs. Among the sorts of policies promoted by the World Bank included the 'privatization of state mining interests, enactment of laws affecting the mining sector and the environment, and measures that lift almost all fiscal burdens from mining companies' (SAPRIN 2004: 155).

By 1995, the government passed Republic Act 7942, commonly known as the Mining Act of 1995. The act ultimately expanded the terms of foreign ownership of mining operations. It was incredibly successful (at least from the perspective of foreign investors). The number of foreign mining countries increased by 400 percent by the end of 1996 (Holden 2005). After the passage of the Mining Act of 1995, the Philippine government implemented the 2004 National Mineral Policy Agenda and the Mineral Action Plan, both meant to further liberalize the mining industry ostensibly to fuel economic growth. The policies resulted in the increase of large-scale mining operations in the country, from 17 in 1999 to 46 in 2015 (Simbulan 2016).

The most recent Philippine President, Benigno Aquino III, introduced a mining policy in 2012 by executive order, bypassing the legislative process. Executive Order (EO) 79, according to critics, including environmental groups and even the Catholic Church (through the Catholic Bishops Conference of the Philippines), is far worse than the Mining Act of 1995 when it comes to liberalizing the mining sector in the country. Among their critiques is that although EO 79 appears to expand areas that will be off-limits to mining, it still honors existing mining claims, as well as grants new ones. Indeed, small-scale miners are critical of EO 79 because it ultimately favors bigger operations, even when the worst mining disasters have occurred at large-scale mines. Perhaps not surprisingly, however, the Chamber of Mines of the Philippines, which represents the interests of big mining firms, supported the President's move.

In sum, whether under the control of a ruthless dictator or democratically elected president, it is clear that the labor and land of the Philippines have been up for grabs for multinational capital, and the Philippine state has actively facilitated the process.

Neocolonialism in the Philippines: Bell Trade Act, Parity Agreement, and legal foundations of dispossession

To fully appreciate contemporary neoliberal state formation, particularly the liberalization of mining in the Philippines, however, it is important to understand the history and legacy of US imperialism in the country. In 1898, the United States acquired the Philippines, along with Puerto Rico and Cuba, with the conclusion of the Spanish–American War. It was the Americans who introduced industrialized mining to the country. The colonial state offered much access to foreign investors. By 1941, the country became the fifth largest producer of gold in the world. Emerging victorious from World War II, the United States could let go of its erstwhile colony while maintaining its military, economic, and political dominance of the Philippines (thereby commanding great influence in the region) through treaties, legislation, and provisions in the newly drafted Philippine constitution. The Philippine Trade Act of 1946 (also known as the Bell Trade Act) included provisions such as a Parity Agreement that allowed citizens of the United States to, among other things, dispose, exploit, develop, or utilize all agricultural, timber, and mineral lands of the public domain (Golay 1955). Indeed, laws such as the Philippine Mining Act, in some ways, merely reiterate terms already laid out in the Philippine Constitution.

Consequently, US corporations dominated the control of strategic sectors of the Philippine economy, including mining in the decades immediately following 'independence'. This has remained unchanged (and indeed worsened) ever since.

Mining in the Philippines

The Philippines' mining potential is estimated to be $840 billion. According to data from the Philippines' Department of Environment and National Resources Mines and Geosciences Bureau, as of 2014, the country's mineral exports amounted to $4 billion, with copper, gold, and nickel being the top. Mining operations are disproportionately centered in the Mindanao region.[2] Large-scale mining, which was facilitated with the passage of the 1995 Mining Act, has had numerous negative impacts on communities in the region, particularly the Lumad population. Mining operations displace people from their ancestral lands. Open-pit mining, the method typically deployed in large-scale mining operations, moreover, has been found to also have major environmental impacts. Researchers associated with the Massachusetts Institute of Technology (MIT) have found that throughout the mining process, toxins can leak into bedrock and are released into the air. Additionally, mining, which is intrinsically invasive, can cause much damage to the natural landscape. The mining of gold, which is one of the country's top mineral exports, has long been singled out by environmental activists globally for its deleterious effects on the environment. Gold mining requires that enormous volumes of earth are dug up and processed. Consequently, the resulting erosion clogs streams and rivers, and can eventually taint marine ecosystems far downstream of the mine site. Exposing the deep earth to air and water also causes chemical reactions that produce sulfuric acid, which can leak into drainage systems. Air quality is also compromised by gold mining, which releases hundreds of tons of airborne elemental mercury every year. Environmental groups in the Philippines have raised concerns specifically about the ways open-pit mining, such as that used to mine gold, poisons the Philippines' waterways and causes erosion, as well as furthers deforestation. Mining, therefore, is among the factors that exacerbate environmental catastrophe in the region, which displaces indigenous peoples.

Indigenous resistance and its repression

It is important to underscore that indigenous communities throughout the Philippines have actively engaged in resistance struggles against US imperialism and the neocolonial state, particularly natural resource extraction and its impacts. For instance, indigenous communities were central players in the anti-Marcos struggle. The Marag Valley in the northern Philippines, which is populated by a number of indigenous groups, was an important site for resistance (both armed and legal) against the dictatorship. Opposition to the Marcos regime in Marag was as much about the dictatorship as it was about logging activities in the region. Several logging companies close to the government were operating in the Valley by the mid-1980s. Given the government's failure to recognize their land rights, many indigenous communities were compelled to join the NPA in armed struggle.

Not surprisingly, the Philippine state has violently quelled indigenous communities' resistance. Military presence in the Marag Valley began in 1982. Marcos' drive to consolidate his political power, as well as his economic interests, led to troops being deployed in the valley to protect Marcos' cronies' logging interests. Bolstered by the political, economic, and military imperatives of the United States at the height of the Cold War, the Marcos dictatorship had the support of the US as one of its committed bulwarks in the Asia-Pacific against the communist threat. With that support, Marcos could legitimately, and conveniently, crush all forms of resistance to his regime under the guise of combating 'communist' terrorists. The United States merely turned a blind eye to egregious human rights abuse and the denial of democracy – the very principle that the United States believes itself to be emblematic of – to the Filipino people.

In 1984, Marcos increased troops to Marag, and peasant communities were forced to evacuate the area. A second evacuation order was issued in 1985. Peasants, including indigenous communities of Isnegs and Aggays, who refused to leave their homes and their land were automatically suspected of being 'terrorist', or at least sympathetic to the 'terrorists' (which often meant that they might as well be terrorists).

The largest military operations in Marag were deployed in 1987, ironically under the democratically elected Corazon Aquino presidency. Committed to 'total war', continuing her predecessors' alliance with the United States in the then 'war on terror', Aquino effectively waged war against the most economically, politically, and culturally marginalized sectors of Philippine society as the long-standing, deeply rooted sources of poverty continued to compel people to join the armed revolutionary movement. Despite a newly established 'democratic' government, Aquino's economic interests varied little from the dictator that came before her – her own personal fortunes relied on sustaining and deepening the country's underdevelopment. Aquino launched a second military campaign in Marag Valley in 1989, and in 1990 bombs were rained on peasant communities for 37 days as part of the Philippine government's continued, 'anti-terrorist', counter-insurgency campaign. Within this period, 100 children died and 300 families – civilians – were left hungry and homeless. People were driven to live in caves, and have as recently as the late 1990s emerged, shell-shocked, only to find their homes destroyed and their crops and livestock decimated. Worse, they had to live under the heavy hand of the Philippine military, which had surrounded their valley to allegedly protect them from 'terrorists' (after nearly two decades of being identified as 'terrorists' themselves) and the forests from logging (since banned by the Philippine government). Yet, the military was ultimately responsible for terrorizing the people becoming the armed vigilantes of loggers, and themselves perpetrators of illegal logging.

I witnessed the continued militarization of the valley under the Ramos administration in 1997. After three military checkpoints and nearly six hours of travel by *banca* (canoe), my companions and I found ourselves in the heart of the Marag Valley, where we did project evaluation work for a rural health program sponsored by the Ecumenical Movement for Justice and Peace. It was June 1997. We were among the handful of outsiders allowed into the valley during this period. The military did not even allow priests and nuns to enter for fear of the seeds of 'terrorism' in preaching from their gospel. There were few schools and no health centers. Indeed, at the start of our journey into the valley, we passed the *banca* of an Issneg family who, after already traveling for several hours out of the valley, had to travel several hours more to seek care for their infant child.

Since the declaration of the global 'war on terror' in the early 2000s, once again the world is divided into US-allied and enemy camps, with the Philippine government of Gloria Macapagal Arroyo proudly boasting of being among the first to join the United States in its biblical 'Campaign for Everlasting Peace'. Perhaps not surprisingly, old Cold War logics (and indeed, even personnel, as Bush's administration during this time proved with the appointment of Dick Cheney, for instance) prevail. If Cold War heroes in the US resurrected themselves in the war on terror, so they did too in the Philippines. It is no small wonder, then, that one of the leaders in combating the 'terrorists' plaguing the Marag Valley led the Armed Forces of the Philippines under the regime. Moreover, as the United States' 'second front' in the global war on terror, the United States sent thousands of troops to the Philippines ostensibly for training purposes. What has in fact occurred is that civilians and militant activists have been used for target 'training'. Indeed, the Macapagal-Arroyo administration would be marked by a sharp spike in extrajudicial killings, under her '*Oplan Bantay Laya*'. Political killings have hardly waned under the more recent administration of President Benigno Aquino Junior, as the cases described at the outset of this chapter illustrate. We have yet to see what the newly elected president will do with his political detractors, but what is clear is that violent repression of indigenous dissent has become a normalized aspect of political life.

Anti-mining activism

Indigenous resistance to mining specifically has a long history and is a national phenomenon. Groups such as the Cordillera Peoples Alliance (CPA) have resisted incursions by the US mining company Newmont in the northernmost areas of the island of Luzon. Indeed, CPA had already been actively engaged in struggles against commercial logging in the region, as well as the fight against the Chico River Dam project under the Marcos regime, before extending their resistance to mining. In other regions of the Philippines, such as Mindoro, the indigenous community established the Unity of Mindoro Against Foreign Mining coalition together with its allies, despite heavy militarization.

In Mindanao, the Lumad community has engaged in a range of activities to resist dispossession from preserving their cultures and ensuring the basic daily survival of their peoples to fighting against mining corporations' incursion on their lands. Long neglected by the central Philippine government, the Lumad community has taken it upon themselves to provide their members with basic social services. For example, the Alternative Learning Center for Agricultural and Livelihood Development (ALCADEV) is an initiative that offers secondary education to indigenous youth from 32 Lumad communities, including members of the Manobo, Banwaon, Higanon, Talaandig, and Mamanwa groups. In addition to teaching students subjects typically offered by the Philippine public school system, ALCADEV offers them instruction in sustainable and organic farming. While the establishment of schools may not seem to be immediately related to anti-mining efforts, ALCADEV ensures that students understand and fight for their rights as indigenous people. Discriminated against and reviled by those identified with mainstream Filipino culture, through their own autonomous schools, Lumads reclaim a sense of dignity and pride in their indigenous roots. Indeed, even as ALCADEV is not conspicuously connected to anti-mining activism in the region, the Philippine state sees it as an institution that poses a great threat to the local social, economic, and political order. It was ALCADEV's former school director who was murdered by paramilitary forces, as mentioned earlier in this chapter.

Anti-mining activism, however, has taken different forms and taken place at different scales. Indigenous activists have engaged in judicial, legislative, and administrative struggles, even as they have mobilized in the streets. They have appealed to international bodies such as the United Nations while also engaging in people-to-people connections with other indigenous communities around the world. They have built coalitions among themselves and other social justice movements nationally and transnationally. In the mid-1990s, Lumads, specifically the B'laan people, engaged in both armed and legal struggles against the Tampakan Copper-Gold Mine Project. If opened, the project would be the fifth largest copper mining operation in the world (Wenk and Shirler n.d.).

The B'laan resisted the early exploratory efforts of the Australian mining company Western Mining Corporation. Their resistance efforts did not cease when the WMC was later replaced by Philippine-based Sagittarius Mining Inc. (SMI) to serve as the project's administrator in 2002. Most recently, the British-Swiss mining giant Glencore Xstrata, together with SMI, has pursued the project.

On the judicial front, the B'laan people, with support from the Catholic Church (specifically the Diocese of Kidapawan), filed a Supreme Court case challenging the constitutionality of the 1995 Mining Act. On the legislative front, they were able to garner support from local governments to pass resolutions against SMI operations and, most significantly, a provincial-level ban on open-pit mining.

Besides building a strong alliance among progressive forces in the Philippines, the B'laan were also able to build international opposition to the project. For instance, while it was filing its class action against WMC at the Supreme Court, representatives of the B'laan community traveled to Australia to make direct appeals to Australian social justice activists for support. They have even caught the attention of the United Nations Special Rapporteur on the human rights of internally displaced persons. For two decades, the B'laan have been largely successful in their bid to slow down, if not entirely halt, the project (Wenk and Shirler n.d.).

The state, meanwhile, has engaged in numerous tactics to push the project through. Due to an appeal by the Arroyo administration, for example, the Supreme Court was forced to overturn its earlier ruling to stop WMC's operations. Incidentally, it was Arroyo who introduced the 1995 Mining Act while she was a senator. With the recent passage of current President Aquino's EO 79, activists fear that the state can overturn the provincial code that has prohibited open-pit mining. The state has, moreover, resorted to the militarization of the area, and members of the group have been killed as a result.

By 2010, the B'laan were forced to engage in armed resistance in response to the militarization of their communities. Indeed, armed struggle has been very much a part of the Lumad's arsenal of strategies to resist mining. Philippine scholar Roland Simbulan (2016) explains:

> The AFP claims that more than 70 percent of the New People's Army (NPA) rebels in Mindanao are from the Lumad tribes. But in fact, the Philippine military has, by its actions, become the number-one recruiter of the NPAs coming from the Lumads. It is the mining companies and the militarization of their communities that have pushed Lumads into armed resistance. (p. 34)

Even as indigenous people engage in highly localized struggles to protect their ancestral domains against foreign mining corporations, they have attempted to coordinate their efforts nationally through formations such as KATRIBU (*Kalipunan ng mga Katutubong Mamamayan ng Pilipinas*, or Conglomerate of Indigenous People of the Philippines).[3] KATRIBU (formerly known as KAMP) is a national alliance of more than 500 regional, provincial, and local indigenous people's organizations. The regional organizations that are part of KATRIBU include the CPA (mentioned above), *Bigkis at Lakas ng Katutubo sa Timog Katagalugan* (Balatik), Central Luzon Aeta Association (CLAA), and Punganay-Cagayan Valley, all of which are located in the region of Luzon. Meanwhile, *Tumandok nga Mangunguma nga Nagapangapin sa Duta Kag Kabuhi* (TUMANDUK) is from the Visayas region. Five regional organizations representing the Lumads of Mindanao are also part of the alliance: PASAKA Regional Confederation of Lumad Organizations, *Kahopongang Lumad sa Halayong Habagatang Mindanao* (KALUHHAMIN), *Kahogpongan sa Lumadnong Organisasyon* (KASALO), KALUMBAY Lumad Organization in northern Mindanao, and *Salabukan Nok G'taw Subanen* (SGS).

KATRIBU launched a nationwide anti-mining campaign in 2009 called ALARM (Ancestral Lands at Risk of Mining) to respond to the influx of large-scale mines on indigenous people's land across the Philippines. Later, KATRIBU created a broader anti-mining campaign network called Scrap the Mining Act Network. This network extends beyond the indigenous community to include individuals, institutions, and groups from the religious community, academia, elected officials, the legal community, environmentalists, journalists, cultural workers, and others. Its primary goal is to fight for the repeal of the Mining Act of 1995. In 2012, the network launched a massive signature campaign to rally Filipinos against the Act and for more progressive mining legislation. Among other activities, members of the network mobilize on key 'red-letter' days to raise awareness about the deleterious consequences of the Mining Act of 1995, including 3 March, the anniversary of the signing of the act, 5 June, Environment Day, 9 August, International Indigenous People's Day, and the second Sunday of October, Tribal Filipino Sunday.

Lumads, moreover, have been part of broader movements for social transformation and justice in the Philippines. Notably, KATRIBU is a member of BAYAN (Bagong Alyansang Makabayan, or the New Patriotic Alliance), a transnational, multisectoral alliance of radical grassroots organizations. BAYAN has stood staunchly and militantly against the Philippine state's neoliberal agenda more broadly. BAYAN links environmental (in)justice and climate change, for example, to natural resource extraction encouraged by the state through its neoliberal policies. For example, in 2009, Typhoon

Ondoy wreaked havoc on the Philippines. The capital of Manila and surrounding areas were particularly hard hit. According to the Philippines' National Statistics Office, 4,929,382 people were affected by Ondoy, leaving nearly 1,000 individuals dead. Though mainstream media outlets attributed the devastation suffered by many Filipinos to poor disaster planning on the part of local and national government, progressive groups attributed it to climate change exacerbated by natural resource extraction. According to Danilo Ramos, the Secretary General of the *Kilusan Magbubukid ng Pilipinas* (Peasant Movement of the Philippines), 'Though it looks like that we are helpless with weather conditions, we firmly believe that there are man-made causes that brought further disasters such as mining, logging, land use conversion and the irresponsible operation of dams'.[4]

Indeed, it is perhaps as a consequence of their connection with militant movements in the Philippines such as BAYAN that the Philippine state has come to see Lumads as especially threatening. Successive Philippine presidential administrations have targeted many Lumad activists for assassination. As of this writing, the most recent spate of violence against Lumads that garnered international attention took place in Bukidnon and Surigao Del Sur, under the Aquino regime, as stated earlier. However, the police, armed forces, and paramilitary forces have systematically targeted anti-mining Lumad activists since the Macapagal-Arroyo administration. Recall that Macapagal-Arroyo was a major supporter of mining in the Philippines even prior to becoming president. Like both her predecessors and successors, Macapagal-Arroyo aggressively pushed through neoliberal economic policies, including the liberalization of the mining industry, even as it bolstered police and military forces to ensure that opposition to those policies would be quelled (Holden 2012). According to progressive lawmakers, by 2008 (six years after Macapagal-Arroyo launched her *Oplan Bantay Laya*), over 600 activists across the country had been killed. These activists include Lumad anti-mining activists in Mindanao. In 2009, Leodinio 'Manong Dos' Monson, the chairperson of *Nigkahiusa Koy Mag-uuma to Boston* (NIGKOMB), council member of PASAKA and *Kusog sa Katawhang Lumad sa Mindanao* (KALUMARAN), and a staunch anti-mining leader, was killed. Mining activists' family members have not been spared. In 2012, the pregnant wife and two young children of a B'laan leader and anti-mining activist, Daguil Capion, were killed. By 2015, Lumad leaders began to characterize their plight as a form of ethnocide. Even when Lumads are not necessarily mobilizing against mining activities, they face the threat of death. In April 2016, thousands of farmers marched demanding government relief to address widespread hunger as consequence of El Niño conditions in the North Cotobato, Mindanao city of Kidapawan, which caused massive crop failures. Police and the armed forces violently dispersed the protesters, leading to deaths and injuries. The incident has come to be known as the Kidapawan Massacre.

Mobilizing in the 'belly of the beast'

Despite the threat of death, anti-mining activists in Mindanao remain undeterred. Lumads, along with the broader national democratic movement represented by the BAYAN alliance in the Philippines, have made concerted efforts to globalize their resistance to mining, relying in particular on BAYAN's international member organizations in the diaspora, most notably those in the 'belly of the beast', the United States. BAYAN-USA has deep links with other Filipino organizations. Indeed, many, if not most, Filipino organizations, regardless of their ideological and political orientation, share a common concern with homeland issues. BAYAN-USA works closely with those groups who share its analysis of Philippine issues and programs in whole or in part.

Following the Kidapawan Massacre, for instance, BAYAN's US-based member organizations immediately launched a letter-writing campaign addressed to President Aquino and copied to key US members of congress. BAYAN-USA noted, 'As people in the U.S. we are the constituents of these congresspeople, and our letters and letters especially from organizations based in the U.S. help convey how important this issue is and that there are people in the U.S. who care about'. In their letters to the Philippine president, BAYAN members made the following demands:

An immediate investigation of the incidents above to be conducted by independent bodies;
An end to the continued harassment and intimidation of Lumad in and out of their communities;
The immediate withdrawal of government troops from the Lumad communities;

Unconditional release of the more than 70 Kidapawan farmers brutally dispersed, illegally arrested and unjustly detained;

The disbandment of all paramilitary groups;

The Philippine Government to terminate its counterinsurgency program Oplan Bayanihan, which victimizes innocent and unarmed civilians; and

The Philippine Government to adhere to the Universal Declaration of Human Rights and all the major Human Rights instruments that it is a party and signatory.[5]

Beyond BAYAN-USA, the International Coalition for Human Rights in the Philippines (ICHRP) was formed in 2015 by concerned Filipinos in the Philippines and throughout the diaspora, together with Lumad community representatives, to specifically raise awareness about human rights abuses under the Aquino government and, more importantly, to highlight the complicity of the US government in those abuses. Indeed, it was prompted in large part by a Philippine police campaign, 'Operation Exodus', which occurred in Mamasapano, Maguindanao, in the Mindanao region, and led to the deaths of 60 people, military personnel, guerillas, and civilians alike. The area is controlled by the Moro Islamic Liberation Front, or MILF, with whom the government had signed a 2014 ceasefire and peace treaty. What has surfaced is that prior to what has now come to be known as the 'Mamasapano incident', the Philippine National Police-Special Action Force (PNP-SAF), which carried out the campaign, involved US military personnel in campaign planning. 'Operation Exodus' was supposedly aimed at the capture of two of the United States' Federal Bureau of Investigation's (FBI) 'most-wanted' persons. However, the PNP-SAF failed to coordinate with the Armed Forces of the Philippines or the MILF in their capture. Instead, a 12-hour firefight ensued, leaving dozens dead. Investigations of the incident have not only revealed US involvement, but that the Philippine president was briefed about the planned operation, and ultimately sanctioned it. For communities in Mindanao, 'Operation Exodus' is evidence both of the Philippine state's utter disregard of Lumad life, as well as of the United States' continued intervention in Philippine affairs to advance its own geopolitical agenda. ICHRP was formed to expose this. Its first major activity was to convene the International Peoples

Tribunal (IPT) on Crimes of the US-Aquino Government Against the Filipino People in Washington, DC. As stated by Vanessa Lucas of the US-based National Lawyers Guild, one of the conveners of the IPT together with ICHRP, 'The Mamasapano operation raises questions over the extent of the US military's involvement in Philippine domestic security'.

In addition to working with groups such as BAYAN-USA and ICHRP, the Lumad community, moreover, sent representatives to appeal directly to the American people, including its sizeable Filipino-American population. While the Lumads have gone through conventional channels to secure international support (e.g. appealing to the United Nations, international human rights groups, and the like), what is distinctive about their work is their direct connections with members of the Filipino diaspora. For the Lumad community, US-based Filipinos are an especially important constituency to organize and mobilize support from, given the United States' role in militarizing Mindanao. In the southern Philippines, as in Marag and other areas of the Philippines, the United States' 'global war on terror' has served as a pretext for the Philippine government to sanction military and paramilitary activities such as *Oplan Bantay Laya* (and later *Oplan Bayanihan*) that ultimately aim to quash anti-mining and other forms of indigenous resistance.

Through the progressive coalition of Filipino-American organizations, the National Alliance for Filipino Concerns (NAFCON), as well as the BAYAN-USA and ICHRP network and the Lumads, toured university campuses, including Stanford University, as well as churches, to speak about their struggles as part of the 'Lakbay Lumad USA' campaign.

Even before the Lumad's 2016 tour of the United States, however, NAFCON had already launched an 'Adopt a Community' campaign in 2015 to provide material support for Lumad communities. According to Ryan Leano, NAFCON Southern California Coordinating Staff Member, the focus of the project for 2016 is to 'bring clean water to 300 members of the Talaingod-Manobo tribe who have very little access to water and are struggling to protect their ancestral land from militarization and multinational logging and mining companies'.[6] Indeed, Lumad leaders joined 200 allies in the 'Lakad: 5K for the Lumad' walk-a-thon organized by NAFCON to raise funds for its clean water campaign for the Talaingod-Manobo tribe. A June 2016 report from a NAFCON member who visited Sitio Dulyan, Talaingod, Davao Del Norte in Mindanao indicates that a new water system was completed and now serves the four hundred residents of the community.

Beyond the Lakay Lumad USA tour, Filipino-American urban-based cultural workers, such as those associated with URBAN x INDIGENOUS (UxI), have taken the initiative to draw connections between their experiences of displacement as a consequence of gentrification with the Lumad experience of displacement.[7]

Postscript

As I was completing the research and writing for this chapter, the Philippines elected a new president, Rodrigo Duterte, in May 2016. While many have debated why this outsider to national politics managed to win the elections, arguably the strength of the Philippine left more broadly, as well as Lumad mobilization in Mindanao more specifically, can be said to have played an important role. Duterte was the mayor of Davao City in Mindanao when he launched his campaign. Though his abrasive language has invited comparisons to US President Donald Trump, Philippine President Duterte and Trump radically diverge in terms of ideology. Duterte is a self-described socialist. Indeed, he garnered support from radicals and progressives across the country for his anti-mining stance and his support for the Lumad community. Since he has come into office, he has appointed an anti-mining advocate, Gina Lopez, to the position of Department of Energy and Natural Resources Secretary. Moreover, he publicly declared, 'I have a big problem with mining companies. They are destroying the soil of our country'.[8]

The Duterte administration has also demonstrated openness to resuming peace talks with the National Democratic Front (NDF), which has served as the governing body for many Filipinos, including Lumad communities, where the Government of the Republic of the Philippines (GRP) has completely abandoned them. The NDF is led by the Community Party of the Philippines (CPP), and its armed wing, the NPA, has been engaged in an over 40-year-old civil war with the Philippine state. Even the GRP, under Duterte, recognizes that the civil war in Mindanao is fueled by the social and cultural marginalization of Lumad communities and, perhaps more importantly, the complete disregard to, and respect for, their ancestral domain claims. Organizations such as the ICHRP and NAFCON have been mobilizing US–Filipinos to sign online petitions to support the peace talks.

How the Lumads actually fare under this administration remains to be seen. As former Congressman Mong Palatino puts it, '*Ang lumalabang Lumad, hindi si Duterte, an tanglaw ng Mindanao*' (Lumad fighters, not Duterte, are the torch for Mindanao).[9]

Notes

1 These incursions are legally sanctioned as a consequence of liberalized mining policies, but are also illegal in the sense that they sometimes fall outside the scope of legal mining.

2 See www.mgb.gov.ph/images/links-images/ThePhilippineMinerals IndustryAtAGlance.pdf [accessed 14 April 2017].

3 See www.katribu.org/content/about-us [accessed 14 April 2017].

4 Excerpted from press statement issued on 13 October 2009, 'Peasant groups to launch 2-day caravan for relief, struggle for land reform and justice to victims of human rights abuses',

forwarded by a university professor based in the Philippines.

5 *Ibid.*

6 Excerpted from a press statement issued on 25 April 2016. Alex Montances, NAFCON Southern California, sc@nafconusa.org, is listed as contact.

7 See www.somarts.org/urbanxindigenous/ [accessed 14 April 2017].

8 See www.reuters.com/article/us-philippine-politics-mining-idUSKCN0YQ0MZ [accessed 14 April 2017].

9 See http://bulatlat.com/main/2015/11/13/ang-lumalabang-lumad-hindi-si-duterte-ang-tanglaw-ng-mindanao/ [accessed 14 April 2017].

References

Golay, F. (1995). 'Economic consequences of the Philippine Trade Act'. *Pacific Affairs*, 28(1): 53. doi:10.2307/2753711.

Gonzalez, V.V. (2013). *Securing Paradise: Tourism and Militarism in Hawai'i and the Philippines*. Raleigh, NC: Duke University Press.

Harvey, D. (2003). *The New Imperialism*. Oxford: Oxford University Press.

Hawes, G. (1987). *The Philippine State and the Marcos Regime: The Politics of Export*. Ithaca, NY: Cornell University Press.

Holden, W.N. (2005). 'Civil society opposition to nonferrous metals mining in the Philippines'. *VOLUNTAS: International Journal of Voluntary and Nonprofit Organizations*, 16(3): 223–49. doi:10.1007/s11266-005-7723-1.

Holden, W. (2012). 'A neoliberal landscape of terror: extrajudicial killings in the Philippines'. *ACME: An International E-Journal for Critical Geographies*. Available at: http://ojs.unbc.ca/index.php/acme/article/viewFile/924/778 [accessed 8 August 2016].

Holden, W., Nadeau, K., and Jacobson, R.D. (2011). 'Exemplifying accumulation by dispossession: mining and indigenous peoples in the Philippines'. *Geografiska Annaler: Series B, Human Geography*,

93(2): 141–161. doi:10.1111/j.1468-0467.2011.00366.x.

McKay, S. (2006) *Satanic Mills or Silicon Islands? The Politics of High-tech Production in the Philippines*. Ithaca, NY: Cornell University Press.

Padios, J. (2012). *Listening Between the Lines: Culture, Difference, and Immaterial Labor in the Philippine Call Center Industry*. PhD Dissertation, New York University. Available at: http://search.proquest.com/docview/1038821783?accountid=14505 [accessed 8 August 2016].

Rodriguez, R.M. (2010). *Migrants for Export: How the Philippine State Brokers Labor to the World*.

Minneapolis, MN: University of Minnesota Press.

SAPRIN (2004). *Structural Adjustment: The SAPRIN Report: The Policy Roots of Economic Crisis, Poverty and Inequality*. London: Zed Books.

Simbulan, R.G. (2016). 'Indigenous communities' resistance to corporate mining in the Philippines'. *Peace Review*, 28(1): 29–37. doi:10.1080/10402659.2016.1130373.

Wenk, I. and Shirler, L. (n.d.). *The Tampakan Copper-Gold Mine Project in Mindanao, Philippines*. Available at: www.academia.edu/22416968/The_Tampakan_Copper-Gold_Mine_Project_in_Mindanao_Philippines [accessed 8 August 2016].

8 | COAL POWER AND THE SUNDARBANS IN BANGLADESH: SUBALTERN RESISTANCE AND CONVERGENT CRISES

Sourayan Mookerjea and Manoj Misra

Introduction

On 4 April 2016, police opened fire on a demonstration by a group of landless labourers, farmers, fisherfolk, and salt producers against a proposed coal-fired power plant in Banshkhali, Bangladesh. Four people died and more than 30 were injured. The villagers had good reasons to fear that the power plant would irreparably damage the local environment, and would therefore destroy their livelihoods. A few days before, on 10 March, the National Committee to Protect Oil, Gas, Mineral Resources, Power and Ports (henceforth NCBD) and other like-minded groups organized a 145-kilometre, four-day 'long march' from the capital city of Dhaka towards Rampal, the site for another 1,320-megawatt (MW) coal-fired power plant. The Rampal plant is facing intense resistance in Bangladesh, both from the grassroots and civil society groups. The plant would not only endanger the livelihoods of locals, but also adversely affect the ecosystem of the Sundarbans, a UNESCO world heritage site. In a separate incident on 26 August 2006, three people were killed and hundreds were injured as law enforcers opened fire on agitation against an open-pit coal mine and an associated power plant in Phulbari. The protesting villagers argued that the open-pit mine would dangerously threaten the livelihoods of more than 500,000 people living in the area. The common thread that unites these three struggles is the opposition to land acquisition by the state and the fear of livelihood losses in the wake of coal power development.

It would hardly be an exaggeration to argue that cheap fossil fuel – predominantly coal-powered capital accumulation – lies at the heart of industrial capitalism's spatial expansion from the nineteenth century onward. Bangladesh is rather a late entrant in this long history of coal. However, the moderate but consistent economic growth that Bangladesh has been having over the past two decades has greatly increased its appetite for cheap electricity. According to the 2010 Power System Master Plan (PSMP), the country aims to achieve a long-term gross domestic product (GDP) growth rate of 7 per cent up to year 2030. This would require electricity supply in excess of 37,500 megawatts (MW) vis-à-vis the current (2016) installed capacity of 12,000 MW. The PSMP envisions domestic and imported coal fuelling 50 per cent of this increased capacity. For the record, coal's contribution to electricity generation is presently around 3 per cent (MoPEMR 2011). As of now, the current government has initiated 10 separate mega coal-fired power plant projects across the country to generate 11,370 MW of electricity.

Yet, Bangladesh is also extremely vulnerable to climate-change-related flooding, sea-level rises, tropical cyclones, tidal surges, and saline water intrusion (Misra 2016b). It is among the top five climate-vulnerable countries on the Global Climate Risk Index (Harmeling and Eckstein 2012). Coal power is a major source of greenhouse gas emissions and therefore a major contributor to global warming. A series of World Bank studies indicate that climate change will increase salinity and will thus contribute to drinking and irrigation water shortages in the coastal regions. This will in turn adversely affect agricultural and fisheries production, the main sources of livelihoods there. The reports conclude that such changes will lead to increased incidence of poverty, out-migration of working-age adults, and dependency ratios (Dasgupta *et al.* 2010), undermining the benefits, if not prospects, of growth, as well as rendering the prioritization of extending the rural reach of electricity supply for household consumption, an oft-cited justification for the coal power buildup, pointless.

This chapter examines the politics of resistance to this contradiction and to the convergence of social, ecological, political, and economic crises in play therein. We retell here the story of the emergence of local resistance to the Rampal power plant project, its articulation with a nationwide protest movement primarily through organizational efforts of the NCBD, which then brings on board the support of Bangladesh's more mainstream environmental organizations, and ultimately attracts an international campaign opposing the development carried on through the transnational networks of a globalized environmental movement. The chapter focuses on the *network* form of resistance and interrogates its ideological-political constellation by contextualizing this development and its resistances, both in our current great recessionary conjuncture and in the *longue durée* of the colonial-capitalist world system. We propose a *post-Western* Marxist and *decolonizing* critique, and resituate the local resistance to the power plant project as also resistance against forest destruction *and* a neocolonial land grab, a local-global networked multitude's resistance against accumulation by dispossession, *but resistance limited by neocolonial accumulated violence.* Crucial to our interrogation of local resistance here is its inability to invent a politics that would address the problem of landlessness and informalization that is interwoven with this instance of development dispossession but remains invisible to the network of national and transnational politics. This local mode of subalternization holds important movement building lessons for the networked multitude form of social justice environmentalist activism. We take these up in our conclusion. The chapter begins by providing background on the Rampal coal-fired power plant project and the criticisms of it.

Rampal power plant in the neoliberal vortex

The proposed 1,320-megawatt (MW) Rampal thermal coal-fired power plant is a joint venture initiative between the Bangladesh Power Development Board (BPDB) and the Indian National Thermal Power Corporation (NTPC) at a cost of US$1.68 billion. The governments of Bangladesh and India signed a Memorandum of Understanding (MoU) on 11 January 2010 to set up two 660 MW capacity coal-fired power plants in the Sapmari Katakhali and Kaigar Daskati areas of Rampal upazilla (sub-district) under Bagherhat district in Bangladesh. Later, on 30 August 2010, the BPDB and the NTPC signed another MoU as the lead agencies on behalf of their respective governments. On 29 January 2012, the two state-owned companies formed a private joint venture company on a 50:50 equity basis – the Bangladesh-India Friendship Power Company Pvt. Limited (BIFPCL) – under the Bangladesh Companies Act 1994 to build the power plant. The BPDB and NTPC will supply 30 per cent of the project cost and the remaining 70 per cent will be financed through external loans (CEGIS 2013).

The Rampal plant is an integral part of the government's larger plan to set up a special economic zone (SEZ) in Mongla to transform the southwest region of Bangladesh. The plant is strategically located 14 kilometres northeast from the existing Mongla sea port. The government has signed another contract with the Orion group, a private sector firm, to set up a separate 630 MW coal-fired power plant in Burirdanga, Mongla. The planned Mongla SEZ will be initially established on an area spanning 205 acres, gradually extended to 9,098 (base case scenario) acres by 2020 (PwC 2015).

This preoccupation with economic growth and energy development is a product of Bangladesh's recent neoliberal reintegration into the world economy. One of the defining moments of this reintegration occurred when the country implemented an IMF-sanctioned three-year medium-term adjustment programme under the Structural Adjustment Facility (SAF) loan in 1986–1987, followed by another three-year loan in 1990 under the Enhanced SAF loan initiative. The adjustment programmes aimed to transform Bangladesh from a primarily agricultural protectionist to a market-oriented economy, and to stimulate growth powered by the private sector. During the first SAF loan, agriculture constituted 42 per cent of the country's GDP, which declined to 12 per cent by 2014–2015. Concurrently, the industrial sector's contribution tripled from 10 per cent to 28 per cent, while employment in this sector increased by a modest 6 per cent (Misra 2016a).

Despite GDP growth rates hovering in the 5–6 per cent range over the past two decades, the formal sector currently employs 7.3 million workers, while the informal sector employs 50.8 million (BBS 2015). Moreover, a significant number of these formal sector jobs are concentrated in the export-oriented ready-made garment industry, which pays below poverty line wages. Further, the neoliberal reforms have led to increased income inequality and pauperization, particularly in rural areas. Between 1991–1992 and 2010, the Gini coefficient (an index of 'zero'means no inequality and 'one'denotes absolute inequality) for income inequality in rural areas increased from 0.243 to 0.431, indicating a sharp 77 per cent increase in rural areas vis-à-vis 47 per cent in urban areas. The same trend is visible in the declining share of income accruing to the bottom five deciles of rural households (Misra 2016a). Moreover, according to World Bank data from 2000, fully 50 per cent of rural agricultural households are functionally landless (Khan 2004: 85). Thereby, the growth-oriented economic policies have led to a systematic dispossession of peasant farmers, and the subsequent increase of rural wage dependency, landlessness, internal migration, and informalization of the workforce (Misra 2016a).

There is also an important geopolitical dimension to the Rampal development. Several commentators argue that the Rampal plant is meant to be a demonstration of India's firm backing of the current Sheikh Hasina-led Awami League government. India–Bangladesh relations have seen major improvements under Hasina's rule. Bilateral relations between the two countries nosedived during the previous Bangladesh Nationalist Party (BNP) regime, as India accused the BNP of colluding with the Inter-Services Intelligence agency of Pakistan and harbouring anti-India elements to destabilize the northeastern states of India. After the Hasina government returned to power in 2009, it cracked down on anti-India elements in Bangladesh and handed over several arrested separatist leaders to India. It also reoriented the country's foreign policy focus by visibly adopting a pro-India stance. In return, India rewarded the Hasina government by exporting electric power and providing coal energy development aid in order to help it retain the support of middle-class civil society.

The Sundarbans in danger The Rampal project has attracted intense local, national, and international criticism over its possible adverse effects on the ecosystem of the Sundarbands – the largest contiguous mangrove forest in the world and the natural habitat of the Royal Bengal Tiger. The Sundarbans is a protected wetland under the Ramsar Convention. In 1999, the government classified the Sundarbans Reserve Forest and a buffer zone extending up to 10 kilometres of its perimeter as an Ecologically Critical Area (ECA) (CEGIS 2013: 1–2). Although the Rampal plant is located 14 kilometres north of the remaining expanse of the Sundarbans, it is only 4 kilometres away from the ECA. Besides the Royal Bengal Tiger, the forest is home to 334 plant and 693 wildlife species, the endangered Ganges and Irrawardy River dolphins, and many other fish, reptiles, birds, amphibians, and invertebrate species (Banktrack 2015; Shafi *et al.* 2009). Already, industrial activity around the forest, conversion of forest land for agricultural purposes, illegal timber harvesting, poaching, shrimp farming, and increasing salinity resulting from the diversion of Ganges River water by India are endangering the forest and its flora and fauna (Biswas *et al.* 2007; Shafi *et al.* 2009). Civil society and environmentalist organizations argue that the establishment of the coal-fired power plant in such close proximity to the Sundarbans ECA will further damage the vulnerable biodiversity of the forest.

The Sundarbans protects the coastline and acts as a natural defence against soil erosion and saltwater intrusion from the Bay of Bengal (Shafi *et al.* 2009). It also shields the mainland from the devastating impacts of tropical cyclones, storms, and tidal waves (Banktrack 2015). The forest offers a range of products, including 'timber, pulpwood, fish, thatching materials, and honey' (SAHR 2015: 8), which supports the livelihoods of 500,000 people in the surrounding areas (Chowdhury 2015). The Rampal plant will use 4.72 million tons of imported coal annually. This massive amount of coal will be transported through the Passur River and other waterways that bisect the Sundarbans. The extensive dredging required to restore navigability of the Passur River for coal transportation would impact fish habitat (CEGIS 2013). Environmentalists worry that any accidental spillage of this coal will cause irreparable damage to the sensitive ecosystem and fish habitat of the Sundarbans region, thus jeopardizing the livelihoods of fisherfolk. As such, on 9 December 2014, an oil tanker carrying 350,000 litres of furnace oil capsized in the Shela River in the Sundarbans, which quickly spread oil throughout 500 square kilometres of the forest (Chowdhury 2015). The government, lacking expertise and capacity, asked the local community to clean up the spill. An official assessment noted that the spill led to severe loss of income and adverse health impacts for the local community (UNEP/OCHA Environment Unit 2015: 5). On 19 March 2016, another cargo vessel carrying 1,235 tons of coal capsized in the same river. These frequent accidents betray the government's assurance that no harm will come to the Sundarbans from the transportation of coal.

According to the eminent environmental scientist Dr. Abdullah Harun Chowdhury (2016), who has been studying the impacts of climate change on the flora and fauna in the Sundarbans region since 2007, the Rampal plant will have grave consequences on the livelihoods of communities living in and around the Rampal area. The plant will withdraw 9,150 cubic metres of water per hour from the Passur River, and in turn will discharge 5,150 cubic metres of water back into the river after treatment. The temperature of this cooling water will be considerably warmer than the normal river water. This discharge of water at an elevated temperature is likely to cause thermal pollution by altering the ambient temperature of the river water, thus endangering fish and other aquatic life. Further, the leaching of toxic-heavy metal residues – arsenic, lead, mercury, nickel, radium, cadmium, chromium, etc. – from the fly ash generated by the power plant will severely pollute the river and nearby agricultural fields. Moreover, people in this region generally use surface water sources for drinking and household purposes due to the brackish water in shallow underground aquifers. Dr Chowdhury thus argues that the power plant will not only lead to the destruction of livelihood options of local communities by contaminating the fish habitats and agricultural fields; it will also lead to public health emergencies in the surrounding areas by having harmful health effects. The power plant therefore renders the people of Rampal doubly victim – an unnecessary anthropogenic victimization of a community that faces the wrath of nature on a regular basis and whose future is disproportionately mortgaged to climate change.

The Rampal land grab The process by which land was acquired for the Rampal project played an important role in generating resistance to the development. On 2 January 2012, 1,834 acres of land in Rampal district was handed over to the BPDB in a process fraught with irregularities, and even before the project obtained site clearance and environmental clearance (SAHR 2015: 9). Only 86 acres of this acquisition was *khas* land (state-owned), and the rest was privately held for residences, agriculture (rice and vegetables), and shrimp farming (Chowdhury 2012: 2).

Land acquisition by the government of Bangladesh falls under two juridical domains. First, Bangladesh's constitution establishes both the right of private ownership of land and establishes the power of the state to acquire privately held land for a public purpose, with compensation. Second, the Acquisition and Requisition of Immovable Property Ordinance of 1982 defines the contemporary statutory regime for land acquisition by the state (Al Atahar 2013: 308).[1] This act specifies a two-step process for acquisition whereby the local district administration must give notice of the government's plan allowing for affected local people to register objections and apply for compensation, the second step of the prescribed process. Once this is completed, the district administration is supposed to issue a second notice, ordering the payout of compensation and concluding the transfer. According to local accounts, however, thousands of landless people were driven off the land between the two prescribed steps with the help of police and mercenaries through force and intimidation. Landless people with traditional, customary, and wage-derived entitlements to land and forest have no standing in the land acquisition law, and these people seem to have completely disappeared from the arena of the conflict and its space of politics. They were not even extended the inadequate World Bank devised Project Affected Persons resettlement and rehabilitation scheme, established after the Jamuna Bridge project fiasco (Al Atahar 2013: 312).

The Environmental Impact Assessment (EIA) report eventually conducted by the government agency CEGIS estimates that the Rampal project displaced about 150 households, or about 700 people (CEGIS 2013: 362). A grassroots leader interviewed for this research disputed this figure, and claimed that the actual number of displaced households was in the order of several thousands. Most independent reports also corroborate his claim. Interestingly, instead of performing an actual headcount of the displacees, the EIA cites the 2011 national census to estimate the number. However, the government had already forcibly acquired the land and had begun to evict people living in the project area well before the impact assessment began. This perhaps better explains the unusually low number of households reported in the assessment. The government, moreover, chose not to carry out any studies of the possible impact on livelihoods in the area or of the scope of potential displacement, either before or during the acquisition process. The government reportedly relocated 18 landless households to nearby Foyla cluster village. However, a monitoring report by CEGIS notes that four of these households have already left the cluster village, lacking any income-generating opportunities. The rest are also feeling insecure as the government has yet to transfer the legal title of allocated houses under their names (CEGIS 2015: xx–xxi).

According to locals, many of the over 3,500 claims for compensation by landowners were refused. Those who received compensation were given substantially less than the market value of land and the government did not set up any independent land valuation process. The compensation was further reduced by as much as 20 per cent by the necessity to pay out bribes to move the claims forward. In the first phase of the project, 400 acres of land was acquired in this way and was passed into the hands of ruling party members, who are now operating shrimp farms while the project is delayed (SAHR 2015: 11). The CEGIS monitoring report further notes that the compensation the landowners received was inadequate to purchase land in neighbouring areas. The prices of land in neighbouring districts were already higher than in Rampal, and the construction of the power plant and other infrastructure in the area further increased land prices. Most landowners could not profitably invest the compensation money in the absence of suitable investment opportunities. They ended up depositing the money in banks, which they are using to meet up their everyday consumption needs (CEGIS 2014: xviii, 179–180).

Loss of livelihood, the actual and substantial costs of resettlement, and training for and finding new work are not addressed by the legislative framework at all, which otherwise provides no check preventing more land being acquired than actually needed, as reported is the case here by a fact-finding mission by the South Asians for Human Rights (SAHR 2015: 10).

Network resistance of the multitude

We turn now to the story first of the emergence of local resistance to the Rampal development, and then its articulation to national and ultimately to transnational networks. The story begins with a rumour: according to a local resistance leader, the government apparently claimed some time in early 2010 that it would acquire land in Rampal to set up a car manufacturing plant. Later, locals learned that the land would be used for a coal-fired power plant. Since the majority of the land within the project site is privately owned agricultural and shrimp-farming land, affected landowners approached the local member of parliament (MP) to arrange relocation of the plant in the nearby government-owned *khas* land. However, the MP turned them away, demanding they drop their opposition to the power plant. At this point, in 2011, landowners in the area decided to organize themselves and form a protest committee under the banner of *Krishi Jomi Roksha Sangram Samity* (Association for the Protection of Agricultural Land).

This *Sangram Samity* mostly consisted of members of the existing *Sapmari Katakhali Shrimp Gher Defence Committee*, an association for shrimp-farm owners in the area. Initially, they staged demonstrations within the locality with the limited aim to save their land from acquisition. Interestingly, this threat of dispossession brought two usually antagonistic classes – landowners and labourers who work for the former – in an uneasy alliance against the power plant. In an interview with us, a leader of the *Sangram Samity* narrated their continual experience of violence, intimidation, and harassment ever since they launched the resistance. He recounted how law enforcement agencies and local goons of the ruling alliance violently pursued protesters, physically assaulted them, and vandalized their property. One leader's house was burned down during the visit of an anti-Rampal civil society delegation. When he went to report the incident, police officers interrogated him about his political affiliations and involvement with the delegation instead. False court cases were filed against several leaders to weaken the resistance. As these pressure tactics proved ineffective, the government forcibly evicted landless labourers from the area to break this key political alliance and restrict the ability of the movement to organize mass demonstrations. Support for the movement, however, was thus far scant outside the immediate locality of the project, since others were yet to comprehend the broader environmental implications of the power plant.

Soon thereafter, *Sangram Samity* leaders made a strategic decision to open a parallel legal battle. They contacted lawyers in Dhaka, and through them filed a writ petition with the High Court in February 2011 seeking an injunction on the Rampal land acquisition and power plant construction. The Court passed an interim stay order following a hearing; however, the Attorney General hastily moved the Court, successfully arguing that the stay order would jeopardize bilateral relations between Bangladesh and India on the eve of the Indian Prime Minister's impending visit later that year. The Court then recanted its previous order. Subsequently, *Save the Sundarbans*, an environmental organization, filed two other writ petitions with the High Court against the Rampal power plant, all of which are pending as of writing this chapter (SAHR 2015: 31).

While the *Sangram Samity* leaders were in Dhaka for the court case, they met with several national organizations. Until this point, the environmental ramifications of coal power were unknown to the *Sangram Samity*. They were primarily concerned about saving their land. Interaction with the NCBD, the Center for Human Rights, and other environmental organizations helped them grasp the grave environmental catastrophe facing them. Soon, they formed alliances with these organizations and transformed the localized resistance into a national movement. Fortunately for them, the NCBD had already amassed considerable experience in organizing broad-based resistance movements.

With the entry of these national organizations, the protagonists and the framing of the story of protest would change. With the landless labourers driven off, the local protesters now grew to include not only agricultural-aquacultural landowners, but also other occupational groups living in nearby areas – such as honey collectors, woodcutters, and fisherfolk – whose livelihoods would be equally affected in the long run. Of course, this network of stakeholders' engagement with and commitment toward the resistance varies greatly. What catalysed their participation, however, is a concerted awareness campaign launched by the environmental organizations. The timely release of Dr Chowdhury's research on the ecological implications of the power plant played its part in galvanizing public opinion. Not surprisingly, therefore, saving the Sundarbans and the Royal Bengal Tiger became the sound-bite demand, displacing the earlier focus on land issues.

The role of the NCBD in the protest needs to be distinguished from other environmental organizations. As its member-secretary Anu Muhammad noted to us, it is a loose collective of leftist activists and intellectuals who are in principle opposed to foreign ownership of national resources. Its origin is rooted in the mid-1990s struggle against the foreign corporate takeover of natural gas fields in Bangladesh. Since then, it has led several vigorous resistance movements, the most notable of which is the anti-Phulbari coal mine protest. So far, the NCBD has organized two successful mass protest marches (in 2013 and 2016) to Rampal, thereby garnering attention from prominent domestic and international media outlets. The government tried to block these agitation plans by resorting to violence and cracking down on protest marchers at different stopovers. While the NCBD's involvement and its mass support pushed the government onto the back foot, it has also allowed the latter to deliberately mischaracterize the protest as an anti-India movement.

As opposed to the confrontational and popular front approach of the NCBD, other participating environmental organizations in the Rampal protest can be roughly characterized as pro-development, green capitalist, reformist, and more attuned to educated middle-class interests. These organizations include the Bangladesh Poribesh Andolon (environment movement) (BAPA), the Bangladesh Environmental Lawyers Association (BELA), Waterkeepers Bangladesh, and several other foreign-funded environmental nongovernmental organizations (ENGOs). These groups enjoy considerable support among environmentally conscious urban middle-class constituents. In most cases, they adopt quieter, behind-the-scenes, and litigation-based protest tactics, preferring to avoid any direct on-the-street confrontation with the authorities. There are nevertheless some crossovers between the memberships of the NCBD and the main-stream environmental organizations.

These national organizations and ENGOs belong to transnational environmentalist networks, and through them accounts of protest marches and demonstrations organized by the NCBD began to circulate in both activist circles and the international media. Consequently, transnational advocacy organizations, such as the Sierra Club, Greenpeace, 350.org, and UNESCO, openly criticized the Rampal project, effectively forcing several prominent international financiers to pre-emptively disassociate from the project. This network-of-networks configuration of protest has been theorized as 'the multitude' (Hardt and Negri 2004; Virno 2004), a conceptualization that, despite its problems, to which we return later, usefully frames such protests in relation to the question of class politics, which many strands of green thinking of course claim to have become irrelevant. Nonetheless, in our appropriation of the concept here, we use it to name a character, indeed a network of characters, in our story of resistance (Mookerjea 2013).

Which then brings us to the antagonists of this story, the constellation of interests pursuing the construction of this and other coal-fired power plants, as well as a growth-at-all-costs development agenda. While the current government of Bangladesh is the one actor most commonly invoked here, especially in news accounts of the issue, the notorious difficulty of naming this character of the story holds an important political lesson standing at the heart of this chapter's argument, as we shall see. This group includes the majority members of the ruling alliance – the Bangladesh Awami League and its allied parties – from the national to the local levels, who are one of the most obvious beneficiaries of the current development agenda. We would also classify the de facto opposition party, the Bangladesh Nationalist Party (BNP), in this group. Although the BNP voiced its opposition to the Rampal plant, this seems to be empty rhetoric aimed at scoring cheap political points. The party has yet to announce any substantial agitation against the plant, nor does it have any intention to do so. Moreover, we have already noted the role of the government of India, as well as industrial interests in both countries and elsewhere. But along with the political establishment is an affiliated techno-scientific community that is predominantly in favour of the Rampal plant, including experts from the World Bank, to those in Bangladesh's universities, professions, middle-class urban neighbourhoods, and agencies such as the Power Board. That such a (trans)national hegemonic bloc of political identities would also qualify for designation by the concept of the multitude is not only its key problem, and indeed its contradiction, but would also seem to confirm those green arguments ready to declare the irrelevance of class politics to that of environmental conservation and climate change. The burden of our argument in the rest of the chapter will then be to explore how the political struggle over the Rampal project is also shaped by the deepest stakes of class politics. But in order to grasp how so, we will need to go beyond the limits of contemporary Western Marxism and understand how capital's colonial history remains at work as a modern cultural infrastructure of power in world capitalism today.

Reflections on subaltern multitude contradictions of local resistance

As we have noted above, this local development conflict needs to be understood both in terms of the broader (geo)politics of planetary scale energy transition and its regional unfolding. India, in particular, has rivalled the People's Republic of China in building coal-fired electric power generators in the name of development, and both India and Bangladesh have commitments to the construction of a contiguous industrial and transportation corridors with mega-ports in the

Bay of Bengal able to access world markets. Such spatial restructuring of built and natural environments and the forms of development dispossession that frequently enough attend them are often critically analysed in terms of David Harvey's (2003) theory of 'accumulation by dispossession'.

Harvey's conception of resistance to accumulation by dispossession, however, remains colonial-Western. We argue here that both the conflict surrounding the Rampal power plant project, as well as the conjunctural situation in which countries such as Bangladesh are placed in the crossfires of development interests in favour of expanding coal-based power and green and social justice interests opposing such development, can be best understood by supplementing the theory of accumulation by dispossession with the theoretical perspectives of the colonial matrix of power (Quijano 2000) and social reproduction or 'subsistence perspective' ecofeminism (Federici 2004; Mies 1998). At stake here is not merely the opposition, indeed, contradiction, between two visions of development, progress, the good life, collective flourishing, or the satisfaction of needs. Rather, this opposition between subaltern and governmental visions of the good life or of development entails a contradiction between common wealth and capitalist wealth, and presupposes the history of colonialism, which sets in place the terms of this opposition in the first place. In this regard, the paramount importance of Federici's and Quijano's feminist and decolonizing interventions rests with their critical demystification of the appearance of the inevitability and historical necessity of capitalist development, a perspective they share with the local honey collectors, fishers, and others directly dependent upon the Sundarbans itself.

There can never be any resistance or protest without there also being stories of resistance, through which those who resist understand what they are doing and what else they might be able to do. In this chapter, we have retold such a story as it was told to us, and as it is being retold in Bangladesh and elsewhere. But in our telling of it, we introduced the character of the multitude to describe the network of networks form of the resistance. The character of the multitude, moreover, also poses a question regarding the relationship of this resistance to class politics. The relevance of this question may not be obvious since the issues at hand may seem quite distant, say, from the sweatshops of Bangladesh's ready-made garment export industry, even though any buildup of electrical power capacity would continue to be allocated for the productive consumption of that industry. From the theoretical perspective of post-Western Marxism (and a social reproduction feminist one at that), the question of gendered class is not primarily a question of *who* resists, nor a question *how* one resists, though these obviously remain important matters. But when one is preoccupied with question of who resists or with questions of how to resist power, which strategies and tactics to take up, thinking about resistance as a story is helpful, as it enables us to consider the question of *what the stakes of the story of resistance are: what in the world actually happens in and through resistance?* In the case of this story about Rampal, this is where the second character we have introduced, the subaltern, becomes significant.

In this regard, it is important to note some of the contradictions of the resistance to Rampal across each scale. Both the national and transnational mobilizations made much of the Sundarbans as a special place in their rhetoric and their publicity, but in different ways. While international media accounts and environmentalist websites refer to the Sundarbans in terms of UNESCO world heritage and environmental conservation discourses (Kelly 2011), emphasizing the importance and rarity of mangrove forests, tigers, and dolphins, the people who also belong to this ecosystem are most often represented by an estimation of their demographic magnitude. All this is reproduced in the national environmentalist mobilization. But now the resistance discourse also borrows heavily from a recent symptomatic formation of Bangladeshi nationalism. In the decades following neoliberal structural adjustment, and as social inequality has deepened, a compensatory hegemonic nationalism has been constructed around the Sundarbans as an imaginary and affective landscape with the formidable Royal Bengal Tiger (now also the namesake of Bangladesh's national cricket team) as its emotional mascot. While this formation reaches back to literary and aesthetic reimaginings of the Sundarbans by an anti-colonial Bengali nationalism dating from the late nineteenth century, this imagined and felt landscape gained new powers during the global campaign to elect seven natural wonders by a Swiss-based marketing organization – the New7Wonders foundation. Prime Minister Sheikh Hasina seized this opportunity and launched an ambitious countrywide campaign in October 2010, and instructed every ministry to pitch in. Massive numbers of Bangladeshis voted in the campaign to elect the Sundarbans as one of the new seven wonders of the world. Bangladesh was thereby globally rebranded as an emergent market, a full member of the pride of Asian Tigers, especially in the eyes of the hopeful urban middle class.

The significance of this strange symptom of Bangladeshi nationalism may be unpacked this way: as a place in the world economy that was deindustrialized over the eighteenth century and then experienced the colonial restoration of serfdom, after which the vast majority of people depended upon subsistence agriculture and agroforestry for their livelihoods, even during its more recent step into dead-end industrialization, it is not at all surprising that the Sundarbans would occupy the place it does in the Bengali political unconscious. In the direct and vital conflict between land ownership and landlessness, the lines of division and struggle are clear-cut to both parties. But for a collectivity where this social relation has been not only urbanized, but further subjected historically to the accumulated violence of patriarchal colonialism, partition, war, and most recently structural adjustment, the question of where one belongs, socially and politically, becomes in emotion and imagination as convoluted and as ever-snaking as the famous waterways and sandbars of the delta itself.

The social and political relation of subalternity is always articulated by a historical and cultural space. Even for urban Bengalis, the deltaic ecosystem remains a half-remembered dream, in the stories of Bonbibi and Dokhin Rai (Jalais 2010), for example, of a different possibility of collective identity and common wealth from that promised by capitalist-corporate development that also remains as elusive as a dream. In leading the national-scale mobilization, the NCBD tapped this ideological complex with resounding success, especially among urban multitudes, but not without paying a high price. For its professed official positions are somewhat contradictory, opposing the Rampal project on environmental grounds and yet failing to categorically reject coal power on nationalist ones or break with the dead end of 'catch-up' development and growth. This contradiction in the position of the left wing of the urban national resistance is shared by some elements of the transnational environmental left as well, who have been persuaded by Indian and Bangladeshi capital that there are no other alternatives for the development of the poor in these countries.

Rampal's invisible and disappeared: resistance to coal power development sets the stage for social revolution

As we have noted, the first group of people to have been dispossessed as land began to be taken up for the Rampal power plant were landless labourers, men, women, and children working on the margins of shrimp aquaculture, agroforestry, and rural services. No one seems to know where they have gone, and we can only presuppose that they now swell the ranks of the informal sector in urban centres in Bangladesh and India. The luckiest of them may have found employment in the sweatshops of Bangladesh's export manufacturing sector. In this way, the world-scale process of proletarianization predicated on industrial development also gives rise, as Federici and social reproduction feminism argue, to innumerable processes of subaltern feminization, through which women, but not only women, continue to be relegated to invisible or informal or precarious zones of the global social division of labour.

In the case of Rampal's disappeared, they are invisible to the justice offered by Bangladesh's laws; they are invisible to the architects of the government's Vision 2021 and the Perspective Plan of 2010–2021, and other economists and planners who are proud of Bangladesh's steady 6 per cent growth rates, and for whom coal energy remains a cheap and necessary strategy of development (Rahman 2016); they are invisible to consultancy firms such as PricewaterhouseCoopers and the McKinsey group who develop policy for hapless governments; they are invisible also to mainstream environmental conservation movements and other such friends of the Royal Bengal Tiger (Chakrabarti 2009); they have even slipped through the cracks of the NCBD's capacities to mobilize a broad-based 'multitude' to protest the Rampal development. This invisibility is the dialectical obverse of the colonial visibilities generated by the East India Company's land survey attending its translation of the colonial principle of eminent domain to the subcontinent (Bhattacharyya 2015), which disenfranchised the landless from legal justice.

Moreover, this colonialist invisibility continues as the modern, cultural matrix of power for contemporary postcolonial governance of what Partha Chatterjee (2008) describes as 'political society'. This process of subalternization-feminization is a symptom of the impossibility for national development within world capitalism to ever be in any way universal, to ever be anything more than the power and privilege of a minority. The mobilization of resistance against the Rampal power plant has not as of yet developed a political strategy that addresses this problem. While the state's land grab, a class project, initially provoked a moment of tactical solidarity between small farmers and landless labourers, this was soon broken up by the state's repressive apparatus. But in the subsequent mobilization, especially at the national scale, the potential to build a strategic politics of solidarity between Bangladesh's subalternized landless multitude and the (trans)national multitude remains within reach, given the Sundarbans' utopian intermediation of commongrounding (Mookerjea 2016). This is where social reproduction feminism's distinction between common wealth and capitalist wealth provides a useful turning point for resistance. The creation of common wealth, as opposed to capitalist wealth, requires a national power development plan that would prioritize the immediate subsistence needs of the 50 million Bangladeshis relegated to the informal sector, instead of intensifying the export sector. It would need to prioritize the food sovereignty of all Bangladeshis, but especially the 50 per cent who are essentially landless. The protection of the Sundarbans points towards such an eco-political-economic restructuring. Resistance to coal power development in the Sundarbans sets the stage for such a social revolution.

Note

1 The Ordinance was amended in 1994. In addition, the government enacted two separate infrastructure development project-specific land acquisition laws, the Jamuna Multipurpose Bridge Project Land Acquisition Act of 1995 and the Padma Multipurpose Bridge Project Land Acquisition Act of 2007.

References

Al Atahar, S. (2013). 'Development project, land acquisition and resettlement in Bangladesh: a quest for well formulated national resettlement and rehabilitation policy'. *International Journal of Humanities and Social Science*, 3(7): 306–19.

Bangladesh Bureau of Statistics (BBS) (2015). *Labour Force Survey 2013*. Dhaka: Ministry of Planning, GoB.

Banktrack (2015). *Equator Principles Analysis of the Rampal Coal-Fired Power Plant Project, Bangladesh.* Available at: www.banktrack. org/ems_files/download/rampal_ equator_principles_full_analysis_ pdf/rampal_equator_principles_full_ analysis.pdf [accessed 30 June 2016].

Bhattacharyya, D. (2015). 'History of eminent domain in colonial thought

and legal practice'. *Economic &
Political Weekly*, 50(50): 45–53.

Biswas, S.R., Choudhury, J.K., Nishat,
A., and Rahman, M.M. (2007).
'Do invasive plants threaten the
Sundarbans mangrove forest of
Bangladesh?' *Forest Ecology and
Management*, 245(1): 1–9.

Center for Environment and Geographic
Information Services (CEGIS) (2013).
*Final Report on Environmental
Impact Assessment 2X (500–660)
MW Coal Based Thermal Power Plant
to Be Constructed at the Location
of Khulna*. Dhaka: Government of
Bangladesh.

Center for Environment and Geographic
Information Services (CEGIS) (2014).
*First Quarterly Monitoring Report of
Second Year*. Dhaka: BIFPCL.

Center for Environment and Geographic
Information Services (CEGIS) (2015).
*Third Quarterly Monitoring Report of
Second Year*. Dhaka: BIFPCL.

Chakrabarti, R. (2009). 'Local people and
the global tiger: an environmental
history of the Sundarbans'. *Global
Environment*, 3: 72–95.

Chatterjee, P. (2008). 'Peasant cultures
of the twenty-first century'. *Inter-
Asia Cultural Studies*, 9(1): 116–126.

Chowdhury, A.H. (2012). 'Environmental
impact of coal based power plant
of Rampal on the Sundarbans and
surrounding areas'. Unpublished
article.

Chowdhury, A.H. (2015). 'Study
of impacts of oil spill on the
Sundarbans mangrove forest of
Bangladesh'. *Journal of Asiatic
Society of Bangladesh*, 41(1): 75–94.

Chowdhury, A.H. (2016). Personal
communication, 17 February.

Dasgupta, S., Huq, M., Khan, Z.H.,
Ahmed, M.M.Z., Mukherjee, N.,
Khan, M.F., and Pandey, K.D. (2010).
'Vulnerability of Bangladesh to
cyclones in a changing climate:

potential damages and adaptation
cost'. *World Bank Policy Research
Working Paper No 5280*.

Federici, S. (2004). *Caliban and the
Witch: Women, the Body and
Primitive Accumulation*. New York:
Autonomedia.

Hardt, M. and Negri, A. (2004).
*Multitude: War and Democracy in the
Age of Empire*. New York: Penguin.

Harmeling, S. and Eckstein, D. (2012).
*Global Climate Risk Index 2013: Who
Suffers Most from Extreme Weather
Events? Weather Related Loss Events
in 2011 and 1992 to 2011*. Bonn:
GermanWatch e.V.

Harvey, D. (2003). *The New Imperialism*.
London: Verso.

Jalais, A. (2010). *Forest of Tigers: People,
Politics and Environment in the
Sundarbans*. New Delhi: Routledge.

Kelly, A.B. (2011). 'Conservation practice
as primitive accumulation.' *Journal
of Peasant Studies*, 38(4): 683–701.

Khan, M.H. (2004). 'Power, property
rights and the issue of land reform:
a general case illustrated with
reference to Bangladesh'. *Journal of
Agrarian Change*, 4(1–2): 73–106.

Mies, M. (1998). *Patriarchy and
Accumulation on a World Scale:
Women in the International Division
of Labour*. London: Zed Books.

Ministry of Power, Energy and Mineral
Resources (MoPEMR) (2011). *Power
System Master Plan 2010*. Dhaka:
Government of Bangladesh.

Misra, M. (2016a). 'Is peasantry dead?
Neoliberal reforms, the state and
agrarian change in Bangladesh'.
Journal of Agrarian Change.
doi:10.1111/joac.12172.

Misra, M. (2016b). 'Smallholder
agriculture and climate change
adaptation in Bangladesh:
questioning the technological
optimism'. *Climate and Development*.
doi:10.1080/17565529.2016.1145101.

Mookerjea, S. (2013). 'Epilogue: through the utopian forest of time'. *Canadian Journal of Sociology*, 38(2): 233–254.

Mookerjea, S. (2016). 'The convergence of crises and the crisis of representation'. *Toxic Media Ecologies Symposium*. 12 March, Intermedia Research Studio, University of Alberta.

PriceWaterhouseCoopers (PwC) (2015). *Pre-Feasibility Report: Mongla Economic Zone*. Dhaka: Bangladesh Economic Zone Authority.

Quijano, A. (2000). 'Coloniality of power and eurocentrism in Latin America'. *International Sociology*, 15(2): 215–232.

Rahman, M.M. (2016). *Outlook of Bangladesh Economy in the 'Double-Dip' Global Recession*. Dhaka: Microcredit Regulatory Authority of Bangladesh.

Shafi, M., Islam, N., and Gnauck, A. (2009). 'Threats to the Sundarbans mangrove wetland ecosystems from transboundary water allocation in the Ganges basin: a preliminary problem analysis'. *International Journal of Ecological Economics & Statistics*, 13(W09): 64–78.

South Asians for Human Rights (SAHR) (2015). *Report of the Fact Finding Mission to Rampal, Bangladesh*. Colombo: SAHR.

UNEP/OCHA Environment Unit (2015). *Sundarbans Oil Spill Assessment: Joint United Nations/Government of Bangladesh Mission December 2014*. Geneva: UNEP/OCHA.

Virno, P. (2004). *A Grammar of the Multitude: For an Analysis of Contemporary Forms of Life*. New York: Semiotext(e).

PART II

AFRICAN REGION

9 | RESISTING ACCUMULATION BY DISPOSSESSION: ORGANIZATION AND MOBILIZATION BY THE RURAL POOR IN CONTEMPORARY SOUTH AFRICA

Lalitha Naidoo, Gilton Klerck, and Kirk Helliker

Introduction

The extreme levels of socioeconomic inequality in South Africa are strikingly epitomized by the access to and use of its land. The legacies of colonial conquest, primitive accumulation, and racial oppression were crystallized in legislation, dating back to the nineteenth century, which systematically confined 80 per cent of the population to 13 per cent of the land. The destructive consequences of and the internecine struggles against the racial inequalities in land distribution in South Africa are extensively documented in scholarly publications. To be sure, the ways in which these processes unfolded in South Africa are paradigmatic examples of accumulation by dispossession (Arrighi *et al.* 2010). The conditions and struggles of (black) workers and dwellers[1] on (white) commercial farms, especially during the post-apartheid period, have not received the same levels of scholarly attention. Yet, the appalling working and living conditions of many farm workers and dwellers in South Africa are vividly captured in official statistics and formal enquiries. For example, research by the Employment Conditions Commission in 2001 found that the average farm worker earned as little as ZAR 544, or US$39[2] per month! The Commission also found: farm workers generally did not receive any overtime pay; there was widespread employment of children of 14 years and younger; pregnant female workers did not get paid maternity leave; only one in four children on commercial farms had a secure source of food, and almost a third were at risk of hunger; farm workers had the lowest rates of literacy in the country; there were stark gender differences in the allocation of employment benefits; and there was a cycle of debt, together with high interest rates, either to farm shops or directly to the farmer (Department of Labour 2001).

Notwithstanding the subsequent introduction of mandatory minimum wages, little has changed in the fortunes of most farm workers since 2001. Violent protests in 2012 by workers on some Western Cape farms received extensive media coverage and underscored the continuing plight of farm workers. Such palpable and collective forms of action by farm workers, however, are exceptional, sporadic, and largely disconnected from the day-to-day struggles and experiences of the vast majority of farm workers. The working and living conditions of these workers resemble those of a pre-industrial proletariat. The far-reaching controls exercised by farmers over the *working and living conditions* of farm workers permeate all aspects of their employment relationship. Consequently, the plight of farm workers is rooted not merely in their employment conditions, but also in their want of tenure security, their position at the fringes of national priorities, and the woeful inadequacy of infrastructure and services in the rural areas. Moreover, reframing dispossession and reparation in terms of both a social wage and a secure livelihood, as Hart (2004) convincingly shows, is an effective way of rearticulating race and class.

Despite formidable obstacles, farm workers and dwellers have opposed the impositions of their employers and the government through variegated forms of resistance and social mobilization. This chapter focuses on the modes of organization and the modalities of resistance deployed by *Phakamani Siyephambili*[3] in opposition to the enduring processes of deprivation, oppression, and exploitation. The discussion draws on research conducted by the East Cape Agricultural Research Project (ECARP), a non-profit organization based in Grahamstown, which supports farm workers, dwellers, and small-scale farmers in the Eastern Cape by promoting agrarian transformation. The rise of oppositional movements in South Africa demanding the redistribution and decommodification of (among others) land, water, electricity, medical services, and education typify precisely what Harvey (2003) identified as the struggles generated by accumulation through dispossession. However, as Hart (2004: 13) cautions, accumulation through dispossession may be 'a useful first step in highlighting the depredations wrought by neoliberal forms of capital, but it needs to be infused with concrete understandings of specific histories, memories, meanings of dispossession'. If we are to take seriously the notion of dispossession as a recurrent process, it must be understood as spatio-temporally specific, emergent, and multifaceted. In practice, therefore, strategies that draw on dispossession as a continuous process must engage with 'specific local configurations of social forces and material conditions, but also extend out from there to connect with forces at play in regional, national, and transnational arenas' (Hart 2004: 16). Part of the reason for this, according to Hart, is that 'developmental local government', as espoused by the African National Congress (ANC) government, has become 'a key locus of contradictions of the post-apartheid order, helping to expose the vulnerable underbelly of neoliberal capitalism' (Hart 2004: 16).

Accumulation by dispossession in South Africa's agrarian political economy

Accumulation by dispossession, as a hallmark of the increasingly predatory 'new imperialism', forcefully promotes the 'super-exploitation' of labour, especially in developing countries. The gendered and racialized modalities of contemporary capitalist accumulation, as well as the increasing number of landless rural workers in the South, bear testimony to the scale of dispossession and accentuate the increasing interrelationship between (uprooted or marginalized) small-scale farmers and precarious wage labourers (Batou 2015). *Phakamani Siyephambili*, located in the Eastern Cape province of South Africa, is a social movement that rose out of and through the struggles of farm workers and dwellers on commercial farms, as well as small-scale farmers, who received land through the post-apartheid government's land reform programme. While the current context and experiences of these rural social groupings are partially divergent, they are confronted by and vulnerable to, similar forms of dispossession; hence, their united action to form a social movement. In addition to the fact that most small-scale farmers, who are members of *Phakamani*, were farm workers or dwellers before acquiring land (i.e. common experiences of class), the sweeping and militant struggles against apartheid provided fertile soil for solidarity in the contemporary struggles of the rural poor in South Africa (i.e. common experiences of race). The struggles of *Phakamani* are informed by both the colonial past (which, in South Africa, includes the periods of segregation and apartheid) and the waves of dispossession wrought by the neoliberalizing regulatory changes intensified under the ANC government.

The evolution of agriculture under colonialism and apartheid-capitalism has been documented in detail (e.g. Beinart *et al.* 1985; Bundy 1988; Greenburg 1980; Morris 1976). Dispossessing African peasants of their means of subsistence (shelter, land, tools, etc.) and the commons (fuel, water, game, etc.), thereby converting them into a labour force, was a necessary but not sufficient condition for the establishment and consolidation of (white) capitalist farming. A politico-institutional factor (in the form of the state, law, police, taxation, etc.) was additionally required to link dispossession to accumulation. Under apartheid, the institutional framework of power ensured that white farmers were highly organized and subsidized, sheltered by price controls and protected markets, and guaranteed a captive and disempowered workforce. This situation was obviously untenable after the abolition of apartheid. When the ANC-led government assumed power in 1994, it pursued a dualistic reform strategy: accelerated neoliberal restructuring of the agrarian political economy and the introduction of a series of labour market changes. On the one hand, the extension of labour laws to the agricultural sector and the introduction of land and tenure reforms were significant departures from the apartheid era, when farm workers and dwellers were subjected to super-exploitation, systematic discrimination, and grinding poverty (Marcus 1989). On the other hand, market-led land reform, liberalized agricultural product markets, the elimination of subsidies, appallingly low agricultural minimum wages (AMW), and the privatization of some essential services led to the persistence of previous forms as well as the emergence of new manifestations of accumulation by dispossession in contemporary South Africa. Arguably, the post-apartheid era has brought on multiple dispossessions for low-waged, landless farm workers and dwellers, as well as the 'beneficiaries' of land redistribution. These conditions constitute the terrain on which the rural dispossessed seek to 'rise up and move forward' in the quest to forge alternatives to contemporary forms of capitalist accumulation.

Multiple forms of accumulation by dispossession prevail in contemporary South Africa. In the agrarian political economy, the critical areas of collective insecurities felt by the rural poor and that arise through various neoliberalizing policies relate to landlessness and tenure insecurities, liberalized product markets, the segmentation of agricultural labour markets, low wages and unfair labour practices, and a generalized absence of essential services (such as decent housing, water, energy, schools, and medical services). Government-driven restructuring is locked into a neoliberal framework that fosters the continuation, from the apartheid-capitalist era, of various forms of dispossessions and associated power inequalities (within and between classes and racial groups, women and men, and urban and rural communities). In this chapter, two critical issues (to farm workers/dwellers and small-scale farmers) are singled out for discussion: namely, land and labour. These issues bring to the fore the neoliberalizing agenda of transformation and the various manifestations of accumulation by dispossession in the agrarian context.

Labour and dispossession Contemporary South Africa is one of the most unequal societies in the world. Low wages and disparities in wages across labour markets are major contributors to the high levels of inequality in the country. Historically, agricultural wages have been the lowest of the goods-producing sectors of the South African economy. In addition to the dynamics of dispossession, there were also certain sectorally specific dynamics to wage formation. As Arrighi *et al.* (2010) show, most of the increases in African wages after the early 1950s occurred in industries that were most in need of a stable workforce (manufacturing, transport, and communication), whereas in agriculture, where the stabilization of labour mattered least, the increase in wages was minimal. These sectoral disparities continue into the present. For instance, in 2013, the median monthly earnings in the agricultural sector was ZAR 1,733 while it was ZAR 3,672 for manufacturing and ZAR 6,000 for mining (SSA 2014). As Harvey (2003: 149) notes, low wages are one of the inevitable outcomes of the processes of accumulation by dispossession.

Given the absence of collective bargaining and the unacceptably low wages engendered by market forces, the ANC government intervened by setting statutory minimum wages for the agricultural sector. The AMW rates are adjusted annually in March, and for March 2015 to February 2016 the hourly rate was ZAR 13.37 and the monthly rate amounted to ZAR 2, 606.78. The AMW received

an unprecedented increase of 52 per cent in March 2013 following
the extraordinary 2012 uprising of farm workers in the Western Cape
over 'starvation wages'. The striking workers demanded ZAR 150
per day, and in so doing were revolting against the low statutory wage
(Visser and Ferrer 2015). While the demand for ZAR 150 per day
was not met – partly because economists advising the Department
of Labour predicated major job losses if that rate was imposed – the
strike projected farm workers and low wages in the sector into the
public arena and compelled the Department to re-examine statutory
wage rates for the sector.

An extremely modest AMW as well as non-compliance with
statutory duties combine with poor and substandard living conditions
to depress the overall quality of life of farm workers and dwellers.
ECARP's work on the living conditions of workers and dwellers
supports the findings of an ILO report on the mushrooming of
squatter camps in and around commercial farms that are devoid
of essential services and amenities, such as housing, water, and
sanitation. Most of those who are compelled to set up shelter in these
camps are farm workers and dwellers who, despite the protections
contained in the Extension of Security of Tenure Act (ESTA), have
been evicted from farms. Hence, a growing mass of landless, under-,
and unemployed people are forced to sell their labour power for
exceedingly low wages and work under conditions akin to sweating.
Other features in the sector emulating the 'sweated trades' of the
eighteenth and nineteenth centuries include the harsh and strenuous
nature of work tasks, especially in horticulture and packhouses (tied
to global value chains), where the pressure to meet targets is extreme
and relentless. In many cases, workers are not adequately protected
against the pesticides used to spray fruit and vegetables, and workers
in the Sundays River Valley complain of outdated and dangerous
machinery used in the orchids, farms, and packhouses.

Land and dispossession Land and agricultural reform in post-
apartheid South Africa are shaped by a neoliberalizing 'rule regime',
which was heavily influenced by the World Bank, IMF, and other
Northern regulatory institutions. Land redistribution is based on
the 'willing-buyer, willing-seller' principle, which has been widely
condemned by land rights activists as the major obstacle to a
redistribution programme that will transform the racially skewed

agricultural land ownership patterns in South Africa. The state-led land reform programme, in each of its many iterations, remains firmly wedded to neoliberalism. Following the introduction of the current land redistribution strategy, known as the Proactive Land Acquisition Strategy (PLAS), the Recapitalisation Programme (Recap) was set up ostensibly to support PLAS tenants in consolidating a productive farming system. In terms of Recap, tenant farmers are to elicit the services of mentors or strategic partners, who will 'train' them to be 'productive'. But, in reality, there is little or no support for PLAS farmers in general, and only a mismatched and haphazard extension service exists for aspiring farmers who received land through this programme. All the small-scale farmers and micro-food producers, who are members of *Phakamani Siyephambili*, lack basic farming equipment and are therefore unable to increase the productive capacity of their plots. Consequently, they invariably remain outside established agricultural value chains and are unable to tap into formal markets. Furthermore, the land and agricultural reform strategies pursued by the post-apartheid government are largely inimical to small-scale farming based on the principles of ecologically sustainable food sovereignty.

Two immediate implications arise from the above-mentioned conditions, which have a direct bearing on the dynamics of accumulation by dispossession in the South African agrarian context. First, land reform and distribution as well as agricultural restructuring, as regulated through PLAS and the Recap, entrench the extant industrial complex of farming and food production, which pits large-scale farms and intensive production processes against small-scale, agro-ecology and micro-food producers. Extensively liberalized product markets in the sector only serve to bolster the market position and power of the well-established, large-scale (predominantly white) farmers and agro-processors. Second, and relatedly, most mentors and strategic partners tend to be white males, who are deeply entrenched in the prevailing, Fordist models of farming. This, as the findings from ECARP's research on PLAS and Recap show, entrenches the inequalities between strategic partners and small-scale farmers, farm workers, and dwellers, thereby exacerbating the collective insecurities of poor, rural social groups (ECARP 2013). For example, landless stockowners have been deprived of the land they used to graze their livestock, and hundreds of farm workers and dwellers working and living on farms in the Sundays River Valley have been evicted. Consequently, these people were compelled to set up a squatter settlement on privately owned land. They face another round of evictions as commercial farmers seek to 'enforce their property rights'.

Similar examples are the farm worker equity schemes and Agri-BEE (the ANC's agricultural version of Black Economic Empowerment). These form part of the market-driven land reform programme and involve the government purchasing shares in farming or agro-processing businesses on behalf of workers. ECARP has identified a number of cases where little, if any, benefit accrues to farm worker 'shareholders' (Naidoo 2006). Even in the highly profitable, export-orientated sub-sectors, such as citrus and deciduous fruit, workers complained bitterly about flaws in the equity schemes, ranging from not being fully informed about their purposes and functions to not receiving any dividends since the schemes were introduced.

Formation of *Phakamani Siyephambili*

On 16 March 2013, *Phakamani Siyephambili* was launched by farm workers and dwellers from 65 farm committees and 11 area committees located in five local municipalities and two district municipalities (Amathole and Cacadu), together with small-scale farmers from collectives that make up the Cacadu Small-Scale Farmers' Association. With the support of ECARP, a great deal of groundwork aimed at organization and mobilization preceded the setting up and launch of *Phakamani*. This signals an alternative way of initiating democratic and 'bottom-up' collectives among rural social groups, which have historically proven to be very challenging to organize and mobilize.

The manifesto of *Phakamani Siyephambili* notes that it is a 'non-partisan, non-sexist movement that brings together farm workers, farm dwellers, and small-scale farmers in and around the districts of Cacadu and Amathole . . . who strive for a society in which unity, equality, and democratic values thrive'. Furthermore, it will 'fight for a society in which all and not a few benefit'. *Phakamani* works towards arriving at a comprehensive understanding of the underlying causes of structural poverty, systemic inequality, and continuing discrimination in South Africa in general, and in the agrarian political economy in particular. It consciously adopted a broad and inclusive view of these underlying causes and their consequences for the rural poor. In large measure, this thinking bears the mark of the social groups that comprise the movement; that is, people living and working on commercial farms and small-scale farmers, who fall outside or operate on the periphery of organized civil society and prevailing value chains.

Phakamani Siyephambili has its roots in the grassroots structures that began to emerge on commercial farms in the Makana Municipality in the Eastern Cape soon after the AMW became mandatory in 2003. Frustrated by commercial farmers' selective compliance and/or non-compliance with core labour standards, including the mandatory wage rates, farm workers and dwellers began to organize and mobilize into farm committees. By setting up these collectives, workers and dwellers resisted and dismantled the committees set up by farmers, which were designed to meet farmers' needs and satisfy their interests to the detriment of the interest and needs of workers and dwellers. Thus, in setting up collectives, workers and dwellers took action to tackle a long-standing lack of collective organization and the persistent inequalities in bargaining power between them and commercial farmers.

Overcoming divisions and finding new ways of organizing Naidoo's (2011) account of the early formation of the farm committee movement in areas around the Makana Municipality not only points to the conditions that inspired the formation of these collectives against neoliberalizing processes and multiple dispossessions, but also depicts the resolve of farm workers and dwellers to build solidarity and unity among all who lived and worked on the farms. Hence, farm committees comprise both workers and dwellers, workers on standard and non-standard contracts, and men and women who are connected to the farm. Building solidarity between the different groups of people on the farm through the farm committee served to undermine the divisions between the people who resided and worked on the farm. The all-inclusive strategy pursued in the formation of farm committees may be distinguished from the traditional, trade-union-based model of organizing on farms, which tends to prioritize full-time, permanent (often male) workers on large-scale farms and agro-processing industries.

Social relations among farm committee members, especially between women and men, also began to transform. On many farms, women, who are often underemployed or unemployed (dwellers) on the farms, were the prime drivers in the formation of the committees. Men, in many instances, feared that the employer would victimise them and dismiss them if they played a leading role in setting up collective structures on the farms. Women recognised the significance of organizing into collective structures to challenge and resist neoliberal forms of restructuring by both commercial farmers and government officials. Social mobilization as a countermovement to neoliberalization and prevailing labour market divisions propelled women into leadership roles in the formation and functioning of the committees. Even in the early stages of the farm committee movement, women assumed positions in the executive structures of the committees.

The formation of the farm committees and the structures that followed are radically different from the traditional ways of organizing at the site of production followed by trade unions in South Africa. For farm workers, as Klerck and Naidoo (2003) point out, the sites of production and social reproduction are combined at the same geographical location. Historically, workers on commercial farms were dependent on farmers for both employment and for other essential human needs such as housing, transport, and food. The production/social reproduction nexus necessitates alternative forms of collective organization that are grounded in the realities of the low-waged agricultural labour market. The collectives at the different levels that now make up *Phakamani Siyephambili* represent an example of an alternative, perhaps more appropriate way to organize, mobilize, and struggle in the agrarian context of contemporary South Africa.

The notion of the collective began to spread to other farms and areas as word got around about the efficacy of farm committees in challenging commercial farmers' non-compliance with labour and tenure laws. Workers and dwellers on other farms learnt how the farm committees started to make rights self-enforcing (i.e. not reliant on external agencies), thereby compelling farmers to pay them independently of impositions by external agents such the Department of Labour, NGOs, and/or trade unions. As the number of farm committees increased, they began to consolidate to form area committees. Mobilization at the grassroots levels unfolded across multiple geographical locations in the Cacadu and Amathole districts. In certain areas and agricultural sub-sectors, mobilizing and organizing were adapted to suit the varying conditions of workers and dwellers. For example, in the large-scale, export-oriented citrus sub-sector, it is not always possible to set up farm committees that link to an area committee. This is because of the large number of seasonal and migrant workers who are present in the orchids and packhouses for short periods in the production process.

Moreover, in citrus-growing areas at a distance from major towns and cities, worker and dweller fears about reprisals from farmers, should they initiate any form of collective organization and action, are more intense as compared to areas closer to major towns. For these reasons, workers in the citrus orchids and packhouses, and on vegetable farms, in the Sundays River Valley and Ncxuba municipalities opted to join existing area committees, or set up area committees without farm committees. The specific structure that collectives assume, therefore, differs in the various areas and sub-sectors of agriculture to suit local conditions.

The flexibility in forms of mobilization, membership, and organizational structure of *Phakamani Siyephambili* is further reflected in the participation of small-scale farmers in the movement. Close to 90 per cent of the small-scale farmers with *Phakamani Siyephambili* membership are former farm workers and dwellers who lost jobs and tenure on farms. Small-scale farmers, as with workers and dwellers on farms without farm committees, participate in *Phakamani*'s activities in the area and municipal committee levels. *Phakamani*'s broad-based membership displays solidarity building among and across the different categories of the rural poor and/or dispossessed. At the same time, it denotes a level of homogeneity in the extent of insecurities, vulnerabilities, and inequalities that result from multiple forms of accumulation by dispossession at the sites organized by *Phakamani Siyephambili*.

Structure of Phakamani Siyephambili Established relationships between the members of *Phakamani Siyephambili* predate the setting up of the social movement. To be sure, the farm workers, farm dwellers, and small-scale farmers who launched *Phakamani* had an established record of joint struggle and campaigning (discussed below). A deep sense of camaraderie was forged among members before setting up the movement. This solidarity also had a profound impact on how members viewed their representation in the executive or leadership of the movement. As the leadership of the area committees comprises representatives of each farm committee in a particular geographical area, the leadership structure of *Phakamani* comprises of representatives from each area committee. Small-scale farmers from each farm also have their representatives in the executive structure of *Phakamani*. A flat or horizontal executive structure exists – there is no chairperson, vice chairperson, or secretary. Members are adamant that these roles are shared so as not to create differences in power and authority in the movement. Women and men have 50 per cent representation on the executive structure, as is the case with the farm and area committees.

Since its inception in 2013, *Phakamani Siyephambili* has continued to expand, numerically and geographically. This is due to the increasing number of farm and area committees that linked up with the movement at the different levels. Established members play an active role in initiating structures and encouraging and advising others on the formation of collectives. At the time of writing, the movement comprises of 75 farm committees and 16 area committees stretching across five municipalities.

The movement has links and networks with similar movements across the Eastern Cape province and South Africa. The interactions with other movements require that the members of *Phakamani Siyephambili* continuously reflect on its distinct identity, aspirations, political beliefs, and action plans so as not to compromise its own transformation agenda, while simultaneously being supportive of and involved in common struggles. Similar issues face the movement as it participates in multi-stakeholder dialogue forums, which require the members to guard against co-option or becoming 'soft' on the transformation agenda through their engagements with government officials and commercial farmers.

Politics of rural struggles and resistance

Humble beginnings As mentioned above, members of *Phakamani Siyephambili* started campaigning for decent working and living conditions, as well as for access to land for agriculture, years before the launch of the movement in 2013. The significant year for the future members was 2003 when the AMW became binding. From the early 1990s, a series of labour laws was extended to the agricultural sector, including the Labour Relations Act, the Basic Conditions of Employment Act, and the Unemployment Insurance Act. With the introduction of these laws, farm workers were regarded as 'employees' – as opposed to 'servants' who were subservient to their 'masters' – for the first time in South Africa's history. A simultaneous process unfolded on the land front with the promulgation of ESTA, which regulated the tenure conditions of farm workers and dwellers on commercial farms.

Yet, workers and dwellers on commercial farms are unable to enjoy the provisions of the various labour and land legislation fully for a variety of reasons. A primary reason is the gross inequality in bargaining power between workers (and dwellers) and commercial farmers, which prevented the institutionalization of a rights-based culture in the sector. This situation was compounded by the absence of vigorous and consistent enforcement strategies by the labour and land ministries. Consequently, workers continue to labour and live under conditions reminiscent of apartheid-capitalism. The AMW changed this and gave workers and dwellers the necessary power to organize, made labour and tenure rights self-enforcing, and encouraged them to think (and act) beyond simply ameliorating the prevailing state of affairs.

The first campaign that workers and dwellers embarked on was to enforce the AMW. They directed their dissatisfaction with the lack of proper labour inspections on farms at the Department of Labour at a meeting held in 2004 in Grahamstown. The Masonic Hall in the town was packed with hundreds of workers who came from across the Makana municipality and from various livestock and game farms. They were mandated to inform the Department of Labour about the lack of government enforcement and non-compliance by farmers with all the major labour standards (Naidoo 2011). Much to the chagrin of the Department of Labour officials present, workers sang freedom songs that spoke of their dispossessions and collective precariousness and insecurities, and they demanded the immediate enforcement of labour standards.

Building on early victories This engagement was a success for workers on many levels. First, they took their dissatisfaction with the dismal state of labour relations on commercial farms in post-apartheid South Africa directly to the provincial head of the Department of

Labour. ECARP's fieldwork shows that this engagement yielded positive results as labour inspections were intensified, resulting in improvements in working conditions and in levels of compliance with the AMW rates. Second, the engagement and improved labour inspections lifted the spirits of workers and dwellers, and increased the numbers joining the struggle. Social mobilization intensified as an increased number of workers and dwellers began to organize and debate the next moves to claim their labour and land rights. Labour provisions were invariably targeted for enforcement because they had clear implementing mechanisms in contrast to those for land, housing, and other services that were highly centralized and bureaucratized.

In 2005, farm workers and dwellers, supported by small-scale farmers and ECARP, took to the streets when they marched to the offices of the Department of Labour demanding more labour inspections and alternative methods of conducting inspections (Makana Farm Committees 2005). They carried banners and placards with words displaying their anger at low wages, substandard working and living conditions, the racist attitudes of farmers, and the seeming inability of the Department of Labour to enforce its own legislation. This was the first overt form of struggle that farm workers embarked on in the province, empowering them to shed off the sense of intimidation and fear they harboured in asserting their rights. Workers' actions were path-breaking in the context of the almost invisible and totally disempowered position that (black) people living and working on (white) commercial farms have experienced historically. The 2005 march was followed by a series of other marches and demonstrations against the slow pace of socioeconomic redress in the agrarian sector in various areas of the Eastern Cape. Alongside the campaigns and engagements, social mobilization gained new momentum as the idea of the collectives and the power to march and demonstrate began to expand to other geographical sites and incorporate other agricultural sectors such as dairy, fruit, and vegetables. As a result, farm and area committees emerged in other municipalities in the Cacadu district from 2003 onwards, and these became adept at making labour regulations self-enforcing.

Broadening and deepening the struggle Questions around land rights, access, and control started to gain increasing prominence in the agenda of the collectives from 2004/2005 onwards. Workers and dwellers were particularly concerned about tenure insecurity and the eviction of workers and dwellers from farms. Hence, land campaigns soon took hold in the collectives. Through this, a critique of the industrial complex of agriculture started to develop and links with small-scale farmers began to emerge. Solidarity with small-scale farmers started to be solidified in the struggles over pro-poor land reform and agricultural restructuring. At a dialogue forum in 2006, small-scale farmers joined forces with farm workers and dwellers in challenging the provincial Land Affairs Minister regarding the neoliberal land and agricultural reforms pursued by the government.

This gathering brought together farm workers, farm dwellers, and small-scale farmers from across the Eastern Cape and various government departments concerned with agricultural and land issues. The event, organized with the support of land rights NGOs, provided the platform for people to articulate their dissatisfaction with the pace, direction, and outcomes of the government's land and agricultural reform strategies. Moreover, it sparked the process that enabled committee members to frame an alternative agrarian transformation agenda with the birth of *Phakamani Siyephambili* several years later. The demands made by people on land and agricultural support at the event clashed with the neoliberal framework and policies of the government. A schism began to emerge between poor rural people's vision of agrarian change and the requirements of the government's market-led land and agricultural reform programme, which was intensified in the years to follow with the implementation of PLAS and Recap.

Campaigning and social mobilization started to intensify in the Sundays River Valley in the Cacadu district and in municipalities in the Amathole district. Workers in the citrus packhouses and orchids began to join workers and dwellers from livestock, dairy, game, and fruit and vegetable sub-sectors, as well as small-scale farmers, in broadening the agrarian transformation agenda. Workers in the export-oriented citrus sub-sector initiated a series of engagements and campaigns, which effectively challenged the structure of the citrus value chain, the distribution of wealth along the chain, and the power vested in retailers nationally and internationally that source citrus from South Africa. These struggles are ongoing and target retailers, labour standard audits, the Department of Labour, the national Directorate of Labour, the Employment Conditions Commission, and organized citrus growers' associations.

Overt struggles and daily forms of resistance are now acted out at multiple levels by all farm and area committees across geographical scales under the banner of *Phakamani Siyephambili*. Farm and area committees continue to self-enforce and defend labour and tenure rights at farm, packhouse, and area levels. There are many examples of the stronger and more confident members safeguarding and protecting the rights and interests of the unorganized and less powerful. For example, members of well-established area committees in the Zuney and Groetvlei areas recently challenged farmers, who violated several labour and land rights of workers and dwellers in less established structures in these areas. Apart from ongoing struggles to enforce labour and tenure rights, *Phakamani* also strengthens struggles around land access, service delivery, housing, education, and access to medical services.

Building democratic structures and cultures   Phakamani Siyephambili and the various structures that comprise the movement emanate from grassroots, bottom-up, and organic processes. The struggles that are waged are rooted in the real experiences of farm workers, dwellers and small-scale farmers, and they direct and control these struggles. The movement in many ways exemplifies alternative ways of organizing by virtue of its grassroots embeddedness, the countermovement it poses to neoliberalization and accumulation by dispossession, and the deep sense of solidarity and comradeship resonating in and through the movement. The orientation of *Phakamani* stems as much from the processes and social mobilization strategies that its founders and members pursued (and continue to pursue) as from the value base and ethos of the movement and the people it represents. The deep-seated solidarity among members of *Phakamani Siyephambili* – across the different places, structures, and scales – stems fundamentally from the socioeconomic and political context that (re)produces the shared forms of dispossession experienced by the rural poor. This unity was forged in the struggles against apartheid, and is being honed by opposition to contemporary neoliberalizing processes in the agrarian political economy.

The farm and area committees were able to seize available opportunities and spaces for consolidating and expanding organizational structures, and deepening democratic values and norms. Crucially, farm and area committees provided a forum for their members collectively to develop an alternative vision of the agrarian political economy. Additionally, they devised processes and systems to facilitate, encourage, and enhance the participation of all on the farms and surrounding areas. The processes that members followed in the farm and area committees were instrumental in strengthening bottom-up collectives and the adoption of a conscious and clear commitment to participatory democracy, which is ingrained in and filters through all the actions of *Phakamani Siyephambili*.

Between 2010 and 2012, farm and area committee members engaged in intensive processes and discussions on the nature and type of relationships they desired for their movement and campaigns. In light of the growth and geographical expansion of the collectives, they found it necessary first to articulate the values and norms governing their relationships, which would facilitate the forging of a radical transformation agenda. Each farm and area committee discussed, developed, and adopted Memoranda of Democratic Codes that spell out how members will relate to each other in the development of a shared transformation programme. The codes entail norms and values such as mutual respect, full participation, equal benefit, dedication to inclusive transformation processes, and a commitment to 'practicing what you preach'. In important ways, this marks the first level of social mobilization in the setting up of *Phakamani Siyephambili* and points to the ethos and political orientation of the grassroots structures that make up the social movement.

Once the codes were adopted by the collectives, discussions on framing their vision of and aspirations for the future agrarian political economy began in earnest. Farm and area committees met repeatedly for a year to analyse the contexts in which they work, live, sustain themselves, and socialize. In these processes, they reflected on their campaigns and struggles (discussed above) and sought clarity on the following (among others): the underlying causes for their unequal access to resources, the low levels of the AMW and the poor working conditions on offer on commercial farms, the absence of support for small-scale farmers that is nurturing and affirming, the assumptions underlying the formulation and implementation of land and agricultural policies, and the lack of decent living standards.

Confronting the state By intensifying the demands for land and agrarian transformation, the struggles of *Phakamani* are, in an important sense, an attack on the prevailing agricultural production system and its politico-juridical foundations. In this regard, small-scale farmers on PLAS farms have resisted the Department of Rural Development and Land Reform's imposition of mentors and strategic partners. A particularly bitter and protracted struggle was launched by the farm workers and dwellers on Yarrow Farm, in the Seven Fountains area, to take over the farm and to practise agro-ecological farming without mentors and strategic partnerships (ECARP 2013). They barricaded the farm to prevent officials from the Department of Rural Development and Land Reform and Makana Municipality from entering the farm. These actions signalled a refusal by the workers and dwellers to tolerate the continuing dispossession, job losses, and evictions that occurred on the farm after it was acquired by the government under PLAS.

PLAS and Recap opened old wounds in the minds of *Phakamani Siyephambili* members and NGOs seeking radical agrarian transformation. When the Green Paper on Land Reform was released for comment in 2011, it drew widespread criticisms from grassroots organizations. Collectives questioned both the consultative process of the Department of Rural Development and Land Reform and the manner in which the decision to involve white commercial farmers as mentors was reached. Interviews and engagements with farm workers and dwellers and small-scale farmers reveal the high levels of mistrust they harbour towards white commercial farmers as a direct result of historical relations of domination and subjugation. As a small-scale farmer explained, the idea of 'mentorship':

> came to our farm, and we told the Minister that we do not want to be the servants of white farmers again. We worked hard for them previously and now we want to work hard for ourselves. We just want the support directly from the government. (small-scale farmer, Masizake Farm, October 2011)

This view resonates throughout much of the Eastern Cape and is not confined to small-scale farmers; it is a shared belief of farm workers and dwellers. One farm worker said that the mentorship programme 'will continue to make us slaves to white farmers as we will never be able to own land of our own for housing, to graze our livestock, and for ploughing' (farm worker, October 2011). Another farm worker (July 2013) noted that:

I sometimes hear people say white farmers are productive, but it is not white people that are doing the work on the farms. It is us [farm workers]. All white people do is issue orders about what needs to be done. We know how to make farms productive so the government does not need to [provide] people to oversee us.

The committees also started questioning the Integrated Development Plans of municipalities and the practices of district officials insofar as they exclude/disregard farm workers, dwellers, and small-scale farmers. Through this challenge, the technical and neoliberal approach to 'development' pursued by government departments was further exposed. The collectives also attempted to engage commercial farmers in an effort to transform working and living conditions. However, farmers declined invitations to participate at that time and distanced themselves from the calls for changes in the sector by arguing that farm workers are the responsibility of the Department of Labour.

Not discouraged by the constraining actions by government departments and the refusal of commercial farmers to enter into dialogue, the farm and area committees used these experiences and subsequent assessments to shape and develop their vision for a transformed agrarian production system and wider society. The committees resolved to campaign for a living wage and not merely a minimum wage, for decent jobs and employment security; they committed to struggle for dignified living conditions; and they articulated a land and agricultural transformation agenda that is fundamentally different from government-led reforms. In the escalation of their struggles, the movement launched a multi-stakeholder dialogue forum in December 2015 to engage commercial farmers and government structures on a living wage for workers; positive and substantive land access, control, and independent use; and to promote and foster agro-ecological farming as an alternative to the existing industrial complex of farming and food production. Finally, the committees deployed the vision encapsulated in these collective actions to develop the manifesto, which *Phakamani Siyephambili* adopted and the movement now uses in its mobilizing efforts, struggles, and engagements.

Conclusion

Accumulation by dispossession is not a one-off event located in the annals of the history of capitalism, but rather an ongoing process intrinsic to the very character of capitalism. However, it takes on contingent forms and dimensions under specific spatial and historical conditions, and these therefore cannot simply be read off the logic of capitalism in an unmediated way. Ultimately, then, in-depth empirical analysis is critical for identifying and understanding specific forms of accumulation by dispossession, as we have sought to do in the case of land and labour themes among the rural poor in contemporary South Africa. At the same time, accumulation by dispossession is based not only on the coercive powers of the state as it is also legitimized through state policies and programmes, including those relating to land redistribution and commercial farming enacted by the post-apartheid state over the past 20 years. Crucially, accumulation by dispossession is invariably contested, as is the ongoing dispossession and marginalization of the rural poor in South Africa by social movements such as *Phakamani Siyephambili*.

As the discussion above shows, the forms of struggle and sites of resistance for *Phakamani* are diverse and wide-ranging. Each struggle and act of resistance serves as a building block in developing a critical consciousness that reflects a countermovement to the neoliberal orientation of the ANC government. Through such struggles and social mobilization, the members of *Phakamani* build the confidence to initiate new and creative campaigns. The principal lessons to be learned from the experiences of *Phakamani Siyephambili* include engaging in protracted and meticulous preparatory work before establishing formal structures; ensuring that all facets of the movement stem from bottom-up initiatives and are subject to democratic control by its membership; tying campaigns directly to the most pressing and immediate challenges confronted by the rural poor; linking local and issue-based struggles to broader, transformative objectives; and targeting, through sustained collective action, not only direct employers and their organized representatives, but also the state and its agencies.

To be sure, the resistance and struggles of *Phakamani* against dispossession remain fraught with a multiplicity of challenges and are perhaps only chipping away at the edges of the dispossession architecture. However, there are signs in present-day South Africa of diverse localized struggles taking place in the rural areas of the country and of connections being drawn between them. It is quite likely that the future course of accumulation by dispossession in

South Africa, at least when it comes to agrarian spaces, depends fundamentally on the capacity of the rural poor to organize on different and interconnected spatial levels, if only because the power of both state and agrarian capital is also so organized.

Notes

1 A 'farm dweller' is either not employed on the farm of residence or employed on a non-standard contract, but has the right to reside on the farm in terms of the *Extension of Security of Tenure Act* of 1997.

2 Exchange rate in December 2001: US$1 = ZAR 13.84.

3 This is an isiXhosa phrase meaning 'rise up and move forward'.

References

Arrighi, G., Aschoff, N., and Scully, B. (2010). 'Accumulation by dispossession and its limits: the Southern Africa paradigm revisited'. *Studies in Comparative International Development*, 45(4): 410–438.

Batou, J. (2015). 'Accumulation by dispossession and anti-capitalist struggles: a long historical perspective'. *Science and Society*, 79(1): 11–37.

Beinart, W., Delius, P., and Trapido, S. (eds) (1985). *Putting a Plough to the Ground: Accumulation and Dispossession in Rural South Africa, 1850–1930*. London: Longmans.

Bundy, C. (1988). *The Rise and Fall of the South African Peasantry*. Cape Town: David Philip.

Department of Labour (2001). *Recommendation of Employment Conditions Commission on a Determination for the Agricultural Sector*. Pretoria: Department of Labour.

East Cape Agricultural Research Project (ECARP) (2013). Presentation made to the Portfolio Committee on Agriculture and Rural Development. Eastern Cape Provincial Legislature, Bhisho, 12 September.

Greenburg, S. (1980). *Race and State in Capitalist Development: South Africa in Comparative Perspective*. Johannesburg: Ravan Press.

Hart, G. (2004). 'Denaturalizing dispossession: critical ethnography in the age of resurgent imperialism'. Revised paper prepared for the *Conference on Creative Destruction: Area Knowledge and the New Geographies of Empire*. Center for Place, Culture and Politics, CUNY Graduate Center, New York, 15–17 April.

Harvey, D. (2003). *The New Imperialism*. Oxford: Oxford University Press.

Klerck, G. and Naidoo, L. (2003). 'In search of greener pastures: trade unionism in the agricultural sector'. In T. Bramble and F. Barchiesi (eds), *Rethinking the Labour Movement in the 'New South Africa'*. Burlington, VT: Ashgate, pp. 150–167.

Makana Farm Committees (2005). 'Memorandum of demands presented to the Department of Labour by farm workers in Makana Municipality'. Unpublished document.

Marcus, T. (1989). *Modernising Super-Exploitation: Restructuring South*

African Agriculture. London: Zed Books.

Morris, M. (1976). 'The development of capitalism in South African agriculture: class and struggles in the countryside'. *Economy and Society*, 5(3): 292–343.

Naidoo, L. (2006). 'The Kransdrift Equity Scheme'. In East Cape Agricultural Research Project (ECARP), *Advancing Positive Land Rights and Sustainable Livelihoods for Rural Communities*. Unpublished position paper prepared for the 2006 Land Summit, Grahamstown. Available at: http://ecarp.org.za/wp-content/uploads/2013/03/Dossier-Land-Campaign-2005.pdf [accessed 20 October 2015].

Naidoo, L. (2011). 'Social mobilisation of farm workers and dwellers in the Eastern Cape'. In K. Helliker and T. Murisa (eds), *Land Struggles and Civil Society in Southern Africa*. Trenton, NJ: Africa World Press, pp. 71–112.

Statistics South Africa (SSA) (2014). *Poverty Trends in South Africa: South Africa Winning War on Poverty*. Available at: www.statssa.gov.za/?p=2591 [accessed 20 October 2015].

Visser, M. and Ferrer, S. (2015). *Farm Workers' Living and Working Conditions in South Africa: Key Trends, Emergent Issues, and Underlying and Structural Problems*. Available at: www.idll.uct.ac.za/sites/default/files/image_tool/images/3/ILO_Farm%20Worker s'%20Living%20and%20Workin g%20Conditions%20in%20SA_14%20July%202015.pdf [accessed 20 October 2015].

10 | FOOD SOVEREIGNTY THROUGH ECOFEMINISM: RE-COMMONING AS RESISTANCE TO AGRIBUSINESS DISPOSSESSION IN KENYA

Leigh Brownhill, Wahu Kaara, and Terisa Turner

Introduction

This chapter examines the process by which peasant farmers in Kenya have turned, in the first decades of the twenty-first century, from resistance against accumulation by dispossession within capitalist agricultural value chains, towards those chains' outright replacement with horizontal social relations and subsistence-oriented farming systems, within ecofeminist 're-commoning' initiatives. Through the recovery of age-old indigenous forms of overlapping entitlements to land, some urban youth are finding their ways back to rural areas in search of food self-sufficiency and 'cultural independence' (Shiriki). We argue that Kenyan 're-commoning' initiatives prefigure a global transition to post-fossil fuel farming systems, using means that create peace, and pursuing ends that are both socially and ecologically just.

Marx's observations in *Capital, Volume 1*, Chapter 32, on the 'Historical Tendency of Capitalist Accumulation', focuses on what 'the primitive accumulation of capital' will 'resolve itself into' (Marx 1867/1967: 761). He illustrates how 'capitalist production begets, with the inexorability of a law of Nature, its own negation' (Marx 1867/1967: 763). In his dialectical thinking, Marx argued that the overcoming and transformation of capital 'is accomplished by the action of the immanent laws of capitalistic production itself, by the centralization of capital' (Marx 1867/1967: 763).

Along with the constantly diminishing number of the magnates of capital, who usurp and monopolize all advantages of this process of transformation, grows the mass of misery, oppression, slavery, degradation, exploitation; but with this too grows the revolt of the working-class, a class always increasing in numbers, and disciplined, united, organized by the very mechanism of the process of capitalist production itself. The monopoly of capital becomes a fetter upon the mode of production, which has sprung up and flourished along with, and under it. Centralization of the means of production and socialization of labor at last reach a point where they become incompatible with their capitalist integument. (Marx 1867/1967: 763)

In the Kenyan food sovereignty struggles considered here, not only the agribusiness sector, but importantly finance capital, serve as central drivers of accumulation by dispossession and new enclosures. Both sectors conform to the imperative of exponential growth. In East Africa, capital's antagonists at first appear as disorganized commoners, the 'lumpen' or worse, but Kenyan peasant farmers are far from 'potatoes in a sack'. They are inheritors and stewards of a great store of indigenous knowledge, ecological practices, agronomic technologies, and local seed varieties and seed saving systems. That is exactly why Big Ag wants in, though they prefer to represent African farmers' priceless seeds, indigenous technical knowledge, and 'ecosystem services' as unvalued 'free goods' prior to and outside of their capitalist market valuation.

In food sovereignty initiatives in Kenya, by building cross-gender and intergenerational alliances, young farmers are reproducing, popularizing, and preserving the ancient seeds that have long been stewarded by elderly rural women. They are reinventing seed commons, and in so doing re-establishing farmer control over key life needs. These and other aspects of one case study of the transition from corporate to commoners' value chains are analysed below, with the aim of illustrating Marx's unique theoretical insight as it is actualized in 2016, here shown within an organic farming initiative in Kenya.

More precisely, the analysis examines the ways and extent to which 'capital's monopoly' has socialized peasant producers in Kenya into a centralized mode of production, and that in so socializing and centralizing them, another mode of production 'has sprung up and flourished along with, and under it' (Marx 1867/1967: 763). This new mode of production, according to Marx, 'does not re-establish private property for the producer, but gives him individual property based on the acquisition of the capitalist era: that is, on cooperation and the possession in common of the land and of the means of production' (Marx 1867/1967: 763). In the case we examine here, we find a creative resolution to the 'historical genesis' of capital in an ongoing effort towards re-commoning.

Kenyan social movements are directly engaged in challenging the imposition of corporate agricultural value chains, and in so doing are propelling a transformation of the agricultural economy. Food sovereignty movements are well grounded within peasant farmer groups. Nongovernmental organizations have been instrumental in civic education, which has informed critiques of TNCs' new seed imperialism. But it is among peasant producers themselves, and within their groups and networks, that we find the most effective efforts to reject the official global market initiatives of Big Ag and international financial institutions, and instead to pose plausible alternatives not only in theory, but in practice. This chapter features the case study of an organic farm collective in Maragua, Kenya, as an entry point into a wider consideration of the direction of change in contemporary globalized grassroots initiatives to break links along the capitalist value chains and reimagine and rebuild links on commoners' value chains. These alternative or commoners' value chains carry not only commodity exchange values, but agricultural products specifically endowed with non-priced use values such as nutrition, local adaptability, biodiversity, and cultural relevance. Commoners are rebuilding these value chains by (re)establishing horizontal social and economic relations and reviving local farming practices, knowledges, technologies, and markets.

A more exhaustive overview would examine the ways and extent to which commoners are breaking all links on the capitalist value chains, from finances to research and development, soil sciences, seeds, inputs, technologies, irrigation, post-harvest processing, markets, producer-consumer links, and post-consumer actions (e.g. waste, recycling). But in this brief chapter, we concentrate on just three crucial links: seeds, finance, and markets. Our analysis examines local and global contexts in each instance, as well as the social relations characterizing the reconstitution of commoning.

For many decades, the subsistence-informed perspectives of rural small-scale farmers have been represented merely as the voices of the 'powerless'. Or they have been drowned out and discredited as fringe and backward; scorned with stereotyped views of 'conservative' peasants who are uninformed about the benefits of 'development' (see, for example, Seavoy 2000). But in the twenty-first century, the increasingly extreme impacts of climate change have brought global attention to the need for alternatives to the fossil fuel dependence of the global capitalist political economy. Rural commoners have organized internationally to lead farming policy and practice towards 'the peasant way' (La Via Campesina). In Kenya, youth and women peasants have also put paid to the 'powerlessness' meme by expressing their strong commitment to indigenous, organic, biodiverse, and locally oriented farming systems. Far from being inert or 'chained to drudgery', Kenya's small-scale producers and peasant farmers are self-organized into thousands of farmer groups that are actively engaged in explicit and implicit food sovereignty activities, networks, and campaigns. Their work goes beyond critiquing and lobbying against the corporate agenda for agriculture, towards replacing it in practice by 're-commoning' and re-establishment of local food sovereignty.

Postcolonial anatomies of agricultural dispossession

Food struggles in Kenya find grounding in a history of farmers' dispossession of land, first by imperial companies, then by white settlers' large-scale plantations and ranches, and then at independence, by African industrial agribusinessmen and agents of international capital. Colonial processes of primitive accumulation continue in the twenty-first century in new and varied forms, including through land grabs, carbon trading, enclosure of genetic materials, and debt financing (Bond 2006; Klopp 2000). 'Private multiplied debt issuances', as John McMurtry shows, 'are the currency of the global corporate gang's control' (McMurtry 2001: 844–845). Channels of appropriation and accumulation in the twenty-first century are carved out and defended by law and policy pursued by transnational corporations such as Monsanto and Syngenta, by the G7 governments, international financial institutions, and official development agencies (especially the WTO, International Monetary Fund, Gates Foundation, and USAID).

For those who trade on stock markets in capital cities, rather than on kitchen tables in African villages, crop harvests and seeds are worth billions of dollars. The contemporary scramble for Africa's seeds finds transnational corporations and neoliberal institutions using multilateral trade agreements, as well as shaping African countries' national laws, to organize global market value chains and keep them flowing. That capital goes to such lengths to enclose indigenous technical and ecological knowledge, seeds, and financial systems globally is evidence of the monetary value that the people's commons hold. Colonial and postcolonial cycles of capital's accumulation by dispossession in Kenya set the historical background for the emergence in the twenty-first century of ecofeminist re-commoning initiatives.

Male deals: the organization of value extraction and accumulation   Central Kenya was heavily impacted by colonial processes of accumulation by dispossession because of its proximity to the centres of administrative power. Before Nairobi had developed into a habitable town, the British administrative centre was established in Murang'a (called Fort Hall by the British), on the slopes of Mount Kenya. The fertile land was coveted for white settlement, and the able agricultural skills of the people made them prime for exploitation on settler plantations and ranches. The town and district of Maragua lies a few miles from Murang'a. As the British carved up the fertile highlands and allocated the best land to white settlers, the towns and villages that remained were cobbled together in native reserves, from whence many men migrated for waged labour in cities or on the settler plantations, and women, children, and the elderly stayed to continue subsistence agriculture and small-scale trade.

One form of colonial-era land-based accumulation by dispossession involved restrictive legislation that barred Africans from growing cash-generating crops such as coffee. White settlers accumulated wealth by dispossessing Africans of land and excluding them through policy and law from engaging in particular agricultural value chains, except as labourers. Whites grew coffee on large estates and plantations, hired low-waged labourers, and built their own mills and roasters. Kenyan coffees have always been very highly rated, achieving AAA status, in part due to natural features of the soils, and equally to the skilled hand-cultivation methods used in the fields. In Kenya, that labour has long been based on the skilled hands of peasant women and the trained labour of landless rural and urban women and girls.

Through the 1940s, Kenyans organized within political associations, trade networks, and other civic bodies to demand independence and self-rule. The British colonial administration did not give in, but tried to accommodate the economic aspirations of elites among the Kenyan nationalists, by responding to calls for an end to discriminatory legislation. By giving coffee trading licences to Africans who owned larger parcels of land (along with other concessions, such as allowing Africans into the Legislature), the British hoped to satisfy the most well-connected nationalist men, and at the same time to silence the more wide-ranging aspirations of a poorer majority.

The aspirations of the majority were announced in unison during a General Strike across Kenya in May 1950, when Kenyans of all ethnicities closed markets and all other economic activities for over a week. Anti-colonial organizing continued, but British concessions were not forthcoming quickly or extensively enough to contain the aspirations of the people for freedom. In 1952, the British declared a state of emergency, when the Land and Freedom Army emerged from the forests and in the towns to demand, by any means necessary, the end of colonial rule in Kenya. One of the most damaging and long-lasting counter-insurgency tactics the British used at that time was to clear most of the peasants from their land in Central Kenya (including in Maragua) and detain them within forced villages. Once the land was cleared, it was easy for the colonial administration to rush through a land titling programme that reallocated land to those most loyal to the British. When the emergency and the villagization programme ended, many Central Kenyans found themselves landless or with much less land than previously.

In the post-independence era, smallholder farmers were now also included in the coffee economy not only as labourers, but as growers in their own right. But when the industry adjusted to the presence of smallholder growers, the gendered class character of the sector changed. Small-scale coffee growers did not hire labour; they used family labour. Each farmer did not have a mill, but they formed cooperatives and shared the labour, as well as the physical infrastructure of the cooperative's mill. This was the creation, in Marx's terms, of 'capitalistic private property', which was 'already practically resting on socialized production' (Marx 1867/1967: 763). Peasant labour was being socialized, while control over their labour and means of production was centralized.

Cash crop contracts in Kenya were cemented with what we have termed 'male deals' between small farming husbands, government officials, and international agribusinesses. The male deal unequally rewarded the touted beneficiaries. Government officials got big salaries for overseeing coffee co-ops. Bankers were paid interest on loans from the foreign exchange that coffee earned the country. And husbands' names were on the contracts and the bank accounts into which payments were made. Ultimately, coffee's cultivation relied on the marriage contract that gave men access to the freely available labour of women and children. It was up to the men to sign the contracts and share the income – or not.

By the late 1960s, Kenya's small-scale coffee farmers were suppliers of high-quality but low-priced, milled but unroasted coffee beans on regional and international markets. Women maintained their own vegetable gardens alongside the coffee plots, and provided most of the free hand cultivation of the crop. Their beans were seen as raw materials for international buyers' value addition (roasting, blending, packaging, branding, retailing) and food corporations' profits within what was becoming one of the world's most lucrative global commodity value chains: coffee.

Through the 1960s and the first half of the 1970s, though the farm-gate price was relatively low, coffee actually gave farmers a substantial income, sufficient for their basic cash needs. It covered school fees, and typically wives expected to get a new dress after the harvest. The national coffee auction also provided the state with more foreign exchange than any other source. But the village coffee cooperatives became footballs in national and local political contests. Chairmanships in the lucrative cooperatives were handed out as rewards for allegiance, and sometimes taken as opportunities for corruption and theft. In addition to local political pressures on the coffee farmers' livelihoods, between 1980 and 1990, real international prices for Africa's coffee exports fell by 70 per cent (World Bank 1994). An agricultural plan that had begun with the promise of household and national development and freedom turned into a reality of rising impoverishment and indebtedness.

By the mid-1980s, women in Maragua and the surrounding coffee-growing region took matters into their own hands on their families' farms. They began ripping out coffee trees and using them for firewood (see Brownhill *et al.* 1997 for a detailed analysis). At the time, it seemed to be an outlying and unique indication of resistance against structural adjustment programmes and the commodification agenda these programs pushed. They were not entirely isolated examples, as it turns out, and by the early 1990s coffee growers in other East African countries were abandoning the crop, responding to falling international prices and rising hunger, poverty, and debt. By planting bananas and vegetables for home consumption on at least part of their land, the Maragua farmers, with women in the lead, had begun to reclaim sovereignty over their labour and small plots of land.

The male deals that bound farmers into the corporate coffee value chains were broken by women's refusal to toil for a crop that could neither pay them nor feed them directly. Planting food crops was strategic, leading to their choice of a diverse mixed cropping system, including common staple foods such as bananas, tomatoes, and kale, crops that could be eaten or sold to a ready local market (Kabura and Doppler 2005; Nguthi and Niehof 2008).

Tellingly in 1997, at the height of the farmers' retreat from coffee and return to mixed food crop cultivation, Maragua was one of the initial sites for the multinational biotech companies' introduction of 'tissue culture' banana production. 'Tissue culture' is a method of propagation of plant material, done in laboratories in a specially formulated nutrient medium, using the tissue of disease-free plants. Tissue culture bananas produce uniform, disease-free plants and fruits, but require more labour, more inputs, and more expenditures, as planting material must be purchased each season rather than propagated on-farm from suckers from mature banana plants. They produce all their fruits at once, rather than staggered, as is the case with local propagation methods (Indimuli 2013).

Kenyan scientists (in particular, women horticultural scientists) were drafted to study, justify, and promote the adoption of tissue culture banana biotechnology among Kenyan farmers (Wambugu 2003). The corporations also employed 'gender mainstreaming' strategies to enlist women in tissue culture banana production. They devised special commercial microcredit loans for women in order to make possible the initial investment in infrastructure (Kabunga *et al.* 2011; Mbogoh *et al.* 2003). So at the very time that Maragua women were reviving the cultivation of a diverse range of local varieties of bananas and strengthening indigenous cultivation methods and market networks, international biotech companies promoted the benefits of a single (patented) banana variety. The tissue culture bananas were suitable for export due to their durability in transit. Their production is reliant on heavy labour demands and costly external inputs, from chemicals to netting and other physical infrastructure. Many farmers who adopted tissue culture bananas could not keep up with the costs (and debt repayments) and labour (Indimuli 2013). By the early 2000s, many farmers had dropped the crop, and biotech-funded researchers were looking for new ways to exploit social capital and increase information flows in order to 'scale up biotech adoption' (Kabunga *et al.* 2011; Karembu 2007).

Once the farmers had begun to break free of the corporate value chains that kept them bound to coffee production, and had refocused their land and labour on their own preferred subsistence crops, international capital quickly adjusted to the new scenario. They took immediate advantage of the small farmers' general shift from coffee monocrops to mixed food crops by recasting the peasant class as one devoted to select horticultural niche commodities. For the farmers searching for an end to hunger and impoverishment, the struggle was far from over.

Capital persists in efforts to maintain a grip on the collective labour and means of production of the Kenyan peasants, as it does with regard to labour and resources within its ambit. Kenyan peasants, on the other hand, are actively building on the discipline, organization, and unity acquired from the capitalist era to cooperate for their own purposes, and to find ways to possess in common the land and means of production.

Re-commoning, ecofeminist praxis, and food sovereignty as resistance to dispossession in Maragua (Shiriki)

Ecofeminism has a long history in Kenya, if we understand ecofeminism as women's struggle to be free of both gendered and ecological exploitation, as well as the more narrow measure of women's leadership in environmental causes. The Nobel committee, in choosing Wangari Maathai for the Peace Prize in 2004, acknowledged a woman descended from a people and a culture in which love for the environment is second nature. In fact, this 'love' is formally instituted in the spiritual and economic life of her people with such taboos as the cutting of fig trees, or even the burning of the fig's twigs (Maathai 2006). The Green Belt Movement employs (and self-employs) women's and youth groups in tree-planting to provide food, fuel, shelter, and income, and to replenish natural resources (e.g. biodiversity, spring water, forest cover) over time. The Green Belt Movement is but one well-known example of Kenyan women's vibrant feminist and ecofeminist organizing and self-help initiatives.

Every woman 'belongs to at least one woman's group', or so we were told by a Maragua woman in 1996 (Brownhill *et al.* 1997: 41). And there are, across Kenya, tens of thousands of grassroots, self-organized, registered, and unregistered women's self-help societies, savings circles, farmer groups, and other trade and work-related groups (Pala *et al.* 1978). These groups have precolonial and colonial-era roots, but in the postcolonial era have grown in extent, variety, and sophistication among women, urban, and rural, especially among the poor. They are readily available means by which the dispossessed unite in efforts to solve common and collective problems. They represent what Marx might call the 'combined, socialized labour', produced in this case by the synthesis of indigenous cooperative forms (Brownhill 2009: 12) and the imposition of 'the immanent laws of capitalistic production itself, the centralization of capital' (Marx 1867/1967: 763).

With the rise of social media from the 1990s, Kenya's grassroots women's groups have grown more closely integrated locally and with international women's and farmers' movements. These include the World March of Women and *La Via Campesina*, networks that draw together groups from around the world into international campaigns to enact change in practice, on peasant farms, and in trade and environmental laws, to end the unequal terms and extractive tendencies of current corporate and foreign investor-friendly policy frames.

The type of social movement mobilization prominent in Kenya in 2016 finds on-the-ground farmers groups engaged in revitalizing forms of indigenous land-sharing, money-saving, and mixed cropping systems. This creative and socially constructive expression is one of the movement-building results of decades of ecofeminist organizing and activity in Kenya, of which women coffee farmers' rejection of the cash crop in favour of local organic food crops is a concrete example.

As ecofeminist scholars and social justice activists, we as authors have taken a special interest in the gendered transformation of the farm economy in Maragua. Without going too deeply into our personal biographies, suffice it to say that we have maintained kith and kinship ties in the area. We share with the coffee wives of Maragua, and with the Shiriki youth, a dedication to food sovereignty, not only in theory, but more importantly in practice. This gives us our unique perspective on the case as an indication of the 'sounding of the knell of capitalist private property', to paraphrase Marx once again.

Gendered class alliances: unity in diversity in re-commoning initiatives When Maragua wives ripped out their husbands' coffee trees and planted food, they strengthened their position by making new alliances with youthful transporters and traders who helped strengthen the value chains linking banana farmers to consumers in the city. This intergenerational unity that was emerging in Maragua and elsewhere in Kenya between rural peasant women and poor urban and peri-urban young men was based in market relations, but also in overt sociocultural interests, including in strengthening local livelihoods in the face of intense poverty and the criminalization of slum youth. In our analysis of the Maragua coffee strike at that time, we characterized this unity as a 'gendered class alliance', or 'cross-gender alliances amongst the exploited, against class antagonists, aimed at creating new, humane social relations' (Brownhill *et al.* 1997: 41).

The Maragua women's move towards food sovereignty was in part broken up by new accumulation strategies of international capital. Farmers were enticed in different directions into different cash cropping schemes, such as tissue culture bananas, French beans, strawberries, and macadamia nuts. But not everyone accepted the market logic. For many who ventured into the new niche commodities, the costs proved too high and the benefits too small, and a retreat from those crops followed (Indimuli 2013; Komu 2016; Mithofer *et al.* 2008). In the twenty-first century, not only have plots for household food production in Maragua re-emerged as a central feature of the families' subsistence, but some farms refuse exotic cash crops altogether and have gone totally organic.

The Shiriki farm in Maragua is a case in point. This two-acre farm is owned by a widow whose employment keeps her resident in Nairobi. She is among a very small minority of Kenyan women who own agricultural land. Since she works in the city and could not herself live on and operate the farm, she had a few options for how to handle the land. She could have sold the land, or leased it out. She could have hired agricultural labourers and a manager to oversee crop production to supplement her family's pantry and income. But she had seen the struggle against coffee in Maragua, and was not herself convinced of the sense of turning to an alternative cash crop. On the contrary, she was committed to the advancement of organic methods, indigenous crop varieties, and the resuscitation of local markets for local foods. She sought means through which to advance these objectives, and in so doing to follow and extend the example set by the women of Maragua who had rejected coffee in favour of local food production some 20 years earlier.

The widow's work in Nairobi regularly put her in contact with youth organizations, community groups, women's associations, and social movements working towards various objectives under the umbrella of democratization, including civic participation in governance processes. It was in the course of this sort of public engagement that, in 2010, she met a youth group interested in starting a farm cooperative. The Shiriki group, which identifies as a charity organization, is comprised of young Rastafari, most of whom were originally living in urban slums. The youth proposed to the widow that they raise money from their craft manufacture and fundraising events to enable them to farm the land, build houses, storage sheds, and a communal hall. They would live there and operate the farm collectively, and aimed to establish a rural cultural education and media centre. In their own words, they proposed 'to involve the youth in agriculture, the natural prerequisite towards real and tangible development. Out of this involvement, the youth population will be directly engaged in providing and uplifting the basic necessities of food, clothing and shelter' (Shiriki Maragua Project n.d.).

This objective, and the youth group's larger vision of furthering local and continental 'cultural independence', aligned with the landowner's commitment to food sovereignty and community development. What the youth proposed to make happen on the land and in the community was a dynamic realization of what the widow would have wished to do, but could not do on her own.

The Shiriki youth connected rural–urban migration with the rise of chemical-dependent farming, and understood that the rejection of chemical farming would require the return of youth to agricultural pursuits. They reasoned that 'the massive exodus of youth from the rural [areas] to the cities and towns has left the aged and a few youth remnants to be easily deceived into use of chemical[s]' (Gicuki 2012). Organic agriculture and indigenous farming methods are relatively labour-intensive, for instance, in weeding, checking pests, and fertilizing and irrigating the land. Lack of sufficient youthful labour in the rural areas has meant that for generations, 'shortcuts' have been employed, in the form of chemical pesticides, herbicides, and fertilizers.

The solidarity and shared project that drew them together was, in our ecofeminist perspective, a mature expression of the gendered class alliances that emerged in Maragua in the 1990s with the rejection of coffee farming. This alliance was actualized in this case in 2011, when a handful of Shiriki group members arrived in Maragua prepared to clear the widow's overgrown land and camp out until they could build temporary housing. In their own words, as a collective, they aspired to 'the preservation, maintenance and continuance of traditional wisdom, as well as innovation of practical modern resource utilization methods'. On the ground, this meant turning to local farmer seed varieties and adopting technology such as spring water irrigation, solar cookers, and Internet outreach and marketing.

The gendered class alliance between the landowner and the youth is echoed in the group's good deeds and intentions as they integrate into their new rural community. They assist neighbourhood widows and other elders in heavy farm labour. The revival of local indigenous and organic farming requires the return of youth to the land to meet the heavy labour needs of organic agriculture, manufacturing, and collective life. The Shiriki group, comprised largely of young men, sees as a conscious part of their goal the objective of making farming viable to attract both women and men back to farming. To do so, they host volunteers, who stay for varying periods on the farm to contribute general labour, learn local farm practices, and practice small-scale food processing and craft production.

Relinking commoners' value chains: seeds, finance, and markets In this case, we find the rejection of commodified value chains is accomplished through the rebuilding of commoners' value chains in seeds, inputs, and markets themselves. That is to say, capital is usurped by the combination of socialized labour and means of production held in common. The Shiriki youth have consulted with women elders of the area to retrieve local seed varieties. They have likewise consulted with elders, as well as information available from NGOs and civil society, on the composition and use of organic and indigenous pesticides, preservatives, and fertilizers. Markets have also been a major focus of the youth, who are active in weekly local village markets, but also periodically appear in urban centres and combine cultural and artistic events with marketing of crops and crafts. The youth have gone further to participate in East African regional trade fairs, where they have displayed their wares and further built their networks for the circulation of their craft and agricultural products. Commoners' markets are key to the realization of food-sovereign farming systems, insofar as these support farmers' efforts, attract more farmers into cultivation, build spaces for peaceful coexistence, fulfil eaters' cultural and nutritional preferences, and open the opportunity for youth cooperation and self-employment.

A growing number of farmer groups, movements, and networks are forming in Kenya explicitly for the purpose of mutual support to spur the wider return to a food system based on local, organic, and indigenous seeds, farming methods, and local markets. Consumers are also on board for health, ecological, and livelihood reasons, with growing youth interest in small-scale farming in East Africa as much as in North America. In Shiriki's case, distinct local seed varieties, old and new agro-ecological methods, and steps towards energy self-sufficiency, such as solar power, for use on the farm and to build communication channels. Although groups such as Shiriki are 'localized' and indigenous, they also maintain a diverse range of connections to wider farmer, arts, and trade networks on regional, continental, and global levels. These include other farmers, researchers, and fair-traders, as well as public officials and global social movements. Producer–consumer (and rural–urban) relationships built in these initiatives, in farmer market and CSA-type value exchanges, prefigure more fully articulated commoners' value chains and market matrices being established locally, continentally, and globally.

In addition to pursuing the nutritional and ecological benefits of commoners' value chain development, food sovereignty activists in the Maragua case are building these value chains by replacing hierarchical with horizontal gender relations. The Shiriki youth share land with a widow and pursue the kind of agro-ecology that she promotes. The saving of seeds is largely in the hands of women. Much of the knowledge of nutrition and of herbal insecticides and pesticides is stewarded especially by elderly women. Therefore, women and men farmers who rededicate themselves to local crop varieties and farming systems must, of necessity, work positively with the knowledge, power, and practices of elderly women. Testimonies from farmers attest to the fact that their aim in this knowledge seeking is not patents and private rights for agribusinesses' accumulation, nor bio-piracy and the dispossession of peasants of their knowledge, but rather the strengthening of peasant seed and knowledge systems for local subsistence.

The values of human health and ecological resilience, which are externalities in capital's accounts, have been stewarded by women for millennia. These values are the hidden but treasured axes of the newly emerging mode of production that we witnessed in Maragua, and that we call 'solar commoning'. When agricultural development aims to maximize the non-priced values of health and ecology, the kinds of market and financial activities that are organized are those that support and generalize these non-priced values, as well as incomes and savings (Njuguna *et al.* 2016). So the food sovereignty movement in Kenya is not only ecofeminist because African peasant women and dispossessed youth are making alliances to lead the transition to a post-fossil fuel farming future. The movement is ecofeminist because it is imbued with ecofeminist goals and objectives, including, in particular, nutritional health and ecological resilience, as both means and ends.

Climate change, geopolitical instability, and economic volatility all remain external challenges to the transition to post-fossil fuel farming at Shiriki, as elsewhere. But these remain challenges for the capitalist political economy as well. As such, they stand as the clear reasons that youth and farmers are re-commoning, and taking food production into their own hands.

In Kenya, land is such an extremely sensitive matter that suggestions that others should share their land with the landless could easily be met with jeers of derision. And with the recent history of land-based ethnic and political violence in the country, broaching the very topic can bring up fears of dispossession and counter-dispossession. In this regard, what Marx states near the end of his discussion of the historical tendency of capitalist production should be reassuring; that the violence of the creation of the capitalist economy is not an indication of the way in which the transition to post-capitalist society will occur:

> The transformation of scattered private property, arising from individual labor, into capitalist private property is, naturally, a process, incomparably more protracted, violent, and difficult, than the transformation of capitalistic private property, already practically resting on socialized production, into socialized property. In the former case, we had the expropriation of the mass of the people by a few usurpers; in the latter, we have the expropriation of a few usurpers by the mass of the people. (Marx 1867/1967: 764)

Thus, we see the biggest challenge to the wider, immediate generalization of 'solar commoning' as capitalist private property. Kenya has several culturally specific systems of overlapping entitlements to land that are enshrined in custom and history; and despite colonial and continuing enclosure, demarcation, and privatization, many remain extant in 2016. Some practices, such as the intergenerational alliances seen in Maragua, and the 'female husband' or 'house of women' custom found in different forms across East Africa, are on the upswing (see, for example, Haworth 2016). Land-sharing such as this signals the transformation, at least in this corner of Kenya, of what had been capitalist private property into socialized property. The more landowners share their private property with the dispossessed for the 'social reconstruction' of food sovereign farming systems (Turner 1994: 9), the more the 'socialized labour' that capitalism created (on a global scale) can engage with 'socialized property' unfettered from the 'monopoly of capital'. This is re-commoning writ large.

Shiriki and beyond: grounded reflections on the prospects for re-commoning, ecofeminist praxis, and food sovereignty as resistance

Historically, commercialization has been an experience of exploitation for African farmers, and only fleetingly successful but for the very few. However, markets themselves are much older than the colonial processes of commodification, and Kenyans, if anyone, are endowed with a tremendously rich array of indigenous trading networks, practices, and places. It is not the market exchange that must go, but the hierarchical organization of the markets at present that is being changed. The global market integration that continues to produce poverty and malnutrition for Africans is fully dependent on oil for chemical inputs, as energy, and for transportation across planetary value chains. These chains, though difficult to remove, are only a recent manifestation of market relations, one that overrode, upon colonial occupation, the commoners' precolonial trade.

Capital's accumulation by the dispossession of commoners – of their resources, labour, and markets – took place most everywhere, but the history of active trading relationships (practices, networks, rules, routes, sites) is deep, in particular in East Africa, the birthplace of humankind. Though the Kenyan peasants have their own particular history and cultures, the longevity of trade as an economic activity in the area also makes it likely that farmers here share, in one way or another, some of the same concerns, conversations, and constraints as farmers and groups elsewhere in building food-sovereign farming systems. Their example stands as a lesson for others who are as deeply committed to bringing post-oil agriculture into existence, not only as isolated collective experiments, but as a wider answer to more than the question of food, but to questions of building a post-capitalist civilization.

What is most promising about the diverse food sovereignty movements in Kenya, as constituted in the twenty-first century, is not only the strength and creativity of their resistance, but also the power and rootedness of their subsistence alternatives. Food sovereignty movements employ substantive creative energies in recuperating and strengthening indigenous agricultural, environmental, and technical knowledge. Their *raison d'être* is attainment of sovereignty over the food systems that lie within their hands and within their grasps, in well-established and new relationships aimed at self-help, self-sufficiency, and community- and civic-mindedness, with *Ubuntu* principles ('I am because we are'), *harambee* organizational models (community fundraising, an original version of crowdsourcing), and merry-go-round activities ('Table Banking', grassroots group finance).

Conclusion

The concentration of capital serves as a fetter on the full productive power of the global economy, as capitalist private property prevents the real producers from interacting with that alienated property (e.g. land) in the ways they would if they were the 'owners' of these 'socially exploited and, therefore, common means of production' (Marx 1867/1967: 763). What Marx did not say was that the capitalist fetter on the economy is highly gendered, and so too is the process by which socialized labour is freeing itself, and the common means of production, from those fetters in major sectors such as food and finance (not to mention energy), as we have seen in places such as Maragua.

Africa's poorest farmers are being dispossessed by male dealers pursuing policies of strengthening corporate value chain extraction of Africa's agricultural wealth. This dispossession is experienced by peasant women in particular. First, there is the immediate loss when indigenous seed varieties are patented. Farmers' seed systems are then classified as illegitimate because they are not certified, and other farmers urged to plant only 'certified' seeds sold by agro-vet outlets of local and especially multinational seed companies.

Another level of dispossession is experienced by farmers when aid funders' and economic advisors' focus agricultural research, outreach, and education exclusively on the value chains most attractive to corporate foreign investors, instead of on the crops and agronomic questions of the farmers themselves. A market-oriented development strategy that makes money its aim, over the non-priced values of nutritional well-being and ecological assets of farm communities, in turn serves to deny funding and knowledge mobilization to the furtherance of locally preferred and ecologically adapted crop varieties and cultivation practices. Not only funding and research, but also policy framing, legal support, and market development, are being denied to peasant farmers by the monopoly of capital on the economy.

A third dispossession is the loss experienced by women more generally as the primary caregivers and ultimate food providers of their families. By seeking to constrict seed trade by peasants, proposed legislation to protect corporate plant breeders' rights promises to cut off the emergency food sources and famine strategies relied on by farmers during periods of drought. Young mothers, in particular, seek the assistance, knowledge, and old seeds of the women seed savers to carry them through hungry times. All of these experiences of dispossession constrict access to the full range of sources of food, especially for poor Kenyans. This in turn perpetuates and deepens the crises of malnutrition and child stunting, while allowing for the accumulation of profits at the other end of the corporate value chains in which the hungry are bound.

In Maragua, the Shiriki youth group is recovering nearly lost indigenous seed varieties, practising organic farming, and informing themselves, the local community, and consumers on the health, nutritional, sociocultural, ecological, and economic benefits of food sovereignty. This grassroots initiative highlights the wealth of resources, creativity, and capacities present in hunger-prone communities. Commoners' wealth indeed constitutes significant foundations for post-oil agriculture in Kenya, and sets an example for food sovereignty initiatives globally.

Capitalists claim that they can overcome food insecurity through for-profit market mechanisms. In contrast, food sovereignty movements aim to overcome hunger by re-establishing farmers' control over land, seed and other productive inputs, including indigenous agricultural knowledge and commoners' markets. In organizing their livelihoods, based on complex social networking and occupation of farms of varying sizes and fertilities, many Kenyan food producers are engaged in the return to indigenous crop varieties and farming practices. Their decision-making is guided by a logic wider than that of the market metrics of commercial agriculture, in that it includes 'non-priced' ecological, sociocultural, and nutritional considerations.

Groups such as the African Biotechnology Network, the African Food Sovereignty Alliance, La Via Campesina, and the World March of Women are actively engaged in research, civic education, and lobbying for laws to protect farmers' seeds, knowledge, land, and farming systems from ecological threats of climate change and economic threats of privatization and corporate enclosure. While recognizing a diverse range of actors and forms of collective action, political engagement, and social networking in our delineation of a 'food sovereignty movement' in Kenya, in this chapter we have highlighted one example of collective organic farming in Maragua, Central Kenya, to illustrate the practices and social relations associated with the emergence of food sovereignty and commoners' value chains. The scope of food-related initiatives and social movements in Kenya today goes beyond the mainly foreign-funded 'civil society' of the 'NGO fraternity', to embrace the rural peoples' significant self-organization of thousands of farmer groups, producer associations, community-based organizations, and women's self-help groups, with the overall aim of strengthening livelihoods and well-being for individuals, households, and communities.

This chapter traces actors in one twenty-first-century mobilization for food sovereignty in Kenya, and pinpoints the efficacy therein of gender and generational alliances in explicit experiments to (re)create farming practices and systems un-reliant on petrochemical inputs. We see this example as 'larger than the sum of its parts'. On the one hand, there is an incremental impact of yearly planting and harvesting cycles, setting examples for neighbours who witness the efforts and its bounty. On the other hand, there is a perhaps under-measured wider impact of the Maragua case when social networking and social media interaction are taken into account. The small kernel planted in Maragua does more than produce two acres of food crops that feed a band of educated Rastafari; it sows seeds for a much wider recognition of the simple fact that There Is An Alternative to the global capitalist food system, and it lies in the humble and giving hands and minds of groups of farmers, such as those in Kenya profiled here.

Food sovereignty movements in Kenya offer insights into emerging post-oil farming systems in the East African region and on a global scale, as peak oil, economic crises, and political schisms eat away at the undercarriage of the fossil fuel civilization. Pursuing the notion that 'nothing is destroyed until it is replaced', this chapter centralizes the creative force of gendered alliances within food sovereignty movements in recomposing horizontal subsistence commoning relations to meet the challenges of the present and to build foundations for a future of food beyond the oil age.

References

Bond, P. (2006). *Looting Africa: The Economics of Exploitation*. London: Zed.

Brownhill, L. (2009). *Land Food Freedom: Struggles for the Gendered Commons in Kenya, 1870–2007*. Trenton, NJ: Africa World Press.

Brownhill, L., Kaara, W.M., and Turner, T.E. (1997). 'Gender relations and sustainable agriculture: rural women's resistance to structural adjustment in Kenya'. *Canadian Woman Studies*, 17(2): 40–44.

Gicuki, R.B. (2012). *One Year On: Still Going on Strong*. Available at: http://shirikiorganization.blogspot. ca/2012/10/one-year-on-still-going-on-strong.html [accessed 14 April 2017].

Haworth, A. (2016). 'Why straight women are marrying each other'. *Marie Claire*, 25 July. Available at: www.marieclaire.com/culture/a21668/the-tanzanian-wives/. [accessed 31 July 2016].

Indimuli, R. (2013). *Factors Influencing the Discontinuance in Adoption of Tissue Culture Banana Technology: A Study of Smallholder Farmers in Maragwa District*. University of Nairobi.

Kabunga, N.S., Dubois, T., and Qaim, M. (2011). 'Information asymmetries and technology adoption: the case of tissue culture bananas in Kenya'. *Courant Research Centre Discussion Paper 74*, Georg-August-Universität Göttingen, March.

Kabura, E.A. and Doppler, W. (2005). 'Smallholder tea and coffee production and its impact on food production and living standards in Kenya'. In *Conference on International Agricultural Research and Development*, Hohenheim, 11–13 October.

Karembu, M. (2007). 'Enhancing the diffusion of tissue culture banana to small-scale farmers in Kenya'. *The International Service for the Acquisition of Agri-Biotech Applications Newsletter*.

Klopp, J.M. (2000). 'Pilfering the public: the problem of land grabbing in contemporary Kenya'. *Africa Today*, 47(1): 7–26.

Komu, N. (2016). 'Nyeri coffee farmers switch to macadamia citing frustrations'. *Daily Nation*, 4 May. Available at: www.nation.co.ke/counties/nyeri/Nyeri-coffee-farmers-switch-macadamia/-/1954190/3188734/-/1255ypuz/-/index.html [accessed 10 May 2016].

Maathai, W. (2006). *Unbowed: A Memoir*. New York: Knopf.

Marx, K. (1867/1967). *Capital: A Critique of Political Economy, Volume 1*. New York: International Publishers.

Mbogoh, S.G., Wambugu, F.M., and Wakhusama, S. (2003). 'Socio-economic impact of biotechnology applications: some lessons from the pilot tissue-culture (TC) banana production promotion project in Kenya, 1997–2002'. In *Proceedings of the 25th International Conference on Agricultural Economics*, 16–22 August.

McMurtry, J. (2001). 'The life-ground, the civil commons and the corporate male gang'. *Canadian Journal of Development Studies*, 22: 819–854.

Mithofer, D., Nang'ole, E., and Asfaw, S. (2008). 'Smallholder access to the export market: the case of vegetables in Kenya'. *Outlook on Agriculture*, 37(3): 203–211.

Nguthi, F.N. and Niehof A. (2008). 'Effects of HIV/AIDS on the livelihood of banana-farming households in Central Kenya'. *NJAS*, 56(3): 179–190.

Njuguna, E., Brownhill, L., Kihoro, E., Muhammad, L., and Hickey, G.M. (2016). 'Gendered technology adoption and household food security in semi-arid Eastern Kenya'. In J.R. Parkins, J. Njuki, and A. Kaler (eds), *Transforming Gender and Food Security in the Global South*. Oxford: Earthscan/Routledge

Pala, A., Awor, T., and Krystal, A. (1978). *The Participation of Women in Kenya Society*. Nairobi: Kenya Literature Bureau.

Seavoy, R.E. (2000). *Subsistence and Economic Development*. Westport, CT: Praeger.

Shiriki Maragua Project (n.d.). *Using Agriculture and Art as the Key to Community Development*. Available at: http://shirikiorganization.blogspot.ca/ [accessed 14 April 2017].

Turner, T.E. (1994). *Arise Ye Mighty People! Gender, Class and Race in Popular Struggles*. Trenton, NJ: Africa World Press.

Wambugu, F. (2003). 'Food, Africa's most pressing problem and why agribiotech is the catalytic solution required'. In *Proceedings of the International Congress, 'In the Wake of the Double Helix: From the Green Revolution to the Gene Revolution'*, Bologna, Italy, 27–31 May.

World Bank (1994). *Adjustment in Africa: Reforms, Results and the Road Ahead*. Washington, DC: World Bank.

11 | GUIDED BY THE YOMO SPIRIT: RESISTANCE TO ACCUMULATION BY DISPOSSESSION OF THE SONGOR SALT LAGOON IN ADA, GHANA

Jonathan Langdon and Kofi Larweh

Introduction

The sound of drums, musketry, the crowds swelling, necks straining to see the Chiefs of Ada arrive in their colourful palanquins; marching bands from Ada 'diaspora' having returned from across to their motherland to display their pageantry and skills, like the soldiers returning from defending the Songor in conflicts of old. Coming at the beginning of August every year, the people of Ada, living where Ghana's Volta River estuary meets the ocean, mark the commencement of their year with the Asafotufiami Festival. This festival celebrates the historical ability of Adas to unite in the face of threats of dispossession, especially in terms of the nearby Songor salt-yielding lagoon. The Songor lagoon is West Africa's largest alluvial salt producer, and artisanal salt production from the lagoon is a major source of livelihood for the roughly 90,000 Adas who live around the lagoon (Dangme East District Assembly 2012). The festival involves re-enacting historical victories against outsiders trying to take the lagoon from the Adas. It also involves oaths of allegiance, where all of the heads of the various clans in Ada swear to unite behind their king, Nene Ada, should any outside force threaten them. While the pomp and musketry that surround this festival may suggest to a visiting tourist that this unity is a fait accompli, the most recent internal and external attempts at accumulation by dispossession of the lagoon reveal that it is a struggle to unify, and the past two struggles to unify have been led by social movements, and not by the chiefs and their pageantry.

In this chapter, we will share aspects of the precolonial and colonial history that the Asafotufiami Festival celebrates – as well as some of the stories it seeks to gloss over. We will link this complex history to two contemporary periods of social movement mobilization concerning the Songor – both of which underscore how people themselves have come together in the face of adversity despite the complicity or lack of action of leadership in the area. While sharing these contemporary stories, we want to concentrate on what it is people *did* and the strategies they *used* to contend with outside threats, as well as the failure of their leaders. This chapter is based on four years of participatory action research on social movement learning emerging from this struggle and shares specific learnings from the fights to prevent or reverse accumulation by dispossession of the lagoon.

'*E yeo ngo*' – salt is Ada

To the people of Ada, salt is central to their identity. Almost two-thirds of the Ada area's 93,000 residents live in the 35 communities that surround the Songor salt lagoon (Dangme East District Assembly 2012). As noted above, the Songor and its defence are the focus of Ada's yearly festival (in contrast to other Ghanaian cultural festivals most often linked to harvests). However, it goes deeper than that: the relationship between Adas and salt is literally embedded in the Ada language, Dangme. When someone asks if another person speaks Dangme, the speaker will say, '*E yeo ngo?*' The literal translation of this question is, 'Does this person eat salt?' Thus, to speak Dangme, and by extension to be an Ada, is to eat salt. This strong identity connection is further deepened with the lagoon's central role in foundational stories of the Adas.

Though there are some variations to the foundation story of the Adas, depending on which clan you come from, these stories all agree on two central points (ASAF 2016). First, that the original Adas to venture into the area they now call home were met by an old woman, named Yomo. Second, this old woman guided them to the Songor lagoon, and revealed she was the spiritual guardian of the lagoon, as well as the rules Adas must abide by in benefiting from the lagoon. In observing these rules, the King of Ada, Nene Ada, as well as the traditional priests, are barred from using gold – instead being adorned with silver or white beads. By extension, for the people of Ada, salt is spiritually more valuable than gold. At the same time, salt is a physical representation of this old woman's spirit and the rules she handed down. Its crystallization indicates to all Adas that their relationship with the lagoon is on good terms. By the same token, failure to crystalize leads to questions of what has gone wrong.

Manuh (1992: 113) notes that the relationship this fostered between the Adas and the lagoon was one of responsible 'community management of a natural resource'. These rules created a bond of trust between traditional leaders, priests, and the people. For instance, salt would only be collected from the Songor when the priest of the Songor spirit, the Libi Wornor, declared it ready. This ensured the salt formation would not be disturbed before completion. The Libi Wornor is from the Tekperbiawe clan, one of the four original clans of the Adas, and has to undergo years of training, including the secrets of salt winning and lagoon environmental preservation skills. The overlapping responsibility for the lagoon that also emerged in this process, where the four original clans laid claim to different parts and roles towards the lagoon, also added to the effective resource management as all felt responsible for maintaining the lagoon (Langdon 2010).

The precolonial and colonial conflicts alluded to above underscored how important the overlapping claims were at generating a mutual defence pact for the lagoon. Amate (1999) documents several different attempts to defeat the Adas by outside forces, and thus seize the lagoon. The Adas were always successful at defending the lagoon. And yet, it was especially the threat of the growing power of the Ashanti kingdom that led the Adas to join other coastal communities in accepting British protection in the mid-1800s. This was the beginning of Britain's Gold Coast colony. In this sense, the British did not conquer the Adas, but rather entered into a protection, and later judiciary agreement, with them (Amate 1999). Colonial magistrates would supersede local authority if disputes arose that could not be handled locally. This was an important introduction, as it saw the rise of internal conflict concerning the Songor, where different British magistrates, over the later part of the nineteenth and early part of the twentieth centuries, ruled back and forth on behalf of different parties within the ruling structure of the Adas on which of them would control proceeds from the Songor (Amate 1999). This process of creating internal tensions in states through the manipulation of how customary law is interpreted is one of the ways in which the British enacted divide-and-rule processes (see, for instance, Gerschiere 1993, for an account of a similar process in

Cameroon). Of crucial significance to post-independence tensions in the Songor, this colonial interference created growing, though not absolute, power for Nene Ada – the Paramount Chief/king in the area – and diminished the power of the Libi Wornor; competing decisions did not complete this transition of power, thus leaving the door open to ongoing internal tensions, and to the potential for external powers to expropriate the resource through manipulation of these tensions. In the post-independence period, these tensions have been used by both efforts to dispossess the Adas of this resource.

At the same time, the systematic accumulation of 'legal rights' from colonial to post-independence practices disintegrated (dissipated) the ownership and trust bonds inherent in the structured traditional leadership relationships. This has given way to new bonds nurtured by ordinary citizens, galvanized by the spirit of Yomo to become social-justice-seeking, natural-resource-protecting, and livelihood-securing forces (movements) at two different stages in the life of the Ada people to interrogate, challenge, and fight threats to their spiritual and physical identity, and to the resource.

Two tales of dispossession and resistance

A crucial dimension of Harvey's (2004) notion of accumulation by dispossession is the privatization of collective and/or common assets, such as natural resources – thus dispossessing the many to the benefit of a few. Elsewhere, one of us (Langdon 2015) has described the way in which the Songor came to be held in trust by the current Fourth Republic of Ghana for the people of Ada and Ghana. It is through this position of trusteeship that the more recent effort at direct ABD occurred. At the same time, the parallel intentional failure to see through a plan approved by Songor communities for the development of the lagoon has neglected the resource and led to the rise of *atsiakpo*. And yet, ring-fencing the lagoon as a state interest emerged through an earlier privatization process of the lagoon through a series of duplicitous legalistic manoeuvres, at first, and finally through what Mbembe (2001: 79) has called the 'privatization of the means of coercion' – whereby state security apparatus is used to pacify local resistance to private accumulation processes. The whole story, though, begins at independence with a state intervention into the river system that feeds the lagoon.

Domino effect of national development According to Manuh (1992), the large-scale development of the Volta Dam, just up river from Ada, had a major ecological impact on the Songor, severely changing its natural flooding cycle that would replenish salt and then freshwater in the lagoon. Gyau-Boake (2001) has documented the devastating environmental impacts of the Volta project. In the case of Songor, this led to a seven-year period in the 1960s and 1970s when the lagoon failed to crystalize with salt. At the apex of this crisis, an external company approached a section of the local traditional authorities – exploiting colonial divisions described above. A deal was brokered that saw a portion of the lagoon leased to this company, called Vacuum Salt Ltd (VSL). In return for this access, the company promised creating a seawater intake point that would replenish the salinity level in the lagoon and restore salt formation. Although the intake point was created, the deal was broken, according to Amate (1999), by the company, when it changed the demarcation of its concession to now encompass almost the entire lagoon. Emphasizing this betrayal, Amate (1999) describes how C.O.C. Amattey brokered the original deal on behalf of the Tekperpiawe clan, and was later jailed when he fought against the betrayal (cf. Ada Salt Cooperative 1989).

Dispossession and resistance, the first tale Over the next decade and a half, Vacuum Salt Ltd (VSL) used every means at its disposal to maintain its concession, and to dispossess the traditional artisanal salt winners from collecting salt – despite the return to productive salt yields in the years after the saltwater intake point was established. This began with legal battles and convincing the state to use policy to defend its concession. It later turned to violence, with VSL enforcing its claim with the help of state security forces. At the same time, the resistance also became much more active in this period.

The legal and government policy back and forth
The legal battle with C.O.C. Amattey threw some doubt on to the company's concession, so it pressured for central government intervention to take over the lagoon through an Executive Instrument (1974's EI 30) and then to grant a government concession to VSL (1975's EI 57). At this time, resistance by Adas to this dispossession of the lagoon took the same path as VSL, in pleading for government intervention on their behalf. As a result of raising the issue of the

spiritual connection between the Adas and the Yomo spirit of the lagoon, EI 57 also included provision for an artisanal salt-winning section of the lagoon near the location of the Songor shrine. Though this area was not nearly as big as the VSL section, it did give Adas an opening to continue winning salt. Through the remainder of the 1970s, this uneasy balance was in place. It was only when the government changed from a military to civilian government that another opening appeared for appealing to the government. The party that won the election in 1979 also won the constituency, with the local candidate promising to overturn the company concession. This was done in the early part of 1981, through another Executive Instrument (EI 10), though it only abrogated the company concession, but didn't return control of the Songor to the Adas. The state had expanded its legal rights – something PNDC Law 287 would later echo.

The people take action, and the dispossession is violently defended
When the military revolution happened on 31 December 1981, a burgeoning movement of artisanal salt winners and young educated Ada allies was already forming to contest VSL, and therefore responded quickly to the revolutionary spirit. Across Ghana, People's Defense Committees (PDCs) were established to deepen the socialist principles the revolution purported to uphold. In the case of Ada, members of the local PDC – many of whom had the cause of the salt winners at heart – seized the VSL salt works, and opened up salt winning for artisanal salt winners. Unfortunately, those who took charge of the salt works did not effectively manage the place, putting short-term pillaging of the factory over the longer-term success of a people's run production unit. This spontaneous victory was to be short-lived, though, as VSL was working behind the scenes to convince a faction within the People's National Defense Council (PNDC) that its concession should be regranted.

Thankfully, it was in this period of uncertainty that the resistance movement in Ada shifted from spontaneity to strategy. As part of the transformation away from monopoly capitalism, and also to contend with a major return of Ghanaians expelled from Nigeria in 1983, the PNDC called for the formation of various forms of production cooperatives (La Verle 1994). Anticipating a need to secure traditional artisanal salt winner access to the lagoon, as well as taxation and customs forms to trade the salt won from the lagoon, a group associated with the PDC management committee worked to form cooperatives in the lagoon. This action had foresight, as on 1 June 1984, the PNDC government cancelled the EI 10 and regranted the VSL concession, while at the same time stating on radio: 'the traditional salt winners in the Ada Traditional Area must be encouraged to form co-operatives to win salt in the area allotted to them' (Ada Salt Cooperative 1989: 46). Despite having already registered the cooperative at this point, and having mobilized people to join it, the period that followed was still a battle, as VSL tried to eliminate the newly established cooperative through any means it could use, and the cooperative worked through every channel it could to access taxation and custom forms, as well as build up its membership numbers. This was the greatest period of open conflict in the Songor struggle. This was the period that VSL, and the owners of the controlling share of the company, the Apenteng family, used state security forces to try to destroy the cooperative, as well as punish any Ada trying to make a living from salt. Albert Apetorgbor, a long-time Songor activist, described one such incident in a Radio Ada (2002: 3) programme on the Songor:

> The late Apenteng, especially his son Stephen, would not allow anybody [in Ada] to win salt, let alone keep it in stock around the Lagoon for a better price.
>
> One day, in 1982, he brought some soldiers to the Kasseh market some 20 kilometers away from the Lagoon [. . .] The soldiers started beating all the women selling salt at the market and all the vehicles loaded with salt were attacked. Almost everybody took to their heels. Everybody was scared. I gathered courage and [. . .] approached the soldiers to find out what they were looking for. I stood by a man who introduced himself [. . .] open[ing] his palm and hit[ting] his chest boastfully, saying that he was Stephen Apenteng and the whole Ada state was under him and that he could do anything to the people at anytime he wished.

Interestingly, it was from 1982 to 1984 that the supposedly socialist PNDC began to negotiate Ghana's first structural adjustment programme with the World Bank and IMF (Hutchful 2002). This signalled a departure from the revolutionary path that had brought the PNDC to power. It also revealed the inner factions within the regime that would, on the one hand, facilitate ABD, while, on the other, provide some state support for artisanal salt winners and their allies to fight back.

Maggie's death and the near triumph of the salt winners

The conflict in the lagoon came to a head in 1985, when Maggie Kuwonor, an innocent pregnant woman standing in her home, was shot by a stray police bullet from an ongoing raid on salt winners. Her death brought major attention to the dispossession underway in Ada, and led to the Amissah Commission of Inquiry (Government of Ghana 1986). The commission came out clearly in favour of the people of Ada, and against the company, yet VSL still managed to have its concession lease secretly regranted. It was only in 1992, when the government passed PNDC Law 287, that the lease was concretely annulled and the central government took over the lagoon to be held in trust for the people of Ada and Ghana (Langdon 2011). A Master Plan for the Songor was drawn up to accompany this trusteeship; the plan would have seen the salt works of the lagoon have both industrial and artisanal access. This plan is to date the only one residents of the Songor area will attest to, as the Cuban team that developed it consulted with artisanal salt-winning cooperatives extensively, in addition to the industrial sector.

Financial resistance and cooperative schisms

Victory in the Amisah Commission was not easy, though, and involved the mobilization of resources and people, even if lawyers gave their time at greatly reduced rates. In the post-Maggie period, the cooperative was able to get a hold of the necessary customs and tax forms to enable members to trade their salt. It was also able to impose a small toll on top of these fees to pay for local development and maintenance of the cooperative. According to Manuh (1992), at the time, a bag of salt in Ada cost 40 cedis, while in Accra the same bag cost 600 cedis. As a result of collecting these fees and tolls, they were able to cover the basic costs of participating in the Amisah Commission. Seeing that the co-op was mounting a financial as well as a legal challenge to VSL swayed many traditional rulers, who began to unite behind the cooperative cause as the best way to get rid of the company. According to cooperative leaders at the time, this was part of the movement's strategy to unify the Adas – showing there was a viable financial alternative to the company (Manuh, 1992). For instance, the cooperative helped sponsor the 1986 and 1987 Asafotufiami Festival, mentioned at the outset (Manuh 1992). This was a symbolic and material gesture that signalled to the Traditional Council at the time that the cooperative could also help support some of the chiefs – perhaps not to the same extent as VSL, but from proceeds of a people's organization, not an entity dispossessing the people. According to Manuh (1992), these costs and others they took on are likely what led to charges of embezzlement against members of the cooperative leadership at the tail end of the 1980s. Similarly, with the removal of VSL as a threat in the later part of the 1980s, more and more cooperatives began to emerge to challenge the initial Ada Salt Winners Cooperative. With the passing of Law 287, the early 1990s saw the return of artisanal salt winning, and a fading out of the cooperative as a major player in the Ada context. One way of seeing this shift is a reaction to the cooperative loosing touch with the values and traditional way of organizing of the people. Another people's movement and organization wouldn't emerge in the area until a new pointed threat arose.

*The '*trorkpe *period: PND Law 287 and the beginning of intentional neglect*

PNDC Law 287 has been both beneficial in the short term and carried with it the potential of a longer-term threat. Its immediate impact was to remove VSL from the equation, and to allow artisanal salt winning to recommence. At the same time, the Master Plan the community supported, and that Law 287 makes a clear commitment to enact, has not been implemented. The state has acquired legal rights over the lagoon, and even reinforced these rights through the inclusion of salt as a government-owned mineral in the mining act of the PNDC era (Law 153), and restated in the current 2003 Mining Act. And yet, successive governments have failed to fulfil the promises of Law 287 'to ensure the efficient development of the salt potential of the Ada-Songor Lagoon by undertaking infrastructural work to benefit the *contiguous communities* and the public interest' (Government of Ghana 1992, p. 1, emphasis added). Instead, successive governments seem to have been of the same mind, to allow the resource to deteriorate due to neglect, while at the same time making attempts to find an 'investor' to take over the resource; these attempts come with explorations of the repeal of 287 (see below). This has been an ever-present concern of those fighting for communal access to the lagoon. In this sense, this period has become *'trorkpe*, being in the middle between two major events, where people are waiting for the proverbial second shoe to drop. The lack of finality has meant that many of the educated revolutionaries involved in the previous organizing have stayed interested in the fate of the lagoon, even as they have grown older and become more settled – despite the failure of the cooperative. This continued focus suggests the analysis they developed during the revolutionary period was still alive. In this sense, the movement was dormant, but not gone.

A new people's organization emerges
In the mid-1990s, another prospect of a people's organization emerged. Radio Ada, Ghana's first community radio station, was founded in 1997, after a two-year period of participatory dialogue. As part of its mandate to be both the *Voice of the Dangme People* and the *Voice of the Voiceless*, the station regularly broadcasts on Songor issues – keeping the Ada community connected with these issues even when they do not earn livelihoods from it. The presence of the station helped in the early part of the 2000s, when the previous Kufuor government floated the idea of a 'Land Use Plan' that would see the Songor parcelled up as a salt-mining concession, and privatized, while the communities surrounding the lagoon would be relocated. Although large-scale mobilization did not occur at this time, effective use of the media by some of the long-time Songor activists generated a heavy-handed reaction by the government (Osahatey 2006). Radio Ada added to this campaign by airing a number of oral testimonies in this period that reminded people of the previous conflict over the resource (e.g. Radio Ada 2002). None of these attempts to privatize followed through, and the other process of neglect was beginning to bear other fruit helpful for future dispossession: in 2003, *atsiakpo* saltpans – as they are called locally – began on a small scale on the outside of the lagoon, and gradually grew over the period to become a major issue by the time oil in commercial quantities was discovered off of Ghana's coast.

Dispossession and resistance, the second tale A change of government in 2008 came on the heels of Ghana's discovery of oil. The new government was the heir of the PNDC legacy, and therefore Adas hoped the Master Plan would finally be implemented. Working against this hope, as Affam and Asamoah (2011) indicate, was the strong case for linking Ghana's domestic salt industry with the burgeoning oil sector – especially for petrochemical uses. It is rumoured in Ada that many Ghanaian elite, including from the former and current governing parties, moved quickly to secure land in the Ada area to create their own '*atsiakpo*' saltpans to take advantage of this linkage (ASAF 2016). Ada elites also were interested in this prospect, and facilitated this elite process, even as they sponsored small-scale enclosures on the sly (while publicly speaking against them) (Langdon *et al.* 2014).

A people's radio: campaign on the airwaves
In 2008, at almost the same time national elites were developing atsiakpo's in the Ada – taking advantage of the long-term neglect of law 287 – Radio Ada began the campaign against *atsiakpo* with a series of radio programs, followed by broadcast announcements from traditional authorities calling on the practice to stop. At the same time, one of us has written how local youth in the Songor saw the danger of this practice for communal access and resisted it on the ground without much support by the older activist generation (Langdon, 2009). For instance, one young man in Toflokpo said when 'Atsiakpo was being constructed, some of us stood up against it. We destroyed some of the Atsiakpos and were arrested' (Toflokpo meeting, July 10th, 2011). No one came to their aid, or stopped the practice, noted another young man, 'Because when the decision, the chiefs having been making the call because they want to stop the Atsiakpo, but they are not really doing it because those ones are there and they are winning salt from them' (Toflokpo meeting, July 10th, 2011). This duplicity on the part of local authorities undermined Radio Ada's efforts.

Nonetheless, the effort to contest *atsiakpo* by Radio Ada was important both for the way it began the remobilization process in the fight that was to come, and for the way it drew attention to the salt pans being bought up by Accra elite that led to activists realizing there was a link between salt and oil. Unfortunately, when Radio Ada's strategy of working with traditional authorities backfired, the station began thus looking for a new approach to stop *atsiakpo*, even as tensions within salt winning communities, and between older activists and young Songor men who were arrested and not defended created the need for a credible mediator. Radio Ada became this mediator and the Ada Songor Advocacy Forum (ASAF) emerged – a space for dialogue, mutual-education, and organizing on Songor issues. ASAF began meeting in 2010, starting by collectively unpacking the history and contemporary challenges facing the lagoon. This phase of mobilization saw the movement shift from spontaneous reaction to a reflective process of strategizing collectively.

Larger dispossession on the horizon and and the resulting resistance
However, it became clear that the central government had much bigger plans for the salt sector in general and the Songor in particular. The first indication of this was a draft salt bill to regulate salt production that was tabled in 2009 by the government. This was the government's first real attempt to deal with salt as a mineral on par with gold. This bill was never presented to parliament and remains in draft form. Then, in 2011, the government met separately with different elements of traditional leadership to broker a deal to privatize the lagoon by turning it into a concession. Much like the colonial and VSL approach that aimed to drive a wedge between different traditional rulers, this was done in separate meetings with traditional leadership to reignite divisions and tensions. In each meeting, the government delegation stated the communities around the lagoon would be relocated and the artisanal salt producers would be given an alternative livelihood. In other words, they would be dispossessed of access to the lagoon and their livelihood.

Given that the central government signalled its renewed interest in the lagoon in May 2011, the timing of the shift in movement strategy from reacting to *atsiakpo* to being more reflective on the Songor situation could not have been better. While preparing a new campaign to take on *atsiakpo* in early 2011, news reached ASAF of the delegation. After discussing this turn of events, ASAF outlined a course of action that would build on its planned *atsiakpo* campaign. Twelve Songor communities were visited over the course of June and July. In each community, asking for community feeling about the potential of relocation abated the tensions over discussions of *atsiakpo*. At the same time, a groundswell of feeling against the proposed relocation and alternative livelihoods emerged. The reaction of one of the elder priestesses of the Yomo spirit in Lufenya conveys the groundswell:

> What we are hearing is that we will be moved away from here. Because they are coming to move us, are coming to move our Gods, our great-grandfathers? We have buried our mothers, our traditional leaders, our ancestors are here. I don't know how to leave these ancestors. So, if they are coming to move them, we will now be calling our children 'Amake koleki', they are dead, the dead. How are you going to move them? And, we will not agree to leave because our great grandfathers have been winning salt, and we are also part of it and winning salt every since. (focus group discussion, 17 July 2011)

This series of community-level discussions were turned into several broadcasts, where community voices and concerns about the relocation, as well as information about it, were aired on Radio Ada. Despite quick and contradictory on-air responses by local- and national-level officials – some saying they never spoke of relocation, while others confessed they had gone about things the wrong way – the overwhelming negative reaction of communities stalled the plan. While mentioning the plan to turn the Songor Salt Project into a limited liability company, the Vice President (now President) John Mahama remained silent on the prospect of relocation.

Secret plans emerge and are countered with open discussion
The plan, however, had not gone away. ASAF found this out in two separate ways. First, the idea of eliminating PNDC Law 287 was floated by the Minister of Lands and Natural Resources at a national mining forum (Langdon field notes, 2012). The importance of cancelling this law was made clear in a secret attestation and cabinet memo that was leaked to ASAF in July 2012, where it was clearly stated by government legal experts that the law was a barrier to turning the lagoon into a private concession. The attestation attached to this memo contained a statement from Ada traditional and local government authorities stating their support for the plan, and the provision of alternative livelihoods to the contiguous communities around the Songor.

One of the major emergent learnings from the 2011 campaign was the committed response of women across the Songor communities to see *atsiakpo* end, and to defend communal access to the lagoon. Over the course of the year, women, such as the priestess from Lufenya, began mobilizing, and sent representatives to ASAF meetings at Radio Ada making clear their intention to send a potent message to government, as well as *atsiakpo* practitioners, at the 2012 Asafotufiami Festival. This was an idea that first arose in 2011, but took a year to fully plan. At a planning meeting at Radio Ada, one of the women representatives from Toflokpo declared their intentions: 'We said we will wear trousers, we will go with Gong-gongs and some people will carry salt, and some women in Toflokpo said we need to wear red tops so that they know we are very serious' (13 July 2012). A women's collective was formed that planned not only a march at the Asafotufiami Festival, but also a major popular education intervention, by taking over an agricultural display at the festival to share the story of the Songor with visitors to Ada, as well as residents who may not know its full history. A tapestry was commissioned by the women to illustrate this story. It began by depicting meeting the Yomo spirit, and continued through the various eras, including when the lagoon was taken over by VSL and Maggie was killed. It also showed the lagoon chopped up into little *atsiakpo* saltpans, and a woman reduced to labourer status. It carried a final message with the lagoon symbolically locked in a box. Women from various Songor communities developed the story to accompany the tapestry. The narration finished with a declaration that linked the present threats facing the lagoon to the past, and a question enticing the listener to join the action:

> Presently the state of Ada is we are mourning, we are so sad, we are in poverty. The question is should this continue, because in those days people were arrested, people were arrested, this is the police. They arrested people, they chased people, some were asked to eat salt. Some were driven away, and this has continued and continued up to date. We are saying the wealth that we have is encased and locked up in this box, what do we do? (Rev. Sophia Kitcher, 4 August 2012)

This approach was in line with the strategy of the movement at this time: create and maintain an open space of dialogue about Songor issues, where community, activist, and salt winner voices can be heard, and where public debate about the future of this collective resource – literally the touchstone of Ada identity – can take place. This was in contrast to the secret plans of dispossession that both government and local elite in Ada continued to pursue. A major emerging analysis of ASAF members, driven by the on-the-ground knowledge of Songor community members, was that *atsiakpo* was being sponsored by chiefs and other Ada decision-makers – despite their public statements that they were against the practice. This led a youth focus group at one of ASAF's first meetings in 2011 to call the traditional rulers of Ada and the Songor *chameleons* – showing one face in public, and another in private (youth focus group, 9 June 2011).

Roughly 60 women (between 5 and 10 each from the eight main Songor communities) arrived at the festival grounds early on the day of Asafotufiami, and marched around the grounds, wearing red, and carrying signs and salt. The signs read, 'Salt for Sale, Lagoon Not for Sale', 'Okor Forest Sacred, Yomo Place Holy', and 'No Lagoon Privatization', among others. This march, especially that it was women, coupled with the educational approach to their display, meant the police present at the festival could not interfere – though one local administrator knocked over their placards at the educational display. Their presence also attracted a lot of attention, with over 2,000 people visiting the display that day – including the very political leadership from Accra connected to the idea of alternative livelihoods and relocation.

At the same time that the women were planning and engaging in this action, an ASAF team, made up of members of the women's collective, the older generation of male activists, and Radio Ada, visited a series of Songor communities to share this secret attestation with Songor communities. At a meeting in Anyamam, one of the ASAF team, the district director for the National Commission for Civic Education (NCCE), received a phone call from the District Chief Executive, head of the local governance administration in Ada, accusing the ASAF member of causing confusion in the district. The DCE was a signatory of the attestation. The ASAF member told him he was doing the work the local government head should have done – letting the people know what he had in store for them. News of this phone call was shared with the Anyamam community, and people thanked Radio Ada and the ASAF team for bringing what was happening to their attention. Anyamam women also added their commitment to going to Asafotufiami to ensure it was clear they would not agree to an alternative livelihood, nor to relocation.

Community radio deepens open discussion

Another major element of the open, educative strategy used by the current iteration of the movement is the central role of Radio Ada – not only hosting discussions where people from all walks of life can speak on Songor issues, but also in its role as a broadcaster of the voice of the voiceless. As mentioned above, Radio Ada has featured Songor issues in shows since it first went on the air. Its broadcasts were a crucial part of the only briefly successful effort to end *atsiakpo*. By the same token, over the past three years, Radio Ada has contributed enormously to creating an environment for open discussion of Songor issues through its broadcasts. It featured educative discussions on Songor laws in its legal advice show; it hosted call-in shows where ASAF organizers could field questions about the government plans they had uncovered; it created a drama series called *Okor Ng Kor* where issues of trusteeship on the Songor, including the importance of women's leadership, could be highlighted in a humorous and dramatized fashion; it broadcast community opinion from visits to Songor towns; it shared statements by trustees defending actions around the Songor; and it provided airtime for ASAF members to discuss their understanding of Songor affairs. In other words, it took the openness of the ASAF approach and extended it to the airwaves.

Radio Ada has also been adept at using this openness to the movement's advantage. For instance, at a meeting in Goi in mid-August 2012 – just after the Asafotufiami Festival where the women marched – the ASAF and Radio Ada team were met with a major challenge. All of the traditional rulers who had come to the meeting suddenly got up and left, having received phone calls and texts threatening them with the loss of their positions if they stayed. The team present understood this was a rebuke for having caused confusion at the festival, however the Radio Ada team in particular insisted that they should prove to all Ada that what they are doing is for the benefit of all – they are not hiding anything. The station quickly organized and put the whole meeting live on air through a remote link, but also ensured that the show focus on other local concerns in addition to the Songor. The nearby sacred Okor Forest, where legend says the Yomo spirit met the first Adas in the area, is being depleted, through deforestation, just as the lagoon suffers a similar fate. This connection was made in the broadcast, and local residents emphasized the need to respect traditions and maintain the lagoon and forest well to benefit the people of Ada. This open strategy left the Ada elite behind the chiefs' departure flat-footed, as ASAF and Radio Ada had positioned themselves as the defenders of Ada tradition and identity. In fact, a delegation from the station and ASAF, led by one of the women's leaders, visited the Ada Traditional Council later that year and received an apology for the way the Goi meeting was handled. This apology was aired as part of a documentary on the Songor produced by ATV, a national TV station.

Because of these consistent, open efforts, it has become much more difficult for Ghana's government, as well as local elites, to operate in the shadows and decide the fate of the Songor. Indications of the impact of this surfaced in the statement at the 2015 Asafotufiami Festival, where President John Mahama mentioned the need for artisanal salt winners to continue to have lagoon access even as the privatization of the lagoon goes ahead – an indication that they will respect Law 287. This is not the end goal of those organizing around the Songor, where a plan is underway to produce a Songor community manifesto for the future of the resource, but it is an acknowledgement that Songor residents have a right to a salt livelihood – a sacred bond between the Adas and the lagoon that the Yomo spirit is not likely to allow to be taken away.

Dispossession destabilized through livelihood, identity and spiritual defence, and strategic open dialogue

Different conditions of struggle have dictated different strategies in the Songor activism. Where an unstable and militarized state existed, dispossession took the form of outright, unapologetic robbery by a company attempting to take all that it could. Likewise, resistance was necessarily more confrontational, and about contrasting this vision with a local organization that could provide the economic well-being the company promised, but do so for all to benefit. It was the death of Maggie Kuwonor that turned the tides on the company and gave the

Ada Salt Winners Cooperative the opening it needed to supersede the company, and end the dispossession. In contemporary times, where secret dispossession plans are hidden behind policy statements and the illusion of democracy, resistance must take a more open and people-first approach. The community radio station is central to this new form of open activism.

At the same time, grounding activism in Ada identity and spirituality destabilized both eras of attempted dispossession. The cultural power of the Asafotufiami Festival underscores the potential power of such claims. It is not for nothing that national-level politicians use the festival to announce the latest development plans for the area, including plans for the Songor. It is also not surprising that both resistance efforts have used it as a way of announcing their presence, and their approach to resistance. The cooperative insisted there was an alternative to the company to engage in locally profitable salt winning; ASAF and Radio Ada insist that open dialogue about the lagoon's future is the only way to ensure equitable and stable use of the resource, based on a mutually derived plan.

However, dispossession attempts can take many angles to succeed. Current *atsiakpo* processes in the lagoon represent ongoing dispossession of communal access by internal and some external elite. And yet its presence also represents the kind of local chaos and conflict that justified state intervention during the last struggle, leading to the lagoon being held in trust by the state. In other words, *atsiakpo* could well become the latest mechanism of divide and rule by the project of new imperialism to accumulate this space in service of the global oil capital – the latest mechanism of large-scale dispossession.

Akpetiyo Lawer, a brilliant troubadour of the movement, has captured these worries more eloquently than we could. She sings:

Look behind us, there comes Government after us [. . .] But what is the issue? *Atsiakpo* is consuming the whole Songor. And all attempts to stop it have proved futile, the fire rages on. Government could not help but to step in. They told our Elders, they are going to take over Songor, to quell conflicts so that we live in peace. (ASAF 2016: ii)

In response, she says, Radio Ada must put 'on their broadcast armour'. Wearing it, she says, 'we entered the communities and started informing the people; we are spreading it', the ability to see through their plans. This call to open knowledge is echoed in the conclusion of her song, 'I say, what one doesn't know, someone knows!' Finding it out and sharing it is the current armour of this movement against whatever attempt to dispossess is on the horizon.

References

Ada Salt Cooperative (1989). *Who Killed Maggie?* Accra: Ada Salt Cooperative Committee.

Affam, M. and Asamoah, D.N. (2011). 'Economic potential of salt mining in Ghana towards the oil find'. *Research Journal of Environmental and Earth Sciences*, 3(5): 448–456.

Amate, C.O.C. (1999). *The Making of Ada*. Accra: Woeli Publishing Services.

ASAF (Ada Songor Advocacy Forum) (2016). *The Struggle of the Songor Salt People*. Sogakope, Ghana: Comboni Press.

Dangme East District Assembly (2012). 'District development plan'. Unpublished document. Accra: Dangme East District Assembly.

Gerschiere, P. (1993). 'Chiefs and colonial rule in Cameroon: inventing chieftaincy, French and British style'. *Africa*, 63(2): 151–170.

Government of Ghana (1986). *The Amissah Commission Report*. Accra: Assembly Press.

Government of Ghana (1992). *PNDC Law 287*. Accra: Assembly Press.

Gyau-Boake, P. (2001). 'Environmental impacts of the Akosombo Dam and effects of climate change on the lake levels'. *Environment, Development and Sustainability*, 3: 17–29.

Harvey, D. (2004). 'The new imperialism: accumulation by dispossession'. *Socialist Register*, 40: 63–84.

Hutchful, E. (2002). *Ghana's Adjustment Experience: The Paradox of Reform*. Geneva: UNRI.

Langdon, J. (2010). 'Contesting globalization in Ghana: communal resource defense and social movement learning'. *Journal of Alternative Perspectives in the Social Sciences*, 2(1): 309–339.

Langdon, J. (2015). 'Democratic hopes, transnational government(re)ality: grounded social movements and the defense of communal natural resources in Ghana'. In D. Kapoor and D. Caouette (eds), *Beyond Colonialism, Development and Globalization*. London: Zed Books, pp. 49–66.

Langdon, J., Larweh, K., and Cameron, S. (2014). 'The thumbless hand, the dog and the chameleon: enriching social movement learning theory through epistemically grounded narratives emerging from a participatory action research case study in Ghana'. *Interface: A Journal for and About Social Movements*, 6(1): 27–44.

La Verle, B. (ed.) (1994). *Ghana: A Country Study*. Washington, DC: GPO for the Library of Congress.

Manuh, T. (1992). 'Survival in rural Africa: the salt co-operatives in Ada District, Ghana'. In D.R.F. Taylor and F. Mackenzie (eds), *Development from Within: Survival in Rural Africa*. New York: Routledge, pp. 102–124.

Mbembe, J.A. (2001). *On the Postcolony*. Berkeley, CA: University of California Press.

Osahatey, P. (2006). 'Ghana Police at it again: disrupt press conference . . . harass organizers, journalists'. *Chronicle*, Accra, 13 November.

Radio Ada (2002). *Radio Ada Oral Testimony Documentary: Resource Conflict – The Songor Lagoon*. Ada, Ghana: Radio Ada.

12 | CONTESTING DISPOSSESSION: LAND RIGHTS ACTIVISM IN GAMBELLA, ETHIOPIA, AND PUJEHUN, SIERRA LEONE

Rachel Ibreck

Introduction

When peasants cede land to large-scale agribusiness projects, they experience radical changes, whether the deals are imposed or involve consultation. Rural people in Africa often have rights to land, vested in either neo-customary authority or the state, and regard these as both an economic and social asset – a source of heritage, livelihood, and imagined security. This means that whether or not the land in question was in productive use at the moment of its expropriation, the loss can be catastrophic. Monetary compensation may help, but it is insufficient unless people's lives change for the better in an overall sense; the sentiment of loss may only deepen over time. Not least because the rise of foreign investment in plantation agriculture in Africa is taking place alongside present or imminent land shortages. We should therefore expect contestation of large-scale land acquisitions, sooner or later, and examine it closely as it arises.

Transnational activism foregrounded the problem of land grabs in the international media and policy circles, but challenging such deals depends largely upon specific understandings and actual practices at the sites of investments. Local resistance to 'land grabs' is often 'hidden' or fragmented, since the global inequalities that make such land leases possible also inhibit collective action. Critics of the deals risk repression from political authorities that may have political or personal interests in the deals. They are also up against the local beneficiaries: communities are socially differentiated and some people gain directly, whether from jobs, corporate social responsibility initiatives, business opportunities, or more subtle incentives. Additionally, land rights activists risk becoming implicated in violent, ethnic, or patronage politics. Despite these conditions, new social formations and strategies of resistance have emerged that are essentially place-based – animated by imaginings of and attachments to places, and engaged in the defence of local cultures, economies, and communal life (Escobar 2001).

This chapter explores resistance to land grabs 'from below' in Sierra Leone and Ethiopia, capturing a snapshot of multilayered and evolving activist processes that have yet to be closely examined. It surveys a five-year period (2011–2016), drawing on political ethnography and documentary research.[1] The research participants were mainly educated elites and community leaders at the forefront of articulating the resistance related to investments in Pujehun, Sierra Leone, and the Gambella region, Ethiopia. Their views are not deemed to be representative – indeed, they are mostly male.[2] But they are the leading makers of meaning and architects of resistance at the local level, and their perspectives matter as such. The discussion first situates the new struggles in political context, briefly surveying relevant histories of contentious politics. It then examines how people affected by the deals in Pujehun district, Sierra Leone, and the region of Gambella in Ethiopia have mobilized against the deals. It identifies a new breed of land rights activists engaged in largely non-violent place-based struggles, but with networks stretching into transnational movements and the diaspora.

The underlying driver for recent foreign investments in African land appears to be rooted in the logic of global capital (Harvey 2004), yet affected people may not identify this 'new imperialism' as the core challenge. Instead, they and their local advocates are embroiled in contests against a local politics of dispossession, in which the conduct of particular authorities, companies, and local elite brokers is instrumental, and they often use transnational connections to garner support for their cause. As such, people often continue to hope that investments will deliver opportunities, while blaming individual companies or governments for unfair terms. Moreover, because rural communities feel the impact of land investments in their everyday lives in a specific locality, their reactions are shaped by the particularities of the investments and by historical experiences.

Activism in context: political constraints and opportunities

Land grabbing is a long-standing practice of national corporate and political elites in Ethiopia and Sierra Leone. But the recent foreign investments have dramatically increased the scale in both countries.³ And the speed with which the deals have been completed and the negligible compensation also raise many questions. There is good evidence that the land taken was not 'terra nullius'; the leases were not based on 'free prior and informed consent'; and they have already had some negative impacts and implications for the rural poor.

There are still differences of opinion upon whether large-scale agriculture can contribute to development, but even leading proponents recognize that there have been flaws in the acquisition process and many deals have had detrimental impacts (see World Bank 2010). Such problems have been convincingly documented in my two sites, Pujehun district in Sierra Leone (Oakland Institute 2011), a mainly rural area populated by over 228,000 (Sierra Leone Statistics 2004) and the region of Gambella in Ethiopia (Oakland Institute 2013), whose rural population exceeds 229,000 (Ethiopia Central Statistical Agency 2007). In both these localities, there was a sudden and extensive influx of foreign investors in land in the post-2007 period: some 225,012 hectares of Gambella's land were estimated to have been rapidly leased (Davison 2011), while the estimate for Pujehun was 248,294 hectares (Green Scenery 2013). Not all the land leases led to a commercial farming project – some lay dormant – but those that did became the focus of protest.

In Pujehun, the most established project was that undertaken by Socfin Agricultural Company Sierra Leone Ltd (Socfin) for a palm oil and rubber plantation to cover 30,000 hectares. Socfin initially consulted the community on its plans, not least because land in Sierra Leone is governed by neo-customary authority, with a system of family tenure and the Paramount Chief as overall 'custodian'. Nevertheless, the landowners were not well informed on the details of the lease, and they were subject to the power and interests of chiefdom authorities. The company's headquarters were in the town of Sahn Malen, and the land in Malen Chiefdom was the first to be incorporated into the project. Landowners there were induced to sign a lease for 6,500 hectares over 50 years, under pressure and confusion. Socfin's plantations now cover 12,000 hectares, the company has employed close to 4,000 workers, and it has contributed to community development, including through schools and roads. However, the annual rent payments (at US$12.5 per hectare) proved too low to cover the landowners' loss of livelihoods (Yengoh and Armah 2014), and food security and nutrition were found to have been negatively affected (ALLAT 2013).

The Karituri and Saudi Star investments in Gambella proceeded without consultation and met with significant local opposition (Rahmato 2011). In Ethiopia, land is deemed common property of the 'state and peoples', administered by the government (FDRE 1995: Article 40). The deals were initially crafted between the companies and regional government, and later renegotiated with the federal government. Saudi Star was given 10,000 hectares for a 60-year period in 2009, and later added 4,000 more, for which it paid just $3 per hectare. It established its headquarters in Abobo, in the Anuak zone of Gambella. After initial difficulties, it produced some rice for both the domestic market and hoped to export. It employed 1,300 mostly seasonal workers (FT Investigations 2016). Karituri took out a much larger concession in 2008 (renegotiated in 2010), leasing 100,000 hectares at a rate of $1–1.25 per hectare to grow cereals for export. The company's base was in the Anuak village of Ilea, in the district of Itang, and it established a school and some new boreholes under its corporate social responsibility schemes. Despite clearing 65,000 hectares, the company faced setbacks, both in raising the necessary funds to develop the farm, and due to flooding productivity was very low. The government cancelled the lease in December 2015 (Davison 2016).

Land investments on this scale are bound to import alien practices and transform the physical terrain, but they also send tremors through society and politics. People's responses to this shock are informed by the 'cultural material' (McAdam *et al.* 2007: 3) embedded through shared histories and practices, as well as by their contemporary circumstances. And while we cannot hope to describe these intricate cultural legacies here, it is important to note that collective action against land dispossession has previously been violent and revolutionary. 'Land to the tiller' was the clarion call of the 1974 revolution in Ethiopia, uniting the peasantry, pastoralists, and other dispossessed in violent mobilizations against predation and exploitation by a class of feudal lords (Zewde 2002). The 1975 land reform, partly by governmental decree and partly enforced through the action of local people, remains the most dramatic case of land distribution in African modern history. Many of the peasants' gains of that revolutionary period were, however, clawed back by subsequent central government legislation (vesting land ownership exclusively in the state) and policies (for large-scale farming, urban expansion, and resettlement). In Sierra Leone, neo-customary tenure has endured across much of the country (except the Freetown Peninsula). But anger concerning the inequalities and exigencies of the agrarian order fuelled rural insurrections, most notably in that of the Revolutionary United Front (RUF) rebellion (1991–2002) (Peters and Richards 2011).

Looking back, neither Ethiopia nor Sierra Leone have a record of non-violent social movements acting on social and economic issues. Human rights struggles have typically been urban-based, and focused on civil and political rights. These tend to be suppressed in Ethiopia, both by law[4] and by police violence, such as during the elections of 2001 and 2005 (HRW 2005). Sierra Leone is a more conducive environment for human rights campaigning, yet workers and student protests have been harshly dealt with, with repeated assaults upon the rights of people in mining areas. The urban and rural are usually distinct terrains of struggle here, as elsewhere in Sub-Saharan Africa. The international human rights movement has remained distant from rural communities. Meanwhile, rural land conflict has often been violent, triggered by land shortage and shaped by prevailing land tenure regimes (Boone 2014).

New land rights activism The responses to the land deals reflect ongoing changes in the forms and organization of contention. New networks have formed connecting rural peasants and indigenous rights activists to the international human rights movement. Those affected by the land grabs have often (though not exclusively) protested non-violently, and even when land tenure is neo-customary their struggles are not necessarily ethnically defined.

The responses to the Socfin deal in Sierra Leone exemplify the new land activism. Here, opposition towards the plantation coalesced in the formation of a network at chiefdom level, the Malen Affected Land Owners Assocation (later renamed Malen Land Owners and Land Users Association, MALOA) in 2012. MALOA is a voluntary membership organization based on residence, although most people in the area are from the Mende ethnic group. The organization was initially supported by at least 101 male heads of landholding families in Malen, who signed its founding resolutions (MALOA 2012). MALOA supporters include not only landowners, but also land users, and women as well as men; all are farmers, but among them are also community leaders such as town chiefs (lower-ranking members of the chieftancy) and teachers. Chiefdom authorities refused to register the organization, declaring it 'illegal and unknown', and its members have faced pressure and arrests, but they continued to campaign publicly and non-violently. And, importantly, it soon became connected to a national-level organization, Action for Large-Scale Land Acquisition Transparency (ALLAT), uniting people affected by the investments from various localities and groups across the country as part of an unprecedented nascent movement articulating the social and economic concerns of the masses (Abdullah 2014).

In Gambella, the land deals have animated both non-violent and violent struggles by indigenous rights activists. 'Indigenous people's organizations' in the diaspora took the lead in a public campaign against land grabs, in particular the Anywaa Survival organization in the UK and Anuak Justice Council in the US. Less obviously, there are informal covert networks of Anuak activists in Gambella and Kenya, connected to the diaspora, but also pursuing their own ideas and approaches at local levels. There have also been some violent protests – notably, a direct attack on *Saudi Star* on 28 April 2012 by Anuak rebels, in which two Pakistani workers and three Ethiopians were killed. This was followed by a wave of repression by the Ethiopian military against local villagers, including arbitrary arrests and rapes (HRW 2012). There have been a handful of other attacks by Anuak forces, including the killing of 19 people in a bus attack on 12 March 2012, and sporadic conflicts between Anuak and Nuer, during the same period.

The different ways in which MALOA and the Anuak community have mobilized in response to the land deals are apparent in their 'framing' of the problem of the land investments, and interpretation of its causes, as well as in their modes of contention (McAdam *et al.* 2007).[5]

Contesting land dispossession in Pujehun, Sierra Leone

Protecting the community of Malen The chiefdom of Malen was described by MALOA members as fertile and productive, the source of their security and livelihoods. Its land was a 'bank for all villagers' that can 'feed families and children' and the 'as yet unborn'. It provided sticks for firewood and building and nutritious foods, including rice, cassava, pineapples, and coco yams: 'with our bush in our possession we can feed and educate children'. They agreed that development was greatly needed and mentioned a previous commercial project in the area, the small-scale palm oil plantation of the Sierra Leone Produce Marketing Board (SLPMB), as a positive example. But they emphasized the need to protect Malen from 'strangers', keeping it as 'family land'. They expressed pride in their 'bush', which served them 'economically and for consumption', and as a home 'for history and tomorrow'. 'If we sell that bush we have sold our life . . . we don't admire anything more than the land we live in'.

MALOA members made only occasional allusions to past poverty and conflict, for instance noting that 'only two to three houses were left here after the war'. Yet, Malen lies in a marginalized and poverty-stricken area, with a history of slavery, violence, and war. Slavery was only banned in the protectorate in 1928, and its legacies are embedded in Mende social life (Ferme 2001: 82), layered over with the exactions of colonial rule. Pujehun was the site of the bitter political conflict of the 1982 *Ndogboyosoi* war, and the district was destroyed during the civil war, 1991–2002, when some of its youth, joined the rebel Revolutionary United Front (RUF), while others were part of the civil defence forces linked to chiefly authority, the *Kamajor*. Over 300 people were killed in the community during the war (TRC 2004: 476), and many more have endured crippling poverty since: average life expectancy was only 46, with very high rates of infant death and food insecurity (UN OCHA 2015).

MALOA members were angry about the exploitation of their land and labour, describing the investment as a 'land grab' and the Socfin plantation as 'slavery work'. But they sought to distinguish their struggle from past conflict. They emphasized that Malen had recovered socially: 'we don't have divisions in the community; after the war there was CDF and RUF but today we are all one'; 'this is a collective idea – we are all united'. In written statements, MALOA emphasized the need to 'consolidate this hard earned peace' (MALOA 2012), and spoke of 'struggling to set our people free'. They said the Paramount Chief had allowed the company to clear the land regardless of the opposition of individual landowners: 'the chiefs are using the survey team and damaging we poor ones here'; they 'do brushing by force'. They regarded the plantation as a new source of insecurity 'bringing confusion and problems in this chiefdom when elections are fast approaching'. In contrast, MALOA, and their struggle to halt the plantation, was conceived as a means to preserve peace and protect the community.

Betrayed by the chiefs MALOA members were deeply troubled by the opaque relationship between the company and the chiefdom authorities, and blamed these leaders, especially the Paramount Chief (PC), for imposing the land lease upon the people of Malen. The chieftancy is the lynchpin of the agrarian order in Sierra Leone, and is tied into a web of clientelist networks connecting upwards to government or political party elites in Freetown. Chiefs draw legitimacy from social norms and beliefs, but have sustained their power through brokering between the local resources of land and people and external interests – colonial, governmental, or commercial. The Paramount Chief is 'custodian of the land', appointed by landowning, 'ruling' families and holds the position for life, and chiefs also retain central functions in the administration of justice and security (Albrecht 2015). There is variation within chiefly structures, and between different chiefdoms (Acemoglu *et al.* 2014), but they are situated within a political economy of extraction that dates back to the era of slavery, and persists today. It is in this context that we can make sense of MALOA supporters' concerns that the chiefdom authorities were in alliance with the company and government elites for their own benefit, and against the interests of the community.

Although some MALOA supporters were themselves section or town chiefs, there was a consensus that the people had been sold out by the Malen chiefdom authorities, in particular the PC and the Chiefdom Speaker. They described how the PC introduced the company to the people, suggesting it would be a revival of the SLPMB plantation and persuading landowners to agree to the investment on false premises. The meetings between the PC and the company were, they said, 'behind our back', 'there was no transparency in the issue'; they believed there must be a 'hidden agenda in the operation and we are trying to uncover this'.

Most agreed that the reason landowners signed the lease was that they did not understand it, since the details were not fully explained. But they also saw the hand of the PC in manipulating the consultations and pressuring people to sign. They recalled the event at which the lease was confirmed, in which Socfin gave out cash as part of the official compensation, as a chiefdom 'money meeting', where 'piles of leones' (local currency) were handed out to section and town chiefs, as a 'shake hands' to sign the lease (MALOA 2012). It seemed to them that some people simply made a mistake: they signed the deal because they 'wanted money', but later realized that the money was 'not enough'. But others who had been opposed to the deal previously were, according to MALOA members, given incentives or pressured to sign.

There were repeated allegations of corruption. People were suspicious that the Chiefdom Speaker had just built a large new house, while the PC was driving a new car. They suggested that some supporters of the deal received bribes: 'people were squeezed [bribed] to accept'; 'they are getting shares out of this'. They suspected that the practice of bribery was also being used to undermine MALOA's support: 'if you are coming on our behalf they send you a brown envelope (bribe)'. The district council chairman was once 'in our favour' but changed his mind when 'he was sent a brown envelope'. They suggested that even the company survey team was corrupt, underestimating their land and 'pocketing' the difference in payment. They also referred to divisions within families, where one member agreed to the deal and collected money on behalf of others, without their agreement: 'our section chief is our brother, he collects the money'.

Whether because of bribery, or simply differences of opinion about the Socfin plantation, tensions between family members, within villages, and between people and their chiefs were rising: 'the community is divided, we are not on good terms, they have money and we don't have'.

Sticking to the law MALOA members stressed their commitment to legal and non-violent methods of protest and to connecting to other affected people nationally and regionally. The formation of MALOA was itself described as a method of promoting a united and peaceful struggle, and they continued to try to register and build the organization (despite blockages at the district level). They resolved to work closely with civil society organizations and human rights lawyers in Pujehun, Bo, and Freetown (in particular, Green Scenery).

They also sought opportunities to connect to regional networks, for instance welcoming interactions with a representative of REACT who had promised to connect their struggle with affected people at Socfin plantations in Liberia and Cameroon. They held meetings within the community, gathered documentation, shared information, and organized a few public demonstrations. They wrote numerous letters to relevant officials, including the Paramount Chief, District Council, District Officer, and Human Rights Commission (MALOA 2011). In the words of one member, 'we reported grievances to the civil society lawyer, they just advise us to wait patiently and not use violent means . . . no one uses violence, we are sticking to the law'.

However, speaking in early 2013, MALOA members were also concerned about the limited impact of their peaceful strategies: 'we've written, but the company still continues'. They argued that the proponents of the lease were using repressive tactics 'when we complain nothing is done; when they complain they arrest us'; 'we said not to use violence, but this is coming from the side of the company'. While they had decided to 'avoid confrontation', several MALOA members were involved in direct action to stop the bulldozers from uprooting their trees. One woman even threw herself in front of the machines, preventing them from progressing, while several men obstructed the progress of the surveyors or the bulldozers in demonstrations at the site of their family land. Such efforts by landowners to block the operations of the company had already led to intimidation or arrests. In 2011, 40 men were arrested and 15 were charged on counts of 'riotous conduct, conspiracy and threatening language' (Welthungerhilfe 2012). In 2012, four protest leaders were charged with 'riotous and insulting conduct' and possession of 'offensive weapons' (Pujehun Magistrate Court 2012).

In the years since, MALOA maintained its peaceful stance under intense pressure. At moments, it seemed that the strategy was gaining traction – there was even a meeting between MALOA representatives and the Bolloré group (major shareholders in Socfin) to seek a solution to the dispute in 2014. But the company's plantations expanded and tensions rose. In October 2013, six MALOA activists, among them former MP Siaka Sama, were arrested, accused of destroying 40 oil palm trees belonging to Socfin, and in 2015 they were convicted of 'incitement, conspiracy and destruction', and given heavy fines and five to six months in prison each (Foryoh 2016). The situation deteriorated further in January 2015, with the shooting of two Socfin staff. MALOA firmly distanced itself from those responsible and condemned the action, but they were increasingly under pressure from the authorities. By the time the President was invited to open the new oil mill in Malen in 2016, the antipathy of the government towards the resisters was clear: 'President of Sierra Leone Ernest Bai Koroma vows to clamp down on civil society organisations and NGOs championing environment and land justice issues' (Premier News 2016). MALOA's commitment to lawful means did not protect it from the force of the law, or the condemnation of authorities. Perhaps not surprisingly, given the strong political support for the Socfin investment, and the sway that chiefdom authorities have in the fields of justice and security in the rural domain (Albrecht 2015).

While MALOA's methods of contention were mainly civic, there were indications that the organization also drew on cultural resources and appealed to customary notions of 'the law'. This tendency surfaced in a mass protest in December 2013, when opponents of the Socfin plantation initiated the Poro secret society to protect the bush from clearance by the company. The Poro brought together some 500 men in the forest to claim a plot of land for the secret society and to protect it from the expanding Socfin plantation. They blockaded a nearby road, and when the Local Unit Commander of the police came to investigate they engaged him in a dialogue to explain their demands. In so doing, they followed in a historic practice of invoking the Poro as a mobilizing force; the society has at different times been employed by the patrimonial order in 'hierarchical political control' or by its opponents in forms of 'egalitarian resistance', including in anti-colonial insurrections and the civil war. It is perhaps for these reasons that the peaceful Poro protest met with a strong repressive response from the authorities: 57 protesters were arrested, 32 were charged, and police fired live bullets and teargas at the protesters, resulting in several injuries (Green Scenery 2014).

The Poro society is a means of channelling of the spirit world in social regulation, and has an 'unspoken' role in politics and in law and order in Mende society (Fanthorpe 2007: 9). Most importantly, it embodies the 'underneath of things', a deep association in Mende culture between concealment and power (Ferme 2001). Its initiation and suppression speak to the premium on secrecy and the inevitability of silences in MALOA's public discourses. It is also a reminder that the repression of MALOA and apparent community support for Socfin – exemplified in a student protest with banners proclaiming 'We want Socfin for Development' and 'Red Card to MALOA' (Saffa 2016) – may not be seen as the end of the matter. Where concealment and ambiguity are social arts, we may find perpetual 'unpredictability', and subtle 'limits on power' (Ferme 2001: 6).

Contesting land dispossession in Gambella, Ethiopia

Preventing the extinction of the Anuak A group of Anuak educated elites form the backbone of organized local opposition to the land investments in Gambella, and they have also facilitated international human rights reporting on the issue. They describe themselves as the indigenous of the area, 'the owners of the land traditionally', believing that their customary rights retain legitimacy and application, despite the statist land tenure regime. Although many are not currently farmers themselves, and worked in urban development peace projects, or the clergy, their intentions are to represent the Anuak peasantry and they routinely refer to their origins and their lasting connections to families and communities in particular villages. The activists opposing the land deals at the local level comprise an informal covert network based in Gambella, or in exile in Kenya. Some of them have strong connections in the diaspora to the Anywaa Survival organization, UK, or the Anuak Justice Council, US, or associations with a political movement the Southwestern Ethiopia Nilotic-Omotic Peoples Independent Movement (SENPIM), which was established with the aim of representing the indigenous tribes of the southwestern region organizing in exile. Opposition to the land deals has also been expressed by the Gambella Nilotes United Movement/Army (GNUM/A 2013), a member of SENPIM.

All the activists interviewed expressed deep ties to the land and community, identifying themselves as the 'indigenous' of Gambella, and condemning the land leases by Karituri and Saudi Star from this perspective. However, they also made it clear that they do not perceive the deals as a new and external threat; rather, they are deemed an additional 'weapon' in the armoury of the Ethiopian government – a regime they fear is intent upon their destruction.

The land investments were seen by Anuak activists to be consistent with past and present government policy targeting the Anuak community: it is part of 'historical injustices . . . we are not recognized as citizens'. In particular, they were linked to a simultaneous process of villagization. While the government presented the scheme as a practical development strategy, relocating rural people to enable the delivery of services, including health, education, and water, the Anuak perceived it as a means to seize their land. The leases to foreign and domestic investors are thus connected to a process of forced displacement, whether or not investors forced people to leave. They are associated with an existential threat to Anuak lives and livelihoods: 'they want the land but they don't want the people'.

All the activists interviewed began their explanation of the problem of land grabs with their personal memories of the atrocities of 2003, the 'Anuak genocide'. They give detailed records of loss, bearing witness to individual suffering, and to the collective trauma of these events. Most spoke of the event that sparked the violence, the killing of a group of construction workers by rebels, the subsequent mobilization of 'Highlander mobs' in revenge, and an organized reign of terror by the military.[6] It was, they suggest, a systematic attempt at eradication. Some of the initial killings in Gambella town were acknowledged by a government investigation, but these were underestimated. Moreover, they were just the beginning of a genocidal campaign, with killings and abuses in the streets and the hunting down of Anuak by military and civilians in their homes and villages. In the words of one peace activist, '1,500, mostly men and boys, were killed in this period. I collected names'.

The genocide and all that has followed since have given weight to Anuak fears of extinction that are socially embedded and have been articulated since the late nineteenth century. The Anuak sentiment of loss derives partly from historical experience, as a borderland people crushed by the conquest of the Ethiopian imperial state, Nuer territorial expansion, and British colonial repression, even before the extractive and repressive policies of the modern Ethiopian state. In recent memory, Anuak bitterly recall the Derg policy that 'resettled' thousands of Tigrayan 'Highlanders' on Anuak land. They also interpret ongoing conflicts with the Ethiopian Nuer community of Gambella and Nuer refugees from South Sudan through this lens, even echoing the same phraseology: 'they take our land, they take our rivers, and they take our people' (Feyissa 2011: iv). But their perception of deprivation also stems from a deep-rooted 'territoriality'.

To be Anuak is to be intimately tied to the land, to a particular village of origin, to ancestors, and to the 'spiritual and supportive nature of the Earth' (Feyissa 2011: 57); leaving or destroying these places of origin is anathema. The investments are viewed as the latest wave of violent dispossession.

There are also economic and ecological losses to consider: the clearance of land for investors risks eroding ways of life and their environment. It entails the destruction of livelihoods, resources, and ways of living: the shifting cultivation practised by Anuak farmers, their use of the fertile land on the river banks, hunting and gathering, and the gifts of the land, 'roots, medicines, wild fruits, honey, and fish'. Activists expressed concerns about ecological damage, including the incursion of the investment into what should have been Gambella's national wildlife park and its 'endangered animals', as well as the felling of precious 'protected' Shea trees. Some even suggested that the weather had changed, becoming drier since part of the forest was cleared for plantations.

The network of Anuak resisters sought to preserve local resources, and opposed any exploitation of their land for commercial purposes without their consultation. Some people wondered if policies of land clearance are partly designed to enable unfettered access for the exploitation of the region for its oil resources, discovered in 2001 – 'are we being killed because of oil?' And they foresaw further exploitation of their land for domestic investors from the 'Highlands' at the expense of local people. Overwhelmingly, the land leases are regarded as the latest in a pattern of state predation and violence against the indigenous people of Gambella. Even the ethnic conflict between Nuer and Anuak was described as a 'government plan':

> The history of predatory appropriations trace back to the numerous slave raiding expeditions organised by the Monarchies in the past[7] . . . the current land grab and forced villagization programs hold the third wave of the Abyssinian conquest to . . . [make] extinct the indigenous Nilotes from their lands. (SENPIM n.d.: 4)

Persecuted by the state By all accounts, the Anuak blamed the Federal Government of Ethiopia as the leading architect of land grabs. This is perhaps to be expected, since the state is driving the deals, and the alienation of land has some 'political advantage' since the commercialization process undermines customary usage rights and places the land under administrative authority (Rahmato 2011: 5). The Anuak describe forced removals backed by 'federal soldiers and police'; they say 'the government is forcing people to vacate land'. And their complaints go well beyond a failure to consult or compensate, to allegations of intimidation and human rights abuses and forced removals of the villagization policy.

Additionally, the activists criticize the regional authorities who first signed the contract with the investors: 'the regional council is under pressure from the federal government and they benefit from the investors'; it 'can't make any decision by itself'. They also accused officials of corruption, in particular the former President of the Regional Council, an Anuak they label as a 'crook' or a 'traitor': '[he] has a car from Karituri; he was sent to India by the company and also built an apartment in town'.[8] A district administrator in Gok was also said to have exploited funds: 'he was given a "gift" by the investors'; 'he misused it and ended up in jail'. Regional and district (*woreda*) officials also had important roles in implementing the leases and the associated villagization policy; they were used by the government to 'push people'. 'When people asked at the regional council why their land was being taken over they were told "you don't have land, this belongs to government"'.

Criticisms of the investors tended to focus on particular negative impacts (rather than on commercial farming in principle). They were charged with displacing people from their homes, and failing to bring benefits, while employing mainly foreigners and Highlanders rather than the 'indigenous'. And there were specific complaints. For instance, Karituri was condemned for having ignored Anuak pleas to leave part of the national park. The company was accused of seizure of land without warning: 'my elder brother used to have a farm in Karituri area; he suddenly saw bulldozers coming to his place. Their things were destroyed. We already bought this land, it belongs to us'. They cited a notorious incident when Karituri workers dug up sacred land, destroying 'the graves of our forefathers' and an occasion when the community requested Karituri share its leftover maize; the company was said to have refused and burned it although 'people were starving'.

Relatedly, the government's development partners were seen to be implicated in the villagization policy through their support for the 'Provision of Basic Services' programme. And though their intentions were not in question, their methods were. Villagization was interpreted as a land grab in favour of regime supporters: 'meant to drive us from our land so it would be taken by Highlanders'. The government was again principally to blame, but others were tarnished by association.

A fragmented political struggle While Anuak elite narratives of the land grab and its causes are remarkably consistent, their network is fragmented. Many of the leading critics of the government fled into exile, mostly either after the Anuak massacre in 2003, or in a second wave of flight after the villagization policy since 2011, while others remain inside Gambella or Addis Ababa, acting covertly. The activists are divided in their approaches to challenging the deals; some are committed to civil means, while others believe that violence may be necessary. 'Because the government didn't listen despite the advocacy, some want to come by force'.

Anuak activists limited their actions within Ethiopia mainly to documentation and information sharing. Several had already spent time in Ethiopian jails at one time or another and some were (re)-arrested in cases directly linked to their land rights activism, provoking international outcry (see Anywaa Survival Organisation 2015; Oakland Institute n.d.; World Bank 2015).

Yet, the international legal activism of the Anuak on the land grab issue has set precedents. Anuak protests against villagization took centre stage in campaigns with international and diaspora partners, and by 2013 they had launched two cases. The first, Mr O (a refugee in Dadaab, Kenya) vs the UK Secretary of State for International Development, charged the Department of International Development with involvement in the villagization policy, and thus 'severe human rights abuses' (Leigh Day 2014). In the second, the World Bank was accused by refugees of supporting the forcible transfer of people associated with villagization through its PBS funding. It responded by launching an official investigation. In 2015, DFID withdrew its funding for the scheme, citing concerns about civil and political rights (Leigh Day 2015). The World Bank investigation found that there were flaws in the design and supervision of the PBS and promised to take steps to address the 'livelihood challenges' they identified in Gambella. It implemented a plan of action in the area, including such measures as 'training grievance redress officers' (World Bank 2017). But its report was described as 'a whitewash' by the activists (IDI 2015).

In the meantime, plans for armed struggle were being made in various localities in the diaspora. In Kenya, there was the launch of the SENPIM, bringing together the 'deprived and impoverished nations' of the South, including the Anuak, Nuer, and Majenger in Gambella, as well as tribes of neighbouring regions such as the Omo and Gumuz. It regarded the commercial investments as 'deadly weapons' of 'neo-colonialism and exploitation' for the benefit of Northern Ethiopians and demanded 'maximum autonomy' for southerners and the (SENPIM 2012) and promised 'vigorous' armed and political struggle. The Gambella Nilotes United Movement/ Army (GNUM/A 2013) shared a similar perspective, notably accusing the *Saudi Star* for serving as a training site for Nuer armed groups that are employed by the state to ethnically cleanse the state. In addition, there have been Anuak groups of fighters with political programmes centred on the Anuak exclusively; some of their leading members are now in jail while others are dead. As one activist explained, these various groups have won support from diaspora in the US, Canada, Australia, or from the Eritrean government. But their lack of coordination is a weakness: 'I was advising them they should unite'.

The call for unity and dialogue is strong within the network. Some Gambellans who have not fled hold onto a hope that they can negotiate an end to the abuses. They also fear that insurgency will 'bring more problems to this region'. One activist called for an 'elders forum' and an initiative to address matters at the regional level. Another noted that the advocacy had some impact and the government had realized the investors were doing a 'bad job'. They all emphasized that the campaigns needed to be international; you could not speak out 'unless you leave the country or go to the bush', for fear of arrest. Meanwhile, those who did speak risked being 'accused of being a terrorist' and imprisoned; 'if you are educated and vocal, they will kill you'. Fighting was understood as a high-risk strategy, 'generalizing conflict is bad; many lives will go'; 'if we fight we will be finished . . . we will all lose'. But even among the advocates of peaceful methods, the ideal of an independent Gambella was nurtured.

The contestation within the Anuak community and their various approaches can be understood against the background of post-1991 politics. The Anuak leaders of the Gambella People's Liberation Movement (GPLM) displaced the Derg in this region. As 'liberators', they seized the opportunity to dominate the regional council and civil service in the early years of the regime. Yet, violence remained entrenched in the politics of Gambella: there was the 1991 Ukuma massacre by Anuak of more than a thousand 'Highlanders' (who had lost their privileged political status with the end of the Derg). There was a constant tension between the federal government and the regional parties, the EPRDF sent Tigrayan 'political advisors' and routinely intervened in the local parties, disarming the GPLM in 1992, imposing a merger with a Nuer party in 1998, and licensing electoral fraud in the 2000 elections. Both inter-ethnic and intra-ethnic political violence ensued, as some Anuaks broke away to form an opposition party. In 2002, the conflict between Anuak and Nuer in Itang spiked, hundreds died, and thousands were forced to flee. The 2003 genocide followed soon afterwards. The activism against the land grabs in Gambella is, in essence, the latest assertion of Anuak political identity and mobilization, echoing previous resistance 'to state encroachments' (Feyissa 2011: 72).

Conclusion

International advocacy on land grabs tends to conflate the experiences and views of affected people – locals are victims, while international corporations and governments are to blame. The fact that certain members of the local community (such as chiefs) are ready to accommodate foreign corporations for private benefit tends to be overlooked. In contrast, my analysis finds that the meaning and implications of the recent wave of global corporate land grabs are specific to the localities in which they are situated and the responses are profoundly shaped by local politics.

The activists in Malen Chiefdom, Pujehun, and Anuakland in Gambella are led by people who conceive of land and development in terms of sociopolitical relations, histories, and imagined futures. They share commitments to their land as a place of origin and a source of autonomy, and they oppose the investments because they intersect with and reinforce existing injustices, threaten rights, and fuel uncertainties. Their defining characteristic is a shared belief in the historical and enduring relation between land and people. They are not 'anti-development' (as their critics sometimes label them). But while corporate 'accumulation by dispossession' (Harvey 2004) is driven by an imperialist logic of progress, the networks against land grabs rely upon shared memories and the construction of an imagined, enduring community.

Experiences in Pujehun and Gambella suggest both the promise of movements against land dispossession, and the difficulty of sustaining them amid the threat of violence. Activists on the front line of the investments are vulnerable to co-option, given the embedded social inequalities and the penetration of patronage networks, and some may eventually turn to violence in pursuit of solutions. They tend to seek external support, whether from diaspora or international donors and allies, despite the risk that the particularity of their beliefs and agendas may be erased through such encounters.

The struggles in Pujehun and Gambella provide a warning and a source of inspiration. First, they demonstrate that resistance is ignited by the destruction and dispossession associated with large-scale land investments, and is likely to surface eventually, regardless of repression, on the one hand, or consultation, on the other. This indicates that local agency must be central to any form of future development in these contested regions of the global periphery and provides a strong argument for a 'land sovereignty' approach that respects the relations between individuals and communities, encouraging them to be 'active agents in all matters affecting their lives' (Rahmato 2011: 6). Second, some local activists are developing solidarity approaches – rooted in ideas about community, but also connected to wider non-violent struggles on social and economic rights – even as others pursue particularist mobilizations reminiscent of previous eras. In many of their practices and principles, the activists have directly challenged the exploitative and violent politics that facilitated the land deals, although they have been unable to repair the profound damage wrought by land dispossession.

Notes

1 This study draws on research funded by the Irish Research Council and the Conflict Resolution Unit of the Irish Department of Foreign Affairs. I am grateful to the research participants in Gambella, Addis Ababa, Ethiopia, in Nairobi, Kenya, and in Pujehun and Freetown, Sierra Leone, for sharing their ideas and experiences with incredible generosity and courage.

2 The field element of the study was limited not only by time and costs, but by political judgement, which indicated the need for discretion and the risks for security and well-being of participants during and after the research. Since many of the activists have already made public statements, the risks of exposing them to unprecedented attention was reduced. Especially in Ethiopia, several interviewees were concerned about risk, and some of the information they shared required a high level of confidentiality. The main field research took place in February 2013 in Sierra Leone, and in April and June 2013 in Ethiopia. For Pujehun, the research drew on in-depth interviews with 28 individuals, and five focus group discussions, as well as participant observation with civil society organizations. For Gambella, it included 19 in-depth interviews in Gambella, Addis Ababa, and Nairobi, and one focus group discussion. Some of those interviewed in both the Pujehun and Gambella cases were arrested or subject to some form of intimidation either before or since the interviews. I have therefore selected material for citation with caution and not included individual names or roles in references.

3 Both are among the top target countries for international deals and both have some projects in start-up or operation (Land Matrix 2015).

4 The Registration and Regulation of Charities and Societies Law passed in 2009 has limited action and curtailed freedom of speech, as have the Anti-Terrorism Proclamation and the Mass Media Proclamation (Amnesty International 2012).

5 I present a broadly shared narrative of the problem, causes, and solutions; all quotations represent views generally expressed by several members of the network and/or echoed in public statements. Although no individual references are given, note that, overwhelmingly, the speakers were male, aged between 20 and 60 years, and were members of the organization and networks described above.

6 They do not tend to mention other events, such as the killing of 'Highlander' government officials that immediately preceded the violence, or the formation of the Gambella People's Liberation Front (GPLF) in response, and its fight back in the years that followed (see Feyissa 2011: 240).

7 Slavery remained legal in Ethiopia and endured in Gambella until the 1940s.

8 Omot Obang Olum was subject to an investigation for corruption, and later fled Ethiopia to seek asylum (Huff Post/ICJ 2015).

References

Abdullah, I. (2014). *Towards an Understanding of Social Movements and Contemporary Sierra Leone.* Available at: www.rosalux.sn/wp-content/uploads/2014/12/Chap01. pdf [accessed 16 May 2016].

Acemoglu, D., Reed, T., and Robinson, J.A. (2014). 'Chiefs: economic development and elite control of civil society in Sierra Leone'. *Journal of Political Economy*, 122(2): 319–368.

Albrecht P. (2015). 'The chiefs of community policing in rural Sierra Leone'. *The Journal of Modern African Studies*, 53(4): 611–635 doi:10.1017/S0022278X15000774.

ALLAT (2013). *Who Is Benefitting the Social and Economic Impact of Three Large-Scale Land Investments? A Cost-Benefit Analysis.* Available at: www.christianaid.org.uk/images/who-

is-benefitting-Sierra-Leone-report.
pdf [accessed 15 May 2016].

Amnesty International (2012). *Ethiopia:
Human Rights Work Crippled
by Restrictive Law*. Available at:
www.amnesty.org/en/latest/
news/2012/03/ethiopia-human-
rights-work-crippled-restrictive-law/
[accessed 16 May 2016].

Anywaa Survival Organisation (2015)
*Letter to World Bank President Re
Arrest and Prosecution of Pastor
Omot Agwa in Ethiopia*. Available at:
www.anywaasurvival.org/letter-to-
world-bank-president-re-arrest-and-
prosecution-of-pastor-omot-agwa/
[accessed 16 May 2016].

Boone, C. (2014). *Property and Political
Order: Land Rights and the Structure
of Conflict in Africa*. Cambridge:
Cambridge University Press.

Davison, W. (2011). *Is Indian Investment
in Ethiopian Farms a 'Land Grab'?*
Available at: www.csmonitor.com/
World/Africa/2011/1223/Is-Indian-
investment-in-Ethiopian-farms-a-
land-grab [accessed 12 April 2017].

Davison, W. (2016). *Karuturi Challenges
Ethiopia Decision to Cancel Farm
Project*. Available at: www.
bloomberg.com/news/articles/2016-
01-11/karuturi-challenges-ethiopian-
decision-to-cancel-farming-project
[accessed 25 May 2016].

Escobar, A. (2001). 'Culture sits in
places: reflections on globalism and
subaltern strategies of localization'.
Political Geography, 20: 139–174.

Ethiopia Central Statistical Agency
(2007). *Population and Housing
Census Report – Gambella Region*.
Available at: www.csa.gov.
et/newcsaweb/images/documents/
surveys/Population%20and%2
0Housing%20census/ETH-pop-
2007/survey0/data/Doc/Reports/
Gambella_Statistical.pdf [accessed
25 May 2016].

Fanthorpe, R. (2007). *Sierra Leone: The
Influence of the Secret Societies, with
Special Reference to Female Genital
Mutilation. A Writenet Report
Commissioned by United Nations
High Commissioner for Refugees,
Status Determination and Protection
Information Section (DIPS) August*.
Available at: www.refworld.org/
pdfid/46cee3152.pdf [accessed 16
May 2016].

Federal Democratic Republic of Ethiopia
(FDRE) (1995). *Constitution of
the Federal Democratic Republic
of Ethiopia*. Available at: www.
refworld.org/docid/3ae6b5a84.html
[accessed 16 May 2016].

Ferme, M.C. (2001). *The Underneath of
Things: Violence, History, and the
Everyday in Sierra Leone*. Berkeley,
CA: University of California Press.

Feyissa, D. (2011). *Playing Different
Games: The Paradox of Anywaa and
Nuer Identification Strategies in the
Gambella Region*. Integration and
Conflict Studies, Max Plank Institute
for Social Anthropology, Halle/
Saale, Vol. 4 (draft copy).

Foryoh, P. (2016). *Sierra Leone Activists
Released After Six Weeks Jail
for Protesting Socfin*. 21 March.
Available at: https://makonitimes.
com/2016/03/21/sierra-leone-
activists-released-after-six-weeks-
jail-for-protesting-socfin/ [accessed
20 May 2016].

FT Investigations (2016). *The Great Land
Rush: Ethiopia, the Billionaire's Farm*.
Available at: https://ig.ft.com/sites/
land-rush-investment/ethiopia/
[accessed 16 May 2016].

Gambella Nilotes United Movement/
Army (GNUM/A) (2013). *Press
Release 'Unity for Peace and Freedom
for the People of Gambella' Second
Year Anniversary of GNUM/A*.
10 August. Available at: www.
anyuakmedia.com/GNUM_First_

Year_Anniversary_-_August_10th_2012.pdf [accessed 16 May 2016].

Green Scenery (2013). *Press Release: Green Scenery Factsheet on Large-Scale Agri-Investments in Pujehun District, Sierra Leone, April 24.* Available at: www.oaklandinstitute. org/press-release-green-scenery-factsheet-large-scale-agri-investments-pujehun-district-sierra-leone [accessed 16 May 2016].

Green Scenery (2014). *Report on the Incident of Police Arrest and Highhanded Measure of Fifty Seven Citizens in Malen Chiefdom, Pujehun District.* Available at: http://wrm.org.uy/wp-content/uploads/2014/02/Arrest_of_fifty_seven_citizens_in_Malen_Chiefdom. pdf [accessed 16 May 2016].

Harvey, D. (2004). *The New Imperialism.* Oxford: Oxford University Press.

Huff Post/ICIJ (2015). *Rights Denied: New Evidence Links World Bank to Human Rights Abuses in Ethiopia.* Available at: http://projects.huffingtonpost. com/worldbank-evicted-abandoned/new-evidence-ties-worldbank-to-human-rights-abuses-ethiopia [accessed 16 May 2016].

Human Rights Watch (HRW) (2005). *Ethiopia: Crackdown Spreads Beyond Capital as Arbitrary Arrests Continue, Detainees Face Torture and Ill-Treatment.* Available at: www. hrw.org/news/2005/06/15/ethiopia-crackdown-spreads-beyond-capital [accessed 12 April 2017].

Human Rights Watch (HRW) (2012). *Ethiopia: Army Commits Torture, Rape.* Available at: www.zehabesha. com/ethiopia-army-commits-torture-rape/ [accessed 16 May 2016].

Inclusive Development International (IDI) (2015). *World Bank Whitewashes Ethiopia Human Rights Scandal.* Available at: www.inclusivedevelopment.net/world-bank-whitewashes-ethiopia-human-rights-scandal/ [accessed 12 April 2017].

Land Matrix (2015). *Land Matrix Newsletter, November.* Available at: www.landmatrix.org/media/filer_public/95/1c/951c640e-3cda-4a0b-821c-3c5142b901b7/7365_up_ispa_land_matrix_newsletter_261115. pdf [accessed 16 May 2016].

Leigh Day (2014). *Ethiopian Man Wins Right to Take Legal Case Forward.* Available at: www.leighday.co.uk/News/2014/July-2014/Ethiopian-man-wins-right-to-take-legal-case-forwar [accessed 16 May 2016].

Leigh Day (2015). *Victory for Ethiopian Man in Battle Over UK Aid Money.* Available at: www.leighday.co.uk/News/2015/March-2015/Victory-for-Ethiopian-man-in-battle-over-UK-aid-mo [accessed 16 May 2016].

Malen Affected Land Owners Association (MALOA) (2011). 'Grievances of Landowners in Malen Chiefdom', 2 October.

Malen Affected Land Owners Association (MALOA) (2012). 'Letter to the Human Rights Commission', 1 December.

McAdam, D., Tarrow, S., and Tilly, C. (2007). 'Comparative perspectives on contentious politics'. In M. Lichbach and A. Zuckerman (eds), *Comparative Politics: Rationality, Culture, and Structure: Advancing Theory in Comparative Politics.* Cambridge: Cambridge University Press. Available at: http://socialsciences.cornell. edu/wp-content/uploads/2013/06/McAdamTarrowTilly07.pdf [accessed 12 April 2016].

Oakland Institute. (n.d.). *Action on Behalf of Indigenous Land Rights Leader in Ethiopia.* Available at: www. oaklandinstitute.org/action-behalf-

indigenous-land-rights-leader-
ethiopia [accessed 16 May 2016].

Oakland Institute (2011). *Understanding
Land Investment Deals in Africa
Country Report: Sierra Leone.*
Available at: www.oaklandinstitute.
org/sites/oaklandinstitute.org/files/
OI_SierraLeone_Land_Investment_
report_0.pdf [accessed 16 May 2016].

Oakland Institute (2013). *Unheard
Voices: The Human Rights Impact
of Land Investments in Ethiopia.*
Available at: www.oaklandinstitute.
org/sites/oaklandinstitute.org/files/
OI_Report_Unheard_Voices.pdf
[accessed 16 May 2016].

Peters, K. and Richards, P. (2011).
'Rebellion and agrarian tensions in
Sierra Leone'. *Journal of Agrarian
Change*, 11(3): 377–395.

Premier News (2016). *Government to
Clampdown on NGOs.* 12 April.
Available at: www.facebook.
com/MALOAPujehun/ [accessed 25
May 2016].

Pujehun Magistrate Court (2012).
*Statement of Offence against Alhaji
Abubakar, Mohamed Abefuah,
Mohamed Mansaray, Baimba Laiwn*,
4 September.

Rahmato, D. (2011). *Land to Investors:
Large-Scale Land Transfers in
Ethiopia, Forum for Social Studies.*
Available at: www.landgovernance.
org/system/files/Ethiopia_
Rahmato_FSS_0.pdf [accessed 16
May 2016].

Saffa, V. (2016). *Malen Secondary School
Pupils Call for Dialogue Between
Socfin and MALOA.* 3 May. Available
at: http://slconcordtimes.com/
malen-secondary-school-pupils-call-
for-dialogue-between-socfin-and-
maloa/ [accessed 16 May 2016].

SENPIM (n.d.). *SENPIM Political
Manifesto.* Copy on file with author.

SENPIM (2012). *SENPIM Press Release.*
Available at: https://view.officeapps.
live.com/op/view.aspx?src=https://
www.culturalsurvival.org/sites/
default/files/senpim_press_release_
final_sept_2012.doc [accessed 16
May 2016].

Sierra Leone Statistics (2004).
*Population and Housing Census,
Final Results, Sierra Leone Statistics.*
Available at: www.sierra-leone.
org/Census/ssl_final_results.pdf
[accessed 14 June 2016].

Sierra Leone Truth and Reconciliation
Commission (TRC) (2004). *Witness
to Truth: Report of the Sierra Leone
Truth and Reconciliation Commission.*
Available at: www.sierraleonetrc.org
[accessed 12 April 2017].

UN OCHA (2015). *Sierra Leone, Pujehun
District Profile.* Available at:
http://reliefweb.int/sites/reliefweb.
int/files/resources/district_profile_-
_pujehun-_29_dec_2015_.pdf
[accessed 12 April 2017].

Welthungerhilfe (2012). *Increasing
Pressure for Land: Implications for
Rural Livelihoods and Development
Actors. A Case Study in Sierra Leone.*
Available at: www.welthungerhilfe.
de/fileadmin/user_upload/
Mediathek/Welthunger-Index/WHI_
2012/Study_Land_Investment_Sierra_
Leone.pdf [accessed 20 May 2016].

World Bank (2010). *Rising Global Interest
in Farmland: Can It Yield Sustainable
and Equitable Benefits?* Washington,
DC: World Bank.

World Bank (2015). *Statement of the
Inspection Panel Regarding the
Charges Filed Against Pastor
Omot Agwa in Ethiopia.* Available
at: http://ewebapps.worldbank.
org/apps/ip/PanelCases/82-Statem
ent%20on%20Charges%20Filed%2
0Against%20Pastor%20Agwa%20-
%2025%20September%202015.pdf
[accessed 16 May 2016].

World Bank (2017). *Inspection Panel:
Ethiopia: Protection of Basic*

Services Program Phase II Additional Financing and Promoting Basic Services Phase III Project, Case – 82, Case Tracker. Available at: http:// ewebapps.worldbank.org/apps/ip/ Pages/ViewCase.aspx?CaseId=88 [accessed 12 April 2017].

Yengoh, G.T. and Armah, F.A. (2014). 'Land access constraints for communities affected by large-scale land acquisition in southern Sierra Leone'. *Geojournal.* doi:10.1007/s10708-014-9606-2.

Zewde, B. (2002). *The History of Modern Ethiopia 1855–1991, Eastern African Studies.* Athens, OH: Ohio University Press.

13 | LOCAL RESISTANCE TO LARGE-SCALE AGRICULTURAL LAND ACQUISITIONS IN THE BENISHANGUL-GUMUZ REGION, ETHIOPIA

Tsegaye Moreda

Introduction

The politically contested nature of land and land access has become more so in the context of the current global land rush, in which Ethiopia is a global hotspot. The issue of land has gained particular momentum over the past few years, due to the ongoing enclosures by a wide range of actors (such as the state, state-owned enterprises, and private investors). There has been a growing and renewed global interest in land resources related to expanding food demand, high food prices, the growing demand for biofuels and animal feeds, climate change, the expansion of trade regimes, and the emergence of consumer- and corporate-driven food systems (Borras and Franco 2012; De Schutter 2011; McMichael 2010; Visser and Spoor 2011; White and Dasgupta 2010; Zoomers 2010). Analytically, the contemporary large-scale land acquisitions must be situated within the development of capitalism and capital accumulation (Akram-Lodhi 2012; White *et al.* 2012). This growing interest in land resources, both domestic and transnational, has elevated pressures on their availability. Those most threatened are poor rural people who, in fact, need land the most; this includes, among others, ethnic minorities, indigenous people, pastoralists, and peasants (Borras and Franco 2012). In Ethiopia, such large-scale land acquisitions, both by domestic and foreign investors, have been taking place over the last few years, mainly in the lowland regions of the country. While estimates vary, a 2011 World Bank report indicates that the total amount of land acquired by investors in Ethiopia between 2004 and 2008 amounts to 1.2 million hectares (Deininger and Byerlee 2011), while the Oakland Institute estimates that the land transferred to investors, as of January 2011, reaches more than 3.6 million hectares (Oakland Institute 2011; see also Rahmato 2011). Although new opportunities could be created from increases in land investments for national growth broadly, central and critical questions are raised regarding the land rights of poor local communities and their implications for local livelihoods, in addition to the questions whether and to what extent the promised employment creation and infrastructural development in land deals are in fact true. As is the case of Ethiopia, where the state formally owns land and at the same time is sympathetic to large investments in land, it is rather common for local communities to lose out in the process since they cannot effectively negotiate under a situation of wider inequalities in bargaining power (e.g. Von Braun and Meinzen-Dick 2009).

Affected local communities react to changes brought about by the expansion of large-scale land acquisitions in different ways. Communities' responses range from covert to more open forms of outright resistance. Nevertheless, large-scale land acquisitions do not always result in people losing their land. Those people affected by such acquisitions may not also necessarily engage in outright resistance, as this depends on the particular economic, political, social, and cultural contexts in which they are situated (Borras and Franco 2013). When resistance does occur, it occurs in a differentiated way, depending on the economic and political agencies involved. Likewise, the choice of which strategies of resistance to use tend to vary, depending largely on the specific social structures, strengths, and defensive capacities of the resisters (Scott 1987: 422). Although the affected indigenous communities in Ethiopia appear to be 'silent' about the land acquisitions, both covert and overt forms of resistance are taking place. The reasons for the resistance of the local communities are not just because they have been displaced from their lands or are being threatened with displacement, but also because they feel marginalized from emerging (but limited) employment opportunities available because of the 'land investments', and because of the lack of fulfilment of other promises that such investments were purported to bring. As will be demonstrated in this chapter, affected local communities have been challenging the land acquisitions in various ways, challenging the state and social forces, particularly over land and access to jobs, and around state politics.

Through a case study in some selected administrative *woredas* (districts)[1] of the Benishangul-Gumuz region – one of the focus areas of the current land acquisitions in the country – this chapter uses empirical evidence in order to demonstrate the type and nature of reactions by local communities towards large-scale agricultural land acquisitions in the region. Information for this chapter comes from a combination of various data collection methods carried out during intensive fieldwork from April to June 2012, which includes semi-structured, in-depth interviews with key informants, focus group discussions (FGDs), direct field observation, and secondary literature review (see Moreda 2013, for details).[2]

The remainder of the chapter comprises three sections. The first section introduces the socioecological, historical, and political economic context of ongoing large-scale land acquisitions in the Benishangul-Gumuz region. The second section scrutinizes the ways in which indigenous local communities have been reacting to the land acquisitions. The third and final section draws conclusions.

The socioecological, historical, and political economic context of large-scale land acquisitions

The Benishangul-Gumuz region is currently one of the nine administrative regions under Ethiopia's federal political system. This region is located in the north-western part of the country (Figure 13.1). It has a total population of 670,847 (CSA 2008). The population consists of the indigenous ethnic minority groups of Berta, Gumuz, Shinasha, Mao, and Komo. It is also inhabited by settlers from other regions with diverse ethnic origins. The indigenous groups depend on a customary land tenure system of communal ownership and rely mainly on shifting cultivation for their livelihood. This is supplemented with other subsidiary activities, such as hunting, gathering, fishing, livestock raising, traditional alluvial gold mining, and honey production and collection.

The region is generally perceived to have extensive untapped land resources, described as having a great potential for agricultural development: a reality that appears to have shaped the current state policy of leasing vast tracts of its land to investors. In addition to decades of gradual encroachments of highlander plough cultivators and the 1980s forced resettlement programme of the Derg regime that moved tens of thousands of impoverished people from densely populated highland regions to the lowland areas, the indigenous lowland communities of the region have faced additional pressures on their land resources caused by the introduction of private agricultural investment since the early 1990s, which was commonly undertaken by investors who were ethnically from the highland regions (Abbute 2002; Markakis 2011). More recently, large swathes of land across the region have been offered to both foreign and domestic capital for production of food and agrofuels on an unprecedented scale. Much of the land offered for leasing is classified by the state and other elites as 'unused' or 'underutilized', presumably overlooking the spatially extensive use of land in shifting cultivation and agro-pastoralism, which poses apparent threats to the land rights and livelihoods of indigenous communities in these lowlands (Makki 2014). A backdrop to this *terra nullius* narrative is the central – and ongoing – role and extraordinary power of the Ethiopian state to define and determine the allocation and use of all land resources, making it particularly difficult for the weakly organized indigenous communities to negotiate effectively or secure adequate compensation from corporate investors or state actors. However, indigenous communities in the lowlands, particularly the Gumuz people, were historically able, to a certain extent, to resist the subjugation and hegemonic ideologies of the highlanders and the state in order to maintain their material as well as their cultural space.

Generally, in the context of recent large-scale land acquisitions, the Gumuz reflected negative attitudes and hostilities not only towards investors and migrant labourers, but also towards the government, which they perceived as facilitating the land acquisitions that were threatening their traditional land use practices and the natural environment. The Gumuz contend that even before the current displacements due to land acquisitions, the state had been in the forefront of their subordination and subjugation, and that what they are now facing is nothing but the continuation of their long history of exploitation and marginalization.[3] Looking back to the establishment of state farms and state-sponsored resettlements schemes in the 1970s and 1980s and the introduction of private commercial farms in Metekel in the 1990s, some scholars have argued that these initiatives exemplified the central state's desire to consolidate its control over people and territory. Contesting the motive of the 1980s resettlement schemes, Gebre (2003: 54), for example, argues that:

> although the resettlement was portrayed as a response to the famine [that affected the country in the 1980s], the overall

decision to establish resettlement in remote locations may have been partly driven by perceived collateral advantages, such as controlling outpost regions.

In the context of the current ongoing process of land acquisitions, state categorization of land as 'unused' or 'underutilized' in order to lease it out to investors is based primarily on expected short-term economic benefits. It does not take into account the social and cultural dimensions of existing local land uses despite the fact that these are critical for indigenous communities. It is important to note that current government perceptions and discourses favour the highland plough cultivators and commercial farmers while undervaluing the land use of the lowlander peripheral communities such as the Gumuz.[4] It was such a discourse that shaped the recent state policy of making lowland areas major sites for large-scale production of commercial crops and biofuels. As Makki (2014: 89) puts it, 'instead of the alliance between smallholders and the state envisioned in the highlands, the strategic alignment in the lowlands involves a pact between the state and large-scale investors'.

Land transfers to investors across the region have been undertaken by the federal government, on the one hand, and regional and local government authorities, on the other. At the federal level, increasing levels of land transfers in the region have been carried out by the Agricultural Investment Support Directorate (AISD), which was established in 2009 to identify potential investment lands in the regional states. It has been argued that this trend of land administration by the federal government is justified due to the prevailing limited capacity of the regional government to manage substantial land investments. Strikingly, information collected during fieldwork for this chapter revealed that neither local communities nor respective regional authorities have been involved in most of the land deals carried out so far by the federal government. Land transfers negotiated with the federal government were easily able to bypass legitimate rural land administration authorities at the regional government. The regional government was simply notified about the land transfer deals carried out between the federal government and the investor.

This apparently contradicts the clearly stipulated desire both by federal and regional governments to enhance decentralized political power and decision-making in rural land administrations. Due to the inherent power asymmetries in the relationship between the regional state and the federal government, the latter having undisputed sway, local and regional authorities seem to have exerted no or very little influence over substantial land deals administered by the federal government, despite the fact that these could have considerable impact on local land use and biodiversity. While the central state has always maintained its key concern for the 'peripheral' areas in the borderlands in relation to the control of territory and people, recent decisions around land investments have direct consequences for contestations over authority between state actors at federal and regional levels. This serves to illustrate not only how contests over land and authority are played out in federal and regional state contexts, but also its salience as a site for the reproduction of the history of marginalization reflected in the pre-1991 subordinated power relations. Although the federal government may have reasserted its authority over territory and people in this way, the implications of undermining the authority of local and regional state actors over the allocation, use, and regulation of land resources within their jurisdictions may become a focal point of resistance.

At the regional level, before the present regional land administration proclamation 85/2010 that provided the mandate for administering rural lands to the Bureau of Environmental Protection, Land Use and Administration, land investment processes in the region involved different regional government offices. This created overlaps and ambiguities in land acquisition processes and procedures. For example, although the *woreda* authorities were in charge of identifying and facilitating the land acquisition process, there were also cases in which the investors themselves identified the desired investment land and approached local authorities for approval. As these land acquisition processes appear to have lacked consistency and coordination, individuals (investors and representatives of the state acting in their own private interests) were able to manipulate them, exploiting the existing confusions and overlaps in the land administration process.

As will be discussed in this chapter, the reactions of the Gumuz target those individuals and groups, including the state, that have participated and facilitated the land acquisitions in one way or another. In their reactions, the Gumuz try to make their actions

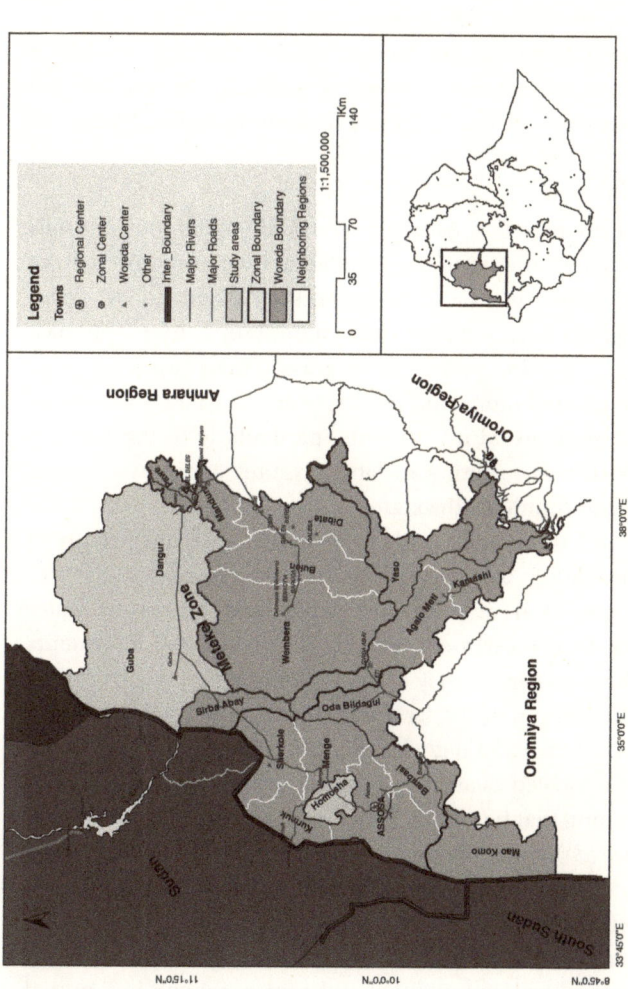

13.1 Map of Benishangul-Gumuz regional state, Ethiopia (showing location of study *woredas*)

Note: This map was created by Nigussie Abdissa, a colleague who works in the Tana-Beles Integrated Water Resource Development Project, Assosa (Ethiopia), using ArcGIS 10.1 by Esri (© Esri).

Source: Boundaries data were obtained from the Benishangul-Gumuz Bureau of Finance and Economic Development (BoFED).

and thoughts be felt by the targets, although they are very careful in maintaining the anonymity of the individuals involved. This bears a resemblance to how Kerkvliet characterized the features of everyday resistance, in which the resisters opt '[to] the extent that the target is rather specific, those who resist imagine that their actions would not be condoned by the target' (Kerkvliet 1986: 108).

The following empirical section scrutinizes the ways in which indigenous local communities have been reacting to the recent large-scale land acquisitions in the Benishangul-Gumuz regional state.

Local resistance

Resistance against investors Although the land rights and natural-resources-based livelihoods of local indigenous communities have been under pressure from encroachments by highlanders, state-sponsored resettlement schemes and state farms over the past several decades (Abbute 2002; Gebre 2003), the pressure is now increasing as more and more land resources are given out by the state to commercial agricultural investments, particularly in the last few years. This in turn is resulting in land disputes and contestations between local communities, the state, and investors.

Interviews and discussions with local individuals and groups in the study areas made it clear that there have been increased disputes over the dispossession of cultivated lands and access to water associated with land investment projects. However, the informants underscored how powerless they are in defending their rights due to the strong politicization of the land investment undertakings, which now also involved the federal government. In this regard, the federal government was viewed as an entity against which it is impossible to dispute, something that has made the Gumuz fearful. As one Gumuz man (Guba *woreda*) concisely puts it: 'We cannot wrestle with these rich investors . . . we know that they have a link with and support from the government. If we wrestle with them, it is obvious that we will lose' (interview, Ayicid *kebele*, 6 June 2012). A similar view was also found among local and regional authorities, though in a muted form, over their reduced influence in relation to land allocations.

Nevertheless, several scattered forms of resistance took place through which the Gumuz people expressed their discontent towards the ongoing land acquisitions. The local reactions targeted all of the actors involved in the land acquisitions in one way or another.

One of the main actors targeted by the local communities were the investors. The local communities generally reflected negative attitudes towards investors operating in their surroundings, and several instances of covert expressions of resistance against them have occurred. Within Dangur *woreda*, for example, informants indicated that local communities sabotaged one of the investment projects that acquired land in their *kebele* (interviews, Gimtiya *kebele*, May 2012). According to informants, a farm machineries warehouse belonging to the Jaba Agro-Industry PLC was set on fire during the night by individuals who still remain anonymous. The manager of the project told me that as a result of the sabotage, machineries such as tractors, threshers, and spare parts, as well as many other valuable goods, were destroyed (interview, Gimtiya *kebele*, 17 May 2012). He believes that this was sabotage carried out by the local community. As the warehouse was the main target, he suspects that the action was mainly orchestrated by former guards working in the warehouse who knew the whereabouts of key machineries. Because of threats of more action, the company was reluctant to make further investments, speculating that more damage might be inflicted. Actually, the manager was well aware of the risks in the area, mentioning that this was not the first incident that had happened in that specific area. He explained that the land that now belongs to Jaba Agro-Industry PLC used to be farmed by another domestic company that left the area some years ago because of the attacks it had faced. The brother of the investor who used to work as the manager on the project was killed on the land by a Gumuz arrow. Soon after that, the investor stopped the project and left the area. Bows and arrows are the main traditional weapon used by the Gumuz for self-defence and hunting. As the case above demonstrates, such sporadic and anonymous actions by local people cannot be overlooked, and could in fact have the potential to have a major impact on projects.

During focus group discussions on the above arson incident, the Gumuz noted that indeed Jaba Agro-Industry PLC had suffered huge losses because of it, but they preferred to be silent on the issue and they did not want to speculate on who may have been behind it (FGD, Gimtiya *kebele*, 20 May 2012). Rather, they emphasized the damage the project had caused them. They were even angry about the name of the project itself: Jaba is the name of a village in another area though within the same *woreda*. The local communities of Gimtiya *kebele* considered this an insult and contended 'how embarrassing it is to hear the name of another place being given to our land while we have our local name'. Some of the informants among the Gumuz during individual interviews indicated that they wanted these people to leave the land as nothing good has happened since their arrival (interview, Gimtiya *kebele*, May 2012).

Damaging field crops is another act of resistance that has been undertaken by the Gumuz people in Belojiganfoy *woreda*. In this *woreda*, for example, an estimated 700 hectares of land covered by maize ready for harvest was destroyed by fire. The investor accused the local community of deliberately causing the fire. Here again, local communities remained quiet when asked for the possible cause of the damage. Their silence cannot necessarily be taken as a sign of their ignorance. Here, it is fairly obvious that, as Scott (1985: 290) asserted, 'the actor is unlikely to admit to the action itself, let alone explain what he had in mind'. From an interview with an official in the regional capital, Assosa, it is clear that the regional government is aware of the hostile attitudes of local communities towards the investors, and thus speculates that the crop damage might have been one of their strategies to chase out investors from the land they were allotted by the government (interview, Assosa, 18 April 2012).

The Gumuz were not only involved in covert forms of reaction; there were also incidents of overt actions taken against the investors. Local people took part in outright conflicts with the investors in villages that were relatively far from zonal and *woreda* towns so that government forces could not easily intervene. Disregarding the claims made by investors, several Gumuz people occupied and cultivated the land already allocated to the investment projects. This was especially the case in Yaso and Belojiganfoy *woreda*, where local people occupied the land, disregarding the investors, in order to counteract them. In Dangur *woreda*, villagers of Gimtiya *kebele* also insisted on cultivating the land that was already cleared by investors in their villages. A key informant from Gimtiya *kebele* administration described it as follows:

> One of the investors who acquired about 3,000 hectares of land in our *Kebele*, for example, tried to clear large part of it. However, this investment project is actually unable to secure this whole land it is trying to develop, as some people in this village defy the land

boundaries claimed by the project. In every direction, the villagers encroach upon the investor's land when the planting season comes in order to take advantage of the already cleared land. We tried to tell them in various community meetings not to encroach on the land already cleared by the investors but they just ignore us. And instead claim that the land originally belonged to them. We even tried to warn the villagers that they must stop this or they will be jailed. (interview, Gimtiya, 16 May 2012)

In interviews, one of the project managers of investment sites in the area complained that it is harder to chase these people from the land without the help of local government authorities, something that might stir even more animosity (interview, Gublak town, 18 May 2012). He indicated that once they sow crop seeds on the field, then it is unthinkable to touch it because their revenge or reaction to that would be so serious. The investors generally refrained from taking measures in such situations for fear of inflaming and provoking violent confrontations. The solution was to compromise, that is, let them cultivate unless they push further, and of course until permanent mechanisms to force the local people to stop such acts were devised. Despite this, there were times in which investors brought in the federal police forces stationed in the nearby town of Gublak to threaten the local people from advancing further into the investment lands already cleared. The villagers, however, claimed that they were cultivating their ancestral land and rejected claims of any wrongdoing. One elderly Gumuz stated that 'it is them who came to us, not us who went to them. We were here, always' (interview, Gimtiya *kebele*, 19 May 2012).

Here, it is worth emphasizing that the shift in the resistance strategies from covert to overt by the Gumuz people, as described, is thus related to the state's inability to exert authority over remote locations, implying that the state's presence and ability to enforce control over territory and people is the defining feature in this instance.

Resistance against seasonal immigrant labourers As a strategy to undermine the land acquisitions, local communities attempt to resist the immigration of seasonal agricultural wage labourers migrating from the central highlands of the Amhara region. In this regard, it is interesting to note that investment projects almost totally depend on agricultural labourers recruited from other regions of the country, particularly neighbouring regions. Following the ongoing land acquisitions, there has been a growing influx of highland seasonal migrant labourers coming to the area for wage employment in areas such as weeding and mowing.[5]

Not only do these migrant workers work as seasonal agricultural labourers, but they also introduce a new form of encroachment on the available land resources. As the jobs are mostly seasonal in nature, many of the labourers stay in the area after the completion of their contracts. They tend to encroach into the forest to acquire land, so that after a year or so of cultivating it they can bring their families, and hence established new settlements.

The creation of such 'illegal' settlements has generated additional challenges for local communities, intensifying the pressure on available land resources. This has been the case mainly in Dangur and Guba *woredas*, where the *woreda* authorities now consider it to be a major challenge to the peace and security of the area, likely to fuel land conflicts (interviews, Manbouk and Mankush towns, June 2012). The Gumuz people are well aware of this kind of encroachment on their land and its implications for them. One informant from the Agriculture Office of Dangur *woreda* illustrates that the people who encroach and establish new settlements tend to over-exploit the local land resources as their continued existence on the land is highly uncertain (interview, Manbouk town, 29 May 2012), and that sooner or later they will be forced to leave. Due to this uncertainty, they resort to using the land and other natural resources more intensively, in contrast to the land use practices of local Gumuz communities. Notwithstanding his earlier argument, this same informant also concedes that these 'illegal settlers' hope that they might claim permanent control of the land they occupy once they have occupied and farmed it for a few years. This did not, however, seem to stop them from exploiting the resources to the greatest extent possible.

Local communities have been reacting against the influx of migrant workers, not just in order to prevent their encroachment on local land resources, but also to undermine the land investment projects by denying the investors access to labour. Several migrant agricultural workers interviewed in Gimitiya and Gublak *kebeles* within Dangur *woreda* stressed that they were 'scared' of the Gumuz people (interview, May 2012). They emphasized that they are fearful to the extent that they felt unable to go on foot from the places where the investment projects are located to nearby towns. According to these informants (seasonal labourers), many migrant workers had been killed by the local communities while they were trying to go back to their home areas on foot. Reacting to these allegations, the Gumuz people contended that the incidents had nothing to do with them. Rather, they explained how migrant workers face challenges when they come to the area (interview, Gimtiya *Kebele*, 21 May 2012). The labourers migrate to these destinations from various areas such as Gojjam, Gondar, and Siemen Shewa, and not knowing their way around is one of the challenges they face. The lowlands are covered in vast expanses of woodlands and forested areas, and the migrants, unfamiliar to the area, get lost in these vast areas, unclear of the direction they need to take. Once they are lost, many do not manage to find their way out. The Gumuz complain that when something happens to these workers, everybody puts the blame on them.

But migrant workers insist that they face intimidation from the local communities every day. Similar attitudes towards the Gumuz was reflected during focus group discussions I held in some selected villages of Tach Gayint *woreda* of the Amhara region, among the main areas of origin of seasonal labour migrants (FGDs, July 2012). The participants stressed that threats from the Gumuz is the major risk factor that they consider when deciding whether to move to the Metekel area, with malaria and harsh climatic condition forming other risk factors. Many labourers, particularly inexperienced young workers, could not withstand the harsh daily labour and long working hours expected on the investment projects and found the harsh climate and cultural shocks they face difficult to cope with. As a result, some decide to return back to their home areas partly on foot in order to save some money. According to the participants, there were cases in which these people were attacked and killed by the Gumuz while they were travelling. However, it should be noted here that such allegations could also be related to the stereotypical views prevalent in the highlands that characterize the Gumuz as hostile. Nevertheless, one local official from Dangur *woreda* administration council admitted that there were a number of such incidents in the *woreda*, but they did not know who was behind them. Whoever is to blame, and whichever group, the Gumuz or the migrants, are right, it is evident from both individual interviews and group discussions with the Gumuz that they have explicit, negative attitudes towards both the migrant workers and the investment projects.

A closer look into the issue reveals that the hostilities of the Gumuz towards the land acquisitions are not only because they face threats of dispossession and displacement from their ancestral lands, but also because they feel marginalized from the employment opportunities brought by the projects. With the exception of a few guard positions, almost all the seasonal wage employment opportunities are filled by labourers from the highland areas. Since I was curious to know the reasons why the projects make use of outside labour coming from as far away as Siemen Shewa, the manager of one of the farm projects located in Gimitiya *kebele* (Dangur *woreda*) explained that they have been forced to bring labourers from other regions because of the lack of interest among the local communities to engage in seasonal labour activities (interview, Gublak town, 18 May 2012). Implicit in his argument is the clear inference that local indigenous people are 'lazy' and have a culture that does not encourage hard work. A highlander himself, his views were no different from those hegemonic ideologies of highlanders in general that considered the Gumuz people 'as little better than animals – unintelligent, ugly, heathen and evil' (Gonzalez-Ruibal 2012: 69). In contrast to this, however, in my own interviews and discussions, most of the Gumuz expressed their interest in making use of the employment opportunities. This is what the following focus group discussion account demonstrates:

> We wanted to work and get some money. . . . But these investors don't like us. They don't want to employ our people. They say this community [Gumuz] is not capable of doing daily wage work and they even went to the extent of calling our people lazy. This is their common response when we approach them for employment. They don't even see us as human beings. . . . That is why they prefer to employ migrant workers. These same investors first promised that they would employ our people and that they would only employ people from other places if there were no enough workers from our communities. But this is not what is happening here. We always ask them for work. Except for a few guard positions in which our people are employed, the

available job opportunities are almost all filled by migrant people
coming from the Amhara region. . . . That is what we see here
in connection with these investors. (interview, Gimtiya, Dangur
woreda, 20 May 2012)

Women in particular stressed that when they approached the
investment projects for employment, they were treated suspiciously
by the employers and even seen as thieves who went there not to work,
but to steal (interview, Gimtiya *kebele*, 21 May 2012). Generally, the
Gumuz informants stressed that this is why they wanted to make the
investment projects leave. So although the investors argued that they
were forced to employ highland migrants for the available seasonal
work because of the lack of local labour, which they attributed to a lack
of motivation among the Gumuz,[6] the fact that local people seeking
the work were not even offered the chance or were less preferred
suggests that the project leaders gave preference to highlanders. In
terms of employment opportunities, therefore, the experience with
existing investment projects is that they appear to have benefited
highland migrants rather than the local communities, at least in the
present study areas.

Resistance against the state As a strategy of resistance and to
undermine its legitimacy, focus group participants in Gimitiya and
Qotta *kebeles*, in particular, expressed their anger at the government,
suggesting that they had been deceived by local officials and had their
ancestral land taken out of their hands. Thus, they threatened not to
pay taxes, although they were aware that this would bring them in
direct confrontation with the government. More than anything else,
the Gumuz were highly irritated by the muteness and, at times, the
role of local authorities in the land acquisitions. This is particularly
so because, in contrast to previous regimes, most of the local
administrative offices are now filled by people from the indigenous
communities themselves. One elderly informant in Ayicid *kebele*
(Guba *woreda*) expressed his sentiment, remarking:

How come a person who is born from us lets their ancestral marks
be destroyed by outsiders, or worse, by those people who enslaved
our fathers and us for generations? We thought a new day has come
for us in which our voices will be heard when our children assumed

government positions and kids started going to school. But these local officials of ours did not stand on our side when our lands were grabbed. They deceived us instead. We don't trust them anymore, I swear! Had it not been to our fierce resistance, we would have disappeared from this area long ago. (interview, 7 June 2012)

This comment highlights how important had been their own agency in defending their territory. Indeed, during group discussions, local communities emphasized that they appealed to local authorities almost every single day. For example, the administrator of Qotta *kebele* particularly stressed that all the grievances of the community are directed at him and that he faces intimidations every day, forcing him in turn to talk to *woreda* and zonal authorities in various instances.

Almost all Gumuz informants interviewed held the view that an effort to relocate many of their villages is a strategy of the government to expropriate their land. Some people who were already relocated to new villages refused to stay and returned back to their previous villages, although in some places, for example Qotta *kebele*, their lands had already been taken by investors. Informants contended that they would not leave their current villages entirely for fear that if they did, they would lose their land and would not be able to come back again (interview, Qotta *kebele*, May 2012). As a result, they comply with local authorities by accepting relocation to new villages as a strategy in order to avoid confrontation, but in practice they also insist on maintaining their previous villages. This is an act of resistance without directly challenging the government's villagization programme. Other people resisted the villagization efforts outright and refused to comply with them.

Historically, the Gumuz have been able to resist pressures from the state at various conjunctures. Gonzalez-Ruibal (2012: 70) describes their resistance as follows:

It is not only strange that the Gumuz have not vanished as a people or their numbers drastically reduced after centuries of enslaving and exploitation. It is equally surprising the degree to which their culture has resisted the pressures of dominant groups, avoiding disappearance or mixture to a large extent.

Although it seems ambiguous, at least for some scholars, to consider flight as a form of resistance, the Gumuz have been able to maintain their moral economies and cultural identities because of their continuous flight to remote areas when the forces they had to fight, including the state, were too strong. The current widespread land acquisitions that have been claiming large tracts of land from the Gumuz appear, however, to have greatly reduced the number of areas to which the Gumuz might flee. It was through flight that the Gumuz resisted and refused to live side by side with other groups in the past. And this resonates with what Adas (1986: 64) once called 'avoidance protest', referring to cases in which peasants used flight as an act of social protest and a means of defending themselves from what they perceived to be exploitative conditions. Indeed, violent forms of resistance against the ongoing land acquisitions have been rare among the Gumuz. This sharply resonates with Scott's argument based on the case of rural Malaysia, in which he argued that the lack of more violent forms of resistance among the peasantry is largely 'the result of a prudent, calculated, and historically tested choice favoring other strategies more attuned to [their] particular social structure, strengths, and defensive capacities' (Scott 1987: 422).

The agitations and discontents of local communities related to land acquisitions, as expressed in various forms discussed above, appear to be shared by some local and regional officials. As indicated earlier, in contrast to earlier regimes, local political power in the region is now in the hands of officials that belong to the indigenous ethnic groups. Some of the officials interviewed admitted their discontent over the land acquisition process, although they were very cautious in voicing opinions that would identify them as being explicitly against the system of which they are a part. For example, two regional government officials interviewed in Assosa and Gilgel Beles, who requested anonymity, expressed their concerns regarding the involvement of the federal government in the administration of investment lands in the region, with particular concerns over the processes and relations of power this implied (interview, April 2012). The officials contended that this current trend of direct federal government intervention undermines the regional government's authority to challenge and negotiate land transfers that may potentially affect local land rights and to promote investments based on distinct regional socioeconomic and ecological contexts. For example, as the fieldwork for this particular study was underway, there was a widely circulating rumour among both experts and *woreda* and zonal authorities related to the transfer of an area that is known for its rich woodland, water, and wildlife resources. Local and regional authorities contended that they would resist such an acquisition by investors if the federal government actually went ahead with it.

This example indicates that local and regional authorities seem to have reacted to some of the land deals that threaten the natural environment. However, their resistance does not seem to have changed or contributed to the rethinking of policies related to the ongoing practices of land acquisitions. It is also not in the open, as most local officials do not wish to openly speak out and oppose the political system of which they are part, but choose, rather, to be silent in order to maintain their position in office. Thus, while engaged in a form of official politics (resistance) backstage, local regional authorities have also been working alongside the federal government in the process of land acquisition despite professing that they do not support many of its aspects.

Although it seems clear that some internal dissension has been occurring within local authorities regarding land acquisitions, in practice such tensions have not been linked to the hostilities of local communities in order to reduce the latter's political and economic marginality.

Concluding reflections on indigenous local communities and resistance to dispossession, displacement, and marginalization

The chapter has examined how indigenous local communities perceive ongoing large-scale land acquisitions, and how these communities, with a particular focus on the Gumuz people, have been reacting to them. The chapter has argued that the apparent silence of the Gumuz people regarding the land acquisitions is misleading. As demonstrated, the Gumuz people, who are now under mounting threats from the current large-scale land acquisitions, are hostile to such acquisitions. They have responded in various ways to threats of dispossession and displacement that have and will continue to occur. These responses range from covert forms (destroying field crops and machineries, attacking/killings) to more open forms (intimidation, refusing to comply with villagization, threatening not to pay tax, encroaching onto land already acquired by investors). However, the emerging discontent of the Gumuz people does not manifest in organized, structured, or large-scale ways. Likewise, the Gumuz are not supported by the local authorities or civil society organizations in defending their local land rights effectively. Despite this, the purpose of their actions is to challenge the land acquisitions taking place on their ancestral lands. The chapter showed that their reactions are not only against investors and migrant seasonal agricultural labourers, but also against the state, challenging its definition of 'development'. Such local reactions prove that the Gumuz have not been entirely helpless. They challenge the recent large-scale land acquisitions, not only because of their implications for possible displacement, dislocation, and the disruptions of their local livelihoods, but also because of the absence of economic benefits from the land acquisitions both in the present and the future. It seems unlikely, however, that the Gumuz will be able to effectively defend their land from the current widespread land acquisitions that involve both domestic and foreign companies with a strong connection to and support from the state. In the current context of the ongoing strong politicization of land investment undertakings involving the federal state, the disadvantages to the Gumuz and other indigenous communities stand out more clearly.

As shown in this chapter, local resistance strategies and investors' capacity to enforce their claims to land vary depending on the state's presence and level of authority. This implies that future expansion of investment (and the subsequent threats to local indigenous communities) depend on the state's continued protection of investors. If investors' performance is perceived as poor, it will likely affect the state's willingness to intervene on their behalf. In light of this study's findings, the local communities' resistance is a potentially important factor that will affect the economic viability of these investment projects.

Notes

1 There are five tiers of government administration in the country, which include (from the highest to lowest administrative unit): federal, region, zone, *woreda*, and *kebele*. *Woreda* is roughly equivalent to district, while *kebele*, especially in rural areas, corresponds to a group of villages.

2 For the intensive fieldwork, two *woredas* from Metekel zone were selected, namely Dangur and Guba. In addition, a short visit was made to the Homosha *woreda* in the Assosa zone, in order to strengthen the findings. These *woredas*, particularly Dangur and Guba, were selected because these areas are the main foci of recent large-scale land acquisitions in the region. Within these *woredas*, some villages were carefully selected based

on investment concentration and expert opinion, particularly regarding accessibility and representativeness. In addition, the Berta ethnic group – which dominates the Tsori-al-metema *kebele* in the Homosha *woreda* – was included in the study. The in-depth interviews were conducted with 17 key Gumuz informants and 14 selected government officials and experts at various hierarchical levels. In-depth interviews with three informants from the Berta ethnic group were also conducted. In addition, in the selected case study villages, a total of seven FGDs were conducted with the communities affected by land acquisitions. Interviews were also conducted with five managers of investment projects operating in the study areas.

3 For further reading as regards to the history of centre/periphery relationships, which was characterized by a long history of inequality, exploitation, and marginalization, see Abbute (2002), Ahmad (1999), Gebre (2003), Markakis (2011), and Pankhurst (1977).

4 The use of land by pastoralists and shifting cultivators in the lowlands is contested by the state, as such existing land uses are perceived to be unsustainable or inefficient (Lavers 2012).

5 Most of these seasonal wage labourers, migrating mainly from the central highlands of the Amhara region, are landless young men or those with small landholdings who are unable to provide for their families from such holdings. For many of these labourers, seasonal migration is the only available source of income.

6 Interview with managers of two investment projects in Dangur *woreda*, May 2012.

References

Abbute, W. (2002). *Gumuz and Highland Resettlers: Differing Strategies of Livelihood and Ethnic Relations in Metekel, Northwestern Ethiopia.* PhD Thesis, Gottinger Studien Zur Ethnologie.

Adas, M. (1986) 'From footdragging to flight: the evasive history of peasant avoidance protest in South and South-East Asia'. *Journal of Peasant Studies*, 13(2): 64–86.

Ahmad, A.H. (1999) 'Trading in slaves in Bela-Shangul and Gumuz, Ethiopia: border enclaves in history 1897–1938'. *Journal of African History*, 40(3): 433–446.

Akram-Lodhi, A.H. (2012). 'Contextualising land grabbing: contemporary land deals, the global subsistence crisis and the world food system'. *Canadian Journal of Development Studies*, 33(2): 119–142.

Borras, S.M. and Franco, J.C. (2012). 'Global land grabbing and trajectories of agrarian change: a preliminary analysis'. *Journal of Agrarian Change*, 12(1): 34–59.

Borras, S.M. and Franco, J.C. (2013). 'Global land grabbing and political reactions "from below"'. *Third World Quarterly*, 34(9): 1723–1747.

Central Statistical Agency (CSA) (2008). *Summary and Statistical Report of the 2007 Population and Housing Census: Population Size by Age and Sex.* Addis Ababa: Population Census Commission. Available at: www.csa.gov.et/pdf/Cen2007_firstdraft.pdf [accessed 19 June 2011].

De Schutter, O. (2011). 'How not to think of land-grabbing: three critiques of large-scale investments in farmland'. *Journal of Peasant Studies*, 38(2): 249–279.

Deininger, K. and Byerlee, D. (2011). *Rising Global Interest in Farmland: Can It Yield Sustainable and Equitable Benefits?* Washington, DC: World Bank.

Gebre, Y. (2003). 'Resettlement and the unnoticed losers: impoverishment disasters among the Gumuz in Ethiopia'. *Human Organization*, 62(1): 51–61.

Gonzalez-Ruibal, A. (2012). 'Generations of free men: resistance and material culture in western Ethiopia'. In T. Kienlin and A. Zimmermann (eds), *Beyond Elites: Alternatives to Hierarchical Systems in Modelling Social Formations*. Bonn: Habelt, pp. 67–82.

Kerkvliet, B. (1986). 'Everyday resistance to injustice in Philippine village'. *Journal of Peasant Studies*, 13(2): 107–123.

Lavers, T. (2012). 'Patterns of agrarian transformation in Ethiopia: state-mediated commercialization and the "land grab"'. *Journal of Peasant Studies*, 39(3–4): 795–822.

Makki, F. (2014). 'Development by dispossession: terra nullius and the social-ecology of new enclosures in Ethiopia'. *Rural Sociology*, 79(1): 79–103.

Markakis, J. (2011). *Ethiopia: The Last Two Frontiers*. London: James Currey.

McMichael, P. (2010). 'Agrofuels in the food regime'. *Journal of Peasant Studies*, 37(4): 609–629.

Moreda, T. (2013). *Postponed Local Concerns? Implications of Land Acquisitions for Indigenous Local Communities in Benishangul-Gumuz Regional State, Ethiopia*. Land Deal Politics Initiative (LDPI) Working Paper No. 13.

Oakland Institute (2011). *Understanding Land Investment Deals in Africa.* *Country Report: Ethiopia*. Oakland, CA: Oakland Institute.

Pankhurst, R. (1977). 'The history of the Bareya, Shanqella, and other Ethiopian slaves from the borderlands of the Sudan'. *Sudan Notes and Records*, 59: 1–43.

Rahmato, D. (2011). *Land to Investors: Large-Scale Land Transfers in Ethiopia*. FSS Policy Debates Series No, 1. Addis Ababa: Forum for Social Studies.

Scott, J.C. (1985). *Weapons of the Weak: Everyday Forms of Peasant Resistance*. New Haven, CT: Yale University Press.

Scott, J.C. (1987). 'Resistance without protest and without organization: peasant opposition to the Islamic Zakat and the Christian Tithe'. *Comparative Studies in Society and History*, 29(3): 417–452.

Visser, O. and Spoor, M. (2011). 'Land grabbing in post-Soviet Eurasia: the world's largest agricultural land reserves at stake'. *Journal of Peasant Studies*, 38(2): 299–323.

Von Braun, J. and Meinzen-Dick, R. (2009). *Land Grabbing by Foreign Investors in Developing Countries: Risks and Opportunities*. IFPRI Policy Brief 13.

White, B. and Dasgupta, A. (2010). 'Agrofuels capitalism: a view from political economy'. *Journal of Peasant Studies*, 37(4): 593–607.

White, B., Borras, S.M., Hall, R., Scoones, I., and Wolford, W. (2012). 'The new enclosures: critical perspectives on corporate land deals'. *Journal of Peasant Studies*, 39(3–4): 619–647.

Zoomers, A. (2010). 'Globalisation and the foreignisation of space: seven processes driving the current global land grab'. *Journal of Peasant Studies*, 37(2): 429–447.

14 | ALL THAT GLITTERS: NEOLIBERAL VIOLENCE, SMALL-SCALE MINING, AND GOLD EXTRACTION IN NORTHERN TANZANIA

Zahra Moloo

This is our home, not his. If I took my property and invested in his home, in Europe, as a white man he would never tolerate the same treatment he gives me as a citizen of Tanzania. (N'gombe Lukala Kadaso)

There is no shop for the souls of human beings. (Leonard Salala)

Introduction

In 2014, at a keynote speech to a room full of private sector representatives, government officials, and civil society actors in Maputo, Mozambique, the Managing Director of the International Monetary Fund (IMF), Christine Lagarde (2014), remarked that Africa was undergoing a 'momentous transformation'. If it managed to harness the potential of its mineral reserves, she said, the continent would experience 'unparalleled opportunity for economic growth and development'.

The conference at which she was speaking was titled 'Africa Rising', a term that has recently been deployed by institutions such as the IMF, technocrats, and journalists. According to *The Economist* (2011, 2013), this term encapsulates several recent changes, including an increase in foreign direct investment (FDI), a retreat from socialist economic models, and a growing middle class of millions of new consumers who can now purchase goods such as iPads and cappuccinos. Colonial tropes of Africa as backward and uncivilized, so frequently used by Western media and NGOs, have given way to an uplifting discourse in which Africans have thrown off their colonial shackles and are finally the authors of their own destiny, forged through trade and foreign investment, rather than aid, and whose emblems of success are the consumer goods that can be purchased in the mushrooming shopping malls of capital cities such as Lagos and Nairobi.

Yet, this optimistic discourse, and its promotion of foreign direct investment (FDI) in the extractive sector, seems starkly disconnected from realities on the ground around mining sites on the continent. Shortly after the IMF conference, an investigation by the organizations Mining Watch and RAID, at a gold mine operated by Acacia Mining (formerly African Barrick Gold (ABG)) in northern Tanzania, found that at least 10 people had been killed by fatal gunshot wounds at the mine in the two months preceding the investigation, and that excessive use of force by police guarding the mine had resulted in the deaths and injuries of villagers from the surrounding area. According to my own investigations in 2013 at Geita Gold Mine, operated by AngloGold Ashanti, a number of small-scale miners reported frequent killings by security guards around the mining site, with bodies, according to one interviewee, thrown in a dam on the mine's concession area. These findings are only the most recent in a long series of allegations and reports of police brutality, human rights abuses, and dispossession around mining sites in northern Tanzania, dating back to the very beginning of these mining operations. The incidents are not much, if at all, talked about among NGOs in urban centres such as Nairobi that are tasked with advocating for communities around mining sites and for greater transparency in the extractive sector.

In this chapter, I will interrogate this apparent contradiction between the reality of resource extraction in Tanzania, a process made possible through incredible violence and the dispossession of small-scale miners and farmers, and the seductive allure of discourses such as the 'African Rising' narrative, which posits that the continent's success will come about through FDI and economic growth. I will delve briefly into the history of mining in Tanzania and demonstrate how the mining infrastructure in place today, including legislation, replicates the colonial system of mining under the Germans and the British; coloniality, as defined by Maldonado-Torres (2007: 243) as the 'long-standing patterns of power that emerged from colonialism', is inscribed in the very legal and policy infrastructure of the extractive sector in Tanzania, and performed through the postcolonial state apparatus.

I will examine in particular two mining sites, North Mara Gold Mine and Geita Gold Mine, where I have reported and filmed, and where violence and the dispossession of farmers and small-scale miners have been features of the multinational extractive project for several decades. Around these sites, small-scale miners and villagers have resisted the dispossession of their lands and livelihoods by continuing to extract gold on the outskirts of mines and by periodically destroying the physical infrastructure of the mines. I will also look at how local resistance to mining has been perceived, described, and criminalized. Finally, I will explore how journalists and media activists can make these stories more visible and counter the neoliberal narrative of a 'rising' continent, a narrative that is especially beneficial to the interests of those who see Tanzania, and Africa, as the final frontier in the quest for profit.

Infrastructures of extraction: from the 1890s to post-independence

When describing the African continent, there exists a common misconception that it has been historically 'marginalized' or 'integrated . . . only superficially' into the global economy (Amin 2013: 37). A study of the evolution of mineral extraction in a country such as Tanzania reveals that specific kinds of integration linked the country to the global economy early on, and private companies in the colonial period 'pioneered methods for securing economic extraction in the absence of modern state institutions' (Ferguson 2005: 380). They laid the foundations for the current economic setup that favours large-scale extraction by multinational companies.

Gold has long been a part of Tanzanian history, beginning with its inclusion in the Indian Ocean slave trade and attracting the Portuguese who settled on the East African coast as early as 1500. While alluvial gold has been mined for centuries by small-scale miners, large-scale mining began in the nineteenth century, with the arrival of German prospectors who discovered gold in the Lake Victoria region in 1894.

In 1895, the German colonial administration established the Imperial Land Ordinance, which stated that all land not already privately owned was owned by the German colonial state (James 1971: 14). The land ordinance paved the way for the concession system, a system that has continued into the present day and has been described as 'the most crucial form of sovereignty for the extraction of mineral wealth by private capital' (Emel et al. 2011: 74). This system used the sovereign power of the colonial government to award exclusive mining rights to private companies in areas containing gold (Chachage 1995: 48). Already, by 1910, 111 claims had been pegged on approximately 76 prospecting fields (Lemelle 1986: 54). In 1909, the Germans opened Sekenke Gold Mine, the very first gold mine in Tanganyika, which became the largest producer of gold in the country before the Second World War. Since commodity gold was 'deeply infused within the international monetary system and central to the gold standard', Tanganyika came to be, quite early on, linked to the prevailing system of global capital (Emel *et al.* 2011: 74).

In 1919, a mandate from the League of Nations turned Tanganyika over to British rule. As under German rule, the British annexed almost all the territory to the state. A 1923 land ordinance declared that an estimated 99 per cent of land in the territory, whether occupied or unoccupied, was public land, with the exception of land that was alienated under the Germans (James 1971: 18). After some debate about the need to develop attractive conditions for large mining companies, the British later instituted the 1929 Mining Ordinance, which granted special prospective licences of up to eight square miles, exclusive prospective licences for areas larger than that, and restricted alluvial mining claims that could be held by small prospectors (Chachage 1995: 60).

After independence, President Julius Nyerere instituted '*Ujamaa*', popularly known as an 'African socialist' method of government. Like the Germans and British before him, he maintained what Emel *et al.* (2011: 74) refers to as the 'national-scale sovereignty' over natural resources. However, although he argued for leaving mineral resources in the ground until Tanzanians themselves developed the skills to mine them, a British company, Tanganyika Concessions, was still producing half the country's gold from the Lake Victoria goldfields during this period (Emel *et al.* 2011: 74). In 1971, demand for gold increased and the World Bank advocated for the country to revise its mining codes to attract private investment. The 1980s was the time of the notorious debt lending crises. In 1986, Tanzania, along with many other countries in Sub-Saharan Africa, was forced to accept the World Bank's Structural Adjustment Policy to dismantle what the Bank termed as pervasive economic controls, and to encourage the private sector's increased participation in the economy. This period heralded the beginning of a neoliberal extractive age, one that continued the colonial method of privatizing land ownership and encouraging large-scale mining, married to a new rhetoric of poverty reduction and development.

Interestingly, although Tanzanians now had to receive permission to sell minerals, artisanal and small-scale miners still had the freedom to operate anywhere in the country (Emel *et al.* 2011: 75). This changed with the promulgation of the 1998 Mining Act, which, like the 1929 Imperial Ordinance, offered attractive incentives to new investors. As well, tenure was given to the mining companies for 20–50 years, or for the life of the mine, with clauses to ensure that incentives would not be changed (Emel *et al.* 2011: 76). Paula Butler (2004: 72) explains that the most significant change in this new act was the 'entitlement of private licence holders to use their mineral rights as collateral and to transfer mineral rights to banks or financial institutions without requiring ministerial approval or consent'. This meant 'a significant erosion of Tanzanian sovereignty over its mineral sector'. By way of example of just how far this 'erosion' went, the 1998 law itself was written by Transborder Associates, a British firm specializing in privatizing and liberalizing developing economies (Emel *et al.* 2011: 76). Versions of the Act were vetted by Canadian mining company Sutton Resources and by the Canadian High Commissioner (Butler 2004).

The 1998 mining legislation has coloniality inscribed in its very details. Such is the genius of weaving colonial codes of practice in law: the law itself becomes, as Karl Marx describes it, an instrument of theft. The most recent 2010 Mining Act does not substantially waver from former legislation, and makes it illegal for local artisanal miners to explore for minerals. Civil society organizations are said to have called it 'the beginning of the end' for small-scale miners (Olan'g 2010). Working in tandem with existing laws governing land ownership and compensation, and tax incentives that encourage private companies to invest in the mining sector, the current legal infrastructure is set up to ensure that private companies headquartered in London, South Africa, or Toronto reap enormous profits from the extractive sector, with state officials, police officers, and private security companies carrying out the work of managing the process of dispossession and its casualties, a setup that resembles indirect colonial rule.

'Africa Rising': financial actors, NGOs, and neoliberal myths

The existing infrastructure, designed to favour the interests of private companies, has been complemented by the work of international financial institutions and the 'myths' that they have constructed (Bush 2015: 46). Since the end of the colonial era, international financial institutions (IFIs) have argued that mineral exploitation by transnational corporations will lead to progress and poverty reduction; according to Ray Bush (2010: 238), they have 'consistently promoted' the 'holy trinity of the market, property rights and foreign direct investment'. Mining companies, he argues, depend on the 'ideological hegemony of modernization' and claim that they will 'promote growth with equity, development with justice and sustainability with employment'. The inclusion of 'justice', 'sustainability', and even 'human rights' in the ongoing operations of multinational mining companies means that these companies, 'labeled as corporate predators during the anti-colonial and anti-imperial struggles', have now been 're-designated' as 'development partners' (Marshall 2015: 65).

Colonial style extractivism can in this way coexist with efforts towards poverty alleviation and development. NGOs tasked with advocating for the rights of communities at times even partner with mining companies. In Tanzania, the NGO Search for Common Ground partnered with mining company Acacia Mining with a motto to 'transform conflict through cooperation'. Through activities such as joint stakeholder meetings, sport, and capacity building, the organization supports the company in improving its relationships with communities near its four mines located in Mara and Shinyanga. In 2011, the Canadian International Development Agency announced a multimillion-dollar grant to three NGOs that partnered with mining companies. The deal enabled World University Services Canada, Plan Canada, and World Vision Canada to receive funding for projects with Rio Tinto Alcan, Iamgold, and Barrick Gold (Schulman and Nieto 2011).[1]

In Kenya, where NGOs have received more donor funding to work on advocacy in the extractive sector, debates revolve around improving company practices rather than challenging them outright. At a 2014 NGO conference in Nairobi on mining, during which communities impacted by mining operations were notably absent, one NGO actor took the room through the World Bank's redress mechanisms for human rights abuses, without the slightest hint of irony. The NGO sector, with few exceptions, appears to present a perspective that fits well with the approach promoted by the IMF, that is, enabling large-scale mining to proceed as previously, with cosmetic changes such as improved corporate social responsibility and redress mechanisms for human rights abuses, crafted by the very institutions responsible for destroying the public sector in many African countries (Moloo 2014). The Tanzanian government, for its part, has its own vision to transform the country into a middle-income nation by the year 2025, an ambition that corresponds with the African Development Bank's conclusions that the emergence of a strong middle class in Africa has 'generate[d] . . . long-term poverty reducing benefits' (African Development Bank 2011: 15). The way to foster the growth of this new middle-class sector, according to the Bank, includes the 'promotion of private-sector growth'.

In this way, the work of advocacy organizations, transnational mining companies, IFIs, and governments do not contradict each other. Instead, they come together under the same neoliberal ideology. Kapoor (2013: 20) characterizes this 'state-market-civil society nexus' as a commitment to the 'reproduction of a colonial-capital modernity'. The belief that private sector development, economic growth, and the rise of a consumer class constitute the path to long-term progress underlies policies on poverty alleviation and development in Africa, and has provided the impetus for the relatively new 'Africa Rising' discourse. This trope of a continent on the rise, advancing through self-sustaining economic growth, and promoted by the IMF, the African Development Bank and media outlets such as *The Economist*, is, in the words of Sasha Breger Bush (2015: 46), one of many 'free market myths' that 'reinforce the power, allure and thus popular acceptance of finance'. The 'Africa Rising' myth is based on findings that Africa's middle class now number in their millions, that foreign investment, manufacturing, and the service sectors are growing rapidly, and that, from 2001 to 2011, according to *The Economist*, 6 of the world's 10 fastest-growing countries were African. The general consensus is that Africa's time is now, that it is no longer a peripheral backward destination. It is not only a seductive myth, but also a dangerous one, particularly when applied to the extractive sector, because by focusing on the 'rising' classes, it deletes the stories of the 'resource poor' and presents the state as a body whose work is to create an investment-friendly environment for business (Lemma 2013). The Africa Rising myth is the quintessential neoliberal trope; its popularity, ubiquity, and allure have made it acceptable to mainstream public discourse, obscuring the violence and colonial continuity of the economic logic that underlies it.

Coloniality in practice: violence and dispossession in northern Tanzania

AngloGold Ashanti's Geita Gold Mine (GGM) sprawls over 196 square kilometres in the northeastern Mwanza region of Tanzania. To reach this 'enclave of mineral extraction' (Ferguson 2005: 378), one has to meander through a landscape absent in infrastructure and similar to the surroundings of other mines in the north of the country. These mines, both at the moment of their establishment as well as in the present day, are places of extraordinary violence and dispossession. This is not coincidental. While Ferguson (2005: 379) argues that there is now 'increasing acceptance of the idea that effective mineral production and endemic violence can coexist', in fact, violence is a *necessary* and *intrinsic* feature of multinational extractivism, in the same way it was instrumental to the colonial project, rooted 'deep in colonial encounters' (Ndlovu-Gatsheni 2013: 134). Present-day open-pit mining sites are among the many flagrant examples of how violence has 'migrated' from the 'colonial period into the post-colonial neo-colonized present'.

Violence is at times direct and unmediated, and at other times enacted through the aforementioned laws and codes governing mining and land acquisition. For instance, the initial granting of the GGM concession to AngloGold Ashanti (AGA) in 1999 required the forced removal of thousands of farmers and small-scale miners extracting gold from the mining area. Under the country's 1998 Mining Act, the company was permitted to lease an area of 196 kilometres over 25 years, including 'exploration tenements' surrounding the concession. In an interview with AGA (9 May 2013), they specified that in the case that 'an appropriate opportunity with sufficient economic potential were identified in future', they would apply for a 'special mining license'. Land already inhabited can simply be reconceptualized solely for its economic potential, an extension of the 'cartesian-capitalist colonial conception of global space as terra nullius', a 'space emptied of histories, peoples and cultures', and 'free for capital to exploit' (Kapoor 2013: 20).

Other activities taking place on the concession area, including small-scale mining dating back several years, were deemed illegal. In

2007, farmers from a village called Mine Mpya, which lies on AGA's concession, reported that they were attacked by police at 5 a.m. and evicted from their homes to make way for the concession. According to 75-year-old farmer Mwajuma Hussein, 'GGM gave instructions and the police came to attack [us]'. They were then dumped in a small patch of land near Geita town, known as Sophiatown, or colloquially 'Darfur', forced to construct makeshift houses out of plastic sheeting (personal interview, April 2013). Unable to go back to their farms, these formerly self-sufficient farmers, many of them elderly people who inherited land from their parents, said they never received any compensation for losing their land and had to look for daily contractual labour to feed themselves. AGA pointed out in an interview via email (2013) that they had followed 'due legal process' and had observed the provisions of Tanzania's Land Acquisition Act 1967 and Land Act 1999, which puts the responsibility for resettling and compensating displaced villagers on the state. After a protracted legal battle, it was found that the displaced farmers could not claim compensation, as they 'had no legal rights of occupancy' on the land, according to the company.

Such legal codes are very convenient for private capital. By conceptualizing land as property to be leased away for years to private capital, they effectively replicate colonial models of resource extraction, which ensured that large-scale mining took place efficiently in the absence of a strong state. At the same time, they ensure that it is the Tanzanian state in the present day that is responsible for managing the impacts of dispossession. The state in this way '[emerges] as an apparatus of violence', relying 'on coercion rather than consent' (Ndlovu-Gatsheni 2013: 74), while the company acquires the advantages of extraction, but evades responsibility for the people rendered disposable to the extractive project. Since this relationship is embedded in law, it becomes unquestionable.[2]

The process of dispossession is aided in large part by state agents acting on behalf of the 'independent state', which stands as 'the primary conduit of foreign direct investment' enabling transnational corporations to extract mineral wealth (Emel *et al.* 2011: 77). Many farmers from Mine Mpya described how local officials, such as the village chairman, colluded with the company and were given bribes, and that the government and GGM 'had an agreement'. Villagers also complained of corruption and suspicious meetings 'behind closed doors' involving their attorney, the judge, and lawyers representing the company (Lissner 2008). In other cases involving over 800 evicted villagers, AGA said that the money they paid in compensation to these villagers was never given to them, and that government officials in their 'lust for money' were to blame (Lissner 2008).

The militarization of mining sites and their outsourcing to private companies provides yet another means for companies to evade responsibility for the violence that takes place on their concessions. When a 16-year-old boy, Mhoja Leonard, was shot and killed by a security guard working for AGA, the company claimed it was 'not liable' for his death because the guard was employed by a private security company, G4S, and not by the mining company itself. In this way, violence, surveillance, and militarization around mining sites become unquestionable, a way for 'power to be exercised with impunity' (Depelchin 2013: 195). The mining company is protected on multiple levels: by legislation that favours large-scale extraction, by the outsourcing of their security, and by a government that favours the interests of the company over rural Tanzanians.

Everyday resistance: 'intruders' and small-scale miners

Despite the heavy militarization of mining sites and the intricate setup that over time has consolidated large-scale mining interests, resistance to dispossession at these mining sites has been varied and prolonged, and has helped to propel the incidents in northern Tanzania into the public domain and into the media. As James C. Scott (1985: 17) explains in *Weapons of the Weak*, 'everyday forms of resistance make no headlines', but 'multiple acts of peasant insubordination . . . create political and economic barrier reefs of their own'. In the case of northern Tanzania, these acts can be situated on a continuum, ranging from small-scale miners defying laws that favour multinational companies, returning to lands from where they have been evicted, and continuing to find areas to mine gold, to venturing into the company's mine pits to extract gold and directly attacking mine infrastructure.

In both Acacia Mining's North Mara Gold Mine and Anglogold Ashanti's GGM, small-scale miners have continued to mine their own gold or to harvest gold pieces from waste left over by the mines. In

Magema, which in 2013 was one of the last remaining strongholds of artisanal and small-scale miners on the Geita concession area, hundreds of people were mining gold on the slopes of the gold mine. The contrast was stark: green hills teeming with people venturing deep into gold pits in the earth, or running down the hills carrying large sacks of stones, while on the other side of the hills sprawled the open-pit gold mine continuing its separate extractive operation.

Some miners had been evicted by police, but eventually returned, while others believed it was their right to continue mining gold on the slopes of the mine, in defiance of the law. The small-scale miners had an intricate and efficient setup. Hussein Makonda, who had invested a lot of his own money in the smaller mine pits, explained the process:

> When the rocks come from the ground, there are women who pound the stone. That is their job. Then the stone is taken to the machine to be crushed. The grinder has a job. Then when it goes to be sorted, the washers have a job. (personal interview, April 2013)

Contrary to the claims of many companies and IFIs that large-scale mining creates thousands of jobs and is beneficial to the economy, a study by the International Institute for Environment and Development (2013) found that the small-scale mining sector employs 10 times more people than large-scale mining. In many areas, however, the legal bias towards large companies, and the resultant criminalization of mining and farming activities on concession areas, has resulted in small-scale miners being squeezed off their lands. 'We don't know where we will go', Makonda told us. 'This is the only area we have left. All the other areas, GGM has already taken'. One small-scale miner from Magema described the eviction process, with state agents facilitating the acquisition of mineral-rich areas by multinational corporations, and small-scale miners acting as conduits. 'When we discover gold somewhere, we are chased away and the government sells it [to the company]. So we are recognized as those who find the gold, but we are not allowed to mine it'. According to the miners, their own contribution to the economy of Geita was far greater than that of AGA, which, after several years, had not even paved the roads or provided a steady electricity supply to the residents of Geita town.

When resistance takes a more confrontational approach, such as when miners venture directly into the mine's waste dumps, the response is often predictably violent. Both Acacia Mining and AngloGold Ashanti deploy private security companies or local Tanzanian police to 'protect' their concessions from what the companies and the media call 'scavengers', those who scour the mine waste dumps for flakes of gold. At Geita Gold Mine, numerous small-scale miners and villagers around the mine reported beatings and killings by company security guards whenever they went to look for pieces of gold in the waste dumps. One man described how he used to extract pieces of gold, but stopped after he witnessed people being killed. Other people from Magema said that when the security officers catch five people, only one is sent to court. 'The others are shot', he said. He added that many people who had gone to look for gold had drowned in a dam on the company's concession area. AngloGold Ashanti itself states in an online report that 24 third-party fatalities had occurred on their site in 2012, and that more fatalities resulted from people drowning in the Nyankanga Dam.

As in many instances where the dispossession of a native population takes place through the language of violence, resistance to it is likewise fashioned through the 'language' of 'force' (Fanon 1963: 42). The tactic that small-scale miners and 'scavengers' deploy, of physically resisting the mines themselves by attempting to harvest gold, have previously gone beyond efforts at eking out a living from the waste dumps; in 2008, thousands of villagers raided the North Mara Gold Mine and allegedly damaged mining equipment worth more than $16 million. A spokesperson for (former) African Barrick Gold in Tanzania said that some machinery was set on fire.

This 'spontaneous civilian movement', as it was called by activists, resembles confrontations of the colonial era, and is criminalized in much the same way that resistance movements against colonial rule were criminalized; a spokesperson for African Barrick Gold complained in an article for the *Dow Jones Newswire* that the incident was undertaken by 'well-organized' groups that 'relentlessly' attacked security personnel and would lead to a 'loss of production and revenue'. On its website, the company mentions long-term challenges it has had to contend with, such as 'vandalism by intruders seeking to unlawfully take gold' (Acacia Mining n.d.). This criminalization occurs not only in the language used by companies themselves, but also in local and international media; the villagers are described as 'intruders' with 'crude weapons' that 'invade' and 'attack' mine infrastructure and 'steal' gold (Bariyo 2008; Ng'wanakilala 2011).

In erasing the historical context of the dispossession of small-scale miners from North Mara, and displacing the attribution of violence from the company and its agents to the villagers, this narrative legitimizes the violence that lies at the heart of extraction, thereby justifying the continued militarization of mining sites. This process is further aided by imagery all too familiar in the African context: that of irrational, uncivilized villagers brandishing 'machetes', 'rocks', and 'hammers'. One media agency refers to the resistance by small-scale miners as 'small-scale gold looting by locals' (Jamasmie 2014). The dehumanizing language used to refer to villagers around mining sites is echoed by the words miners themselves use to refer to their relationship to the mining companies. At GGM, one small-scale miner said that the company sees them as 'animals' or 'bait'. Yet, it is through these daring and confrontational actions that the villagers around the mining sites demonstrate their agency and sovereignty over the land that has been taken from them.

From the mine pits to the high court

After years of confrontations between villagers and state or private security officers, the struggle in North Mara took a new turn when 12 villagers, including relatives of people who died in incidents near the gold mine, sued African Barrick Gold in the British High Court in 2013. The villagers argued that the company's subsidiary, the North Mara Gold Mine, had 'failed to prevent the use of excessive force by police and security which had led to six deaths and other injuries in 2008'. The company denied the claims, and the case was settled out of court for an undisclosed sum of money. While some welcomed the settlement, others found it disappointing and noted that human rights abuses were only acted upon when taken to 'rich countries like Britain'. The court case publicized the killings in the UK and internationally, helping to deepen the debate on multinational mining in East Africa, but it also demonstrated that resistance through legal means has its limits. The confidential nature of the settlement meant that it could hardly set a precedent for future cases and the payouts to the individual victims involved in the court case did not lead to systemic changes on the ground; in 2014, the organization RAID documented 10 killings at the North Mara Gold Mine in the two months following their June investigation, and in November 2015, during a second human rights field assessment, RAID and Mining Watch conducted more than 50 interviews with the victims of violence by mine security and by police guarding the mine, and noted that victims who had been promised remedy by the North Mara mine were made to sign documents giving up their right to take legal action against the mining company and its subsidiaries.

While the court case did not elicit the kinds of systemic changes that activists would like to see, the miners' diverse and ongoing strategies of contesting the legitimacy and authority of the mining company constituted a threat substantial enough to prompt stringent responses by African Barrick Gold. The company decided in 2011 that in order to 'improve security' and 'extend the life of the mine', it would allocate $14 million for the construction of a three-metre-high concrete wall around the mining site. ABG also hired a consulting firm to train Tanzanian police on international human rights standards and announced a new series of community projects to improve relations with villages around the mining site. In 2014, the company changed its name from African Barrick Gold to Acacia Mining, enabling it to distance itself from its tainted reputation,[3] and announced that it would move its North Mara operations underground. In 2014, according to a report by journalist Geoffrey York, ABG said it had reduced the number of 'intruders' by 35 per cent. While these changes are no doubt in part motivated by the need to maintain an attractive image to investors, and while they will certainly make it more difficult for villagers to make a living from the waste dumps and to bring the company to justice, they nevertheless demonstrate the extent to which ongoing local resistance has impacted company operations. The company's response combines increased militarization with efforts at improving relations with villagers; it is in keeping with the new neoliberal model of extraction where sustainability and human rights are absorbed into the operations of companies, but where the endemic violence of extraction continues.

Investigative journalism and cross-border networks

Despite the incredible violence at North Mara and Geita gold mines, media coverage of incidents at northern Tanzania's mining sites remains limited. The Tanzanian media only occasionally reports on these incidents, and the international media less so. One major challenge is logistical; mines are often located far from urban centres and are difficult to access. Another challenge is that investigative journalism on the African continent is a highly dangerous venture. The few investigative journalists working on the continent operate in contexts where public narratives and discourses promoted by the media and government tend to be skewed in favour of powerful government and corporate interests. While one major story could make a significant dent in this overarching trend, it is still necessary to have continuous and contextualized reporting on the extractive industries, rural dispossession, and neoliberal economic policies, in order to create a substantial impact in public understandings of how coloniality persists in the present day.

A handful of investigative and independent journalists, and activists organizing campaigns on mining struggles in the Global South, do the essential work of ensuring that stories of rural communities around mining sites remain continually visible. The process of rendering these struggles visible on a consistent basis feeds into organized campaigns for justice by activists in the Global North, such as the Protest Barrick campaign, which aggregates 'news articles, testimonies, and backgrounders about Barrick's operations worldwide' and forms part of a Toronto-based network, the Mining Injustice Solidarity Network. In Tanzania, journalists, lawyers, and human rights activists have continued to monitor and report on the operations of mining companies in northern Tanzania. One journalist in particular, Dotto Bulendu, who accompanied me to the GGM, has continually reported on the incidents at both GGM and North Mara Gold Mine for Tanzanian television and radio, and frequently accompanies activists and journalists from the Global North to mining sites in order to gather information. His work has been instrumental in bringing stories from the ground to activists in the North. During my own investigation, his initiative and expertise, along with that of two independent Geita-based human rights activists, enabled us to produce multiple reports in different formats, generating both long investigative reports for mainstream media, as well as an independent film consisting of testimonies from around the mining site.

These journalists and activists cement networks of exchange, communication, and organizing between the Global South and the North, and act as a thread connecting rural communities on the ground to groups of activists and journalists in urban centres and in other countries, who would otherwise remain disconnected from rural communities that are not formally organized or represented by an association or organization. Journalists and media activists could also play a role in more nuanced analysis and reporting on, for instance, the role of larger NGOs in subverting resistance of communities in East Africa, or colluding directly with mining companies, or on the innovative solutions that companies invent to continue evading justice.[4] Such analysis is not easily available to the public in East Africa.

Conclusion

There is no doubt that the neoliberal economic architecture that has been transforming economies towards increased privatization, foreign investment, and free trade is becoming more entrenched in East Africa, including Tanzania. In the extractive sector, the neoliberal turn has served to further develop an already existing, decades-old colonial infrastructure set up to guarantee the interests and wealth accumulation of multinational mining companies. Their legitimacy has been consolidated more recently through neoliberal discourses embraced and promoted by IFIs, NGOs, and the media. But while in urban centres NGO workers engage in advocacy work and government officials review and revise mining codes, in rural areas mines such as Geita Gold Mine and North Mara Gold Mine continue to produce more casualties. It is here that rural Tanzanians are continuing to assert their agency over their land and resources. Written out of both the 'Africa Rising' discourse, and marginalized from NGO conferences, the small-scale miners around GGM and NMG mines have continued to resist the dominance of the mines, insisting on their right to extract gold on their own land. Their very survival constitutes a form of resistance.

Local and international efforts to address the exploitative logic of extraction in Tanzania will have to put these rural communities at the forefront, while also challenging mainstream neoliberal discourses that depict foreign direct investment as beneficial to the economy, and villagers as 'intruders' standing in the way of development. Some global initiatives are already challenging the economic logic of extraction;

the 'Yes to Life, No to Mining' movement and allied campaigns such as Protest Barrick have been instrumental in supporting grassroots resistance to multinational mining. In East Africa, however, so pervasive are the myths and economic logic of neoliberalism that a real transformation of the extractive sector will have to begin first and foremost by a process of unlearning and, simultaneously, of remembering; remembering the *raison d'être* of multinational mining and its colonial roots, and unlearning the economic neoliberal logic that pervades mainstream thinking. Investigative journalists and media activists are well placed to bring up and critically frame some of the issues around coloniality, especially in the extractive sector, but this must be part of a longer and sustained effort at understanding and connecting coloniality and dispossession to their historical roots, and their present-day manifestations through legalized theft and neoliberal economic discourses. Such efforts are fundamental for longer-term decolonization. Without such a transformation, any change will remain cosmetic and multinational companies such as Acacia Mining will simply change the rules of the game, as they do already, by incorporating noble concerns about human rights into a fundamentally unjust and extraordinarily violent practice. In the words of Fanon (1963: 56), 'Everything has to be rethought'.

Notes

1 Another platform, the Information Centre for the Extractive Sector, an initiative funded by the African Development Bank, the UNDP, and the governments of the US, UK, and Canada, seeks to promote 'informed polices' for the extractive sector in Kenya, which can be used to 'drive continental development'. It is now housed within Adam Smith International, a group that grew out of the free-market think tank Adam Smith Institute.

2 While writing an article about the displaced farmers for a media agency, one editor pointed out that 'under the law – which, however unfair, is the law – they shouldn't have been there because it was already a mining area'.

3 Barrick Gold Corporation is still the majority shareholder in Acacia Mining. Its tainted past includes its controversial acquisition of Bulyanhulu Gold Mine three years after Sutton Resources, with Tanzanian authorities, forcibly evicted a community of small-scale miners and filled in their mining pits. Reports emerged that 52 people were allegedly buried alive inside the pits.

4 One example is Acacia Mining's use of 'grievance mechanisms', which is a non-judicial mechanism that enables communities to demand compensation from the company provided they sign away the right to ever sue the company in a court of law.

References

Acacia Mining (n.d.). *Security and Human Rights*. Available at: www.acaciamining.com/sustainability/our-material-areas/security-and-human-rights.aspx [accessed 17 September 2015].

African Development Bank (2011). *The Middle of the Pyramid: Dynamics of the Middle Class in Africa*. Available at: www.afdb.org/fileadmin/uploads/afdb/Documents/Publications/The%20Middle%20of%20the%20Pyramid_The%20Middle%20of%20the%20Pyramid.pdf [accessed 19 April 2016].

Amin, S. (2013). 'Class suicide, the petit bourgeoisie and the challenges of development'. In F. Manji and B. Fletcher Jr. (eds), *Claim No Easy Victories: The Legacy of Amilcar Cabral*. Dakar, Senegal: CODESRIA and Daraja Press, pp. 31–60.

Bariyo, N. (2008). 'Tanzania Barrick mine intruders steal gold, disrupt output-co'. *Dow Jones Newswire*. Available at: http://protestbarrick.net/article.php?id=362 [accessed 15 January 2016].

Bush, R. (2010). 'Conclusion: mining, dispossession and transformation in Africa'. In A. Fraser and M. Larmer (eds), *Zambia, Mining and Neoliberalism: Boom and Bust on the Globalized Copperbelt*. New York: Palgrave Macmillan, pp. 237–268.

Bush, S.B. (2015). 'Gambling on hunger and climate change'. In N. Buxton and M.B. Dumontier (eds), *State of Power 2015: An Annual Anthology on Global Power and Resistance*. Amsterdam: The Transnational Institute, pp. 38–49.

Butler, P. (2004). 'Tanzania: liberalization of investment and the mining sector analysis of the content and certain implications of the Tanzania 1998 Mining Act'. In B.K. Campbell (ed.), *Regulating Mining in Africa: For Whose Benefit?* Uppsala: Nordiska Afrikainstitutet. Available at: www.diva-portal.org/smash/get/diva2:240515/FULLTEXT02 [accessed 16 February 2016].

Chachage, C.S.L. (1995). 'The meek shall inherit the earth but not the mining rights'. In P. Gibbon (ed.), *Liberalized Development in Tanzania: Studies on Accumulation Process and Local Institutions*. Uppsala: Institute for African Studies, pp. 37–108.

Depelchin, J. (2013). 'Cabral and the dispossession (dehumanization) of humanity'. In F. Manji and B. Fletcher Jr. (eds), *Claim No Easy Victories: The Legacy of Amilcar Cabral*. Dakar, Senegal: CODESRIA and Daraja Press, pp. 189–202.

Emel, J., Huber, M.T., and Makene, M.H. (2011). 'Extracting sovereignty: capital, territory, and gold mining in Tanzania'. *Political Geography*, 30: 70–79.

Fanon, F. (1963). *The Wretched of the Earth*. New York: Grove Press.

Ferguson, J. (2005). 'Seeing like an oil company: space, security, and global capital in neoliberal Africa'. *American Anthropologist*, 107(3): 377–382.

International Institute for Environment and Development (2013). *Responding to the Challenge of Artisanal and Small-Scale Mining: How Can Knowledge Networks Help?* Available at: http://pubs.iied.org/pdfs/16532IIED.pdf [accessed 19 April 2016].

Jamasmie, C. (2014). *African Barrick is History, Changes Name to Acacia Mining*. Available at: www.mining.com/african-barrick-is-history-changes-name-to-acacia-mining-31334/ [accessed 19 April 2016].

James, R.W. (1971). *Land Tenure and Policy in Tanzania*. Toronto: University of Toronto Press.

Kapoor, D. (2013). 'Trans-local rural solidarity and an anticolonial politics of place: contesting colonial capital and the neoliberal state in India'. *Interface: A Journal for and About Social Movements*, 5(1), 14–39. Available at: www.interfacejournal.net/wordpress/wp-content/uploads/2013/05/Interface-5-1-Kapoor.pdf [accessed 17 March 2016].

Lagarde, C. (2014). *Africa Rising: Building to the Future*. Keynote Address at Africa Rising Conference, 29–30 May, Maputo, Mozambique. Available at: www.imf.org/external/np/speeches/2014/052914.htm [accessed 5 September 2015].

Lemelle, S. (1986). 'Capital, state, and labor: a history of the gold mining industry in Tanganyika, 1890–1942'. Unpublished doctoral dissertation, University of California, Los Angeles.

Lemma, S. (2013). *Against the Gospel of Africa Rising*. Available at: http://africasacountry.com/2013/11/against-the-gospel-of-africa-rising/ [accessed 20 March 2016].

Lissner, A.C. (2008). *Someone Else's Treasure: Photo Essay*. Available at: http://protestbarrick.net/downloads/SomeoneElsesTreasure_tanz.pdf [accessed 19 April 2016].

Maldonado-Torres, N. (2007). 'On the coloniality of being: contributions to the development of a concept'. *Cultural Studies*, 21(2–3): 240–270.

Marshall, J. (2015) 'Contesting big mining from Canada to Mozambique'. In N. Buxton and M.B. Dumontier (eds), *State of Power 2015: An Annual Anthology on Global Power and Resistance*. Amsterdam: Transnational Institute, pp. 63–75.

Moloo, Z. (2014). *Kenya's Civil Societies and Extractive Industries, Buying into Neoliberalism?* Available at: www.codesria.org/spip.php?article1923 [accessed 19 April 2016].

Ng'wanakilala, F. (2011). *Five Killed in Barrick Tanzanian Mine Attack – Police*. Available at: www.reuters.com/article/2011/05/17/tanzania-barrick-attack-idUSLDE74G09W20110517 [accessed 19 April 2016].

Ndlovu-Gatsheni, S. (2013). *Coloniality of Power in Postcolonial Africa: Myths of Decolonization*. Dakar: CODESRIA Press.

Olan'g, S. (2010). *Tanzania Passes a New Mining Law and Builds Capacity for Informed Policy Debate*. Available at: http://archive.resourcegovernance.org/news/tanzania-passes-new-mining-law-and-builds-capacity-informed-policy-debate [accessed 19 April 2016].

Schulman, G. and Nieto, R. (2011). *Foreign Aid to Mining Firms*. Available at: www.dominionpaper.ca/articles/4300 [accessed 9 April 2016].

Scott, J.C. (1985). *Weapons of the Weak: Everyday Forms of Peasant Resistance*. New Haven, CT: Yale University Press.

The Economist (2011). *Africa Rising*. 3 December. Available at: www.economist.com/node/21541015 [accessed 10 April 2017].

The Economist (2013). *A Hopeful Continent*. 2 March. Available at: www.economist.com/news/special-report/21572377-african-lives-have-already-greatly-improved-over-past-decade-says-oliver-august [accessed 10 April 2017].

15 | 'OLOIBIRINIZATION', COLLECTIVE IDENTITY, AND THE FUTURE OF MULTILOCAL RESISTANCE IN THE NIGER DELTA

Temitope B. Oriola

Introduction

The Niger Delta crisis has generated tremendous focus in the last two decades (Frynas 2000; Obi 2008; Oriola 2013). The scholarly literature has articulated issues such as political marginalization (Courson 2011), state excesses (Omotola 2009), social and demographic correlates of participating in armed struggle (Oyefusi 2007), women's response to state violence (Ekine 2008; Oriola 2012), the kidnapping phenomenon (Akpan 2010), and rise of the clearinghouse of the insurgency – the Movement for the Emancipation of the Niger Delta (MEND) (Okonta 2006), among others. This piece contributes to the increasingly robust body of work on the Niger Delta.

This chapter addresses three key issues. It employs the concept of 'Oloibirinization' to interrogate the process of dispossession of the Niger Delta minorities. This chapter also explicates the Niger Delta collective identity and how it shaped the repertoire of protest against dispossession in the region. The concluding section reflects on the future trajectories of the Niger Delta struggle.

Brief history of Delta development, Oloibirinization, and dispossession in the Niger Delta

Crude oil was discovered by Shell D'Arcy (now Shell Petroleum Development Company of Nigeria [hereafter, Shell]) on 3 August 1956 in Oloibiri in the present-day Bayelsa state in Nigeria's Niger Delta. The first tranche of oil from the region reached the global market in 1958. The region was soon found to have more commercially viable oil locations. The discovery of oil, its exportation, the Nigerian petro-state's political process, and attendant political economy have led to fundamental changes in the lives of the peoples of the Niger Delta. The focus of the newly independent Nigerian state quickly shifted from agriculture to ensuring a ceaseless flow of oil. The Niger Delta was transformed from a poor agrarian economy to the playground of transnational oil corporations, such as Chevron, Texaco, Agip, and Mobil, among others.

The consequences have been dire for the Niger Delta (Okaba 2008). Peasant farmers, families, and several local communities have been dispossessed of their lands, homes, and livelihood to facilitate oil drilling, pipelines, and associated prerequisites of the oil industry. Niger Delta communities have also had to live with spectacular levels of environmental hazards: oil pollution on farmlands, gas flaring, and serious climate change (Human Rights Watch 2002; UNEP 2011). Destruction of crops, pollution of rivers that served as the people's main source of water, destruction of marine life relied on for livelihood by fishermen and women, and health hazards are some of the immediate impacts of the oil industry in the Niger Delta.

Studies demonstrate that the dispossession of the peoples of the Niger Delta and environmental degradation from oil production have altered the complexion of the relationship between the peoples of the Niger Delta and the Nigerian state. The peoples of the Niger Delta strongly believe that the British colonial expansionist project christened Nigeria; dominant ethnic groups, transnational oil corporations, and local elites (traditional rulers and politicians) from the Niger Delta have combined to dispossess them of their land and exploit the resources of the region without adequate compensation (Oriola 2013).

The concept of 'Oloibirinization' was coined by Ehwarieme (2008: 158, 161) to signpost the 'decline in economic importance of a town, community or region [which] leads to its political oblivion, social obscurity and developmental neglect and decay . . . because its economic glory has departed'. The concept is eponymous of Oloibiri, the town that has the dubious distinction of being the first location where oil was discovered in Nigeria. Oloibiri is both significant and signifying (Oriola 2013). Its predicament is an algorithm for what may befall resource-rich communities when commoditized resources such as oil dry up. How does a community become 'Oloibirinized'? Although Ehwarieme (2008) does not offer precise details, I build on this concept by articulating the process of becoming Oloibirinized. The effort here is conceptual rather than empirical.

Oloibirinization is a complex sympodial process. There are seven facets in its processual formulation. These are contested legality, state-sanctioned violence, labour market rupture, environmental degradation, co-optation of local elites, adaptation to subjugation, and militant protest. The silhouettes of these facets shape and are shaped by the political process, which serves as the stem of the facets. Therefore, the link between the facets and the stem is synergistic and mutually reinforcing.

The Oloibirinization model   *Contested legality* involves the generation of laws for purposes of dispossessing resource-rich communities of their land and appropriating any legal claims therefrom. These laws/decrees are legal fictions that strip the people of land and other valuable resources and repose ownership in the state. The Oil Pipelines Act 1956 and the Petroleum Act 1969 invented the idea of 'eminent domain' (Frynas 2000: 75). This meant that the government could confiscate private land for public use. The process of overriding private or communal ownership of land was refined in the Land Use Act Decree 6 of 1978 and the Land Use Act CAP 202 L.F.N. 1990 ACT CAP L5 L.F.N. 2004. These laws have been used to dispossess communities of control over their lands.

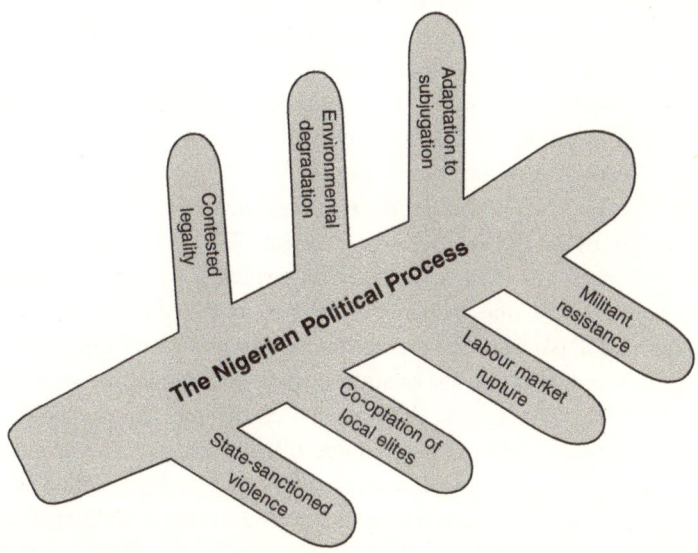

15.1 The Oloibirinization model

A closely related facet is *state-sanctioned violence*. This entails the use of the machinery of coercion to evict rural men, women, and children from their resource-rich land. This includes both human (police and military personnel) and material resources, such as bulldozers, to accomplish the task of dispossessing the poor and occupying land by the preferred new 'owners'. This dimension also involves stationing heavily armed state and non-state forces to secure the newly occupied area. This stage may also involve the use of private military companies to supply armed guards. Such deployment of troops may take days or sometimes years. They are sometimes conducted at the behest of oil corporations. Documents leaked by Wikileaks, for instance, indicate that Shell provided 'logistical support' to state forces in the Niger Delta (Rowell 2009). Part of the routine consequences of such deployment is abuse of local men and women by troops. For instance, state forces (rather than insurgents; see Oriola 2012) are often reported to have carried out sexual abuse of women in the Niger Delta (Omotola 2009).

Labour market rupture is another facet of the Oloibirinization process. This facet involves two processes: the importation of a large number of highly skilled work force from major cities and/or foreign countries, on the one hand, and hiring low-skill staff such as drivers, cooks, cleaners, and minor contractors from the local communities, on the other. This creates a threefold regime of inequality: Profits are appropriated by the oil companies and the state, huge salaries and emoluments are paid to the imported skilled staff, and low-skill staff receive what in the local economy is huge pay, but in the overall resource economy amounts to a pittance.

Consequently, a new form of stratification is set in motion in the local economy. At the top of the hierarchy are Western oil workers who benefit from the normative articulation of race (Li 2003) in Nigeria. Although Nigeria does not have the structural equivalents of the blatant 'racial' issues in Euro-American societies, the remnants of the socioeconomic relations fabricated by slavery and colonialism imply that the world is literally at the feet of such persons in a postcolonial social, physical, and ideational space (Oriola 2013). This group is immediately followed by their equally skilled and privileged local counterparts who also earn huge salaries. A third category comprising minor contractors, cooks, and other miscellaneous low-level staff are next to the skilled local staff. Poor community members occupy the lowest rung of the ladder. This tends to breed widespread discontent in the communities.

The facet *environmental degradation* accompanies mining activities even under the most ethical regimen. The Niger Delta environment has had significant environmental problems since oil drilling began. In particular, the pollution of water sources and farms have affected the livelihood of the people, as earlier stated. Analysis of company documents indicate that the Niger Delta experienced 553 oil spills from the activities of two companies, Shell and ENI, in 2014 (Amnesty International 2015). Shell was responsible for 204 oil spills and ENI 249 (Amnesty International 2015). The numbers are staggering given that between 1971 and 2011, there were only 10 spills per year in the whole of Europe (Amnesty International 2015). Phenomena such as acid rain and dangerous gases negatively impact the health of the local populace (Okaba 2008). A study conducted by the United Nations Environment Programme (UNEP) at the behest of the Nigerian government found that 'heavy contamination [was] present 40 years after an oil spill occurred, despite repeated clean-up attempts' in Ogoniland (UNEP 2011: 9).

Co-optation of local elites is also organically linked to the Oloibirinization enterprise. Local chiefs, traditional rulers, politicians, youth leaders, women leaders, and select human rights activists are targeted for incorporation to accomplish the Oloibirinization process. One of the most striking instances is the case of four Ogoni chiefs within the Movement for the Survival of Ogoni People (MOSOP), who were perceived as sympathisers of the regime of General Sani Abacha. The chiefs were killed by a youth mob on 21 May 1994. Ken Saro-Wiwa was arrested for allegedly instigating the murders. Saro-Wiwa and eight other Ogoni activists were extrajudicially hanged by the General Sani Abacha regime. The action by the Abacha government was congruent with the process of Oloibirinization. It is aimed at consciously suppurating communal tensions and generate schisms among local communities through inter- and intra-elite animus. The final product of this facet is a fractured community with either silenced or co-opted elites. For instance, MOSOP and the movement it represented have been in steady decline since the episode summarized above.

In addition, *adaptation to subjugation* occurs as a major part of the Oloibirinization process. It involves what Pierre Bourdieu calls the somatization of the relations of domination (McNay 1999). The local population imbibes the cardinal tenets of its subjugation. This dimension entails the exacerbation of social vices: drug addiction, alcoholism, prostitution among young adults and prepubescent girls, increased high school drop-out rates, gang-related violence, and increased materialism. These are mainly coping strategies for the lived experiences of alienation and lack of opportunities. Nonetheless, the enemy is now within. This dimension has a concomitant effect: the stereotyping of members of such communities as 'violent', 'lazy', 'drunks', 'incompetent', etc.

The Oloibirinization framework is also undergirded by *militant resistance*. This entails the gradual evaporation of non-violent advocacy as activists reassess their strategies and marginalized youth resort to deploying violent architectures of protest. This dimension is often preceded by one or more watershed moments. The watershed moment in the Niger Delta crisis was the hanging of the Ogoni Nine (Bob 2005; Omotola 2009). Peace activism slowly went into disuse or became degenerate as new actors introduced a different set of techniques. Such tactics include kidnapping oil workers, illegal oil bunkering (theft), and pipeline vandalism, among others. These tactics represent a fundamental shift in the resistance practices against Oloibirinization of the Niger Delta region. These were not entirely new tactics. For instance, kidnapping was a well-known repertoire of contention before the formation of MEND in 2005.

Several groups have been formed since the turn to violent struggle in the Delta. They include the Egbesu Boys of Africa (EBA), Feibagha Ogbo, Feibokirifagha Ogbo, Meinbutu Boys, Alagbabagha Ogbo, and Torudigha Ogbo. Others are Federated Niger Delta Ijaw Communities (FNDIC), the Niger Delta Militant Force Squad (NDMFS), the Niger Delta Strike Force (NDSF), and the Grand Alliance. Others are the Niger Delta Coastal Guerillas (NDCG), South-South Liberation Movement (SSLM), the November 1895 Movement, ELIMOTU, the Arogbo Freedom Fighters, Iduwini Volunteer Force (IVF), the Niger Delta People's Salvation Front (NDPSF), the Greenlanders, Deebam, Bush Boys, KKK, Black Braziers, and Icelanders. Organizations such as the Coalition for Militant Action (COMA), Niger Delta People's Volunteer Force (NDPVF), Joint Revolutionary Council, and the the Movement for the Emancipation of the Niger Delta (MEND) have been at the epicentre of violent resistance in the Delta region (Courson 2007: 25). MEND, in particular, remains the clearinghouse of the oil-related insurgency (Okonta 2006).

The next section explores the link between violent repertoires of protest and collective identity in the Niger Delta region. The aim is to explore elements of the Niger Delta identity that have had an overarching influence on the tactics of protest or resistance.

Multilocal resistance, pan-Niger Delta identity, and unity

Identity construction is an important component of understanding the transformation of grievance to collective action (Taylor and Whittier 1992). New identities are manufactured and older ones reconstructed through this process (Jasper 1997). While a social movement can benefit from pre-existing collective identities, such as gender and ethnicity, recruitment of participants, for instance, requires strategic framing (Polletta and Jasper 2001). Such identities also have to be managed and incorporated with other frames such as the injustice frame to be effective (Polletta and Jasper 2001: 284). Thus, collective identity and framing strategies are not mutually exclusive (Gamson 1995).

Collective identity refers to 'imagined as well as concrete communities, involves an act of perception and construction as well as the discovery of pre-existing bonds, interests, and boundaries' (Polletta and Jasper 2001: 298). The notion of *process* is important in understanding collective identity as it involves ongoing re/de/construction and negotiation. Collective identity entails 'cognitive definitions concerning the ends, means and field of action' (Melucci 1995: 44). This takes place within the boundedness of language accompanied by certain rituals and practices of the group. Collective identity comprises a 'network of active relationships' among actors, who are engaged in negotiation and the onerous processes of decision-making (Melucci 1995: 45). This network encompasses organizational types, leadership, communication, and technologies of communication (Melucci 1995). In addition, collective identity is constitutive and constituted by 'a certain degree of emotional investment, which enables individuals to feel like part of a common unity' (Melucci 1995: 45). This demonstrates that collective identity is necessarily *meaning* work and 'cannot be reduced to cost–benefit calculation' because emotions are also mobilized in the process (Melucci 1995: 45).

The Niger Delta is an aggregate of at least 40 ethnic groups. They include the Itsekiri, Urhobo, Efiks, Ibibios, and Ijaws, among others. These groups speak over 250 languages and dialects in 13,329 settlements (Watts 2008) spread over 12 per cent of Nigeria's land mass, or 112,110 sq km. There are five main linguistic categories in the Delta: Ijoid, Yoruboid, Edoid, Igboid, and Delta Cross (Watts 2004). The Ijaws (Izons) are the most populous ethnic group in the region and have been at the vanguard of the insurgency that erupted in the late 1990s (Okonta 2006). Nationally, the Ijaws rank fourth numerically after the Hausa-Fulani, Yoruba, and Igbo. There are 16 clans in the Ijaw ethnic group. These are Apoi, Tarakiri, Kabouowei, Mein, Gbaran, Okogba, Kolokuma, Ogboin, and Debe. Others are Atisa, Buseni, Kalabari, Okirika, Opubu, Opokuma, and Ogbia (Boro 1982: 60). These groups differ from the Ogoni, under Ken Saro-Wiwa's MOSOP, who gained global attention for protests against Shell and the Nigerian state. The Ogonis are in fact a collection of several peoples across six kingdoms: Babbe, Eleme, Gokana, Ken-Khana, Nyo-Khana, and Tai.

The main question this section seeks to explore centres on how a common 'Niger Delta' collective identity has been formed from such complex ethno-linguistic crossroads. The Niger Delta identity has undergone several changes in nomenclature. The region is called the *Niger Delta* because it is the delta of the River Niger. The region was named Oil Rivers in the days of palm oil trade. The British colonialists called the region the Oil Rivers Protectorate from 1885 to 1893. The Oil Rivers Protectorate was rechristened Niger Coast Protectorate in 1893. Today's Niger Delta peoples were part of the Igbos in the eastern region and the Yorubas in the western region at independence in 1960. The Niger Delta currently has 185 of 774 local governments in Nigeria and nine of the 36 states of the federation. These are Abia, Bayelsa, Delta, Akwa-Ibom, Rivers, Cross River State, Edo, Imo, and Ondo states. Three of these states are recognized as *core* Niger Delta states. They are Bayelsa, Rivers, and Delta states.

In reality, therefore, the idea of the *Niger Delta* is reductionist. It does not refer to one monolithic, linguistically homogeneous group. Nonetheless, several sociopolitical and historical factors have combined to manufacture a *Niger Delta collective identity*, which insurgents have used for mobilization. There are at least several factors that have contributed to the invention of the Niger Delta collective identity.

First, the shared history of marginalization has strengthened the formation of a collective Niger Delta identity. While the question of mapping out ethnic groups is still largely contentious, some of the signifiers include coterminous territory, shared ancestry (Osaghae 1986), and language. Each of the 40 ethnic groups in the Niger Delta is an identifiable group surrounded by other minority groups – a minority among minorities. At the heart of the majority–minority divide in Nigeria is the regionalization that started in the 1940s and finally became law in the 1954 federal constitution (Osaghae 1986).

Historically, each of these groups has often had its sociopolitical and economic interests overshadowed by ethnic politics in Nigeria, which favours larger ethnic groups (Nnoli 1978; Osaghae 2003). The use of controversial population figures in apportioning government largesse: ministerial portfolios, military and paramilitary recruitment, monthly distribution of revenue to states by the federal government and sundry offices, and promotion heavily favours the three major ethnic groups to the detriment of the minorities. The attendant feelings of collective suffering, marginalization, and exploitation constitute a major factor in manufacturing a Niger Delta collective identity.

Delta minorities' fear of domination by majority ethnic groups has also reinforced the Niger Delta collective identity. Minorities in the Niger Delta had genuine fear of domination by majority ethnic groups as far back as colonial times. In July 1956, for instance, the Rivers Chiefs and People's Conference (RCPC) was established to fight against the marginalization of the present-day Delta region (Omotola 2009). The RCPC was part of the 1957 London Constitutional Conference on the invitation of the Colonial Office (Omotola 2009). The result was the Willinks Commission, established to ascertain the veracity of the fear of minorities (Colonial Office 1958). The Willinks Report stated that the fears of the minorities were real, and called for designating the region as a 'special area' and establishment of a special commission to carry out developmental projects (Colonial Office 1958; Technical Committee on the Niger Delta 2008).

Also, the peculiar challenges posed by the difficult geographic terrain and environment of the Niger Delta have fostered a distinct collective identity. The physical space embodied in the Niger Delta region is naturally harsh. General Bello, former Commander of the Joint Task Force (JTF) established to quash the oil-related insurgency agreed that 'life here (the Niger Delta) is harsher than any part of Nigeria'.[1] The life course navigation of a marshy, mangrove terrain where toughness is a prerequisite for survival has contributed to forging a collective Niger Delta identity. In this context, to be Niger Deltan means to have swam and fished in often polluted waters, and navigated one's way through complex creeks. These experiences engender enormous camaraderie.

This is closely intertwined with the rich history of resistance in the Niger Delta, which also enhances the region's collective identity. The peoples and kingdoms of the Niger Delta fought historically against oppressive authorities and/or overlords. For instance, King Frederick William Koko, who ruled the Nembe or Brass people from 1889 to 1898, was staunchly opposed to the 'new order that was creeping in with Christianity, trade and the British consul' (Alagoa 1964: 90). King Koko led the Nembe people to war – the Akassa war – against the Royal Niger Company on 29 January 1895 by 'popular choice of the Nembe people' and cooperation of all the chiefs (Alagoa 1964: 95, 102). The people had decided that 'to die by the sword was far better than to die of hunger' as the Royal Niger Company (RNC) had obtained royal assent from Britain to monopolize trade in King Koko's domain as the sole buyer of agricultural produce (Alagoa 1964: 102).

The RNC shot at canoes suspected of smuggling goods on which it had monopoly, and thereby engaged in extrajudicial killings and public humiliation of the people to protect its interests. The Akassa war was caused by grievances that had been brought to the attention of the government and the RNC. King Koko and his men caused serious damage to the Royal Niger Company's machinery, killed 24 persons, and captured 70 as prisoners of war (Alagoa 1964).

The colonial administration carried out a reprisal attack against the Nembe people to bring them under control. The Nembe people assured the administration that the markets had to be opened up before there could be peace (Alagoa 1964). A commission of enquiry led by John Kirk was set up by the British government. Kirk found that the Royal Niger Company was monopolistic and prevented the Nembe people from their traditional markets, and blamed the British government for granting such concessions to the company. The

Akassa war was 'one of the most important' factors in the abrogation of the charter of the Royal Niger Company (Alagoa 1964: 115).

Suffice to state that the British colonialists encountered a difficult task annexing many of the kingdoms of the Niger Delta. King Dappa Pepple was banished in 1854 and King Jaja of Opobo was dealt a sleight of hands by the British in 1887. He was invited for negotiations over his opposition to British trade monopoly and was promptly arrested and sent to exile (Okaba 2005). The Nana of Itsekiri experienced a similar fate. A British invasion was required to sack Oba Ovvonrannwen Nogbaisi of Benin. The monarch was banished to Calabar. The resistance posed by various kingdoms in the Niger Delta was so strong and costly that the British enacted a poll tax to provide money for combating the insurgencies. Consequently, the Niger Delta collective identity is an *oppositional identity*. This helps in stimulating mobilization of the Niger Delta people against any entity defined as oppressor or opposition.

The Niger Delta collective identity has also been fostered and aggravated as a fundamentally oppositional identity by the ethnic 'chauvinism' (Osaghae 1986: 157) of some leaders of the majority groups. President Shehu Shagari, a Fulani from northern Nigeria, epitomized in 1982 the condescension with which some political elites from major groups viewed minorities:

> it has become a tradition for minorities to complain because they
> were so accustomed to complaining. This behaviour was due
> largely to their past experience, of what they have suffered before.
> They have been victimised by the majority groups for so long. But
> since then, a lot has been done to rectify this apparent injustice.
> But because they are so used to complaining, they cannot help
> complaining again and again, even if things were better.[2]

On Monday 10 March 2003, 21 years after Shagari's statement, President Olusegun Obasanjo, a Yoruba from the South West told Niger Deltans: 'You cannot produce anything because you are lazy. It is your laziness that is making you to make all these demands'.[3] This statement finds visible space on the Internet and other social media platforms as a painful reminder of the arrogance of the state and the disrespect with which leaders of the majority ethnic groups, who run the levers of power, treat Niger Deltans.

Insurgents are not oblivious of the attitude of the state and some elite of the ruling ethnic groups. For example, Asari Dokubo, leader of the Niger Delta People Volunteer Force (NDPVF), demonstrates keen awareness of this attitude and shows how it strengthens insurgent resolve and mobilization:

Interviewer: Now, there is also an aspect of this struggle that I will like you to share, the execution of Ken Saro Wiwa. What role do you think that particular interlude has played in all that is going on here?

Response: I think it is the arrogance of the rulers of the Nigerian State as represented by those who were the direct beneficiaries of the British, the stolen sovereignty of the people. And those who received, this were bequeathed on err [pauses] . . . the particular set of people the Hausa–Fulani, the Fulani ruling Oligarchy in the North. Their belief is that the people must be taught a lesson. They believe that if they killed Ken Saro Wiwa, other people would not rise up against them. Killing Ken Saro Wiwa was to put fear into the minds of the people and to teach them a lesson that anybody who follows this part will be like Saro Wiwa.[4]

MEND's Jomo Gbomo also argues that the Northern ruling elite 'assume(s) leadership of Nigeria to be the birth right' of northern Nigeria.[5] The 'arrogance' of the Nigerian state controlled by majority groups is a rallying point for insurgents. In addition, the hanging of the Ogoni Nine and several military actions in Niger Delta communities such as Odi, Odiama, Agge, Gbaramatu kingdom, etc. have fostered the oppositional nature of the Niger Delta collective identity and exacerbated dissident mobilization rather than dissuading potential insurgents.

The Niger Delta identity is a major beneficiary of the growing consciousness (Taylor and Whittier 1992: 111) of Niger Deltans about other parts of Nigeria and the rest of the world. This awareness is a function of several factors. These include the spread of the Internet, improved tele-density, and 24-hour local, national, and (digital satellite) television. The Nollywood movie industry rather picturesquely displays the 'good life' being enjoyed in cities such as Lagos and Abuja (Ugor 2009). The MOSOP experiment in the

1990s has turned out to be a tip of the iceberg. The current level of awareness of Niger Deltans about their position in the Nigerian sociopolitical and economic configuration is an improvement over previous generations.[6] The level of consciousness of Niger Deltans about their social situatedness and positionality in Nigeria has increased.

Finally, the Niger Delta collective identity has immensely benefited from the unprecedented level of ethnic rancour and polarization in Nigeria. This has led to the *supertribalization* of young people (Osaghae 2003: 55). For instance, Adaka Boro, who led the first Niger Delta insurgency against the Nigerian state, lost the student union presidential elections at the University of Nigeria, Nsukka, because his main opponent campaigned in the largely Igbo student body that a 'stranger' must not be elected. This was the 1960s when the Niger Delta was part of the eastern region. Boro's comment on the ethnic strategy of the eventual winner is instructive: 'Ogbuka won with his tribal majority. One indelible mark, however, had been made on me. If two Ijaws would be regarded in their region as strangers, it was conclusive that *we were the detached members of an ethnocentric society*' (Boro 1982: 47, emphasis added).

The 'ethnocentric society' Boro experienced is alive and well. Various militias and extra-state armed groups have grown in all regions of Nigeria purporting to fight for the ethnic collectivities to which they belong. The Odu'a People's Congress (OPC) provides security and acts as guardian of Yoruba interests. The organization Bakassi Boys performs a similar role among the Igbos in the southeast, while in the Hausa-Fulani-dominated north, the Arewa People's Congress (APC) is the unofficial sheriff of ethnic interests. At the heart of these agitations is the so-called 'National Question' (Osaghae 2003: 55). This implies a cocktail of demands and agitations, ranging from revenue-sharing formula to resource control and state creation.

Although MEND is an Ijaw-led insurgency (Okonta 2006), it purports to fight against the marginalization of whole of the Niger Delta rather than strictly Ijaws. MEND has carefully manoeuvred the differences among the 16 Ijaw clans to produce a united front against the opposition. This process is a delicate balancing act of negotiation involving the use of inclusive language and actions that suggest a 'WE' feeling among people who are generally distrustful of one another. The significance of this achievement becomes accentuated when one considers that the avatar of the Niger Delta struggle, Ken Saro-Wiwa, could not prevent internal divisions among the relatively numerically small Ogoni peoples (Bob 2005).

The invention of a *Niger Delta* collective identity predates present-day insurgents. Several historical, political, economic, ideational, and cultural factors have combined to hand insurgents a potent accoutrement of mobilization. The Niger Delta collective identity symbolizes, for all intents and purposes, generations of struggle against oppression, a quest for justice that has consumed – literally and figuratively – thousands of people and embodies the elemental contours of the Nigerian society. This identity is formed in contra-distinction to the majority ethnic groups. Therefore, the Niger Delta identity is tenaciously oppositional, and signposts a communal response to environmental injustice and economic subjugation.

Future prognostications on the fate of resistance in the Niger Delta

The dynamics and intricacies of the Delta struggle for environmental and social justice have been altered by certain events. In particular, the six-year presidency of Goodluck Jonathan, an ethnic Ijaw from the Niger Delta region, has bequeathed a confounding paradox: it inadvertently brought Niger Delta agitations and actors into mainstream politics, while also failing to bring about concrete development in the Delta region. This is in spite of targeted projects such as colleges and universities that were established by the Jonathan administration. The inadequate attention to the Delta region by Jonathan is arguably embodied in the non-completion of the east–west road, which runs through the heart of the region. This has had the unintended consequence of eroding some of the claims of the Niger Delta people. Questions such as 'What did President Jonathan do for the Niger Delta?' are being asked by Nigerians across the political spectrum.

The federal government's amnesty programme has succeeded in de-escalating tensions in the region by providing vocational training for over 20,000 ex-agitators. This was the first formal education for some of the participants. The programme has, however, been plagued by corruption, over-bloated contracts, and unpaid participant stipends, among other issues. Some participants claimed that individuals who never participated in the insurgency are part of those receiving benefits.

There are other structurally salient issues at stake. The inability of President Jonathan to secure a second term at the polls has contributed to an eerily familiar dynamic: secessionist discourse. A meeting of Niger Delta stakeholders took place at Hotel Presidential, Port Harcourt on 27 April 2015. Ann-Kio Briggs, widely regarded as the 'Mother' of the Niger Delta struggle, addressed the 'Lower Niger Congress' in a video posted by *Sahara Reporters*. Ms Briggs stated that the 'time is ripe for the Niger Delta to secede from Nigeria'. Ann-Kio Briggs requires little introduction. She was appointed Liaison Officer for the Aaron Team set up by MEND to negotiate with the federal government in 2009 during the administration of President Umaru Yar'Adua. Briggs is well respected in the Delta region.[7] Briggs' newfound voice after six years of relative reticence represents a new trajectory in the Delta movement.

This trajectory is marked by a trifecta of issues: President Jonathan's electoral loss has widened the pervasive sense of injustice felt by a huge section of the Delta region. The Ijaw Youth Council (IYC) exemplified this line of reasoning when they released a statement that the 'north conspired with a section of the south west to take over the Presidency from President Jonathan and the minorities of the south-south in an election fraught with irregularities' (Eziukwu 2015a). The statement alleged that 'Northerners created Boko Haram and blamed it on President Jonathan deliberately to incite the northern populace against President Jonathan and make him unpopular in the 2015 election' (Eziukwu 2015a). This suggests that Jonathan's administration was made to fail.[8]

The new trajectory is also shaped by the factionalization of MOSOP, which has contributed to the erosion of the intellectual dimension of the Delta struggle. This removes a key non-violent aspect of the struggle and portends danger. In addition, the empowerment of key insurgent leaders (discussed below) by the Jonathan administration is another factor.

There is a distinct possibility of a return to the period before the amnesty programme was introduced in 2009. There are three categories of actors capable of reinventing the Delta insurgency. The first comprises behemoths or 'Generals' of the last outbreak of war against the Nigerian state and oil corporations. They include Mr Government Ekpemupolo, or 'Tompolo', Alhaji Asari Dokubo, and Ebikabowei Victor Ben (General Boyloaf), among others.

Boyloaf and others were able to change the complexion of violence in the region from internecine conflicts, such as the Warri ownership tripartite debacle among Urhobo, Itsekiri, and Ijaw, into a concise affront against the Nigerian state and its oil interests (Oriola 2013). Nevertheless, such individuals, for reasons explained below, are now a liability on the moral universe of the Delta movement for social and environmental justice.

For instance, Tompolo, who was largely a mysterious apparition during the last insurgency, has learned the politics of the oil industry. He leveraged his closeness to the Jonathan administration to become a security contractor. There were widespread reports in December 2014 that he had purchased six decommissioned Norwegian warships for his maritime security firm (Falayi 2014). This suggests that the weaponry of the insurgent 'Generals' has become more sophisticated. Another example is Alhaji Dokubo, who was the first to explicitly call for the use of violence against the Nigerian state following the hanging of the Ogoni Nine. Dokubo mobilized the NDPVF into an insurgency machine. He is now a security contractor in Nigeria and college proprietor in the Republic of Benin. Top echelons of the Nigerian military are confident that the appurtenances of the good life that these insurgent leaders have tasted may prevent them from returning to the creeks, where conditions are inhuman.

Rank-and-file participants in the last insurgency constitute another category with capacity for another round of violent resistance. They have sedimented knowledge – geographic, operational, and mechanical – from the last exercise. These are battle-hardened individuals. They include over 20,000 individuals who accepted the 2009 amnesty deal. This category also includes those who never accepted amnesty. There are no exact estimates of the number of such individuals.

The last category includes young men and women who have reached maturity since the last insurgency. They were children in the late 1990s to 2009 – a period marked by admixture of non-violent protest and insurgent violence – but have now grown to be aged 18–23. The limited educational and employment opportunities in the Niger Delta may make such youth unable to be unwilling to participate in any violent resistance against the Nigerian state and oil corporations. It is didactic to recall that Tompolo's camp reportedly employed over 3,000 people at the height of the last insurgency

(Oriola 2013). The likes of Tompolo continue to enjoy tremendous public support and may find willing recruits in young adults in the Delta. For instance, oil pipelines were destroyed when a court granted the Economic and Financial Crimes Commission (EFCC) an arrest warrant for Tompolo (*Sahara Reporters* 2016). The federal government in fact urged the people of Delta state to hand over Tompolo to the EFCC (Amaize 2016).

Finally, two of the three broad aspects of the Delta struggle are barely managing to survive. The intellectual dimension of the Delta movement led by MOSOP has become splintered by internal strife. This schism, if left unchecked, may signal the premature end of this vital aspect of the struggle. The organized civil society dimension, which includes women's groups, human rights organizations, environmental justice groups, etc. within and outside the Niger Delta, is also largely demoralized. This is due in part to the failure of the Jonathan administration to transform huge oil wealth and public support into meaningful development in the Niger Delta. Questions about what is next for the Delta are now being asked (Ifowodo 2015). Those questions are in and of themselves quite revealing. Jonathan's six-year presidency, as stated earlier, has taken the bite out of the key moral grounds of the Delta movement, although legitimate grievances remain.

The violent agitation represented by MEND and NDPVF, among others, may experience a change of guards but remains the most vibrant. It is likely to once again find its voice and/or weapons. However, it has lost a significant proportion of its legitimacy in the eyes of the Nigerian public. The co-optation of insurgent leaders into cabinet positions, security contracts, local and national electioneering machinery, arms procurement, etc. has contributed to shifting public perceptions. Public demonstrations by rank-and-file ex-insurgents protesting being left out of financial deals by their leaders have also been particularly damaging. Threats by the likes of Asari Dokubo to go to war should Nigerians fail to re-elect President Jonathan (Eziukwu 2015b) have also undermined their credibility.

Consequently, while violent resisters may find support in the Delta, they will arguably have limited sympathy in other parts of Nigeria. There is a lower probability that they would be perceived as rebels with a cause. What is clear is that every aspect of the struggle for environmental justice and resource control is not quite the same anymore. Nonetheless, violent resistance remains a distinct possibility. The signals sent by new administration of Muhammadu Buhari will be critical in shaping the next trajectory of the Niger Delta movement.

Notes

1 Interviewee 12.

2 Cited in Osaghae (1986: 157).

3 See www.unitedijawstates.com/maps.html [accessed 12 May 2010].

4 Interviewee 11.

5 Jomo Gbomo statement (number 13).

6 Interviewees 17, 18, 25 37, and 38.

7 I interviewed Briggs in 2012 during

my research on women's engagement in the Niger Delta insurgency.

8 The statement revealed divisions within the IYC. A faction led by its president, Udengs Eradiri, had accepted Jonathan's defeat, while another faction led by the group's spokesperson, Eric Omare, rejected the election results (Oduma 2015).

References

Akpan, N.S. (2010). 'Kidnapping in Nigeria's Niger Delta: an exploratory study'. *Journal of Social Sciences*, 24(1): 33–42.

Alagoa, E.J. (1964). *The Small Brave City-State: A History of Nembe Brass in the Niger Delta*. Ibadan: Ibadan University Press.

Amaize, E. (2016). 'Why we can't hand over Tompolo to JTF, EFCC – Ijaw elders, youths'. *Vanguard*. Available at: www.vanguardngr.com/2016/01/why-we-cant-hand-over-tompolo-to-jtf-efcc-ijaw-elders-youths/ [accessed 29 January 2016].

Amnesty International (2015). *Nigeria: Hundreds of Oil Spills Continue to Blight Niger Delta*. Available at: www.amnesty.org/en/latest/news/2015/03/hundreds-of-oil-spills-continue-to-blight-niger-delta/ [accessed 15 December 2015].

Bob, C. (2005). *The Marketing of Rebelion: Insurgents, Media and International Activism*. Cambridge: Cambridge University Press.

Boro, I.A. (1982). *The Twelve-Day Revolution*. Benin: Idodo Umeh.

Colonial Office (1958). *The Report of the Commission Appointed to Enquire into the Fears of Minorities and the Means for Allaying Them*. London: Her Majesty's Stationery Office.

Courson, E. (2007). *The Burden of Oil: Social Deprivation and Political Militancy in Gbaramatu Clan, Warri South West LGA Delta State, Nigeria*. Niger Delta: Economies of Violence Working Papers, No. 15. Berkeley, CA: Institute of International Studies, University of California.

Courson, E. (2011). 'MEND: political marginalization, repression, and petro-insurgency in the Niger Delta'. *African Security*, 4(1): 20–43.

Ehwarieme, W. (2008). 'Oloibirinization: developmental future of a post-oil Niger Delta'. *Proceedings of the International Conference on the Nigerian State, Oil Industry and the Niger Delta*, 11–13 March, Yenagoa Bayelsa state. Port Harcourt: Harey, pp. 157–163.

Ekine, S. (2008). 'Women's responses to state violence in the Niger Delta'. *Feminist Africa*, 10: 67–83.

Eziukwu, A. (2015a). 'Ijaw Youth Council makes U-turn, vows response to Jonathan's election loss'. *Premium Times*. Available at: www. premiumtimesng.com/news/top-news/180526-ijaw-youth-council-makes-u-turn-vows-response-to-jonathans-election-loss.html [accessed 27 May 2015].

Eziukwu, A. (2015b). 'Niger Delta militants meet in Yenagoa, threaten war should Jonathan lose presidential election'. *Premium Times*. Available at: www. premiumtimesng.com/news/headlines/175532-niger-delta-militants-meet-yenagoa-threaten-war-jonathan-lose-presidential-election.html [accessed 27 May 2015].

Falayi, K. (2014). 'Ex-militant, Tompolo, buys six warships'. *The Punch*. Available at: www.punchng.com/news/ex-militant-tompolo-buys-six-warships/ [accessed 27 May 2015].

Frynas, J. (2000). *Oil in Nigeria: Conflict and Litigation Between Oil Companies and Village Communities*. Hamburg: Lit Verlag.

Gamson, W. (1995). 'Constructing social protest'. In H. Johnston and B. Klandermans (eds), *Social Movements and Culture*. Minneapolis, MN: University of Minnesota Press, pp. 85–106.

Human Rights Watch (2002). 'The Niger Delta: no dividend of democracy'. *Human Rights Watch*, 14(7A): 1–39.

Ifowodo, O. (2015). 'So now what becomes of the Niger Delta?' *Sahara Reporter*. Available at: http://saharareporters.com/2015/05/06/so-now-what-becomes-niger-delta-ogaga-ifowodo [accessed 27 May 2015].

Jasper, J.M. (1997). *The Art of Moral Protest*. Chicago, IL: University of Chicago Press.

Li, P. (2003). 'Social inclusion of visible minorities and newcomers: the articulation of "race" and "racial" difference in Canadian society'. Paper presented at the Conference on Social Inclusion, Canadian Council on Social Development, 27–28 March, Ottawa. Available at: www.ccsd.ca/events/inclusion/papers/peter_li.pdf [accessed 2 December 2010].

McNay, L. (1999). 'Gender, habitus and the field: Pierre Bourdieu and the limits of reflexivity'. *Theory, Culture and Society*, 16(1): 95–117.

Melucci, A. (1995). 'The process of collective identity'. In H. Johnston and B. Klandermans (eds), *Social Movements and Culture*. Minneapolis, MN: University of Minnesota Press, pp. 41–63.

Nnoli, O. (1978). *Ethnic Politics in Nigeria*. Enugu: Fourth Dimension.

Obi, C. (2008). 'Enter the dragon? Chinese oil companies and resistance in the Niger Delta'. *Review of African Political Economy*, 35(3): 417–434.

Oduma, I. (2015). 'Buhari divides Ijaw Youth Council'. *Daily Independent*. Available at: http://dailyindependentnig.com/2015/04/buhari-divides-ijaw-youth-council/ [accessed 27 May 2015].

Okaba, B. (2005). *Petroleum Industry and the Paradox of Rural Poverty in the Niger Delta*. Benin: Ethiope.

Okaba, B. (2008). 'Petrodollar, the Nigerian state and the crises of development in the Niger Delta region: Trends, challenges and the way forward'. *Proceedings of the International Conference on the Nigerian State, Oil Industry and the Niger Delta*, 11–13 March, Yenagoa Bayelsa State. Port Harcourt: Harey, pp. 21–39.

Okonta, I. (2006). 'Behind the mask: explaining the emergence of the MEND militia in Nigeria's oil-bearing niger delta'. *Niger Delta: Economies of Violence Working Paper No. 11*. Berkeley, CA: Institute of International Studies, University of California.

Omotola, J.S. (2009). 'Dissent and state excesses in the Niger Delta, Nigeria'. *Studies in Conflict & Terrorism*, 32(2): 129–145.

Oriola, T.B. (2012). 'The Delta creeks, women's engagement, and Nigeria's oil insurgency'. *British Journal of Criminology*, 52(3), 534–555.

Oriola, T.B. (2013). *Criminal Resistance? The Politics of Kidnapping Oil Workers*. Farnham: Ashgate.

Osaghae, E. (1986). 'Federalism, local politics and ethnicity in Nigeria'. *Commonwealth & Comparative Politics*, 24(2): 151–168.

Osaghae, E. (2003). 'Explaining the changing patterns of ethnic politics in Nigeria'. *Nationalism and Ethnic Politics*, 9(3): 54–73.

Oyefusi, A. (2007). 'Oil and the propensity to armed struggle in the Niger Delta of Nigeria'. *World Bank Policy Research Working Paper No. 4194*. Available at: http://ssrn.com/abstract=979666 [accessed 2 January 2008].

Polletta, F. and Japer, J. (2001). 'Collective identity and social movements'. *Annual Review of Sociology*, 27: 283–305.

Rowell, A. (2009). 'Secret papers show how Shell targeted Nigeria oil protests'. *The Independent*. Available at: www.independent.co.uk/news/world/americas/secret-papers-show-how-shell-targeted-nigeria-oil-protests-1704812.html [accessed 29 January 2016].

Sahara Reporters (2016). *Tompolo Accused of Blowing Up Oil Pipelines in Delta*. Available at: http://saharareporters.com/2016/01/15/breaking-tompolo-accused-blowing-oil-pipelines-delta [accessed 21 January 2016].

Taylor, V. and Whittier, N. (1992). 'Collective identity in social movement communities: lesbian feminist mobilization'. In A. Morris and C.M. Mueller (eds), *Frontiers in Social Movement Theory*. New Haven, CT: Yale University Press, pp. 104–129.

Technical Committee on the Niger Delta (2008). *Report of the Technical Committee on the Niger Delta*. Port Harcourt: Prelyn Fortunes.

Ugor, P. (2009). 'Youth culture and the struggle for social space: the Nigerian video films'. Unpublished doctoral dissertation, University of Alberta, Edmonton, Canada.

United Nations Environment Programme (UNEP) (2011). *Environmental Assessment of Ogoniland*. Available at: www.unep.org/disastersandconflicts/CountryOperations/Nigeria/EnvironmentalAssessmentofOgonilandreport/tabid/54419/Default.aspx [accessed 2 January 2016].

Watts, M. (2004). 'The sinister political life of community: economies of violence and governable spaces in the Niger Delta, Nigeria.' *Niger Delta: Economies of Violence Working Papers, No. 3*. Institute of International Studies, University of California, Berkeley, USA.

Watts, M. (2008). 'Imperial oil: the anatomy of a Nigerian oil insurgency'. *Niger Delta: Economies of Violence Working Papers, No. 17*. Institute of International Studies, University of California, Berkeley, USA.

INDEX

Aaron Team, 329
Abacha, Sani, 319
Acacia Mining company, 19, 297, 301, 305, 307, 309, 312
accumulation by dispossession (ABD), 2, 3, 4, 23, 44, 63, 92, 146, 177, 269; definition of, 48; in South Africa's agrarian economy, 189–94; in South India, 123–8; mechanisms and experiences of, 45; multiple forms of, 190; of commoners, 225; resistance to (by fishing communities in Tamil Nadu, 135; in Ghana, 231; in South Africa, 187–208)
acid rain, 319
Acquisition and Requisition of Immovable Property Ordinance (1982) (Bangladesh), 170–1
Action for Large-Scale Land Acquisition Transparency (ALLAT), 256
Ada (Ghana), resistance to dispossession in, 231–50
Ada people, 17, 231; defence of Songor salt lagoon, 233; foundation story of, 232
Ada Salt Winners Cooperative, 239, 248
Ada Songor Advocacy Forum (ASAF), 17, 242–3, 245
addiction, in First Nations communities, 37
Adivasi people, 13; composition of, as development-displaced persons, 71; social networks of, 69
adivasi, dalit and non-tribal forest dwellers (ADNTFD), 67; restriction of forest rights of, 69
Africa, colonial tropes of, 296–7
'Africa Rising': conference, 296; narrative of, 297, 298, 300–3, 311
African Barrick Gold company, 297, 301, 307–8; court case against, 308

African Biotechnology Network, 227
African Development Bank (ADB), 302
African Food Sovereignty Alliance, 227
African National Congress (ANC), 189–90, 206
agency of dispossessed people, 9–10; collective, 61–2
Agrarian Law No. 5/1960 (Indonesia), 104
agrarian wars, escalation of, 119
Agrarische Wet (1870) (Indonesia), 99
Agri-BEE (Agricultural Black Economic Empowerment), 194
agribusiness, 4, 16, 51; in Kenya, 209–30
Agricultural Investment Support Directorate (AISD) (Ethiopia), 279
agricultural labour, exploitation of, 16
agriculture: chemical, rejection of, 220–1; rising costs of, 116 see also organic farming and subsistence-oriented farming systems
agro-extractive sector, 14; dispossession in, 98–121
agroforestry, 179, 180
agrofuels see biofuels, production of
aiga extended family, 52
Akassa war, 324
Akkaraipettai Motorized Boat and Kattumaram Fishworkers Union (India), 137
Aliansa Anti Diskriminasi Petani (Philippines), 115
Alternative Learning Center for Agricultural and Livelihood Development (ALCADEV) (Philippines), 15, 153–4; former director murdered, 154
Amattey, C. O. C., 235
American Indian Religious Freedom Act (1978) (USA), 35
Amissah Commission of Inquiry (Ghana), 238

amnesty programme, in Nigeria, 328, 330
Ancestral Lands at Risk of Mining (ALARM) campaign (Philippines), 156
AngloGold Ashanti company, 297, 303–4, 305, 306, 307 *see also* Geita Gold Mine
anti-colonialism, 21, 95
anti-mining activism, in Philippines, 145–63
Anuak Justice Council, 18, 256, 262
Anuak people: genocide of, 263; preventing extinction of, 262–6; resistance of, 256, 264
Anugrah Saritama Abadi (ASA) company, 104, 113; coconut trees destroyed, 108
Anywaa Survival organization, 18, 256, 262
apartheid, 199; abolition of, 190
apartheid capitalism, 190, 191, 199
Apenteng, Stephen, 237
Apenteng family, 237
Apetorgbor, Albert, 237
aquaculture, 132; as enclosure of commons, 124; promotion of, 123
Aquaculture Authority Bill (India), 132
Aquino Corazon, 147, 151–2
Aquino III, Benigno, 148, 153
Arewa People's Congress (APC), 327
armed struggle, 315
Asafotufiami Festival (Ghana), 231, 239, 244, 245, 247, 248
Asian Development Bank (ADB), 51, 58, 60, 61, 62, 100, 148; challenges to policies of, 43; *Improving Growth Prospects in the Pacific* report, 49
atsiakpo saltpans, 234, 240, 245; as mechanism of divide and rule, 248; campaign against, 241–2, 244, 246
attachment to place, 128
autonomy, of villages, 52
avoidance protest, 291
Awami League (Bangladesh), 168, 176
Away Estate (KOA), 103
Azad, Lingaraj, 75, 89

Bagong Alyansang Makabayan (BAYAN), 156–7; demands of, 158–9
Bagong Alyansang Makabayan–USA (BAYAN-USA) organization, 158, 160

Bakassi Boys, 327
bananas: patenting of, 216; production of *see also* tissue culture bananas
Bangladesh: joint industrial projects with India, 176; Perspective Plan, 180; Power System Master Plan, 165
Bangladesh Environmental Lawyers Association (BELA), 175
Bangladesh Nationalist Party (BNP), 168, 176
Bangladesh Poribesh Andolon (BAPA), 175
Bangladesh Power Development Board (BPDB), 166, 170
Bangladesh-India Friendship Power Company Pvt Ltd, 166
Banshkhali (Bangladesh), proposed coal-fired power plant in, 164
Barrick Gold company *see* African Barrick Gold company
Basic Agrarian Law (1960) (Indonesia), 107
Basic Conditions of Employment Act (South Africa), 199
Bassett, Mary, 37
bauxite mining, resistance to, 13, 67–97
Bay of Bengal Fishworkers Union, 138
Bello, General, 324
Ben, Ebikabowei Victor (General Boyloaf), 329–30
Benishangul-Gumuz (Ethiopia), large scale land acquisition in, 275–95
Bentinck, William, 69–70
Bigkis at Lakas ng Katutubo sa Timog Katagalugan (Balatik) (Philippines), 156
Bill and Melinda Gates Foundation, 212
Bimoli cooking oil, 104
bio-piracy, 223
biodiversity, 62, 218
biofuels, production of, 278, 279
biotechnology, adoption of, 217
B'laan people, 154–5
Black Radical Tradition, 4
Bohotokong Estate (KOB), 103
Bohotokong village (Indonesia), 99; dispossession in, 101–6
Boko Haram group, 329

Bolloré group, 260
Bonbibi and Dokhn Rai, stories of, 179
Borabhata village (India), 76
Boro, Adaka, 327
bounties, 28, 30
bows and arrows, use of, 283
brackishwater aquaculture, 123;
associated with pollution, 124
bribery, 259, 304
Briggs, Ann-Kio, 329
British colonialism, 213, 214, 233, 263,
299, 316, 322; in India, 69–70
British East India Company, 69
Bulendu, Dotto, 310

Cacadu Small-Scale Farmers' Association
(South Africa), 194
call centers, work in, 147
Campaign Against Shrimp Industries
movement, 132
camps, of resistance, establishment of,
109, 110, 114
Canadian International Development
Agency (CIDA), 301
Capion, Daguil, 157
capitalism, 1, 2, 22, 23, 37, 44, 48, 54, 63,
71, 92, 95, 99, 146, 176, 180, 189, 190,
201, 205, 206, 224, 236, 275; colonial,
4, 19, 22, 98; industrial, 15, 164; racial,
4 *see also* apartheid capitalism *and*
petro-capitalism
capitalist production, laws of, 99, 209–10
Cargill Indonesia company, 104
Carlisle Indian Industrial School, 32
cash crops, 214, 219; Africans barred from
growing, 213
caste, 8; among fishing communities in
India, 139
Catholic Church, 148, 154
Center for Human Rights (Bangladesh),
174
Central Luzon Aeta Association (CLAA)
(Philippines), 156
Chasi Mulia Adivasi Sangh (CMAS)
(India), 72
Chatterjee, Partha, 180
Cheney, Dick, 152
Chetty, Marie, 131

Chico River Dam (Philippines), 153
chiefs, 10; conflict with, 258–62; killing
of, 319; paramount, 257, 260
Chiefs of Ada, 231
child stunting, 227
Chinese traders, in coconut trade, 102–3
Chola empire, 123
Chowdhury, Abdullah Harun, 169–70, 174
Christianity, 2, 53, 324
Citizenship, of Native Americans, 32
Citizenship Investment Bill (2014)
(Samoa), 51
citrus-growing, in South Africa, 197, 201
climate change, 157, 165, 170
coal power, resistance to, in Sundarbans,
15, 164–83
Coastal Regulation Zone Notification
(1991) (India), 126
coastline, of Tamil Nadu, respatialization
of, 125–6
coconut plantations, 13–14;
dispossession related to, 98–121
coconut shell briquettes, production of, 115
coconuts: commodification of, 118; trade
in, involvement of Chinese traders,
102
coffee: as monocrop, 217; in global
commodity chain, 215; Maragua
coffee strike, 219, 220, 221; prices of,
215; production of, 213
colonial amnesia, 7
colonialism, 3, 212; connection with
capitalism, 63; etymology of, 21 *see
also* Belgian colonialism, British
colonialism, Dutch colonialism *and*
German colonialism
coloniality, in practice, 303–5
colonization, 95; as modernizing
force, 20; local resistance to, 1–27;
normalization of, 1
commodification, of land, 22, 78
common property, 124
common wealth, creation of, 181
commongrounding, 181
commoning, 130; as resistance, 128–31;
coastal, 129; creation of markets, 222;
rethinking value chains, 221–4; solar,
223–4

commons: enclosure of, 45; politics of, 92
Communist Party of India (Marxist-Leninist), 72
Communist Party of Indonesia, 105, 107
Community Forest Management (CFM), 71
Community Party of the Philippines (CPP), 161
compensation, for dispossession, 73, 74, 86, 105, 171–2, 251, 304; refused by peasants, 113
consultations with the people, in Samoa, 61–2
consumer class, rise of, 302
Coolie Ordinance Acts (1880), 100
cooperatives, 141, 236; formation of, 237; in coffee production, 215
co-optation, 54, 86; of activists, 269; of aims of struggle, 6; of local elites, 319
copra: production of, 101–2, 104, 115, 117; trading in, 55–6
Cordillera People's Alliance (CPA), 153, 156
corruption, 259, 305
counter-violence, 9, 19
credit, access to, 131
Criminal Tribes Act (India), 70–1
criminalization, of peasantry, 105, 110, 118, 308
cross-class organizing, 8–9, 10
customary land: mobilization and securitization of, 43; rights regarding, 262; used as collateral, 43
Customary Land Advisory Committee (Samoa), 50
Customary Land Alienation Act (1965) (Samoa), 48
customary law, 10, 63, 233, 261
customary usage, of Indian fishing communities, 126, 129, 130–1

Dakota Access Pipeline, resistance to, 12, 36
Dalit peoples, 13, 83, 84, 132; social marginalization of, 136–7, 139; social networks of, 69
dams, building of, 23
Darni Penu, 78, 81

De-Notified and Nomadic Tribes Act (1871) (India), 71
deaths see extrajudicial killings and killings
debt, 63, 133, 141, 187, 212, 217; of smallholders, 101; sovereign, 124 (of Philippines, 146–7)
decolonization, 3, 47, 71, 166, 177
deforestation, 247
democracy: critique of, 52; system of, 48
democratic structures, building of, 202–3
Department for International Development (DfID) (UK), 4; withdraws funding aid to Ethiopia, 266
development: critique of, 78; definition of, 293
Diageo company, 4
Dilip Singh Bhuria Commission report, 71
dioxin, pollution by, 38
direct action, 93, 260
disaster reconstruction, in Tamil Nadu, 122–44
displacement of people, 73, 74, 76, 86, 214; associated with Rampal power plant, 171 see also resettlement
dispossession: by shrimp farms, in India, 123–5; concept of, 189; local resistance to, 1–27; of Bangladeshi farmers, 167–8; of Lumad peoples, 145–63; process of, 304–5; related to coconut plantations, 101, 101; related to discovery of oil in Ghana, 240; resistance to, 55 (in Bohotokong, Indonesia, 102; in Ethiopia, 251–71, 292–3; in Kenya, 209–30; in Mindanao, 145–63; in Niger Delta, 315–34; resistance to, in Samoa, 43–66; in Sierra Leone, 251–71; in Sulawesi, Indonesia, 98; in Tamil Nadu, 122–44; local, 1–27)
divide and conquer, principle of, 105
division of marginal social groups, 12
Dokubo, Alhaji Asari, 326, 329, 330, 331
Domb people, 82, 83
Dongria people, 67–8, 75, 79, 81, 84, 85, 86, 87, 88

Down To Earth report on Indonesia, 101
drought, 226
drums, used in protests, 87
Dummer, Lieutenant Governor, 32
Dutch colonialism, 99, 101
Duterte, Rodrigo, 161

East Cape Agricultural Research Project
    (ECARP), 188, 192, 193, 194, 200
East India Company, 99, 180
ecofeminism, 11, 221, 223; considerations
    regarding, 224–5; in agricultural
    contexts, 209–30; subsistence-
    perspective, 177
ecological concerns, 9; in coastal areas
    of India, 130–1
education: for ex-insurgents, 328; girls
    quit school, 112; within movements,
    93
Ekpemupolo, Government, 329
El Niño, 158
elders of the struggle, 113
electric poles, hitting of, 110
electricity, free, switch from, 57
Elisara, Fiu Mata'ese, 53–4, 58, 60, 62, 63
eminent domain, 68; concept of, 317
Employment Conditions Commission
    (South Africa), 187
empty lands, myth of, 3 see also terra
    nullius and unused land
enclosure: of genetic materials, 212; new,
    16 see also commons, enclosure of
endangered species, 168
energy self-sufficiency, 222
Energy Transfer Partners Oil Company,
    37
engaged academics, 7
English language, 36; shift from Native
    languages, 33
ENI company, oil spillages, 319
environmental degradation, 150, 264;
    associated with aquaculture,
    124; associated with mining, 319;
    associated with Rampal power plant,
    174 see also pollution
Environmental Impact Assessment (EIA),
    171
epistemicide, 32, 39

erpatch concession licenses, 102
Ethiopia, 18; land acquisitions in, 275–95
ethnic conflict, 264
ethnicity, 8, 322, 327; mapping of, 323
ethnocide, 158
Eurocentrism of the left, 22
Executive Instrument (EI) 57 (Ghana),
    235–6
export-oriented industrialization, 146
Extension of Security of Tenure Act
    (ESTA) (1997) (South Africa), 192, 199
external actors, role of, 115
external allies, role of, 113–16
extractive industry, 148, 297, 302;
    colonial roots of, 312; infrastructures
    of, 298–300; neoliberal, 299, 311
extractive model of production, 70
extrajudicial killings, 153, 157, 319, 324

fa'alavelave gift giving, 46
fa'alupenga salutation, 56
fa'amatai, 43–66; reassertion of, 51–8
fa'asamoa, 43–66; reassertion of, 51–8
Fanon, Frantz, 94, 312
farm committees, in South Africa, 200,
    202, 203; formation of, 195–8
farm workers: demonstrations of, 200;
    living and working conditions of, 188;
    strikes of, in South Africa, 192
farming see agriculture
fatigue, of activists in struggle, 116
Federici, Silvia, 177, 180
feminism, 178, 181 see also ecofeminism
feminization, subaltern, 180
'fence of shins', 111
feudal production, transformation of, 20
fig trees, cutting of, 217
finance, in commoning systems, 221–4
finance capital, 16
fisher citizenship, 133
fishing, 30; artisanal, 123–8, 141
    (modernization of, 129–30); in
    colonial times, 31–2; pollution
    of habitats, 169; rights to, 38;
    traditional, 117
fishing communities: in India (and state,
    128–31; moral oversight of, 127–8);
    resistance of, in Tamil Nadu, 122–44

fishing industry, commercial, 122, 137; destructive trawling by, 130

fishworker, definition of, 137, 140; inclusion of women in, 141

flight, as form of resistance, 290–1

flooding, 165

fono village council system (Samoa), 58, 59–62

Food and Agricultural Organization (FAO), 123

Food First organization, 4

Food Liberation movement (India), 72

food security, 124

food sovereignty, 11, 24, 209–30; as resistance to dispossession, 217–24, 224–5

Food Sovereignty organization, 4

foreign direct investment (FDI), 23, 107, 297; in plantations, 251

foreignization of space, 23

Forest Rights Acts (India), 69

forest-dependent peoples, 67

Forestry Department interests, in India, 129

forests: appropriation of, 68; destroyed by Vedanta, 84; ecological function of, 169; entitlement to usage of, 171

fossil fuels, 164

free prior and informed consent, 253

Front Perjuangan Pembaruan Agraria Sulwesi (Indonesia), 115

Fulani people, 325, 326

G4S security company, 305

Gambella (Ethiopia): land struggles in, 251–71; resistance to land dispossession in, 262–6

Gambella Nilotes United Movement/Army (GNUM/A), 262, 267

Gambella People's Liberation Movement (GPLM), 268

Ganges River, diversion of, 168

garment industry, 167, 177

Gbomo, Jomo, 326

Geita Gold Mine (Tanzania), 19, 297, 303, 305, 311

gender economy, dual-strategy, 131–5

gender mainstreaming, 216

gendered alliances, creation of, 228

gendered nature of agriculture and economy, 214, 226

genocide, 28, 37

germ warfare, 28

German colonialism, 298, 299

Germany, 46

gheraos encirclement of officials, 88

Glencore Xstrata company, 154

Global Climate Risk Index, 165

Godeffroy & Sohn company, 46

Gogoi, Ranjan, 68

gold: harvested from mining waste, 305, 307, 308; kings and priests barred from using, 232; mining of, 150, 296–314 (artisanal, 298, 306)

Gold Coast colony, 233

Government Order 172 (GO172) (India), 126–7

Government Order 25 (GO25) (India), 125–6

Grahamstown meeting (South Africa), 199

GRAIN organization, 4, 5

Gram Sabha process, 68, 86, 89, 90–1

grazing of livestock, loss of land for, 193

greed, viewed as evil force, 37–8

Green Belt Movement (Kenya), 217–24

Green Paper on Land Reform (South Africa), 204

Green Scenery organization, 259

Greenpeace, 175

Gumuz people (Ethiopia), 18, 277–93; fear of, 287; looked down on, 288–9

gun sales to indigenous peoples, banning of, 29–30

harambee, organization model, 225

Hart, G., 188–9

Harvey, David, 20, 23, 63, 177, 188, 191, 234

Hasina, Sheikh, 168, 178

historiography, colonial, 28

homes, ownership of, 128; among fishing communities, 136

'house of women' custom, 224

housing: post-tsunami in India, 135, 136

human rights, campaigning over, 255

Human Rights Protection Party (HRPP) (Samoa), 48
Human Rights Watch, report on killings of Lumad people, 145
Hussein, Mwajuma, 304
hydropower, in Samoa, 57, 60, 62

Iamgold company, 301
identity, process of construction of, 321
Igbo people, 322
Ijaw people, 322, 327
Ijaw Youth Council (IYC), 329
illiteracy, 85; of tribal peoples, 77
immigrant workers, resistance to, 285–9
Imperial Land Ordinance (1895) (Tanganyika), 298
imprisonment of activists, 111, 112, 114, 116
indentured labour, 46, 47; Chinese, 47
India: building of coal-fired power plants, 176; disaster reconstruction in, 122–4
Indian Nonintercourse Act (1790) (USA), 33
indigenization, 51 see also re-indigenization
indigenous communities, resistance of, 292–3
indigenous crop varieties, 220
indigenous peoples, 44, 145, 262, 265, 278; agricultural systems of, 218 (labour-intensive, 221); legislation against, 35; massacres of, 30; resistance of, 150–3; rights of, 101 see also knowledge, indigenous
indigenous traditional ecological knowledge (ITEK), 32
Indofood Sukses Makmur Tbk company, 104
Indonesia, agrarian conflict in, 98–121
Indonesian Farmers Alliance (API), 115
Indonesian Peasant Front (BTI), 107
informal sector, 167
informalization, 166
intergenerational unity, 219, 224, 228
International Coalition for Human Rights in the Philippines, 159, 162
International Institute for Environment and Development, study of mining industry, 306
International Monetary Fund (IMF), 146, 192, 212, 301, 302; Structural Adjustment Facility (SAF), 167
International Peoples Tribunal (IPT), 159–60
Internet, development of, 326
investors in agriculture, resistance to, 282–5
ipu cup, sharing of, 60

Jaba Agro-Industry company, 283
Jaja, King, 325
Jakeska, Jithu, 85–6
Jayapal, K. A., 138
Jharania people, 83, 84, 87
Jonathan, Goodluck, 328–9, 331
journalism, investigative, 310–11
judicial activism, 98

Kadaso, N'gombe Lukala, 296
Kadraka, Manda, 91
Kahogpongan sa Lumadnong Organisasyon (KASALO) (Mindanao), 156
Kahopongang Lumad sa Halayong Habatagang Mindanao (KALUHHAMIN), 156
Kalahandi Sachetan Nagarik Manch (KSNM) (India), 73, 86, 87–8
Kalimantan island (Indonesia), 100
Kalipunan ng mga Katutubong Mamamayan ng Pilipinas (KATRIBU), 155, 156
KALUMBAY Lumad Organization (Mindanao), 156
Karituri company, 254, 262, 265
Kenya, 267; extractive industry in, 301; grassroots organizing in, 218
Khond people, 73
Kidapawan Massacre (Philippines), 158
kidnapping: in Niger Delta, 315; of oil workers, 320
killings: of anti-power plant activists in Phulbari protests, 164; of oppositionists in Indonesia, 101, 107–8, 157–8; see also extrajudicial killings
Kinari village (India), 75–6
Kirk, John, 324

knowledge: customary, guarding of, 54; indigenous, 35, 59, 210, 216, 223, 227 (enclosure of, 213; recovery of, 36) *see also* indigenous traditional ecological knowledge (ITEK)

Koko, King Frederick William, 324

Kondh people, 77, 78, 82, 83, 91

Koroma, Ernest Bai, 261

Kotduar village (India), 76

Kothari Sugars company, campaign against, 133

Krishi Jomi Roksha Sangram Samity (Bangladesh), 172–4

Kufuor, John, 240

Kutia peoples, 79

Kuwonor, Maggie, 238, 244, 247

La Via Campesina network, 218, 227

labour laws, organizing around, 196

labour market, rupture of, 318–19

Labour Relations Act (South Africa), 199

LaDuke, Winona, 36

Lagarde, Christine, 296

Lakbay Lumad USA campaign, 160

land: alienation of, 63 (seen as breach of social norms, 59); and dispossession, in South Africa, 192–4; as marketable commodity, 21; as private property, 70, 118, 304; commodification of, 22, 46; customary (inalienable, 47; mortgaging of, 46, 50; registration of, 50; used as collateral, 44, 50, 63); marketization of, 50; over-use of, 286; redefined as crown land, 47; redistribution of, in South Africa, 190, 192–4; sacred, desecration of, 265; scarcity of, 251; sharing, 224; tribal, control of, 34 *see also* customary land

Land Acquisition Act (1967) (Tanzania), 304

Land Act (1999) (Tanzania), 304

Land and Freedom Army (Kenya), 214

Land and Freedom for Tillers (LAFTI) (India), 132

Land and Titles Commission (Samoa), 46

land claims, in Maine, 33

Land Claims Settlement Act (USA), 38

Land Commission, international, 46

land grabbing, 3, 5, 9, 15, 18, 23, 212, 264, 265; as national practice of elites, 252; associated with Rampal power plant, 170–2; resistance to, 17, 30–1, 251, 252, 268 *see also* legal activism, on land grabs *and* large-scale land acquisitions

land leases, non-transparency of, 17

land reform, 21, 24–5; in Ethiopia, 254; in South Africa, 189

land rights activism, 251–71; new, 8, 255–6

land sovereignty, 24–5, 269

land tenure systems, 3, 300; bourgeois, 5; collective, 21; customary, 44, 45, 277; defence of, 202; individualization of, 56; laws regarding, organizing around, 196

land titles: programme in Kenya, 214; registering of, 21

Land Titles Registration Act (2008) (Samoa), 50

'land to the tiller', 254

Land Use Decree 6 (1978) (Nigeria), 317

landless people, activism of, 118–19

landlessness, 70, 98–121, 166, 167, 171, 191, 192, 214, 223

Lands, Surveys and Environment Amendment Act (1989) (Samoa), 49

languages, indigenous: loss of, 35–6; revitalization of, 36; right to speak, 35

Lanjigarh (India), 73, 76, 85; refinery in (development in, 77; decommissioning of, 91; ecological impact of, 81; foundation stone laid for, 75; resistance to, 74)

large scale land acquisitions, in Ethiopia, 275–95; resistance to, 282–92

law, used to enact dispossession, 317

Law 287 *see* PNDC Law 287

Lawer, Akpetiyo, 248–9

LBH Bantaya legal aid organization, 113–14

LBH Surabaya organization, 115

Le Tangaloa Dr Pitapola Alailima, 52–3

League of Nations, 299

Leano, Ryan, 160

learning: in action, in Samoa, 62–3; through conversations, 61–2

legal activism: against extractive industry, 308–9; on land grabs, 266
legal aid, 86; as pacificatory measure, 114
Legal and Human Rights Information Centre (Bohotokong), 113
legal recognition, offered in exchange for resettlement, 127
legality, contested, 317
Leonard, Mhoja, 305
Libi Wornor spirit, 233–4
Lilomaiava, Dr Ken Lameta, 58, 61
Lilomaiava-Doktor, S., 51–2
liquor, provided free by companies, 83
local resistance, 1–27, 251; in Bangladesh, 165, 166, 172; in Ethiopia, 275–95; in Ghana, 234; in Niger Delta, 315–34; in Tanzania, 298, 309; primacy of, 6
logging industry, 151, 152
Lok Adhikar Manch (LAM), 69
Lompogan Estate (KOL), 103
London Constitutional Conference (1957), 323
Lopez, Gina, 161
loss, rhetoric of, 35–6
Lucas, Vanessa, 160
Lumad people, 7, 9, 10, 14–15; anti-mining activism of, 145–63; targeted for assassination, 157

Maathai, Wangari, awarded Nobel Peace Prize, 217
Macapagal-Arroyo, Gloria, 152, 157
Magema (Tanzania), small-scale mining in, 306
Mahama, John, 243, 247
Maine, privately owned islands in, 30
Maine Indian Claims Settlement Act (1980) (USA), 33
maize, burning of, 284
Majhi, Abhi, 75
Majhi, Balabhaddra, 75
Majhi, Bhim, 73, 75
Majhi, Dai Singh, 73, 77
Majhi, Gato, 83
Majhi, Kumuti, 74, 80, 85–6
Majhi Khond people, 72
Makonda, Hussein, 306
'male deals', 214–15, 216, 226

Malen (Sierra Leone), land activism in, 256–8
Malen Affected Land Owners Association (MALOA) (Sierra Leone), 255–62
Malen Land Owners and Land Users Association (MALOA) (Sierra Leone), 18, 255
Malifa, Leuluaialii Tasi Malifa, 58
malnutrition, 187, 227
Mamasapano Incident (Mindanao), 159–60
Mamoe, Luaki Namulau'ulu, 56
Mandagi, T. K., 103
Marag Valley (Philippines): militarization of, 152; resistance in, 150–1
Maragua (Kenya), 213; gendered transformation of farm economy in, 218; importance of case, 228; organic farming collective in, 211; women's activism in, 215–16
Marcos, Ferdinand, 146, 151; struggle against, 150–1
Marcos, Imelda, 146
market, hierarchical organization of, 225
market economy, insertion into, 46
markets, in commoning systems, 221–4
marriage, 215
Marx, Karl, 20, 146, 210, 218, 223–4, 226, 300; *Capital*, 209; dismissal of rurality, 94; views on India, 92
Marxism, 22–3, 24, 94, 166; definition of workers and owners, 141; post-Western, 178; Western, 176
Master Plan for the Songor (Ghana), 238, 239, 241
matai: system of, 10, 13, 47, 52, 55–8, 59, 60, 62, 63; use of title, 48, 57 (prohibited, 47)
Mau a Pule movement (Samoa), 47, 56
Maulolo Tavita Amosa, 53
McKinsey group, 180
Memoranda of Democratic Codes (South Africa), 203
Mende people, 18
mentorship, concept of, 204
merry-go-round activities, 225
meta-dispossession, 11–12, 28–40

migrant labour, 100, 102, 106;
agricultural, 18
migrant workers, 4, 197; encroach on
land, 286; Filipino, 147; killing of, 287
see also immigrant workers
migration, 22, 23, 49, 86; related to
climate change, 165; rural-urban,
220
militarization, 318; of mining areas, 305,
308, 309
Mindanao, 153; anti-mining activism in,
158–61; dispossession in, 145–63
mining: artisanal (criminalization of,
306; in Tanzania, 296–314); open-
pit, 68, 164, 303, 306 (ban on, 155;
environmental impact of, 150) *see
also* mining industry
Mining Act (1998) (Tanzania), 300, 303
Mining Act (2003) (Ghana), 239
Mining Act (2010) (Tanzania), 300
Mining Action Plan (Philippines), 148
mining industry, 5, 13, 14; activism
against, 67–97; in Philippines, 149–50
(liberalization of, 157); liberalization
of, 148–9
Mining Injustice Solidarity Network, 310
Mining Ordinance (1929) (Tanganyika),
299
Mining Watch organization, 297, 309
Mishra, Rakesh, 85
Mishra, Sarat Chandra, 89
Mishra, Saswat, 77
missionaries, 2, 45
mixed cropping, 216
modernization: of fisheries, in
Coromandel coast, 129–30; trope
of, 301
moneylenders, dependence on, 133;
reduction of, 131
Mongla (Bangladesh), special economic
zone, 166–7
Monsanto company, 4, 17, 212
Monson, Leodinio 'Manong Dos', 157
Moro Islamic Liberation Front (MILF), 159
Mother Earth, 25
Movement for the Emancipation of the
Niger Delta (MEND), 19, 315, 320–1,
327, 329, 331

Movement for the Survival of the Ogoni
People (MOSOP), 19, 319, 322, 326–7;
factionalization in, 329, 331
Muhammad, Anu, 174
Multi Nabati Sulawesi company, 104
multitude: subaltern, 176–9; theorization
of, 175
muththi (handful) collections, 80

Nagapattinam (India), disaster
reconstruction in, 122–44
Nambiyarnagar (India), housing complex
in, 136
Nana people, 325
Narayanpatna people, land rights of, 72
National Alliance for Filipino Concerns
(NAFCON), 160–1, 162
National Committee to Protect Oil, Gas,
Mineral Resources, Power and Ports
(NCBD) (Bangladesh), 164, 165, 174,
175, 179, 180
National Democratic Front (Philippines),
161
National Forest Policy (India), 70
national liberation movements, 23
National Mineral Policy Agenda
(Philippines), 148
National Thermal Power Corporation
(NTPC) (India), 166
Nayak, Siddartha, 73, 76–8, 86
Nayoan, Theo, 103, 104
Nembe people, 324
Nene Ada, 231, 232, 234
neo-customary governance, 253, 255
neocolonialism, 12; definition of, 2–3; in
the Philippines, 146–9; new forms
of, 2
neoliberalism, 191, 192, 206; in extractive
sector, 311; in the Philippines, 146–9;
opposition to, 156
network of networks, 15
networks: against land grabs, 269; cross-
border, 310–11; resistance form of the
multitude, 15, 172–66
New Order (Indonesia), 108
New People's Army (NPA) (Philippines),
145, 151, 155, 161
New Zealand, 46, 47

New7Wonders foundation, 178–9
Newell, Wayne, 37
Newmont company, 153
NGO Coordination and Resource Center (NCRC) (India), 134
non-governmental organizations (NGOs), 108, 125, 127, 128, 134, 135, 140, 211, 228, 297, 301, 311; activism of, 139 (limitations of, 136); competing for territory, 134; environmental, 175; in disaster reconstruction resistance, 122–4; local, role of, 10; rejection of, 91; viewed as distraction, 115
Niger Delta, 19; activist groups in, 320; collective identity (construction of, 321–8; oppositional, 325–6); conditions in, 324; development in, 315–21; ethnic groups in, 322; resistance in, 315–34 (future of, 328–32); secession of, 329
Niger Delta People Volunteer Force (NDPVF),19, 330, 331, 326
Nigeria, regionalization in, 323
Niyam Raja, 67, 77, 78, 81
Niyamgiri: declared National Park, 72; resistance to mining industry in, 67–97
Niyamgiri – The Mountain of Law documentary, 69, 76
Niyamgiri Surakhya Samiti (NSS) (India), 13, 67; development of leadership, 92–3; growth of, 77–81; origins of, 73–7; strategy, mobilization and tactics of, 81–95; resistance to bauxite mining, 72–9
Nogbaisi, Oba Ovvonrannwen, 325
non-violence, 9, 259, 260, 269, 329; evaporation of option, 320
North Mara Gold Mine (Tanzania), 297, 305, 308, 309, 311
Nuer people, 263, 264, 267
Nyerere, Julius, 299

O le Mau movement (Samoa), 56
Oakland Institution, 275
Obansanjo, Olusegun, 325
Objects of Agrarian Reform (TORA) program (Indonesia), 116

occupations of land, 108, 109
oceans, access to, 32
Odisha Mining Corporation (OMC), 13, 67–8, 77, 90
Odu'a People's Congress (OPC) (Nigeria), 327
Ogoni Nine, hanging of, 319, 320, 326, 330
Ogoni people, 322, 328
oil: discovery of (in Ethiopia, 264; in Ghana, 240–1; in Nigeria, 315–21); theft of, 320
Oil Pipelines Act (1956) (Nigeria), 317
Oil Rivers Protectorate, 322
oil spills, pollution arising from, 319
Okor Forest (Ghana), 247
Okor Ng Kor drama series, 246
Oloa movement (Samoa), 55
Oloibiri town, significance of, 316
Oloibirinization, 19, 315–34; complexity of, 317
Ong Soen Hie, 103
Operation Exodus (Mindanao), 159
opium, growing of, 69
Oplan Bantay Laya, 153, 157, 160
Oplan Bayanihan, 159, 160
organic farming, 210, 219, 220, 222, 227; labour-intensive, 221
Organisasi Tani Buruh dan Nelayan (ORTABUN), 13, 109–19; challenges for, 116–18; organization of resistance through, 106–18
Orion group, 167
Orissa Government Land Settlement Act (1962) (India), 70
Orono, Joseph, 30
Oxfam organization, 5

Palatino, Mong, 162
palm oil, 322; production of, 99 (gendered effects of, 101)
panchayat village bodies, 131, 133, 137; constrain possible social change, 139; elections in, 138; represent centralized male authority, 132
Papua, 100
paramount chiefs *see* chief, paramount
participatory action research, 98

Particularly Vulnerable Tribal Groups (PVTG), 67

PASAKA Regional Confederation of Lumad Organization, 156

Patnaik, Naveen, 75

Patnaik, S. K., 85

Pattanaik, Kishen, 76

Pattinavar sub-caste, 123

peasantry: viewed as inert, 20; viewed as revolutionary, 94

Peasants' Alliance Against Discrimination (Indonesia), 14

pemandu leadership system, 108–9, 113

Penobscot Nation, 38–9

Penobscot people, bounties for scalps of, 30

People's Defence Committees (Ghana), establishment of, 236–7

People's National Defence Council (PNDC) (Ghana), 236, 237–8

People's Union for Civil Liberties (PUCL) (India), 75

Pepple, Dappa, 325

Permanent Settlement Act (1894) (India), 70, 89

pesticides, indigenous, use of, 222–3

petitions, use of, 116 (online, 162)

petro-capitalism, 19

Petroleum Act (1969) (Nigeria), 317

Phakamani Siyephambili organization (South Africa), 16, 188, 189–90, 193, 194, 203; creation of, 194–8, 201; structure of, 197–8 (horizontal, 198); lessons of, 206; manifesto of, 205

Philippine National Police-Special Action Force (PNP-SAF), 159

Philippine Trade Act (Bell Trade Act) (1946) (USA), 149

Philippines, anti-mining resistance in, 145–63

Phulbari (Bangladesh), anti-mining protest in, 174

Plan Canada, 301

plantations, 69, 70; ex-colonial, redistribution of, 107; for palm oil and rubber, 253; labour relations in, 117; shortages of labour in, 55;

struggles against, 258 *see also* coconut plantations

PNDC Law 287 (Ghana), 236, 239–40, 243, 247

police, 89, 113; non-linear responses to, 114; strategies designed to confuse, 110; taken hostage, 111 *see also* violence, of police

pollution: associated with mining industry, 67, 87; associated with oil industry, 316; associated with shrimp farming, 130; campaigning against, 133; of rivers, 316; of water, 319; of waterways, 169; thermal (of coastal waters, 124; of waterways, 170)

Poro secret society (Sierra Leone), 261

poromboke land, 126

poverty, 107, 257; reduction of, 302; rural, pathways out of, 22

Presidential Decree 32/1979 (Indonesia), 107

PricewaterhouseCooper, 180

primitive accumulation, 2, 20, 23, 92, 108, 146, 209, 212

private property, under capitalism, 224, 225

privatization, 147, 190, 300; of common assets, 234; of land, 299; of mining in Philippines, 148; of Songor salt lagoon, 240, 242, 243, 245, 247; of the means of coercion, 234

Proactive Land Acquisition Strategy (PLAS) (South Africa), 193, 201, 204

production/social reproduction nexus, for farmers, 196

proletarianization, 95, 180, 190

protected areas, mining in, resistance to, 91–5

Protest Barrick campaign, 19, 310, 312

public transport, right to utilise, 140

Pujehun (Sierra Leone), land struggles, 251–71

Pule, use of term prohibited, 56

pulp and paper mills: closing of, 38; pollution deriving from, 38

Punganay-Cagayan Valley organization, 156

Quijano, A., 177

race, 3–4
racial capitalism, 4
Radio Ada, 240–4, 246, 249
Rahardja, Rudi, 103
RAID organization, 297, 309
Ramos, Danilo, 157
Rampal (Bangladesh) coal-fired power plant: land grab associated with, 15; resistance to, 164–83 (contradictions of, 178; lack of strategy, 181)
Ramsar Convention, 168
rape, 256
Rastafarians, in Kenya, 220, 228
REACT organization (Sierra Leone), 260
Recapitalisation Programme (Recap) (South Africa), 193, 201, 204
reclaiming of dispossessed lands, 108
re-commoning, 9, 11; as ecofeminist practice, 217–24; considerations regarding, 224–5; in Kenya, 16–17, 209–30
re-indigenization, 58–63
relocation *see* resettlement of communities
remittances, of migrants, 48, 147
remittance-based land purchases, 23
rentals for land, 253–4
Republic Act 7942 (Mining Act) (Philippines), 148, 150, 155; call for repeal of, 156; constitutionality of, challenged, 154
reservations, for indigenous peoples, 32, 33, 38
resettlement of communities, 100, 128, 135, 240, 243, 278, 290; after Indian tsunami, 122, 125–8; disruption of, 88; forced, 303; policies of Derg in Ethiopia, 263, 277
resistance: definition of, 9; everyday, 282, 305–8; forms of, 276 (covert, 284); in rural struggles, 198–205; to dispossession *see* dispossession, resistance to
resources, loss of, through resettlement, 129

Revolutionary United Front (RUF) (Sierra Leone), 255, 257
right to vote, of indigenous peoples, 33
Rio Tinto Alcan company, 301
rivers, restoration of, 38
Rivers Chiefs and People's Conference (RCPC) (Nigeria), 323
roadblocks, as means of protest, 57–8
Robinson, Cedric, *Black Marxism*, 20
Royal Bengal Tiger, 178–9; preservation of, 168, 174, 180
Royal Niger Company, 324
rural struggles, politics of, 198–205

S. Jagannath v. Union of India (1996), 132
SABMiller company, 4
sabotage: of crops and machinery, 9, 88, 283, 292, 307, 324; of oil pipelines, 320, 331
Sagittarius Mining Inc (SMI), 154
Saifaleupolu, Telei'ai Sapa, 52, 58
Salabukan Nok G'taw Subanen (SGS) (Philippines), 156
Salala, Leonard, 296
Salim Group, 104
Salim Ivomas Pratama Tbk (SIMP) company, 104
salinification, 124, 168, 169
salt, trading in, 238
salt lagoon *see* Songor salt lagoon
Saluang people, 106, 118
Sama, Siaka, 260
Samoa Act, 47
Samoa National Party (SNP), 48
Samoa, 13; part ceded to Germany, 46; resistance to dispossession in, 43–66; Spanish influenza in, 47
Samoan Individual Property Ordinance, 47
Samoan Offenders Ordinance, 47
Saro-Wiwa, Ken, 319, 322, 326, 328
Saudi Star company, 254, 256, 262
Save the Sundarbans organization, 173
Scott, James C., *Weapons of the Weak*, 305
Scrap the Mining Act Network (Philippines), 156
Search for Common Ground organization, 301

secrecy of movements, 261
security companies, private, 307
seed, 221–4, 221, certified, 226, elderly women, role of, in preserving, 210, 222, 223, 226; indigenous, 222 (patenting of, 226; recovery of, 227); trade of peasants, constricted, 226
seed commons, reinvention of, 210
seed imperialism, 211
Sekenke Gold Mine, 299
self-financing of movements, 93
self-help groups (SHG), 14, 141; of women, 131, 133, 142
sexual harassment, of women activists, 111
Shagari, Shehu, 325
shaming, in public, 88
shea trees, felling of, 264
Shell company: protests against, 322; relation to military, 318; oil spillages, 319
Shell D'arcy company, 315
Shiriki Farm (Maragua, Kenya), 219–20, 222–3
shrimp farming, 122, 168, 170, 172, 173, 180; mass movements against, 132–3; pollution deriving from, 130
Sierra Club, 175
Sierra Leone Produce Marketing Board (SLPMB), 257, 258
Sikoka, Lado, 80, 89
Sili, village (Samoa), 62
Sindhabahali village (India), 76
Sioe The, 103
sit-downs (*dharnas*), 88
slave revolts, 2
slavery, 4, 22, 257, 258, 298, 318
slaves, emancipation of, 25
Socfin Agricultural Company Sierra Leone Ltd (SOCFIN), 253, 255, 257, 260, 262; palm oil and rubber project, 18; two staff shot, 261
social media, 218
social movement activism, 93–4
social movements, 231–2; mobilization of, 218
Social Needs Empowerment Human Awareness (SNEHA) (India), 14, 131, 132, 136, 138, 140, 141, 142

soil erosion, 169
solar power, use of, 222
solidarity, 20, 94; creation of, 195, 197, 201; in Phakamani Siyephambili, 202
somatization of relations of domination, 320
Songor salt lagoon (Ghana), 17; fails to crystallise, 235; organizing against appropriation of, 10, 17; resistance around, 10, 17, 231–50; trusteeship of, 234; weaving of tapestry, 244 *see also* Master Plan for the Songor (Ghana)
songs of struggle, 87, 112–13, 199, 248–9
Soto, Hernando de, 21
South Africa, organization by the rural poor in, 187–208
South Asians for Human Rights (SAHR), 172
Southwestern Ethiopia Nilotic-Omotic Peoples Independent Movement (SENPIM), 262, 267
sovereignty, 43, 56, 300, 308; in land, 24–5; indigenous, 24; politics of, 43–66 *see also* food sovereignty
special economic zones (SEZ), 23, 166–7
squatting, 88
ssipsis, an elder, 38
Standing Rock, 36, 37
state: confrontation with, in South Africa, 203–5; resistance against, 289–92; role of, 280, 291 (in determining land allocation, 278)
Sterlite company, 72 *see also* Vedanta/Sterlite company
stories, of resistance, 177
Strategy for the Development of Samoa, 49
stratification, racial, 318–19
strikes: general strike, in Kenya, 214; of farm workers, in South Africa, 192
structural adjustment programmes, 49, 147, 148, 178, 179, 215, 237
subjugation, adaptation to, 319–20
subsistence crops, farmers' preference for, 217
subsistence farming perspective, 209; disparaged, 211–12
Suharto, 99, 100, 107

Sukarno, 107
Sulawesi (Indonesia), dispossession in, 98–121
Sulawesi Agrarian Reform Struggle Front, 14
Sumatra, 100
Sundarbans (Bangladesh), 179; a UNESCO world heritage site, 164, 178; ecological threat to, 168–70; resistance to coal power in, 164–83
Sundarbans Reserve Forest, 168
Sundays River Valley, 192, 194, 197, 201
supertribalization, among young people, 327
Supreme Court of India, 91; mining judgement of, 89, 90
Survival International, 100
Suryanagar housing complex, 139
Sutton Resources company, 300
sweated trades, 192
Syngenta company, 4, 17, 212

Taking of Land Act (1964) (Samoa), 48
Talaingod-Manobo tribe, 160–1
Tampakan Copper-Gold Mine Project (Philippines), 154
Tanganyika Concessions company, 299
Tanzania, Northern, mining in, 296–314
taxation, 57, 69; refusal of, 56; threatened non-payment of, 289, 292
Tekprepiawe clan, 235
terra nullius, 21, 22, 253, 278 *see also* unused land
tissue culture banana production, 216–17, 219
Toeaina Club, 56
Toe's, Koh, 105
Toi Gen Keng, 103
Toleofa, Afamusunga, 54
torture, 101
trade unions *see* unionization
trade-union models of organizing on farms, 195–6
Transborder Associates, 300
Transformasi untuk Keadilan (TuK), 99
transnational activism, 7
transparency, 258
Trask, Huanani-Kay, 2–3, 59

Treaty of Berlin, 46
trees: of plantations, destruction of, 260; planting of, 217 *see also* uprooting
Trump, Donald, 34
tsunami, in India, 5, 14; displacement resulting from, 125–8, 132; teconstruction following, 122 (struggles within, 133–5)
tsunami housing, 128
Tumandok nga Mangunguma nga Nagapangapin sa Duta Kag Kabuhi (TUMANDUK) (Philippines), 156
Tumew, Budi, 103
Tumua, use of term prohibited, 56
Tumua and *Pule* and *Aiga* (TPA) movement (Samoa), 56
Typhoon Ondoy, 156–7

Ubuntu principles, 225
Ujamaa, 299
Ukuma massacre (Ethiopia), 268
United Nations (UN), 154
UN Declaration on the Rights of Indigenous Peoples, 24
UN Development Programme (UNDP), 134
UN Environment Programme (UNEP), 319
UN Special Rapporteur on the rights of IDPs, 155
Unemployment Insurance Act (South Africa), 199
UNESCO, 175
Unilever company, 4
unionization, 11
United Nations (UN), establishment of, 47
United States of America (USA), 151, 158; military intervention in Philippines, 153, 159
Unity of Mindanao Against Foreign Mining coalition, 153
Universal Declaration of Human Rights, 159
unused land, 279 *see also terra nullius*
uprooting: of coffee trees, by women, 215, 219; of trees, resistance to, 260

URBAN x INDIGENOUS (UxI)
organization, 161
USAID, 17, 212

va, concept of, 51
Vacuum Salt Ltd (VSL), 17, 235; legal
challenge to, 238; seizure of plant,
236
value chains: planetary, operation of,
225; preferred by corporations,
226
Vedanta/Sterlite company, 13, 67, 79, 88;
cricket club involved in violence, 75;
destruction of forests by, 84; setting
fire to machinery of, 76
Via Campesina organization, 24; Final
Declaration of, 24
villagization, 214, 263, 265–6, 290; non-
compliance with, 292
violence, 1, 18, 87, 98, 235; against anti-
shrimp farm activists, 133; against
Dalit families, 136; against Lumad
communities, 145–63 *passim*; against
power plant activists, 173; against
protestors, 75, 79, 88; against women
salt sellers, 237; associated with
extractive industry, 303–5, 308,
309; associated with gold mines,
297, 307, 308; colonial, 15; deaths
in First Nations communities, 37;
domestic, campaigning against, 140;
gang-related, 320; language of force,
307; neocolonial accumulated, 166;
neoliberal, 296–314; of police, 80,
91, 117; of resistance movements,
321, 330, 331–2; of rural land conflict,
255; of state, 304, 318; sabotage as,
9; state monopoly of, 118 *see also*
counter-violence, non-violence *and*
torture
Vision 2021 (Bangladesh), 180
Volta Dam (Ghana), 17; ecological impact
of, 235
volunteers, working in organic farms, 221

wage labour, 22, 117; resistance to, 47
wages: agricultural minimum wage in
South Africa, 188, 190, 191–2, 195, 198,
199, 200; of farm workers in South
Africa, 187, 188
wall, building of, at North Mara mine,
309
Waponahki Confederacy, 30
Waponahki people (Wabanaki), 11–12;
anti-colonial resistance of, 28–40;
dispossession of, 29; generosity of,
34–9; history of, 29
'war on terror', 151–2, 160
War on Want organization, 4
Washington Consensus, 146
water: access to, 87, 160; shortages of, 165
water resources, protection of, 36–7
Waterkeepers Bangladesh organization,
175
West Java, land occupations in, 108
Westbrook, Thomas, 32
Western Mining Corporation, 154–5
Wikileaks, 318
Willinks Commission, 323
women: activism of, in Songor,
243–6; as coffee farmers, 213, 218;
as fish vendors, 140; as horticultural
scientists, 216; as movement leaders,
83; dispossession losses of, 226;
encircle police, 88; in the forefront
of organising farm committees, 196;
included in definition of fishworkers,
141; increased cohesiveness of,
131; involvement of, 8; maintain
vegetable plots, 215; response of, to
state violence, 315; rights of, 140; role
of, in struggle, 111, 198; sexual abuse
of, 318; work of, 215 *see also* seed,
elderly women, role of, in preserving
and self-help groups, of women
women's groups, 133
World Bank, 21, 100, 123–4, 146, 148, 167,
176, 192; associated with villagization,
266–7; report on Ethiopia land
acquisitions, 275; Structural
Adjustment Policy, 299; studies on
salinity, 165
World March of Women, 218, 227
World Trade Organization (WTO), 212
World University Services Canada, 301
World Vision, 135

World Vision Canada, 301
World Vision organization, 135, 136, 139

Yar'Adua, Umaru, 329
Yarrow Farm (South Africa), takeover of, 204
'Yes to Life, No to Mining' movement, 19, 312

Yomo spirit, 231–50 *passim*
Yoruba people, 322, 325
young people, returning to the land, 221

zamindars, 70, 71; reparations from, 72
Zoomers, A., 23